GOING TO WAR: CREATING COMPUTER WAR GAMES

JASON DARBY

Course Technology PTR
A part of Cengage Learning

COURSE TECHNOLOGY
CENGAGE Learning™

Australia • Brazil • Japan • Korea • Mexico • Singapore • Spain • United Kingdom • United States

COURSE TECHNOLOGY
CENGAGE Learning™

Going to War: Creating Computer War Games
Jason Darby

Publisher and General Manager, Course Technology PTR: Stacy L. Hiquet

Associate Director of Marketing: Sarah Panella

Manager of Editorial Services: Heather Talbot

Marketing Manager: Jordan Casey

Acquisitions Editor: Heather Hurley

Project Editor: Sandy Doell

Technical Reviewer: Joshua Smith

Editorial Services Coordinator: Jen Blaney

Copy Editor: Melba Hopper

Interior Layout Tech: Macmillan Publishing Solutions

Cover Designer: Mike Tanamachi

CD-ROM Producer: Brandon Penticuff

Indexer: Larry D. Sweazy

Proofreader: Sandi Wilson

For product information and technology assistance, contact us at
Cengage Learning Customer & Sales Support, 1-800-354-9706

For permission to use material from this text or product, submit all requests online at **www.cengage.com/permissions**
Further permissions questions can be emailed to
permissionrequest@cengage.com

All trademarks are the property of their respective owners.

Library of Congress Control Number: 2008928829

ISBN-13: 978-1-59863-566-9

ISBN-10: 1-59863-566-2

Course Technology, a part of Cengage Learning
20 Channel Center Street
Boston, MA 02210
USA

Cengage Learning is a leading provider of customized learning solutions with office locations around the globe, including Singapore, the United Kingdom, Australia, Mexico, Brazil, and Japan. Locate your local office at: **international.cengage.com/region**

Cengage Learning products are represented in Canada by Nelson Education, Ltd.

For your lifelong learning solutions, visit **courseptr.com**

Visit our corporate website at **cengage.com**

Printed in Canada
1 2 3 4 5 6 7 11 10 09

To my wonderful family, Alicia, Jared, Kimberley, and Lucas for all their support.

ACKNOWLEDGMENTS

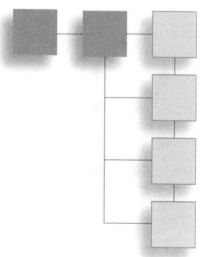

I would like to thank the following people who helped me in the creation of this book. Without their help this book would not have been written.

To my wife, Alicia, and my children, Jared, Kimberley, and Lucas, who supported me through another book project.

To Chris Branch, who wrote the Wargame Map object extension on short notice. This made computer-controlled movement a lot easier for people to implement in their own games.

To Adam Lobacz, who made the war game graphic tile sets that you see in the book.

To my good friends Yves Lamoureux, Francois Lionet, and Jeff Vance, who provided help and support to ensure that this book is as complete as possible. Sorry for all the questions, guys!

To the professional and very friendly staff at Course Technology PTR, who always provide excellent support throughout the whole writing process.

ABOUT THE AUTHOR

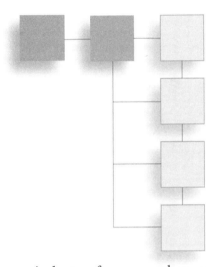

Jason Darby has been working in the IT games industry for more than a decade, writing user and systems documentation for users. For a number of years, he has been director of his own company, Castle Software Ltd, focusing on the games and application creation market, where he has been making games, applications, and CD-ROM demos.

Jason is the author of *Make Amazing Games in Minutes; Power Users Guide to Windows Development; Awesome Game Creation,* 3rd Edition; *Game Creation for Teens;* and *Picture Yourself Creating Video Games,* all published by Course Technology PTR.

Jason has also had several articles published in the UK press, including *Retro Gamer*® and *PC Format*®, both leading magazines in their field.

Contents

INTRODUCTION

Welcome to *Going to War: Creating Computer War Games*. This book is aimed at anyone who wishes to make exciting war games for Windows. In the pages that follow, you will learn how to make games in a drag and drop game creation system that requires no programming knowledge. You will learn how to make the components of your war game, such as a map, player and computer movement, and attack phases. By the end of the book, you will be ready to make your own war game and add your own features to it.

Audience

If you've purchased this book or are reading it in a bookstore, then we can assume you're interested in making computer war games. You may be interested in war games or like to re-create battles from the past or have ideas on creating your own future or fantasy war game. You may be someone who wants to make your own computer war games either for yourself or for other people. You may be someone who hasn't programmed a computer before (you do not need to be a programmer to use this book) or you may have some background in traditional programming such as C++ or Visual Basic.

Aim of the Book

The aim of the book is to allow anyone with no programming background to make exciting war games for Windows.

Some of the things that are covered in this book are:

- Different types of war games

- Introduction to MMF2

- Program basics in MMF2

- Using history or creating your own story

- Hexagon maps and how to create them

- Player movement

- Using the terrain to speed up or slow down movement

- Using money to finance a war

- How weather might impact your fighting force

By the end of the book you should be very comfortable with the Multimedia Fusion 2 software and able to begin to make your own war game ideas a reality.

This book does not:

- Teach more complex programming languages like C++, C#, or Java and isn't meant to. This book is aimed at those who want to make games easily without needing to learn those more complex languages. If you are interested in C++, consider *C++ Programming Fundamentals* by Chuck Easttom.

- Teach you how to be a graphic artist or music creator. Look at *Composing Music for Video Games* by Andrew Clark or *3D Graphics Tutorial Collection* by Shamms Mortier.

- Show you how to become an Indi Developer or build a team (if you want more information on being an Indie Developer read *The Indi Game Development Survival Guide* by David Michael).

- Assume you are an expert at game creation. This book is aimed at those with little or no knowledge of game creation but also those who might have an idea how things are put together but need more information.

Chapter Overview

This book runs in a simple yet effective order to allow you to get the most out of reading it. Because many of the chapters build on example files from previous chapters, it is not recommended that you skip chapters.

Chapter 1: Welcome to War Games: An introduction to the different types of war games and how they made their arrival on the home computer.

Chapter 2: Introduction to Multimedia Fusion 2: An introduction to the program that we are going to use to make our war games, Multimedia Fusion 2.

Chapter 3: Your First Creation: Learn all of the basics needed to begin making your own war games.

Chapter 4: Creating Ideas: Deciding what type of war game you will make and how you might get some ideas for a game if you don't currently know what to make.

Chapter 5: Your First Hex Map: The war games in this book all use hexagon tiles for the maps. In this chapter you will learn how to make your very first map.

Chapter 6: Movement: How to get player units to move on the map, while taking into consideration differing movement points and multiple units on screen at one time.

Chapter 7: Terrain Effects: How the terrain the units are moving on can affect the speed of the units. This chapter looks at various terrains, such as mountain, river, and forest tiles.

Chapter 8: Weather: How weather plays a part in your war games. This chapter also takes a look at how to change the scenery of your hexagon map tiles to represent the right weather. We will also look at dates and time, where you can change the weather based on the time of year.

Chapter 9: Enemy Movement: Controlling enemy forces to move around the screen. How to give orders and starting and destination points to computer units.

Chapter 10: Attack and Defense: This chapter details how to bring combat into your games, including how to implement computer-controlled attacks.

Chapter 11: Generals and Officers: How officers have an effect on the battlefield, and how to implement them in your own war games.

Chapter 12: Digging In: This chapter takes a look at how you can provide additional features in your games that give your units additional cover, such as buildings, sandbags, and other fortifications.

Chapter 13: Maps: How to create a larger scrolling map so that you can have a large battlefield. This chapter also covers how to create your own mini map, so the player can see a small version of the whole battlefield.

Chapter 14: Money: Soldiers and equipment must be paid for, and here you learn how to implement simple and easy to use money and financial code to your game.

Chapter 15: Testing and the Debugger: With all of the objects and data needing to be used in your war games, you need to take extra care tracking and finding bugs in your games. We will be looking at the built-in debugger program that can help you find those pesky bugs.

Chapter 16: Editors: A chapter on how to create an editor for your games, which will allow you to make the data for your game quickly and easily, rather than manually typing it in for each game.

Chapter 17: All at War: A look at other types of war game ideas you can use for your own games, such as sea, air, and space battles.

Appendix A: War Game Engine: An overview of the war game engine, which will help you remember what different aspects of the engine accomplish.

About the CD-ROM

The companion CD-ROM contains everything you need to make all of the programs included in this book.

General Minimum System Requirements

You will need a computer that can run Windows 95 or better with a CD-ROM drive, a sound card, and a mouse.

Multimedia Fusion 2 (www.clickteam.com) Trial

The filename for this application is MMF2Demo.exe, and it is located in the Demos folder.

Minimum System Requirements

- Windows 95 with IE 4.0+ / Windows 98 / Windows NT4 SP3+ / 2000 / XPZ Pentium

- 32 MB with Windows 9x, 64 MB with Windows NT, 128 MB with 2000 and XP.

- CD-ROM drive

- Graphic card with 8 MB+ memory

- 50–100 MB free hard disk space

Recommended System Requirements

- Windows 98 or Windows 2000/XP

- Pentium 4

- DirectX 9.0

- 64 MB RAM with Windows 98, or 256 MB RAM with Windows 2000/XP

- CD-ROM drive

- 3D accelerated graphics card with 32+ MB memory

- Sound card

- 100–200 MB free hard disk space

Folders

There are a number of folders on the CD-ROM that contain important files for use within this book but also useful information.

- **Color Figures:** In the Figures folder on the CD-ROM, you will find color versions of every figure seen in the book.

- **Demos:** Location of the demo file that you can install.

- **Examples:** All of the example files needed to follow the instructions in this book as well as completed versions of the code.

- **Import:** Two images used for importing into the picture editor.

- **Sound:** Two .wav sounds to use in the examples.

- **TileSets:** A number of graphic libraries for use in the example files.

- **Wargame Object:** An MMF object used to add additional functionality to MMF2 for the A* movement algorithm.

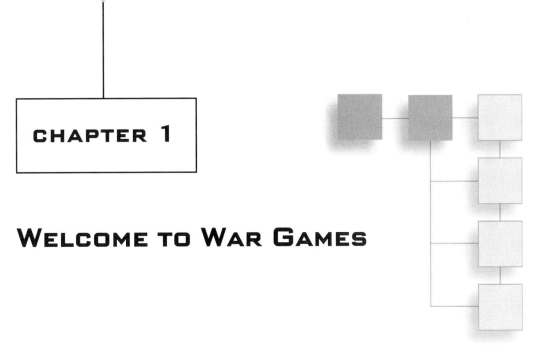

CHAPTER 1

WELCOME TO WAR GAMES

Welcome to war games! We assume you are reading this book because you want to make your own computer war games for the PC platform. Using this book and the accompanying software, you will be able to create your very own battles from single-soldier skirmishes to large campaigns featuring many units.

You don't need any programming knowledge to learn how to create your war games because you will be using a special software programming language called Multimedia Fusion 2, which is all about creating games using an event-based system that is easy enough for anyone to use to make games. This does not mean that the program lacks power. On the contrary, games and programs made with Multimedia Fusion 2 can be very complex and powerful. The main benefit of the program is that it's very quick and easy to use so you don't spend lots of time trying to learn to program, leaving you to concentrate on making your war games.

In this book we will also be exploring the rules and concepts that you might want to include in your own games, as well as look at various time periods that you could recreate. By the end of this book you will be able to make your own war game battles and understand how to make your own war game editor.

A Brief History of War Games

War games have been around for a very long time and in many different forms. It is perhaps impossible to know when, where, or in exactly what form the earliest of war games might have existed, but it is quite possible that they used counters made of wood or even bone and might have resembled today's board games. One such game that still survives today is chess. You may not consider chess to be a war game, but think about it; chess is all about making moves, attacking, defending, and surprising the enemy (other player).

War games became an important aspect of military life beginning in the 1800s as the various European countries fought for control of territory. Since then, they have grown from a military battle tool into a hobby form as non-military types wanted to recreate famous battles.

Since the early days of war and strategy games, different types have appeared that appeal to new groups of players and that take advantage of new technology.

New Model Army

One type of war gaming system, which has been popular since the early 1900s, was the type that required metal or plastic soldiers on a battlefield. Players would move their soldiers certain distances on the battlefield, working out firing rates, distances and a multitude of other rules to try and recreate the battle as authentically as possible.

Such battles could take from a few hours to several days, depending on the size of the battlefield. Players would need to take into account such issues as the number of model soldiers required, a person to play against, and somewhere to play the game.

This form of war game was popular because it wasn't a simple case of moving wooden blocks around a board. It was very visual, and you could see the battle progress right before your eyes. It was a visual experience like no other and a leap forward for people wanting to recreate certain battles. The logistics of getting started on the road to such a hobby, however, were not easy or cheap.

Model soldiers were pretty much the mainstay of any war game hobbyist for many years, but finally, as better production techniques came along and board games became more complex (and more accurate for those wanting to recreate historic battles), they started to become less attractive. A further competitor to the traditional war game came in the form of the home computer in the 1980s.

The tabletop war game was starting to look as if it finally had its day. The younger generations no longer wanted to recreate past battles and were more interested in fantasy and futuristic stories and battles. Just as it was looking like the model soldiers were going to be resigned to history and a small band of dedicated users, a British games company released a set of products that would set the table top gaming world alight. Games Workshop, which had been successful in distributing American products, decided to create two of their own games as both role-playing and table top miniature soldiers. Warhammer was a medieval fantasy-based game, and Warhammer 40K (40,000) focused on futuristic wars.

Both proved to be very successful and transformed the table top game. Recently, they have also released miniature soldiers based on the Lord of the Rings tale, which has again brought in many new players who may not otherwise have considered playing this type of game.

Board and Hex Wars

Board games took away some of the hassles from having model soldiers taking up floor space or even a whole room. Depending on the game, they used plastic or metal models to represent battle units, which would be placed on a battlefield or map area. In some cases, these games required imagination; you had to imagine that one plastic item could equate to a few hundred or a few thousand soldiers, tanks, or planes.

One of the most popular board war games is Risk. It is played on a world map by two or more players. Playing against or with other players, the game calls for world domination. One of the fun aspects of this game is creating alliances to attack other players. These alliances are generally fragile and short-lived, but this gives the game an amazing edge and makes it a lot of fun to play.

It was probably because of games like Risk that games designers were encouraged to look for new gaming ideas. Risk really captures the idea of armies moving across land and fighting, but ultimately is fighting at a country level. It's no surprise that game designers came up with the concept of fighting various battles within a board game setting, but at a battle level. This is where the Hex game appeared, using a board map of a battlefield. Each space on the map was drawn using a square or hex. The units were represented by a cardboard square or hex shape. These games were very popular and allowed people to recreate famous battles throughout history, including the American Civil War, the battle for Stalingrad, and even science fiction battles from the future.

Hex games were particularly successful because they didn't have the start-up costs or room issues of the model soldier games, and they allowed the player to really see the battle landscape, which board games like Risk couldn't.

Hex games proved popular for quite a while and really hit their peak in the 1980s. Unfortunately, another advancing technology, the home computer, took the limelight and provided a new way of playing war games.

People are still making hex board games today, and you can find these online using a search engine. Independent game developers make many hex-board war games. Unfortunately, many of the companies that used to make these types of games no longer exist, so it is rather fortunate that the individual game creator is still creating these products.

Computer War Games

The war game landscape was forever changed with the arrival of the home computer. These early computers, such as the Spectrum 48K, Electron, and the BBC computers had very small memory constraints and limited graphical ability. These machines had many benefits over model soldiers and board games, but the one factor that made a big difference was that the computer could control the opposing side in battle. Until this point, war gaming was generally a group affair, either finding other groups or friends to help you play. If you weren't a member of a wargaming group or your friends were not interested in this type of game, it could be very difficult to get to play any war games. Computer AI (Artificial Intelligence) provided someone to play against, with settings that could make easier or harder challenges.

Early computer war games were very simple affairs, with basic graphics and soldiers usually in a single color. These images were typically made up of simple blocks, and though they are very basic compared to today's computer graphics, were still impressive in their day.

As technology improved, so did the accessibility, type, and scale of such war games. Computers also meant that the traditional war game could be played, as well as new and different types of war games, such as arcade battles, flight simulators, and role-playing games.

With fast processors and the larger amounts of computer memory that computers can handle these days, directing a battle with hundreds or even thousands of individual soldiers is now possible. One of the best computer war games available is the Total War series, which has covered both medieval and Roman warfare on a scale that has yet to be beaten in a computer game. Not only can you control hundreds of soldiers, you can also attack cities and use siege warfare or even diplomacy if you prefer.

As computers continue to become more powerful and graphics become more photorealistic, home computers will continue to lead what is now the most popular way of playing war games.

Battle Card Games

Some might not consider card games to be war games, and that might be true in the traditional sense of needing toy soldiers or a hex board game. Card games can range from a very simple set of rules such as cheat, to card games which have more in depth and complex rules, like World of Warcraft battle cards. They can require calm, strategy and an amount of risk, which any armchair general would need in a traditional war game.

One of the most well-known battle card games is Top Trumps, which involves a set of simple cards on a subject matter such as dinosaurs, fighter jets, tanks, or planet seach—subject matter that has several categories. Each player selects a category in turn and the one with the higher figure for that category wins the cards. The player wins when she has collected all of the cards.

More complex card games like Pokemon and Yu-Gi-oh have arrived on the scene and have proved very popular. Cartoons and computer games based on these card games have increased in popularity over time.

Computer and Board Games

In the 1980s when the home computer started to become a useful way of playing war games, developers tried other methods to make the war games come alive. Early computers, such as the Sinclair Spectrum, had very limited memory and only a small number of colors, so they could not convey the battlefield danger and excitement to the player.

Some developers decided to go for a dual approach, using the home computer to do the calculations and odd special effects, while having a board to move around your pieces. The computer would keep track of the pieces on the board as well as working out the battlefield computations, such as weather effects, morale, and unit strength.

Making War Games Using Multimedia Fusion 2

In this book we will be making our war games using an easy-to-use programming tool called Multimedia Fusion 2. This product allows even those with no programming knowledge to make their own computer games. Multimedia Fusion is great because you will be able to spend more time concentrating on what you need for your games rather than trying to learn how to program. Making a game is not just about being able to program, but about coming up with a structure to your game so that you can accurately create the environment that your war games will take place in.

In this book we will be concentrating on Hex-based war games, which are one of the most popular types of war games played in both computer and board game form. This doesn't mean that what you learn in this book cannot be applied to other types of war games; on the contrary, you will be able to use the concepts and ideas on other games that you might want to make. This is because many of the concepts that are covered are very typical of other war games.

Multimedia Fusion 2 is also called MMF2 throughout this book. More information about Multimedia Fusion 2 can be found at www.clickteam.com.

We will be taking a closer look at Multimedia Fusion 2 in Chapter 2, before we begin making our war games.

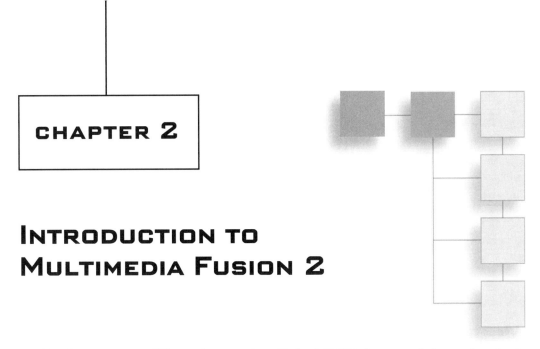

CHAPTER 2

INTRODUCTION TO
MULTIMEDIA FUSION 2

In this chapter you will learn how to install the MMF2 demo and then take a look at the process you can use to build your games from the bottom up, allowing you to understand what you need to do at each stage of the process. You will also learn about all the editors, toolbars, and screens available, some of which you will spend a lot of time in, while you may only use others intermittently. Finally, you will get to see the objects that are available; these objects are the cornerstone to any creation within MMF2 and are essential to getting features like text, graphics, and buttons in your war game.

Installing Multimedia Fusion 2

Before you can begin to create your programs, you will need to install the trial version of MMF2. Place the CD-ROM that comes with the book into your computer's CD-ROM drive.

 Browse the CD and navigate into the \Demos folder. In this folder, you will find a file called MMF2Demo.exe. Double click on this file to start the installation. A Welcome dialog box will appear as shown in Figure 2.1; click on the next button to continue with the installation.

Note

As detailed in Figure 2.1, you must ensure you are logged in as a user with Administrator rights. If you are not logged in as an Administrator, the installation may fail.

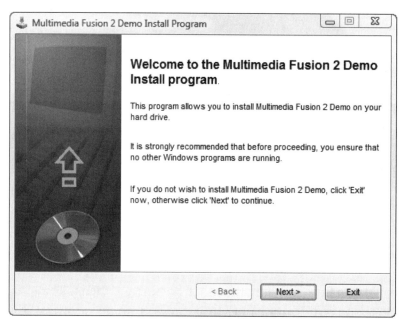

Figure 2.1
The Welcome dialog box.

The next dialog box, shown in Figure 2.2, provides information on the trial version and details on purchasing the full version of the software. Click on the Next button to proceed to the next dialog box.

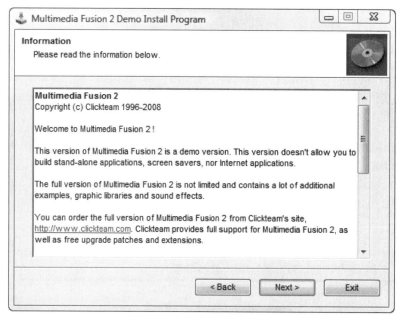

Figure 2.2
The information dialog box.

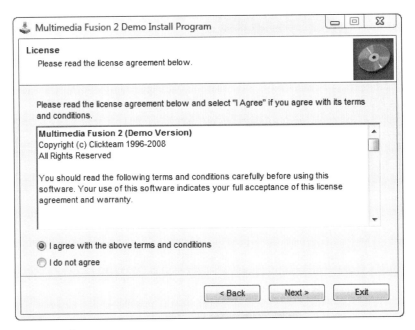

Figure 2.3
The license agreement dialog box.

When the License dialog box appears, as shown in Figure 2.3, read the terms and conditions carefully, then check the "I agree with the above terms and conditions" radio button (this is the round box). You will then need to click on the Next button to proceed.

You will now need to decide where you wish to install the trial version of MMF2 as shown in Figure 2.4. The program will have already decided on a potential installation path and drive. If this location is acceptable, click on the Next button to continue with the installation.

If you wish to select a different drive and folder location, click on the small rectangular box (which contains three dots), and select a new installation path. A Browse dialog box will appear, as shown in Figure 2.5; select the disk where you wish to install MMF2 (in this example there is a C, and a recovery disk on D) and then locate the folder. Click on OK to continue.

After you select the new location, you may receive a message advising you that the folder where you want to install MMF2 doesn't exist, as shown in Figure 2.6. This is nothing to worry about, and you should click on the Yes button.

You will be taken back to the installation path dialog box as shown in Figure 2.4. Click on the Next button to continue. At this stage you will get confirmation of

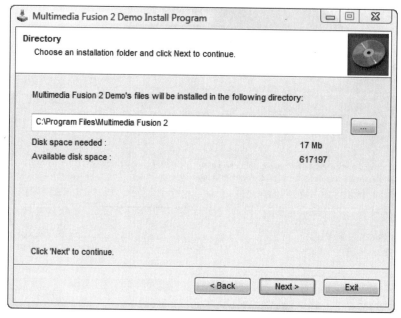

Figure 2.4
The installation path dialog box.

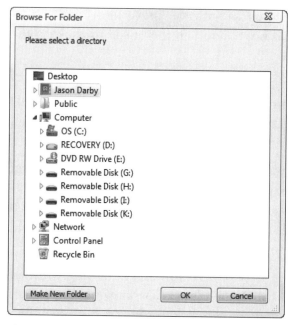

Figure 2.5
The Browse For Folder dialog box.

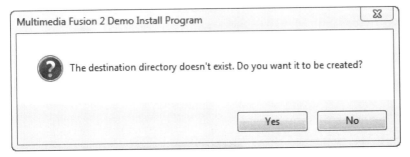

Figure 2.6
Create new folder dialog.

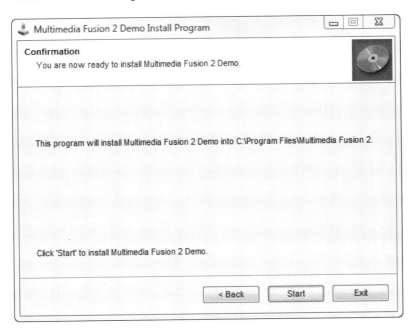

Figure 2.7
Confirmation dialog box.

where the files for MMF2 will be installed, as illustrated in Figure 2.7. If you agree with the selected path, click on the Start button to let the installer start copying files. If you want to change the location, click the Back button to reconfigure it.

The installation files will now be copied to your computer's hard disk as shown in Figure 2.8. This may take a minute depending on the speed of your CD-ROM drive and computer.

Once the installation has been completed, a final dialog box will appear, as shown in Figure 2.9. This dialog box provides some information that may be of use to new users. Click on the link to visit Clickteam's web site for support; if you want

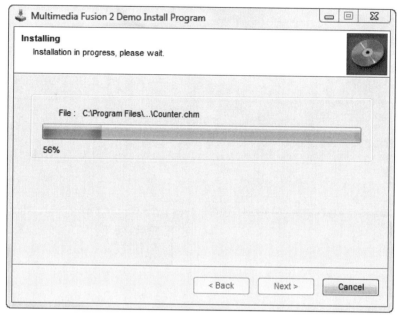

Figure 2.8
Installation copying files.

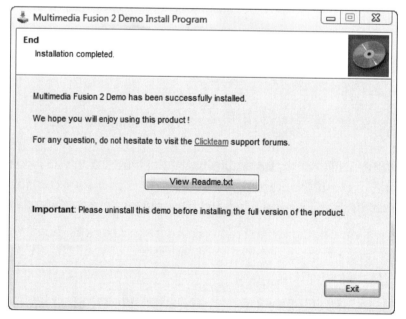

Figure 2.9
End Installation dialog box.

to know the latest details on the trial software, click on the View Readme.txt button.

We will launch Multimedia Fusion shortly, so for now click on the Exit button.

Program Creation Process in MMF2

Creating war games, or, in fact, any type of game, in MMF2 follows the same process. This process can be categorized as follows (but not necessarily in this order):

- **Creating a New Application:** An application in MMF2 is effectively a new blank worksheet to create your program.

- **Creating the Frames:** A frame is a self-contained level or screen within your program. You can create a single frame or multiple frames for your application. Frames can be linked to and jumped back and forth from.

- **Setting the Scene:** This may involve importing images, drawing images, or placing graphics on different frames.

- **Adding Functionality:** You can add extra power and functionality to Multimedia Fusion using Objects, which are placed within the frames. These objects are covered later in this chapter.

- **Coding:** At this stage you begin coding your creation. This is so MMF2 knows what to do when a certain event happens. This event could be when a user clicks on the mouse or exits the program.

- **Testing:** You will need to test your creation to make sure it works correctly and that no programming errors exist.

- **Compiling:** After you complete your testing, you will need to compile your program. This changes the MMF2 formatted file (which can only be opened on a computer running the MMF2 program) to either an executable or screensaver formatted file. At this stage it can be given to a user to run on her own computer without the need for MMF2 to be installed locally.

Note

When using the trial version of MMF2, you will not be able to compile your creations into either screensavers or executable files. To do this, you will need to purchase the full version of the software from Clickteam.

■ **Distribution:** After you compile your program, you will need to think about how you are going to distribute your file. Will you upload it to the Internet? Provide it on a CD-ROM? Perhaps you are going to create a special installer program to make it easier to install on the end user's computer.

Starting MMF2

You can start MMF2 in either of two ways, either from an icon on the Windows desktop or from the Start/Programs menu bar. If you choose to start MMF2 from the desktop, double click on the icon. If running from a Windows XP PC use the Start menu, click on Start|All Programs|Multimedia Fusion 2|Multimedia Fusion 2. If you are running the trial version on Vista, click on the Start button then click on All Programs, and from the menu bar, find Multimedia Fusion 2. Clicking on this folder reveals several options, one of which is the Multimedia Fusion 2 icon.

Note

Depending on what version of Windows you are running, the location of the program on the menu bar may be placed under Start|Programs rather than Start|All Programs as previously stated.

An example of the files located under the Multimedia Fusion 2 folder is shown in Figure 2.10.

The MMF2 demo screen will appear as shown in Figure 2.11.

The Demo dialog box details the limitations of the trial version, and also gives details of where a full version can be purchased. You will notice that Always show the tutorial at startup is currently enabled. If you leave this option checked, MMF2 will load a help file explaining how to make a simple Bat & Ball game. We do not wish to run the tutorial at this time, so ensure that the Always show the tutorial at startup is not checked and then click on the Continue button.

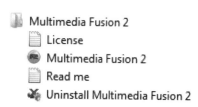

Figure 2.10
Example of the files installed under the MMF2 folder.

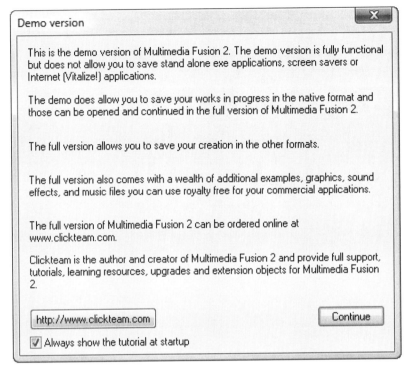

Figure 2.11
Demo-version dialog box.

Note

You can run the tutorial at any time, by going into the menu system and selecting Help|Tutorial; alternatively, you can check the Always show the tutorial at startup checkbox when you next start MMF2.

The MMF2 interface will now run and should look similar to that in Figure 2.12. This is the default interface when no programming has been started or when you start the program each time.

Program Walkthrough

In this section of the book, you will take a tour of the MMF2 interface and the screens you will encounter when using the product (the different screens are called Editors in MMF2). You will also learn when you might use different parts of the application as future reference.

Note

If you forget which part of the application does a particular task, you should refer back to this section for advice on which editor to choose.

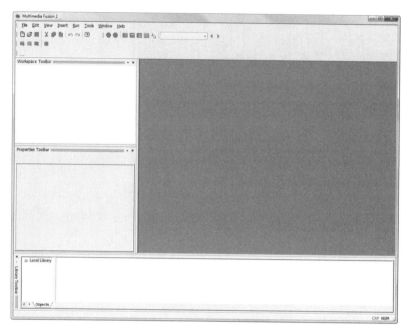

Figure 2.12
The MMF2 interface.

MMF2 has several editors and toolbars that will be used to create your programs. In this section, you will learn about each of them and how they interact with Windows programs and when you might use some editors and toolbars and not others.

Note

An editor is a special screen in MMF2 for completing a specific task. This could be creating a picture, programming some interactivity or placing your images on screen. A toolbar is used for accessing specific information and data in MMF2.

The following sections contain more details about the individual toolbars and the editors that are available.

Program Areas

Figure 2.13 displays what you can see when you first load MMF2; these are:

1. The Menu Toolbar

2. The Menu Button Toolbar

3. Workspace Toolbar

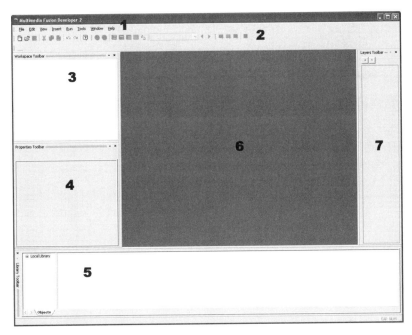

Figure 2.13
Various editors and toolbars in MMF2 highlighted.

4. Properties Toolbar

5. Library Toolbar

6. Workspace/Editor Area

7. Layers Toolbar

N o t e

The actual layout of the screen may differ slightly in the trial version of the software. The Layers loolbar may or may not be automatically displayed.

You will come into contact with the majority of these toolbars throughout the use of the product and will use some more than others.

- **The Menu Toolbar:** This is the text menu at the top of MMF2 program, which configures the general layout and program preferences. From the menu toolbar, you can also load and save programs. An example of the menu toolbar in action can be seen in Figure 2.14.

Figure 2.14
The File option from the menu toolbar has been selected.

- **The Menu Button Toolbar:** Just under the text menu is the button toolbar. Depending on which editors are open, different buttons will be present. These buttons provide quick access to various settings and other editors. An example of some items in a menu button toolbar can be seen in Figure 2.15.

- **Workspace Toolbar:** The workspace toolbar provides a view of your program and its contents. In the toolbar you will see objects and frames; these are discussed later in this chapter. An example of an application structure in the workspace toolbar is shown in Figure 2.16.

- **Properties Toolbar:** Different items within MMF2 contain properties. The properties toolbar provides a quick way of accessing them. An example of the properties toolbar is shown in Figure 2.17.

- **Library Toolbar:** From the library toolbar you will access pre-made objects and graphic libraries; these can be either using those that come with the product or by creating your own. An example of a library already selected can be shown in Figure 2.18.

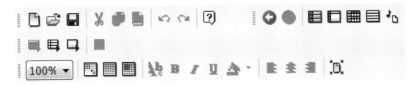

Figure 2.15
A selection of menu buttons.

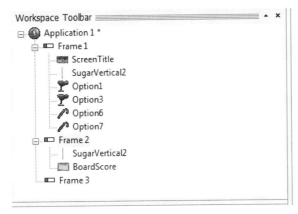

Figure 2.16
An example application loaded into the workspace toolbar.

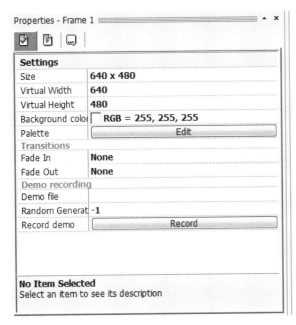

Figure 2.17
An example of frames properties.

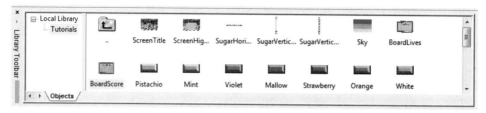

Figure 2.18
A set of game items loaded into the library toolbar.

■ **Workspace & Editor Area:** This is where a number of the editors will appear (one at a time), and allowing you to make your creation (by placing the graphics on the screen) or program it. Examples of the editor are discussed later on in this chapter in the Editors section.

■ **Layers:** The layers toolbar allows you to create multiple layers to place your objects and graphics on screen. This is very useful for graphical effects or for grouping graphic items. An example of two layers in use can be seen in Figure 2.19.

The Editors

The editors within MMF2 are:

■ Storyboard Editor

■ Frame Editor

■ Event Editor

■ Event List Editor

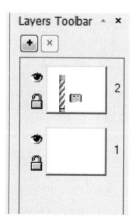

Figure 2.19
A two-layer program.

- Picture Editor

- Expression Evaluator

Storyboard Editor

The storyboard editor allows the programmer to see the structure of all the screens in their games; these screens are called frames in MMF2. These frames could be levels of a game, different pictures in a screensaver, or various screens within a multimedia tutorial (an example of a three-frame program can be seen in Figure 2.20). The storyboard editor allows you to visualize from above the order of frames within your program. The editor also gives you the ability to drag and drop frames into a specific order, or insert additional frames. The storyboard editor can help provide a useful insight into understanding the amount of work you still have left to do to complete your program (for example, working out the percentage of frames still left to program).

If we take a closer look at the storyboard editor, shown in Figure 2.21, you will notice a number of configurable options are available from this screen. These

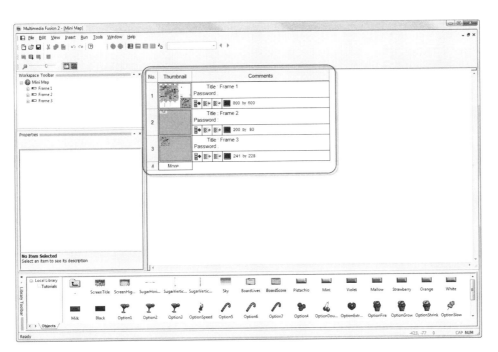

Figure 2.20
Example program displayed in storyboard editor.

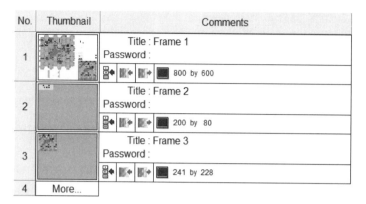

No.	Thumbnail	Comments
1		Title : Frame 1 Password : 800 by 600
2		Title : Frame 2 Password : 200 by 80
3		Title : Frame 3 Password : 241 by 228
4	More...	

Figure 2.21
Storyboard editor close up.

include the name of each frame, the size of the frame, password, and transitions for the start or end of each frame.

If you were going to change the frame size or the title of a frame, you probably would do this in the Workspace editor, and you would generally only use this editor to assign a password, add a transition, or change the order of a frame.

Frame Editor

The frame editor is one of two core editors that you will spend the majority of your time working in (the other one is the event editor). The frame editor is where you place all of the graphical objects for your program. Within the frame editor you may also add any additional objects that are required for the frame to function. These objects could allow you to display a picture, open a file, and create a text file. These objects will be covered shortly. Figure 2.22 shows a program displayed in the frame editor.

After you drag the items from your library toolbar to your frame or import them using the built-in picture editor, you will see them in the left-hand pane. This windowpane allows you to select individual objects, which can be quite useful if you have a lot of items placed on top of each other. You can also create object folders, which allow you to organize relevant items in one place.

Event Editor

The event editor is where all the coding is done in MMF2. The coding is not what you might normally expect of a programming language because you won't need

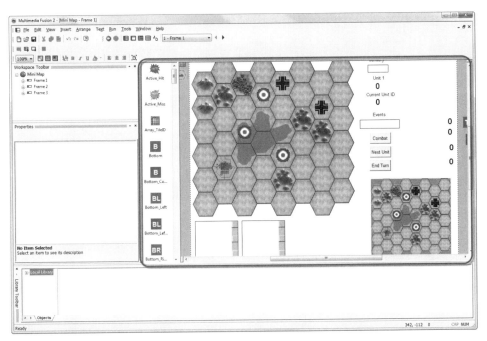

Figure 2.22
A program displayed in the frame editor.

to do lots of typing in of text. The majority of the programming within MMF2 takes the form of left and right clicking of the mouse buttons. The event editor is based on an eventing system, which makes it an easy system to understand for anyone with no programming background. Although the programming side may seem simplistic, it actually makes programming very quick. Because of the work already done by the programmers of MMF2, there is a lot of power in the product. This means that you do not sacrifice the power of the program because of its ease of use, which is very important when you start getting into very complicated programming projects.

An in-progress project displayed in the event editor is shown in Figure 2.23. A closer look at the event editor can be seen in Figure 2.24.

The event editor is split into several rows and columns. Down the left hand side, as shown in the gray shaded boxes in Figure 2.24, are several events. These events contain conditions. Across the top are objects (these are the core components that are required in our programs, such as graphics, multimedia, and text video), and the grid-like area between those two areas are where the actions are placed (where a check mark is displayed). The first seven objects across the top are called system objects and are always present in your creations. Listed after these seven

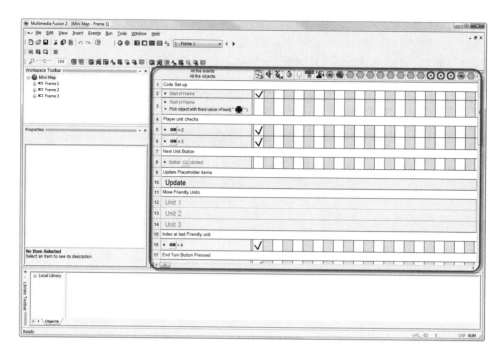

Figure 2.23
Event Editor within the MMF2 interface.

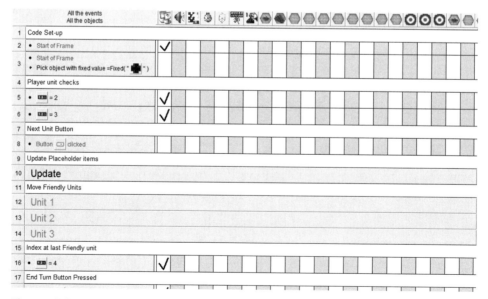

Figure 2.24
Close-up look of the event editor.

system objects are any additional objects that you have added to that specific frame. To the right of the events and directly below the objects (the white boxes) are action boxes. Where you see check marks in Figure 2.24 are where actions have been assigned to a condition.

Beginning with the events and conditions; an event is simply a container which holds one or many conditions that tell the program to wait for something to happen. Some examples of possible single conditions might be:

- The program has just appeared

- Ball graphic stops moving

- User exits program

- Music is playing

- Internet is loading

- User clicks on a button on a CD-ROM menu

Note

These are example conditions to illustrate what you might find within your games and are not examples of conditions shown in Figure 2.24.

You can also use multiple conditions in MMF2:

- Music is playing and user clicks on button

- Ball graphic hits bat graphic and current score

- Graphic has disappeared off screen, and player's lives equal zero

Note

You can create more than two conditions in an event; the ones mentioned shown as an illustration of their structure.

Having defined a condition, you will then want something to happen and this is where actions come into play. The whole reason you are trapping conditions is because you want something to happen at that point.

Some examples of action are:

- Lose a life

- Add 20 to player score

- Exit the program

- Play a sound or music

Some examples of how actions and conditions work together can be seen in Table 2.1.

Table 2.1 Conditions and Actions

Condition	Action
User clicks on button	Go to different screen
User clicks on exit button	Exit that screen or exit the program
Ball goes out of play	Remove 1 life from player's life total
No lives left	Display hi-score
Song has finished playing	Play next song
File has downloaded	Display a message to say Download complete

The importance of the action box is that it is directly under a specific object. Perhaps we have a graphic of a plane and when it gets to the edge of the screen we want that plane to bounce back so that it doesn't leave the frame. The condition might be as follows:

Is the Plane object about to leave the playfield?

Note

This is an example of a condition and action and not the actual text that will appear in the MMF2 program.

When placing the actual action, we need to place it in the action box that directly relates to what we want to happen. In this case, we want the Plane object to bounce back. So moving across from the condition, we would ensure that we are directly below the Plane object and then find the action Bounce. You can see an example of this code and what it would look like within the event editor in Figure 2.25.

Event List Editor

The event list editor is a refined view of the event editor that allows you to see your conditions and actions in a list. Figure 2.26 shows where the event list

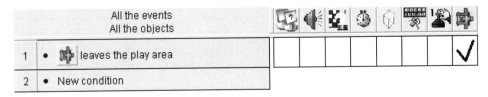

Figure 2.25
Plane object with action.

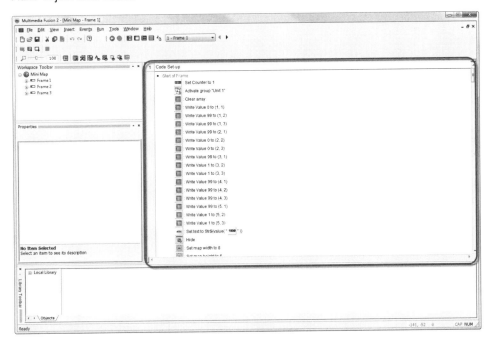

Figure 2.26
The event list editor.

editor is displayed in the MMF2 application. Figure 2.27 shows a close up view of this screen.

One of the things you need to consider in an event-based programming system is that the code is executed in the order that it is placed in an event or action box. This is fine for conditions because in the event editor you can change the order of the conditions, but for actions, you can only add new ones, which are then displayed as check marks or colored blocks. The event list editor allows you to change the order of created actions (by dragging and dropping them in the order that you want them). Another advantage of the event list editor is that it is graphically stripped down which is perfect for printing your events out so you can study them away from your computer. Except for printing or ordering

Figure 2.27
Close up view of the event list editor.

actions (conditions and events can be ordered easily from within the event editor), you will not need to use the event list editor.

Picture Editor

When you want to import graphic images or perhaps draw your own, you will use the picture editor as shown in Figure 2.28. To use the picture editor, you must first have placed an object of a graphical nature onto the frame play area. Once you have done that you can then double click to edit it (more information about objects is available later on in this chapter).

The picture editor contains similar tools that a normal drawing program might have, including pencil, paint brush, fill, text, and shapes. You can also select different colors to apply to your images as well as implementing picture transparency.

Included within the picture editor is an animation editor which allows you to create multiple pictures in a single animation and also set the speed of that animation. You can create multiple animations for the same object, so you could, for example, create a robot with walking, jumping, and running animations. This would all be kept within the same object and you would then use MMF2 to select which animation you want to play at a particular time.

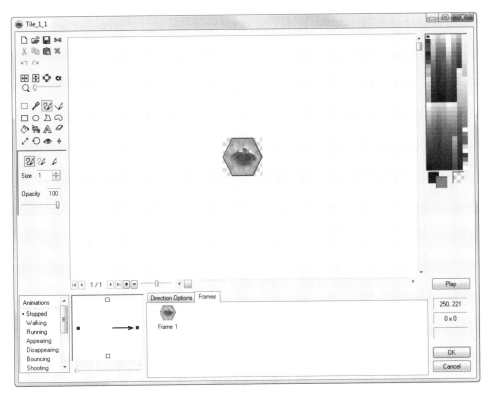

Figure 2.28
Picture editor for drawing or importing graphics.

Expression Evaluator

The expression evaluator resembles a scientific calculator with a selection of numeric- and calculation-based buttons. You will use the expression evaluator when you want to compare different types of data, do calculations, or set data into a specific object. An example of the expression evaluator can be seen in Figure 2.29 and Figure 2.30. You will notice that the buttons are the same, but the expressions are different. The type of calculations you are trying to do will depend on the expression evaluator that is displayed.

Some examples of when you might use the expression evaluator are

- To set a number in the score object

- Set a text word, for example Hello, in a text object

- Compare two numbers and see if one is greater than, less than, or equal to the other number

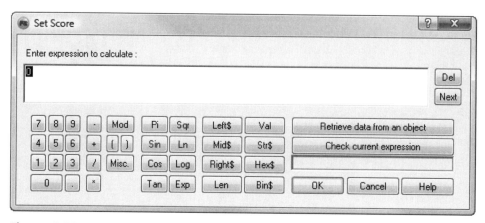

Figure 2.29
The basic expression evaluator.

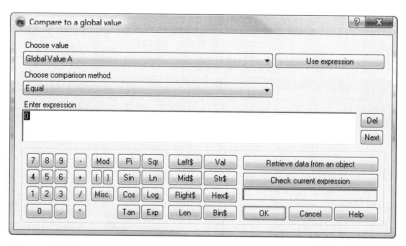

Figure 2.30
More complex expression evaluator.

- Compare two pieces of text

- Find the location of a file (the current drive where the application is installed)

- Obtain specific information from an object

Objects: The Key to Development

Objects in MMF2 are the core components for creating your program. When you look closely at any program in MMF2, you may notice that every item on the frame editor is a separate entity. These entities are all objects. Some examples of objects being used within a program could be:

- A score counter

- A background graphic

- A player-controlled graphic

- A button for clicking next

- An animation

- A high score table

- A drop-down menu box

- A video box

It makes no difference if you are making a war game, multimedia application, video player, kiosk system, or an arcade game; every program will utilize objects. Objects are what make MMF2 extremely powerful because, not only does it have a large number of already included objects, anyone with a knowledge of C++ can also create additional ones. If you purchased the full version of the product, you can download the Bonus Packs to gain this added functionality.

Note

The demo comes with a standard set of objects and will allow you to make all of the programs detailed in this book as well as a wide and varied number of other programs you might make yourself.

Note

Objects are also referred to as extensions or extension objects.

Approximately sixty objects are available in the trial version of MMF2, some of which will be covered in more detail throughout the book. You will learn how to add an object in Chapter 4. Until then, here is a quick rundown of each of the extensions.

- **AVI:** AVI is a video format and is used to display and play video files within the MMF2 application.

- **Active:** The word is very appropriate for this object type because it is associated with any graphic object that is going to move across the screen or be animated.

- **Active Picture:** You can load a picture from the hard disk and then rotate, resize, and manipulate it in real time. You can either load the picture in to the program when you are developing or get the object to ask the user to specify a file when the program has been compiled.

- **Active System Box:** An object that is generally used for application toolbars or toolbar buttons, which can contain check boxes and hyperlinks.

- **Active X:** Active X objects are a specially formatted file created by Microsoft and other software vendors. Using Active X gives you the ability to add functionality from applications that the user might have installed. For example, it is possible to use the Internet Explorer Active X control to create a web page display within an MMF2 application. To be able to create a web browser within MMF2, you need to have IE installed; this will allow you to insert the IE Active X control in your own programs.

Note

Not all Active X objects are available on every user's machine; the number of objects is dependent on the applications the user has installed. Additional license restrictions or requirements may be assigned to Active X controls and care should be taken when using them.

- **Analog Joystick:** This object reports specific information about the movement of the joystick and which buttons are pressed. Support for standard joysticks is built in to the Player object.

Note

The player object is part of a special group of objects that are always present in an MMF2 program and will be discussed shortly.

- **Animation:** The animation object is used to display FLC and GIF still images and display them as if they were animated; it does this by showing each of the images quickly to give the illusion of a smooth animated movie. If you are going to animate bmp or other file formats, you should use the Active object.

- **Array:** When you want to store information that you might want to retrieve in your creation at a later stage, you can use the array object. Arrays store either numbers or text. You can write to and read from the array file at runtime. The array is an efficient way to store and retrieve information that is used regularly.

- **Backdrop:** This is used when you want to display a graphic or background image that you don't need to animate.

- **Background System Box:** Used in conjunction with the Active Background system object. Used if you want to attach buttons and move the object with the active buttons attached to it. This object is also used for toolbars like the active system box.

- **Button:** Used when you want to use various button types, either standard ones within Windows applications or your own buttons using your own images. Contains standard Windows checkbox, radio, and push-button types.

- **CD Audio:** Allows you to play audio CDs from within an MMF2 program. You can also use it to open and close the CD-ROM door.

- **Click Blocker:** When you want to prevent the left, right, or center mouse button, you can block it (prevent it) from happening using the Click Blocker.

- **Combo Box:** Standard Windows control used for displaying lists in a drop-down box.

- **Counter:** Number or graphics counter that can be used in a variety of ways: for keeping track of a calculation, scores, or to display a health bar in a game, etc.

- **Cursor:** Allows graphical changes to the mouse cursor.

- **Date and Time:** Ability to add a date or time to your programs or do comparisons of the computer's current settings. The time can be displayed in analog or digital format.

- **Dialogs:** Seen in standard Windows applications.

- **Direct Show:** Allows you to include a wide variety of sound and video file formats within your own creations, including AVI, MPEG, and MP3 formats.

- **Download Object:** An object that allows you to download files from the Internet using the HTTP protocol.

- **Draw Object:** The draw object creates an area of the screen that acts like a paint program where different pen, paint, and fill options can be applied.

- **Edit Box:** Allows you to create a way for the end user to enter text. The object also has the ability to save and load text.

- **File:** Using the file object, you can load, save, append, and delete files as well as a host of other file and folder checking capabilities.

- **Formatted Text:** Ability to add text to the screen which can be given formatting features, such as bold, underlined, and italic.

- **FTP:** FTP stands for File Transfer Protocol and is used to download or upload files to the Internet.

- **Hi-Score:** Adds a Hi-Score table, which can be configured with a predefined set of scores and names.

- **INI:** Special type of formatted file, in which MMF2 can store information and read from at runtime. Used for storing basic program configuration information.

- **Layer Object:** Allows you to change the order of objects on the screen so you can move items in front of or behind other objects.

- **List:** Creates a list which can be sorted. This is a standard Windows control object that you will see in dialog boxes and applications.

- **Lives:** Displays the number of lives that a player has in a game, in text, numbers, or image format. When a player loses a life, you can subtract a number from the number stored in the lives object, which will then update the display to reflect the current state of play.

- **MCI:** An object that allows the MMF2 to control any multimedia device that is connected to the computer. It works by sending a string (text) command to the MCI object. There is a large selection of commands to choose from and advanced documentation can be found on the Microsoft Web site.

- **MPEG:** MPEG is a standard video format (Motion Picture Expert Group) and allows you to play these files within MMF2.

- **Mixer:** Allows you to change the volume control of your sound and Midi formatted files.

- **MooClick, MooGame, and Moosock:** A selection of network-based objects that allow the creation of multiplayer games, chat programs, and special network protocol based applications.

- **Network:** Basic Local Area Network (LAN) communications where two machines can communicate with each other.

- **ODBC:** Stands for Open Database Connectivity, and allows communication with a variety of database files, such as Access, Dbase, SQL Server, Oracle, and Excel databases. Using the object, you can access, update, edit, and create new tables within the database using SQL language.

- **Picture:** An object to load and display a picture that can be resized within MMF2 at runtime.

- **Pop-up Menu:** You can see the pop-up menu in use in the Windows operating system when you right click on the mouse button. The pop-up menu allows you to create your own pop-up menus in MMF2.

- **Print:** Allows you to use specific print options and printer settings.

- **Question & Answer:** If you want to create a program that asks the user a selection of questions, a quick way to create them is to use the Q&A object.

- **Quick Backdrop:** You can create a simple background image for your program which can include gradients or a solid color.

- **Quicktime:** Allows you to implement Quicktime movies in your creations.

- **Quiz Object:** An improved Question & Answer object with multiple choice, true or false, and matching quiz system.

- **Rich Edit:** Rich Edit is a special kind of object that allows advanced text formatting and also allows the loading and saving of text files.

- **Score:** Used to keep track of a player's score and display it as a graphic object.

- **Screen Capture:** Allows you to capture (take a picture of) an area of the screen and save it to a graphic formatted file.

- **Search:** Gives you the ability to search text files for a phrase or word as well as use wildcard options.

- **Shared Data:** Allows you to share data between several files that have been created in MMF2.

- **Static Text:** Basic text display object.

- **String:** Basic text display object.

- **Sub Application:** Allows you to insert another MMF2-created application into the frame of another MMF2-created application.

- **Tree Control:** Allows you to create application-based trees seen in standard Windows applications, using folders and items.

- **Vitalize Plugin:** You can open a URL or download a file using this object.

- **Wargame Map Object:** An object that will make creating Wargame maps and unit movement.

- **Window Control:** Control the size, visibility, and position of the current MMF2 application.

- **Windows Shape:** Create an application with a rounded shape or use another object (graphic picture) to create the shape of your application.

System Objects

The objects that we have just described are those you will add to your program for a specific set of features. If you do add those objects, they will not appear in your program or the event editor object list. There is another type of object called "System Object" which is present in every MMF2 file. These seven objects are not displayed within the frame editor but in the event editor. Figure 2.31 shows a blank event editor with no code written in it but the seven objects already present.

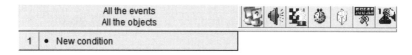

Figure 2.31
The system objects present in the event editor.

The seven system objects can be used in the same way as normal objects and can be used to create conditions or actions. These system objects have the following capabilities:

- **Special Conditions**: Special conditions are a selection of useful commands that you will use in cases of comparing numbers and strings, running external programs, enabling and disabling groups, and checking the clipboard contents.

- **Sound:** If you want to determine whether a sound is playing or apply a sound to be played, select this object.

- **Storyboard Controls:** Movement between frames is handled by the actions of this object. Its conditions check to see if the frame has started or finished.

- **The Timer:** Used when you want to do comparisons on the current time or determine the amount of time that has passed since the application was first started.

- **Create New Objects:** Used when you need to create copies of already created objects or pick or count objects that are already in play on the frame.

- **The Mouse Pointer and Keyboard:** Any actions or conditions that will use the mouse and keyboard will be placed within this system object. Also allows checking for the mouse pointer within a specific area on the screen or identifying when a key has been pressed.

- **Player 1:** Sets up the player controls (joystick or keyboard) and also configures the lives and score of the current player.

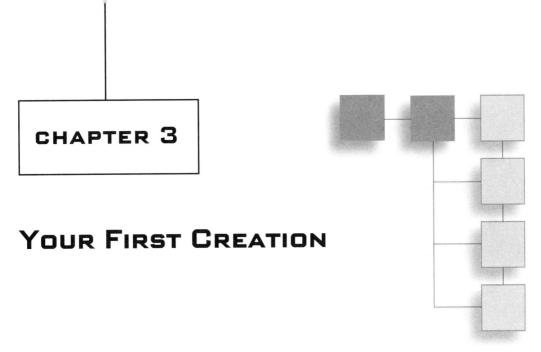

CHAPTER 3

YOUR FIRST CREATION

For your first creation, you will be making a very simple program that will display a text object which contains the words Welcome to my first program and will use a simple movement routine and code to bounce around the screen. This simple creation is to give you a brief look at some of the screens you will use in more depth later on as well as give you a quick look at what you need to do to put your creation together.

For our first project we will use the following process:

1. Create the application file and rename it.

2. Add the text object.

3. Configure the text object.

4. Set its movement property.

5. Code the text to bounce around the screen.

Creating the Application File

The first thing you need to do is create an MMF2 file to work with. This is called an application file.

1. Open MMF2.

2. Click on File | New from the menu toolbar, or alternatively click on the New File icon as shown in Figure 3.1.

You will now get a blank application file with a single frame as shown in Figure 3.2.

The blank application is the starting point of all creations in MMF2, regardless of the type of program you are creating. On the right side, you can see the storyboard editor and the relevant screen size information. It is always a good idea to change the application name to something more appropriate to the work you are doing. You can actually open multiple MMF2 files and display them on the workspace toolbar, so if they all had the title Application 1, it would be quite difficult to distinguish between them without clicking on each one and viewing its contents. So you should change the title of the application to something more appropriate; let's change it to First Program.

1. Right click on the text Application 1 in the workspace toolbar.

2. When the pop-up menu appears, click on Rename.

3. Type the words First Program where the text Application 1 was originally displayed.

Each application can have many frames, but all applications must have at least one frame. A frame is where we place all of our graphics, text, and objects for our

Figure 3.1
The New application icon.

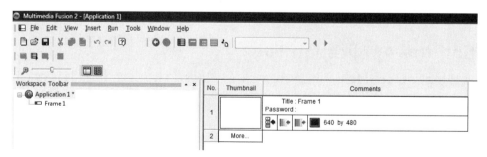

Figure 3.2
Blank application.

creation. A single frame may be all that you require in the whole of your program, or you might have many frames. In this program we only require a single frame, but in a game, for example, you might have many frames: one to represent the loading screen, many to represent the levels, and finally one frame to be the high score table. You could put everything in one frame, but it is useful to remember it is easy to move between frames, and having a single cluttered frame is not necessarily the easiest to work from a workflow point of view.

Let's change Frame 1 to Welcome..

1. Single click on Frame 1 to highlight it.

2. Then right click and select Rename.

3. Type in the word Welcome to replace the word Frame 1.

We won't need to configure any of the application properties for this program (this will be covered later in the book); all we want to do now is begin placing an object on the frame.

Note

Application properties affect how the whole program works, including every frame in the program. Frame properties are the opposite and only affect the actual frame that the configuration is applied to.

Setting Up the Screen

We now need to place our components on the frame editor and begin setting out our scene. To access the frame contents we can double click on the frame text (Welcome in this example), or we can click on the Frame Editor button, as shown in Figure 3.3.

Note

Before you can click on the Frame Editor button, you must highlight the frame itself by single left clicking on it. If you do not highlight the frame text, the Frame Editor button will continue to be grayed out and nothing will happen when you click on it.

Figure 3.3
The Frame Editor button.

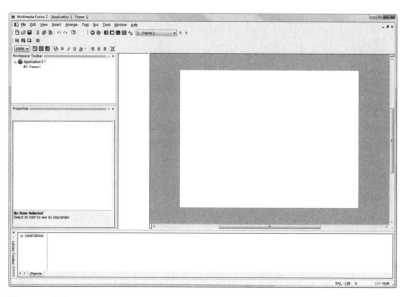

Figure 3.4
Blank frame.

MMF2 will now display the blank frame as shown in Figure 3.4. You will notice a white box, which is the play field/play area and the gray shading, which is the out of frame area. The white area represents the display area, so when you run the program, this is where objects that need to appear should be placed. Objects that don't need to be displayed (either for the moment or at all) can be placed off screen. This does not always have to be the case though, and graphics can be moved in real time from one area to another; additionally, an object can be placed on the playfield, but it can be configured to be invisible until a specific point in time.

Note

Not all objects are visible and even when placed on the play field will still not appear.

In this program we want a piece of text that is going to move around the screen, so we need to add our text, and to do that we need to add a text object.

Right click on the white play area or select Insert I New Object from the text menu.

A large list of objects will appear. These are the objects we detailed earlier, and are the core components for making your programs. Figure 3.5 shows the wide range of objects you can choose.

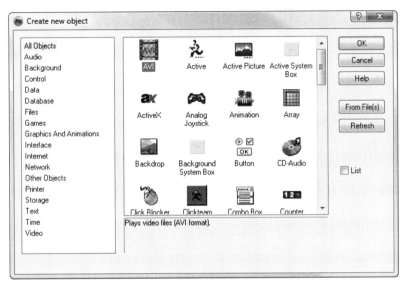

Figure 3.5
The object selection screen.

We want to add an object that will display text; from the list there are a number of objects that potentially could achieve this for us, but in this case we are going to select the String object. The selection box is quite small so we can either change the view (by clicking on List) or move the mouse cursor to the bottom right of the dialog box and then left clicking, holding down the mouse key, and dragging. You should then end up with an object view that looks similar to that shown in Figure 3.6.

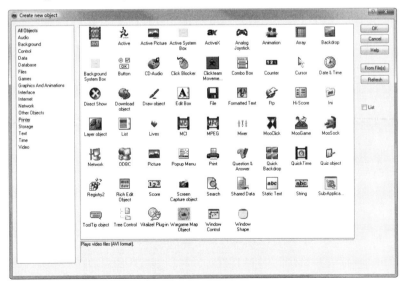

Figure 3.6
An expanded Insert Object dialog box.

String

Figure 3.7
String object icon.

You can find this object by looking through the list alphabetically. The object picture looks like the image in Figure 3.7.

1. To select the string object icon for placement on our frame, double click on the String object icon (or left click on it once and then click on the OK button).

2. The mouse cursor will now change to a cross hair. This means the object is ready to be placed on to the frame area. Click anywhere within the large white box.

3. A box containing the word Text will appear where you clicked. You can also see the object listed in the object list to its left, as shown in Figure 3.8.

Some objects, including the String object, allow you to edit them within the Frame Editor. You can double click on it in the Frame Editor to edit the text directly, or you can single click on it and then access the object properties in the Properties toolbar. For this example, you should change the initial text by double left clicking

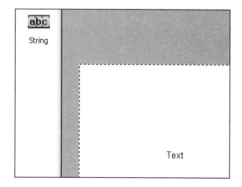

Figure 3.8
The String object on the play area.

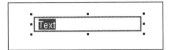

Figure 3.9
The String object has been selected and is ready for text entry.

on it (the dialog box would then be highlighted as shown in Figure 3.9). If you wanted to change anything else about the object, you would then use the object properties dialog.

1. Double left click on the String object, and then type in the text **Welcome to my first program**.

2. To complete entering the text, click with the left mouse button somewhere on the frame. Do not use the Enter or Return key because this will create an extra line within the text object.

You will now notice that the string object is not showing all of the text that you typed in. This is because the object is not big enough to display the amount of text that you entered, so you need to resize it.

1. To resize, single left click on the string object to select it, and then left click on it again. A border will appear around it with a number of small black squares. Left click and hold, and then drag from one of these squares to expand it. In our case, we want to increase the width of the object, so we need the right side, middle, black square.

2. Drag the square a little, then let go; see if it's the correct size and if not, continue until you can see all of the text.

N o t e

You can also change an object's size through the properties window.

When you add an object to the frame, MMF2 gives it a default name based on the object type. In this example, the string object has a name of String. If you add another object of the same type, it will automatically be called String 2. When you have many of the same type of objects on screen at the same time, it is very helpful to rename them so you can identify them when you are adding conditions and actions to them. So change the String name to something more appropriate, and call it Welcome Text.

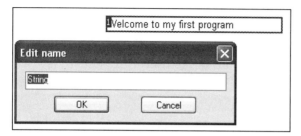

Figure 3.10
Object rename dialog box.

1. Right click on the object and select Rename.

2. The rename dialog box appears, as shown in Figure 3.10. Type in **Welcome Text** and click on the OK button.

N o t e

You cannot have two objects with the same name; MMF2 will not allow it. If you try to change the name to something that already exists, MMF2 will add a number to the end of the name.

You now need to change the properties of the object to apply a movement type to it. Nearly all objects can have a movement type applied to them. We will be using different movements throughout the book, but for now we need to give it a bouncing ball movement. This type of movement will act as a bouncing ball and allow us to bounce the object off the sides of the application frame. By default, all objects have no movement applied, and they are set to static, so when the frame or application is running they do not move anywhere on the screen.

1. Click on the String object.

2. The properties box will display the object properties. This properties box is shown in Figure 3.11.

A number of different items can have properties assigned to them, including:

- **Application Properties:** These properties detail compilation details like compiler settings, compressing the runtime and sounds, including external files, etc. It also allows the user to configure the look and feel of the applications menu bar, maximize and minimize buttons, and background color.

- **Frame Properties:** Configuration options set at the individual frame level, including its size and background color as well as how many objects can be displayed and if it should grab the desktop at the start of the frame.

Figure 3.11
Object properties dialog.

- **Object Properties:** Settings and configuration for the object that has been selected including its size and location on the screen, if it should have movement assigned to it.

The relevant properties will be displayed in the properties dialog when they have been selected and are currently highlighted. As soon as you click off the relevant item the properties dialog will go blank.

The properties dialog for objects is split into a number of tabs. Different objects can have different tabs and not all are available for each object. An example of the tabs being displayed can be seen in Figure 3.11.

Some of the tabs you might come across in your creations are:

- Settings
- Display
- Size/Position
- Text Options
- Movement
- Runtime Options

■ Events

■ About

Note

You can find out what each tab is by leaving your mouse over the tab icon for a few seconds, which will display a text tooltip (this is a piece of text that appears at the mouse cursor location). You will then be able to see the name of the particular tab your mouse is over.

We want to set the position of the Welcome Text object so that it is placed near the middle of the screen. To do this, we would use the Size/Position tab of the object's properties. With this tab you will see an entry called Position. This position heading is set out in two coordinates, the X and the Y position. The X represents the object position from the top left corner of the screen to the top right and the Y is from the top left to the bottom left. Using these two coordinates, you can plot a position on the screen. To change the position of the object, you can either use the mouse and drag the object to the location that you want, single click on it, and then move it with the cursor keys for more precision movement or you can enter an exact coordinate. We will move it to exact coordinates by typing in the X and Y location.

Note

In this book we will identify an object's location by putting the X and Y location coordinates within parentheses(X,Y), to make it easier to read. So if you read in the book to place an object at (20,50), this means you should place an object at the X position of 20 and the Y position of 50.

1. First let's ensure that the object is selected, so single left click on the Welcome Text object.

2. Click on the Size/Position tab within the object's property window.

3. Enter the X coordinate as 250 and the Y coordinate as 220.

Now we need to apply the Bouncing Ball movement.

To apply a movement function to an object, click on the movement tab within the objects properties.

Under type, you will see that it currently states that the object's movement is Static. Click on the drop-down option and select Bouncing Ball, as shown in Figure 3.12.

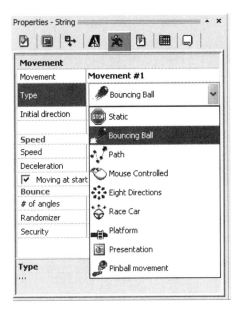

Figure 3.12
Selection of movement objects.

We can leave the rest of the options configured to their default settings for the moment. We have now configured the object's properties and are ready to begin our test run of the program and start programming.

Playback

Playback is running your creation as if the program was a completed compiled file. This allows the programmer to test the program as he goes along. When running the program it will display over the MMF2 program and will act as if it was the final program. However, it can be stopped with a click of a button allowing the programmer to continue coding his creation.

There are three types of playback:

- **Run Project:** A project is a set of MMF2 applications loaded all at once, unless you are running multiple applications at the same time. Then you are unlikely to need this option often.

- **Run Application:** This runs the whole application from the first frame and continues until the application is exited by the user or by code. This is as near as you can get to compiling the file in to an executable and running it.

Figure 3.13
The three options to test your applications.

> ▪ **Run Frame:** You can have many frames within an application. You wouldn't want to go through all of your frames in your program to get to the one you want to test because this would be very time consuming. This allows you to test the current frame you have selected. Of course, if the program is told to go to another frame from the current frame, the program ends. It will only test the current frame you are in and no others.

The three menu buttons shown in Figure 3.13 are currently all enabled; this will rarely happen, and normally you will only seen Run Application and Run Frame enabled. The buttons are in the order of Run Project, Run Application, and Run Frame.

If you run your creation now (by clicking the run application or run frame button), you will notice that the string object Welcome Text flies off in a direction and then disappears off screen. When you assigned the Bouncing Ball movement, it already had a default number of settings to move it in a random direction at the start of the frame. MMF2 does not stop objects moving off the screen by default, and so the object left the playfield when it got to the edge of the frame. To stop the program, you can either click on the X in the top right corner or press the Stop button, which is the black square next to the Run application and Run Frame buttons. You have completed everything you need to prepare them, and now you need to create the logic within your program so it knows what to do when the text touches the edge of the frame.

Writing the Code

To begin writing the code, you need to go in to the event editor. To do this, click on the event editor menu button shown in Figure 3.14.

Figure 3.14
The event editor button.

Note

If the event editor icon is grayed out, it is because the current frame is not selected. Double left click on the Welcome frame in the Workspace toolbar to ensure that you can select it.

Note

Each frame has its own copy of the event editor, so if you have a two-frame program and place code in the event editor of frame 1, there wouldn't be any code in frame 2's event editor.

You are now in the event editor. This is where you create your code to make your programs work. The code to make the text bounce around the screen actually only requires a single event and one action to get working. In addition to that single event, we will add a number of comment lines. These are useful for several reasons including:

- Adding your copyright message

- Adding details about the author and her web site

- Placing a creation date

- Adding comments about difficult to understand code

It is always useful to add comments to your programs because over time you may forget why you created a program and come back to it at a later stage. A few useful reminders can be a great help in trying to decipher your programs if you haven't touched them for a long time. The copyright or date comment lines are useful if you intend to distribute your code online to other developers to help them understand a specific type of code or show a particular feature.

Note

Placing a copyright message in the event editor will not necessarily prevent someone from taking your code and using it in their own programs if you distribute the uncompiled file. It is recommended that you only distribute code externally to other people (online forum groups for instance) if you are happy that the code might be taken and reused by someone else.

Let's add a copyright and date message. You will be in the blank event editor shown in Figure 3.15.

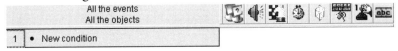

Figure 3.15
The blank event editor screen.

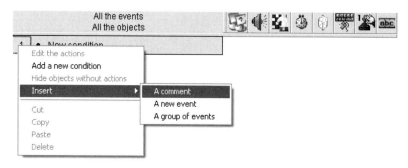

Figure 3.16
Adding a comment.

Right click on the event line number 1. You will see a pop-up menu. Select Insert |
A Comment as shown in Figure 3.16.

When you select A Comment, a dialog box appears, as shown in Figure 3.17. This
is the comment dialog box and is used to add your comment in various sizes and
colors to your creations.

Some programmers find it useful to make their comment lines larger or even
color code them. There is no set formula for doing this, and you should do it in a
way you are comfortable with. Let's now add some comments.

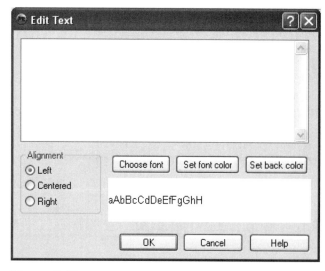

Figure 3.17
The comment dialog box.

In the text box, type in the following:

Author: **Your Name**

Date: **Today's Date**

Program Name: **Welcome Text**

Version Number: **1.0**

Try changing the background color and font color to something you like. Your comment dialog box will now look like the one shown in Figure 3.18. When you are happy with it, you can click on the OK button.

Note

You could also create separate comment lines by adding just the author's name, clicking on the OK button and then following the same procedure for adding another comment line.

You will now see your comments saved in the event editor as shown in Figure 3.19. It is also very useful to use the comment line to add a blank line sometimes to separate code as this makes it more readable. To do this rather than typing any text in to the dialog, you leave it blank and then click on the OK button.

Now you need to create your first line of code. To do this you need to create a condition. In this case, you need to check the current position of the string object

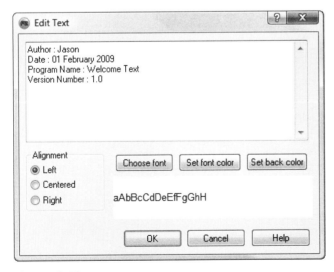

Figure 3.18
The completed comment dialog box.

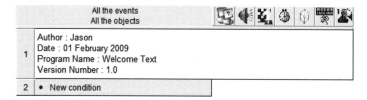

Figure 3.19
The completed comment line in the editor.

Welcome and identify when the object has reached the edge of the frame. Once you know it has reached the edge of the frame, you can then create an action and tell MMF2 to do something about it.

Click on the New condition text. This will bring up the New Condition dialog box as shown in Figure 3.20.

This dialog box displays all the possible conditions you can select from the available objects. As you add more objects to your frames, the number of objects shown in the dialog box increases. This is one of the main reasons for ensuring that objects of the same type have identifying names based on the role they play. If you had 20 string objects, graphically they would all appear the same. The only method you can use to identify the object that you need is by using its name (hover the mouse over it to see its name). If they are named String, String 1, String 2, and so forth, you would not know which item plays which role.

Figure 3.20
New Condition dialog box.

Figure 3.21
The Welcome string object that you need to select.

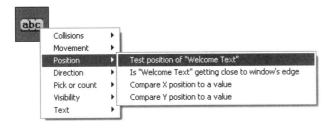

Figure 3.22
The popup menu option.

Now that you have a list of objects, you need to select the object you want to check the condition for. In this case, it's the Welcome Text string object that we need as shown in Figure 3.21.

Right click on the object, and you will see a pop-up menu, which displays a selection of position options. Different objects have different menu options available to them. To test an object's position and determine if it is about to exit the frame, select a specific condition menu option.

Select Position|Test position of Welcome Text as shown in Figure 3.22.

Note

Because the conditions are in a form of English, you can work out where an option might be stored. This can be very useful if you are looking for particular conditions to apply to an object. In this case, we know we need to check the position of the object, so the best place to start was in the Position menu option.

A Test Position dialog box appears, and you will notice a number of arrows positioned around it. If you hold your mouse cursor over one of the arrows, you will receive a tooltip explaining what each arrow checks for.

- There are four arrows around the edge of the white box area (this white area represents the frame edge) pointing inwards. Each one of these arrows checks for an object coming in to the frame from a specific frame side (top, left, right, or bottom).

- There are four arrows around the inside edge pointing outwards. These check for an object leaving the frame in one of the four possible directions.

- There is a large arrow placed in the center of the frame. This checks for objects currently in the frame but not coming in or going out.

- There is a large arrow in the bottom left of the dialog box. This checks for objects that are currently out of the frame.

To check when the object is just about to leave the frame area, select the four arrows that are pointing outwards. These have been marked in Figure 3.23.

After you make the selection, click on the OK button.

The condition will be saved as an event line, which in this case is event line 2. The actual event can be seen in Figure 3.24 and shows the object picture as part of the condition. If you have multiple string objects in a set of code and you want to check which particular object it is, you should use the tooltip; place the mouse over the object and it displays its name.

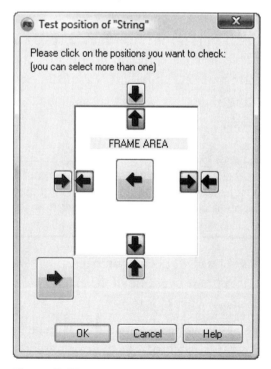

Figure 3.23
The test position dialog box.

Figure 3.24
The single condition event.

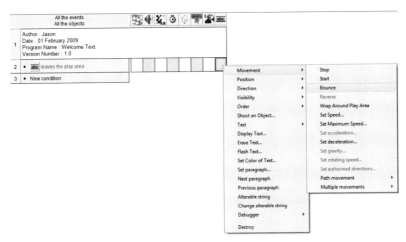

Figure 3.25
Bounce action for the Welcome Text object.

Now that you have your condition, you need to tell MMF2 what you want it to do when the condition is true (remember when the condition is true it runs any actions that exist). You need to make the Welcome Text string object bounce off the edge of the screen, so you should apply the action to its action box.

To do this, move to the right of the condition that you have just entered until you are directly under the Welcome Text object. Right click on the action box, from the menu choose Movement|Bounce as shown in Figure 3.25.

You will now have a Check mark graphic in the action box for this object. If you hold your mouse cursor over it, it will display the Bounce tooltip. On running the frame or application you will now notice the words Welcome to my first program bouncing around the screen.

Congratulations, you have completed your first program.

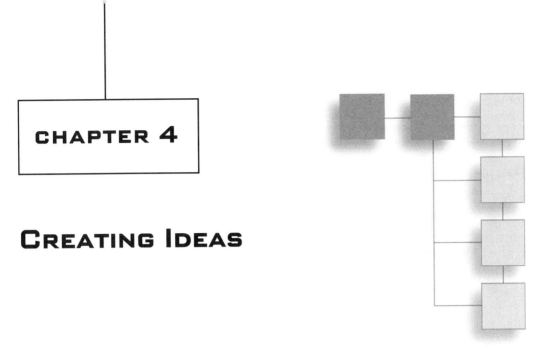

CHAPTER 4

CREATING IDEAS

When designing and creating your own computer war games, you might wonder what type of game to make. Coming up with an idea can be a daunting task. Fortunately, many options are available to the war game creator.

History

Throughout history, there have been many skirmishes, battles, and wars. There is no shortage of information in books, television documentaries, movies, and on the Internet for you to use as inspiration for your game.

History is probably the easiest place to start if you are unsure what type of war game to make. It is very easy to find information on particular timeframes, generals, battlefield maps, and unit types, which you can use to create your own scenarios.

The number of battles and wars over the centuries seems endless, with the great number of wars giving the war gamer many topics to choose from. In most cases, you would pick a timeframe or battle that most interests you. This might be because of the weapons used, a battle shown in a movie or TV program, or some local battle that happened near where you live.

There are many different time periods and battles to choose from, and you will find them listed in this chapter grouped into particular timeframes. These timeframes are not precise historical groupings but a general selection of potential battle types following certain countries or regions. Throughout history, many battles have taken place in many countries and regions of the world. If the battles in the lists that follow do not interest you, there are many other wars and battles to choose from. You should read about and research any time period or battle that interests you.

Ancient Civilizations

A few thousand years ago, the world saw some of the mightiest civilizations rise and fall. It was also a time of great upheaval as countries tried to expand their borders, influence, and income. This is a popular timeframe for those who fight tabletop war games because of the interesting choice of weapons, settings, colorful uniforms, and large scale hand to hand battles that lasted for hours.

Some civilizations of particular interest are

- Gaul

- Roman

- Greek

- Egyptian

Many of these civilizations overlapped and fought each other. Many people find the Roman civilization and its battles intriguing, and they use it as their primary focus. The great thing about many of these civilizations is that they have been depicted many times in TV shows and movies, and a large amount of information is available from which to draw a picture of the times. You might want to base your game on some of the following battles:

- Battle of Lilybaeum

- Battle of Capua

- Battle of Troy

- Battle of Alesia

- Battle of the Nile

Note

It is important to remember that in many cases the amount of information available for conflicts may not be accurate or complete. Some battles and wars have very little information and accounts of the battles are sketchy at best. In the particular case of movies, the film studios often change things to make the story more interesting. If you are creating a war game that you want to be accurate, then it is recommended that you use other sources of information.

Medieval

After the fall of the Roman Empire, many countries went back to their pre-Roman life. In England, for example, many of the buildings and technologies, such as stone working, aqueducts, baths, medicine, and even to some extent law, were forgotten or disregarded. This period was known as the Dark Ages and is considered the early part of medieval life. After this period, European countries such as England started to be ruled again by a single king or head of state rather than different tribal leaders, and the countries began to create laws and build castles to defend various regions within their realms. Europe then went through a long period of upheaval, where borders and countries were in constant change.

The medieval period provides many wars to choose from and covers many different countries, so depending on where you live in the world, you may find many scenarios that relate to your country or region. Medieval times are interesting to research because of siege warfare, missiles, such as crossbows and the longbow, and battles that raged on for hours. Among these are:

- The Battle of Hastings
- The First Crusades
- The Siege of Jerusalem

Renaissance

At the end of the medieval period, Europe began to grow culturally, religiously, and intellectually. The Renaissance lasted roughly from the 14th century to the 17th century. During the Renaissance, armies had early gun powder-based weapons and pikes (large poles with a metal spearhead attached to the end). Some of the famous battles and wars of this time are:

- Agincourt
- Battle of Ravenna
- War of the Roses
- Battle of Tewkesbury

Napoleonic

Though only a very short period in time, the Napoleonic era is a popular timeframe for traditional tabletop war gamers to play. The battles involved large numbers of soldiers, muskets, cannons, and cavalry.

The key battle in the Napoleonic period was the Battle of Waterloo, which took place in 1815. Napoleon Bonaparte was in command of the French forces, while the Duke of Wellington was in charge of British forces. There were also a large number of other soldiers from Prussia (pre-Germany), Russia, Holland, and Austria.

During this time period, sea battles increased in number as well.

Battles to consider:

- Waterloo

- Battle of the Nile

- Battle of Trafalgar

- Battle of Dresden

Americas and the New World

The Americas can be split into three key time periods when considering the types of war games you want to make. The first of these was the early colonization of the Americas by Europeans and the defeat of the native people. Once the European colonies started to become established, they soon reverted to their in-fighting based on what was happening in Europe. The final period can be categorized once America declared its independence from Great Britain in 1776. The American Civil War which saw fighting between the Confederate and the Union forces lasted from 1861 through 1865.

The American civil war is usually a popular time period for war gamers and has been extensively covered in computer games, movies, and TV dramas.

Some famous battles of the Civil War are:

- Gettysburg

- Chickamauga

- Antietam

Recent History

If you are unfamiliar with events that happened a long time ago, you might be interested in more recent events.

Recent history can cover a wide spectrum of periods and timeframes. For the purposes of this book, we are going to classify recent history as anything from World War I (1914–1918) onward. The main consideration for wars and battles during recent history is the change from mainly infantry and cavalry forces to using various other technologies, including mechanized tanks, planes, helicopters, and missiles.

Common wars/battles that you could cover include:

- World War I

- World War II

- Battle of Britain (WWII)

- Vietnam

- Korean War

- The Falklands

- Gulf War

- Afghanistan

- Iraq War

Fantasy Worlds

Rather than create a game based on a past or current war, why not consider making a war game in a fantasy world setting? This allows you to add a number of interesting elements to your game that you wouldn't normally include when creating a war game based on an actual event.

You can create your own fantasy worlds, but you might consider basing your world on some of the many myths and legends told throughout history. Adding in elements such as different animals or creatures, such as minotaurs, dragons, and ogres. You may also decide to include such things as magic.

Science Fiction

Science fiction usually relates to a world or worlds that are more technically advanced than our current civilization. A perfect example of this could be a world in 20 years time that has robots as our helpers, or humans traveling among the stars in their spaceships. The sci-fi genre has been very popular for a long time, and you can easily find movies or books that discuss or tell stories about this genre. You can check out movies such as *Bladerunner, I-Robot, Starship Troopers, Timecop,* and books such as *War of the Worlds, Time Machine, 2001,* and *Neuromancer.*

In your war games you could have a space battle using ships as your units, or you could have planet-based wars using technology such lasers, jetpacks, and portals.

Basic Game Engine Document

In this book you will learn how to create different files that you can then use for your war games. You will learn all the key aspects of what makes up a war game, and how it can be programmed within MMF2. These examples are the basis of your war game engine, which you can then build on to make it more complex or more tailored to the period of time that you have decided to concentrate on. The following information is documented to help you think about some of the basic information and rules that MMF2 needs in order to begin building your engine. The war game examples in the following chapters will draw upon the information listed here.

Once you have completed reading the book and are ready to start making your own games, you should consider documenting some information about how your game is going to work.

Unit Types

For your war game, you will have various unit types. The type of game you make will determine the types of units you will use.

An example of the types of units in a WWII game could be:

- Tanks

- Trucks

- Jeeps

- Mortar units

- Bombers

- Fighter planes

- Boats

- Infantry

An example of the types of units in a medieval game could be:

- Spearmen

- Light infantry

- Mace men

- Archers

- Heavy cavalry

- Crossbow men

Even though the two games are of different time periods, you can still group the different types of units into a set of groups. These groups are mainly important for the movement restrictions we will discuss in more detail in Chapter 6.

- **Infantry**: This covers any soldiers who move on foot.

- **Vehicle**: This may be a vehicle from modern history, such as a tank or jeep, but it can also include anything that moves faster than a man on foot, as do the infantry units. Cavalry and chariots are considered vehicles.

- **Air**: Any unit that can fly; this includes airplanes, helicopters, and barrage balloons or perhaps spaces ships.

- **Sea**: Any unit that can move across water; this may include sea terrain squares.

- **Transport**: This is anything that can carry another unit.

When making a game, you can either use a small set of groups (e.g. vehicles to identify quick moving items) or create an object for each type of unit within your game. So rather than the vehicle group you can have tank, truck, jeep, etc.

Terrain Types

The terrain type will differ, depending on the type of game you are making. Some traditional terrain hexagons could be:

- Sand

- Sea

- River

- Road

- Train track

- City

- Town

- Forest

- Hill

Assume for a moment that you are making a space game; you might have terrain tiles other than those listed, such as space, worm hole, planet, red dwarf, meteorite, and comet. It does not matter whether your game fits in with the normal hexagon units listed here. The war game rules are interchangeable.

Unit Movement

A unit can move a certain number of hexagon tiles each turn. You could either set up a number of movement points for each unit type (for example five points for vehicles and two for infantry), or you can assign different movement points to each individual unit. The second option allows you more scope for giving certain units more or less movement points. These movement points are the initial starting values before you take into account any terrain modifiers (remove points for more difficult terrain). You can see an example movement tables in Figures 4.1 and 4.2.

Unit	Movement Points
Infantry	5
Vehicle	8
Air	10
Boat	6

Figure 4.1
Basic group movement points system.

Unit	Movement Points
Infantry	5
Mortar Team	3
Jeep	9
Tank	8
Truck	7
Airplane	11
Helicopter	10
Barge	3

Figure 4.2
Expanded group movement points system.

It is important to remember when making your war game that you may have to change your initial starting movement points as you test your game. You may find that one side has an unfair advantage and is able to move across the hexagon map too quickly. For now, all you are trying to do is map out your basic game units and any useful information that will make it easier for you to make your game later on.

Terrain Movement Table

Unit movement will be affected by the terrain. For example, if you have an infantry unit moving through a forest, they will be slowed down; if they are moving by road, they will move at their optimum pace. This is also true of vehicles; a truck on a road will move better than a truck off road. This is where the terrain movement table comes into effect; it will identify times when a particular unit will be affected by the terrain. You can see an example of a terrain movement table in Figures 4.3 and 4.4, which lists the cost of moving on a particular terrain hexagon. Where it says NA, this means that the particular vehicle type cannot move on that terrain.

You might also have to consider units that can move on road, river, and sea. Though not common in modern forces, there are different vehicles that can move on these types of terrains. If you are creating a medieval game, you can

Vehicle Type	River	Road	Sand	Sea	Lightwood	Forest
Infantry	3	0	1	NA	1	2
Vehicle	NA	0	2	NA	2	NA
Air	NA	NA	NA	NA	NA	NA
Boat	0	NA	NA	1	NA	NA

Figure 4.3
Terrain Movement Effect Table.

Vehicle Type	River	Road	Sand	Sea	Lightwood	Forest
Infantry	3	0	1	NA	1	2
Mortar Team	3	0	2	NA	1	2
Jeep	NA	0	2	NA	2	NA
Tank	NA	0	3	NA	2	3
Truck	NA	0	4	NA	3	NA
Airplane	NA	NA	NA	NA	NA	NA
Helicopter	NA	NA	NA	NA	NA	NA
Barge	0	NA	NA	4	NA	NA
Warship	NA	NA	NA	0	NA	NA

Figure 4.4
More detailed Terrain Movement Effect Table.

leave out air objects from your movement table. You could expand your table to include catapults, chariots, and siege equipment. These tables are here to provide you with a starting point to make your own tables.

Note

Flying Machines

One thing that you might need to consider is that planes and helicopters are not affected by the terrain; you could also implement a weather effects table; this could slow down the movement of the vehicle or even prevent flying in certain weather conditions.

Game Phases

To make your war game easier to create and easy for the player to understand what they need to do next, you need to create several game phases. These phases are when you will manage all of the different events happening on the screen, from the players' movement, the computer-controlled movement, firing, and player orders. By making several different phases, you will make the game much easier to program because you can then code each one independently.

Note

Creating phases is an example of how you can order your games functionality; the order can be changed or items can be added or removed to match the type of game you are making.

For our design document, we have identified five phases that the computer will need to compute to ensure that the game runs correctly. These phases are:

- Friendly movement phase

- Friendly fire phase

- Enemy movement phase

- Enemy fire phase

- Turn results phase

Within each of these phases are additional checks by the computer to confirm certain rules or aspects of play; for example, you can see the phases you have already detailed with some new items:

Friendly movement phase

Unit movement check

Terrain modifier check

    Enemy opportunity check

Friendly fire phase

    Able to fire
    Attack modifiers
    Morale check
    Enemy retreat
    Remove units

Enemy movement phase

    Unit movement check
    Terrain modifier check
    Friendly opportunity check

Enemy fire phase

    Able to fire
    Attack modifiers
    Morale check
    Enemy retreat
    Remove units

Turn results phase

    Check win conditions
    Display results if a side wins

Continue game if no side wins

Each phase is explained in the following list:

Friendly movement phase: You will be able to move any of your units on the map within their designated movement points. The game will have to determine whether they have enough movement points to be able to move to the map hexagon. There will also be checks to see if the object can move over a particular terrain type. If a unit moves away from an enemy position, the enemy has a chance of firing at that unit when it moves away; this is the enemy opportunity check.

Friendly fire phase: After all movement is completed, the units will be ready for attack. This is the time that each unit will be able to fire at an enemy as long as it is within the range of that enemy's particular weapon system. After the unit fires, a set of additional checks needs to be made to reduce the enemy's strength, check its morale to see if the unit retreats, and finally, remove any units that are no longer able to put up a fight.

Enemy movement phase: Works in the same way as the friendly unit movement phase, except this will have to be fully controlled by the computer. Creating enemy movement is harder than allowing the player to move the units himself.

Enemy fire phase: You need to check each enemy unit and see if it is within firing distance of a player unit. You should test to see if the enemy hit the unit and then take the appropriate actions.

Turn results phase: After all movement and firing is complete, you will check to see if any victory conditions have been met. These victory conditions can be set at the start of a game, for example, total destruction, getting to a particular terrain tile, and holding it for a length of time. If the victory conditions are not met, you can start the whole process again.

Combat Tables

As is true of many of the items discussed in the design section, many of the concepts are interchangeable with your own rules and ideas. Combat is one such area where you might need to make some changes to fit into your own game.

Depending on the type of game and the rules, combat could get quite complex. As a basic starting point, each unit would have the following:

Attack Value: The attack score of each unit. This signifies how strong an attack of a unit is. A rifleman might be given an attack value of 3 while a tank could be given a value of 10 out of 10.

Defense Value: How good a unit is at defending itself.

Unit Size: How large the unit is. Is it a single soldier or a unit of 100 men, 1,000, or more? You could say this is the health of the unit; once this value reaches 0, the unit no longer functions as a force and is removed from the battlefield.

Firing Distance: How many tiles a unit can fire. This is particularly useful for cannons or artillery pieces that can out fire a standard gun unit.

If you have four units, the first with the ID of 1 is a standard infantry unit, the second is a machine gun unit, the third is a tank, and the fourth is an artillery battery. With that setup, you could create the table shown in Figure 4.5.

In some war games each unit is a single soldier on screen, so size can be ignored. If this is the case, then you can use the following to calculate whether an attacking unit has done any damage to a defending unit.

Unit (ID)	Att	Def	Sze	FiD
1	3	2	5	2
2	4	4	5	3
3	7	8	8	6
4	8	1	20	12

Figure 4.5
Basic unit information.

```
Att+(rnd10)+1 = total attack strength :
Compare to : Def+(rnd10)+1 = total defense strength
```

Using the attacking score and then rolling a random number out of 10 gets the total attack strength. Compare this to the defense score and the random roll out of 10. If the attacker gets a higher score than the defender, the attacker has done some damage. In a single unit game, if the attacker wins, the defending unit is destroyed. If you have a unit that consists of a group of soldiers, you might want to deduct a number of points from the Sze (Size) amount. Using Sze as the deciding factor determines the total number of soldiers to remove from the unit.

Note

In MMF2 when you use a random number it always starts from a value of zero. So if you decide to do a random number of (10), then it could give you a number from 0 to 9. In the attack and defense you could use the zero, but if you always want a value that doesn't include zero, you can just add a single number to it. If you do random (10)+1, you will always get a result from 1 to 10, as if the original value was 0; it will automatically add one to the random number value.

The attack factor has already been able to decide whether a specific unit has been able to successfully attack another unit. This is weighted by the strength of the unit, so as previously mentioned, a rifle unit has a lower attack number than a tank unit, but if they mount a successful attack, which initially will be harder for them, then the tank unit would take damage.

The maximum amount of damage a unit will be able to make is up to the maximum Sze value. This is not perfect by any means because a single weapon might be able to destroy additional units. Depending upon the game you are making, you can make certain weapons that can do additional damage and remove additional units when a successful attack has taken place.

So the calculation for the amount of damage a unit can make is as follows:

Attacking Rifle Unit a has Size value of 5, = (RND5)

This means that an attacking unit can do up to five units of damage to the Sze value of the defender. In this case, you don't need to add an additional value to the random number generator. If the size is 5 and you set the random number to (5), the return value could be between 0 and 4 in damage. The reason you don't need to add a single value point is that even though a unit's attack is successful, that doesn't actually mean that any casualties were taken. Of course, in your own games, you can easily add a value to increase the damage taken.

Note

> Different unit types may have a big influence on the attack and defense values of other units in your game. For example, when you think about a defense value of a tank unit in comparison to a rifleman unit, they should be different. You can add additional defensive modifiers when required; for example, a unit in a house, trench, or behind other cover such as a hedge would receive additional defensive points, while a unit in an open field with no cover could lose defensive points because it is an easy target for the enemy units.

Many other factors can be taken into account when you are making a war game: for example the weather, if a unit is dug in or in a fortified position, and the general morale of the unit. We will be covering these issues in this book and showing you how to implement them within your own games. For now, you have the basic information you need to start putting together a war game, so in the next chapter you will be looking at how to make your first hexagon-based map.

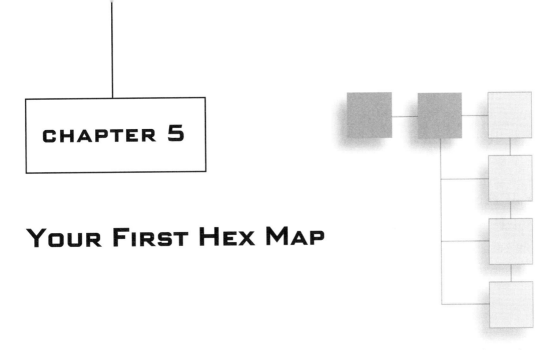

CHAPTER 5

YOUR FIRST HEX MAP

You should now have a basic idea of how to create your games in Multimedia Fusion 2. The basic introduction will be enough to find your way around the interface and begin to place your different game objects on screen. As you move further through the book, concepts will be explained so that you can get on with the important aspect of thinking about how you design the components you want to include in your war game.

Now that we have discussed the different history and genre possibilities, the place to start with your war game is to make a simple map. So in this chapter you will learn how to create a simple hex map manually and how to create a map using an MMF2 shortcut. By the end of this chapter, you will understand how to make your own maps.

What Is a Hex Map?

The war games that you are going to make in this book are based on two key shapes: the hexagon and the square. The hexagon will be used for your maps, essentially the background to your games, while the squares will represent the soldiers, tanks, planes, and boats of your battlefield units.

As discussed in Chapter 1, hexagons are the standard type of shape to use for maps in war games. You can easily connect these hexagons to create a set of tiles that will become your battlefield. You could also use squares to make your maps as some board games did in the past. Overall, hexagons work better when making maps because their slanting sides make connecting terrain tiles much easier. If you have a set of sea tiles and a set of sand/land tiles, it is easier graphically to make the transition from one type of terrain to another.

In Figure 5.1 you can see a single hexagon shape, and in Figure 5.2 you will notice how several hexagons can connect to create a map.

Note
_____

Tile Set

The words *tile set* are used often in game creation. Tile set means a set of graphics that can be connected to create a multiple number of rooms or worlds. Tile sets can be two- or three-dimensional; in this book, we will be using 2D graphics. If you have a set of graphics for sand, sea, and cliffs, you can connect them together to create many different maps using the same tile set. Though it takes longer to generate all of the separate graphics, it speeds the process of world/map creation because you can join the tiles together to create a unique world map.

_____

Figure 5.1
A single hexagon shape that is used in this book for the terrains.

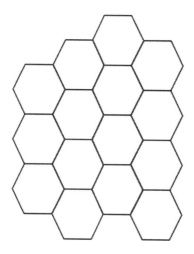

Figure 5.2
A set of blank hexagon shapes connected together to create a tile map.

Creating Your First Hex Map

You are now going to create your first hex map. All of the hexagon tile graphics have already been created, so you do not need to be concerned about your drawing skills or the time it would take to create some images. To create your hexagon map you will use the library feature in MMF2. The library feature allows you access to game content, such as objects and graphics, and then provides a quick way of accessing them and placing them into the frames of your games.

Note

All library files that are used in MMF2 are files that have been saved in the native format of the program. This format is called MFA, and anyone with MMF2 (trial or full version) can access these MFA files, either from the program menus to access it as a game file or through the library system if you want to add the components of that file to another game.

Connecting to the Library File

To begin, you will connect to the library file that has already been created and is located on the CD-ROM that comes with this book. We have created several tile sets that will be used throughout this book, and they can be found in the TileSets folder.

1. Ensure that MMF2 is open, and click on the New Application button or use the menu File|New option. This creates a blank game file ready for you to create your first hexagon map.

2. You will see the Library Toolbar situated at the bottom of the screen, as shown in Figure 5.3.

3. Right click on the left-hand pane of the Library Toolbar; you will see a pop-up box as shown in Figure 5.4. Select New.

4. A Browse For Folder dialog box, as shown in Figure 5.5, appears and allows you to search for your library folders.

5. Browse the CD-ROM drive that contains the CD-ROM from this book, select the TileSets folder, then click on OK.

Figure 5.3
The Library Toolbar.

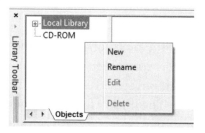

Figure 5.4
The New option on the Library Toolbar.

Figure 5.5
The Browse dialog box that allows you to search for your library files.

6. You will see the words New Library in the left-hand pane of the Library Toolbar, and it will be selected; you can now type the word **Tile Graphics** into the box and press the Return or Enter key to save the library name.

7. If you click on the word Tile Graphics, you will see all of the available tile sets that are included on the CD-ROM for this book, as shown in Figure 5.6.

Figure 5.6
All of the libraries available in this book.

N o t e

As you are reading library files from the CD-ROM drive, there may be a small delay in displaying the graphics or placing them from the Library Toolbar to the frame. You can also copy the TileSets folder from the CD-ROM to your hard disk and connect the Library Toolbar to the disk version of the files.

Placing Your First Hexagon

We shall start by accessing the library file and then placing a single hexagon on the first frame of our game. We will build up from this to create our first map.

1. In the right-hand pane of the Library Toolbar, you should see the library file called Tile_set1; double click on this to display its contents. If you do not see this file, click on the text Tile Graphics; this should display the libraries contained within it.

2. You need to ensure that you can see the frame editor. Either double click on the text Frame 1 in the workspace properties toolbar or click on the box that contains the number 1 in the storyboard editor window.

3. You should now see the frame editor, a blank white area, which is the frame and the gray area that surrounds it, which is the off-screen area.

You will now see nine different tiles that are available in this tile set as shown in Figure 5.7.

We will now place a single tile onto the frame editor.

1. Click on the hexagon in the Library Toolbar called Grass_Full; this is the tile that is colored in green.

2. Hold down the left mouse button when the object has been selected and drag the item onto the frame editor. Release the mouse button, and the object will appear on the frame as shown in Figure 5.8.

Figure 5.7
The collection of tiles in this library file.

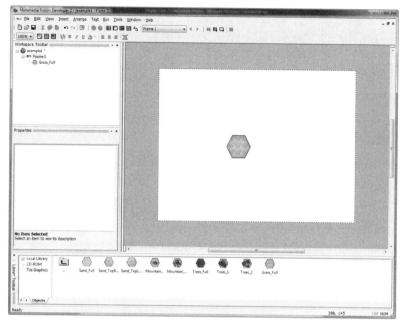

Figure 5.8
The single grass tile placed on the frame editor.

Placing Additional Tiles

We can now drag and drop additional tiles that we require onto the frame editor. In this example, we will drag two additional tiles on to the frame.

Because it is impossible to drag and drop precisely on to the frame editor, we will drag and drop the items we require and then reposition them.

Hold down the mouse button on the Mountain_Small hexagon in the Library Toolbar and then drag and then release the mouse over the frame to place it.

Now follow this same procedure for the Mountain_Large.

You will now have three tiles on the frame, but they will not be precisely positioned, as shown in Figure 5.9.

Note

When you drag and drop graphics from the Library Toolbar, you are creating an exact copy of that object, with the same name. An alternative to duplicating an object is to clone it; we will go into more detail about this shortly.

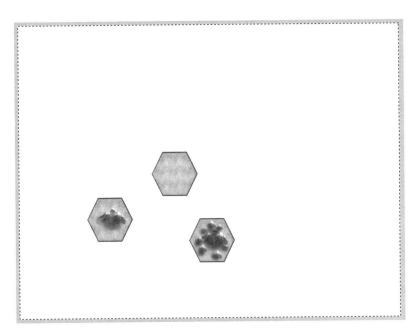

Figure 5.9
Three tiles placed on the frame.

Positioning Your Tiles

The position of the tiles is not as precise as it should be for a map, as shown in Figure 5.9. To create a map from the tiles, they need to be put next to each other. There are two ways to achieve this: precise positioning and coordinate positioning.

Precise Positioning

Sometimes you may want to place an object in a specific area on the frame. In many cases, you might get very close when you have dragged an object from the Library Toolbar, but close is not good enough when working on a computer game. Using precise movement means that you can move an object a single pixel at a time. For example a screen resolution of 640 × 480 has 640 pixels across the top, and 480 lines going down, a total of 307,200 pixels. Leaving only one or two pixel gap between your tiles can make the difference between your tiles looking fine or the background color being displayed, meaning the player will see gaps between your objects.

To move an object on the frame editor, you need to do the following:

1. First click on the object that you want to move.

2. The object that you want to move will be surrounded by a box. This shows that the object has been selected.

3. Press the arrow keys to move the object. If you want to move the item upwards, you can press the up arrow key, and so on.

4. If the selected object is still too far away from the adjacent tile, you can drag it closer using the mouse before using the arrow keys; otherwise it might take you a while to get in the right position.

You can see the three tiles moved into position using the cursor keys in Figure 5.10.

Note

The arrow keys are also called the cursor keys.

Coordinate Positioning

When you click on an object that is placed on the frame editor, it will display its properties in the properties toolbar. Every object has a set of properties that you can configure through this toolbar, and in this case there are properties for moving the object on the screen. If you know the exact position that you wish to

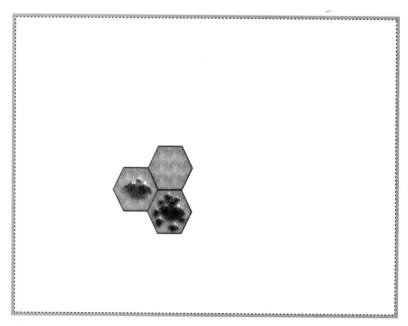

Figure 5.10
The three tiles moved so they are connected to each other.

move an object to, you can type in these coordinates rather than dragging and dropping or using the cursor keys.

In this example, you will learn how to place two new tiles on the frame, and then position it using the properties toolbar.

Start with the three tiles connected together that you created in the last example. As you place items using exact coordinates, you need to close the current file you just created and open another file that you may think looks exactly the same. The reason for this is that you are going to place two new tiles at specific coordinates on the screen, and because you will place your own tiles in slightly different positions, using this next step would not be correct.

1. Close any files you may already have open in MMF2 by selecting File|Close.

2. Click on File|Open from the MMF2 menu, and then browse to your CD-ROM, into the Examples folder and select example1.mfa.

You also need to ensure that you can currently see the correct tiles in the Library Toolbar, so click on the words Tile Graphics in the left side of the Library Toolbar, and then double click on Tile_Set1 to reveal all of the tiles we are using in this example.

3. Drag the object called Trees_1 from the Library Toolbar and then place it anywhere on the frame, as long as it is not touching any of the three tiles we previously placed.

4. Drag the object called Mountain_Small and place it anywhere on the frame. You will now have something that looks like Figure 5.11.

5. Select the Trees_1 object by clicking on it. This will place a box around the object and display the object properties. In the properties window, you will see a number of tabs; if you hold your mouse over them, you will see help text appear that advises you what that particular item is. Click on the tab that has a small box and two arrows pointing downwards and to the right. This is the size and position tab. You will now see a set of properties that you can amend within this tab as shown in Figure 5.12.

6. If you click on the number that is opposite the X position, you can type in the object's new position coordinate. For the Trees_1 object, type the X coordinate to be 282 and its Y coordinate to be 244. As you type in the number and press the Return key, the object on the frame will then move to this particular coordinate.

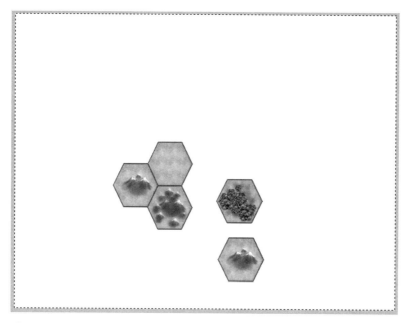

Figure 5.11
The five tiles placed on the frame, ready for you to reposition two of them into place.

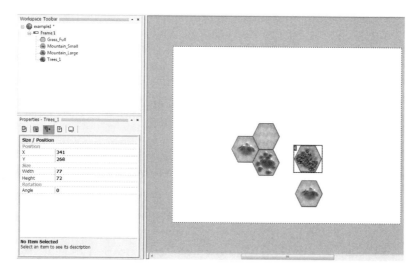

Figure 5.12
The object selected, the current properties of the Trees_1 object, and the size and position tab selected.

7. For the Mountain_Small object, click on it, and ensure that the Size/Position tab is selected. Type in the X coordinate to be 166 and the Y position to be 313.

You should now see your five tiles looking like those shown in Figure 5.13.

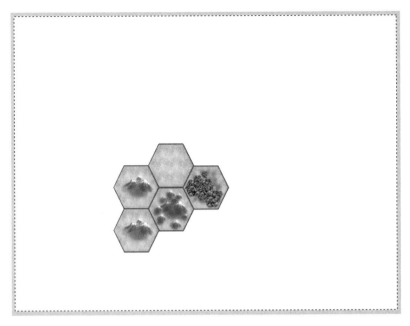

Figure 5.13
Five tiles joined together.

Placing Tiles Using Code

As well as manually placing items around the frame using the precise positioning and the coordinate system, you can also use the MMF2 event editor. The benefit of this is that you can move things in executable time. This means when you have completed your war game and you create an executable file, you can make it move items around when someone is running your game. Moving objects using code is very useful because you can create instances when certain tiles would be placed at certain times. So, for example, you could create different layouts for your war games for different missions. The downside of this is that it is more work because you need to specify in the code where you want the item to be placed. This requires a number of things:

- The tiles that you want to move need to already be on the frame but outside the play area so that when the frame starts the user cannot see them. Normally, you would have a background graphic or loading screen in place while you make the program load the tiles in place.

- All tiles need to be active objects and not backdrop objects; do not worry too much about this now as all of our tiles in the Library Toolbar are active objects. This is because you cannot access backdrop objects at runtime, so therefore you cannot move them. You can use backdrop graphics if you intend to place the graphics at edit time.

■ You need to have the coordinates for where you want to place each individual tile. This can be a lot of work if you want to place lots of tiles. You can do this for each tile, but a quicker way is to use mathematics and loops; we will look at this shortly.

N o t e

When you are creating your game using the editors, this is called edit time. You can place objects and move them about to precisely configure your game. Runtime is when you finish your game and it is running on your computer (or other users' computers) as a Windows executable file.

In this example, you need six tiles; you have already created a file you can use, which is contained on the CD-ROM provided with this book.

1. Close any examples that you currently have open in MMF2, by using File|Close.

2. Click on File|Open and then browse to the CD-ROM drive that contains the CD from this book. Navigate into the Examples folder and select example3.mfa. This will open an example file with six tiles all placed outside the white frame area. You may need to double click on the text Frame 1 in the workspace toolbar to see the same as the image shown in Figure 5.14.

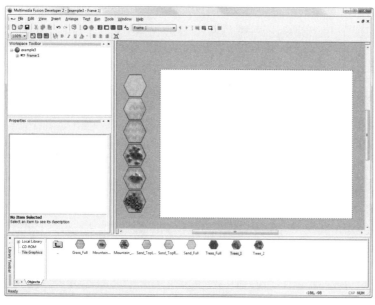

Figure 5.14
The six tiles placed on the side of the frame.

Figure 5.15
Seven system objects and the size tiles we are using to create our small map.

You have your six tiles off to the left of the play area ready for you to move them using the event editor. Because these items are off frame, if you were to run the frame now, all you would see is a blank frame.

Click on the Event Editor button to access the screen where you will create your code.

You will see a single New condition line and the tiles listed after the seven system objects as shown in Figure 5.15.

Note

You will see only six tile objects listed after the seven system objects. This is because when you drag items that are the same from the Library Toolbar, it creates duplicates. These duplicates only take one place in the event editor.

In the following example, we will move the objects at the start of the frame, so that they appear when the frame loads. There are many different options within MMF2, and you could move them once a certain task has completed or when a set amount of time has passed.

1. Click on the New Condition text on event line number 1.

2. The New condition dialog box appears, as shown in Figure 5.16. We are going to move these tiles at the start of the frame, and frame handling conditions are placed under the Storyboard controls object. This is the object that looks like a horse and chessboard icon. Right click on this object to reveal its list of conditions, and then select the Start of frame item.

This now creates the first event that will run as soon as the frame is loaded. We could create multiple event lines with the moving of each item, but we can also put them all under one event. When working with lots of actions for similar groups of items or the same item, you may want to separate them out a little to make the actions easier to read. For this example, we are going to create all six actions under the same event line; each movement will be placed against each tile, so this is very easy to read.

1. On event line 1, move across from the Start of Frame text until you are directly under the sand-colored tile called Sand_Full. Right click on the

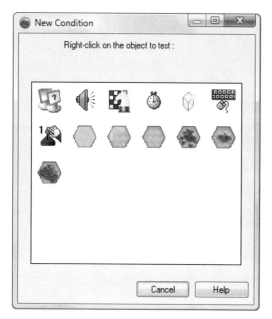

Figure 5.16
The New Condition dialog box.

blank action box to reveal the options in a pop-up box. You can see the pop-up menu in Figure 5.17.

2. In this case, we want to change the location (position) of the object on the frame. So select the position menu option and then click on Select Position. A Select Position dialog box appears, as shown in Figure 5.18, and it will

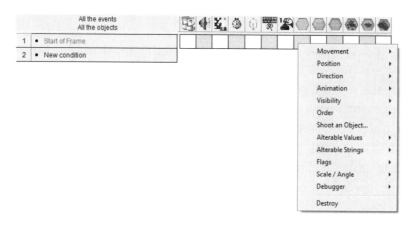

Figure 5.17
The pop-up menu options for this tile.

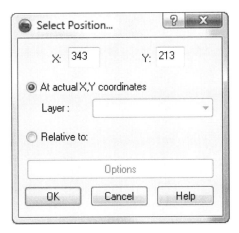

Figure 5.18
The Select Position dialog box that will help you position objects on the frame.

already have At actual X, Y coordinates selected. This means that it will place the object in the exact coordinates that are displayed in the X and Y boxes. X will move an item to the left or right, while Y will move an item up or down. In the X box, type in 216, and in the Y box, type in 168. Now click on OK to save this information to the event editor.

If you run the program using the F8 key, you will see a single hexagonal object on the frame. We now need to do the same for the other items using the same process. Use the coordinates in Table 5.1 to help you with each object's position. Remember that the cursor should be directly under each object where you will add the action to move that particular object. For example, the next item to move will be the Sand_TopLeft object, so move across from event line one and ensure that the cursor directly below the Sand_TopLeft object and access its action box.

Table 5.1 The Coordinates of the Other Five Objects

Object Name	X	Y
Sand_TopLeft	216	239
Mountain_Small	274	204
Grass_Full	274	274
Trees1	331	169
Mountain_Large	331	239

Figure 5.19
The actions for the six hexagons.

After you do this for each item, your event editor will look like the one shown in Figure 5.19. In this figure, we have expanded the contents of each action box to show you what they contain. If you want to check each item, hold your mouse cursor over each check mark to reveal a box that advises you of the action contents.

If you run the program now by pressing the F8 key, you can see the final set-up of the frame, as shown in Figure 5.20.

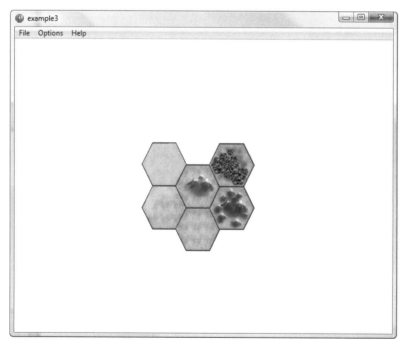

Figure 5.20
The final placement of the six tiles.

Importing New Tiles

Rather than using graphics from a library, you can also directly import graphics into MMF2. This allows you to create your game graphics externally within another program like Photoshop and then import them into MMF2.

There are a number of objects in MMF2 that allow you to display an image on the screen. There are backdrop, picture, and active objects. Each situation determines which item you would use. If you were going to create a hexagon map that does not change, using the backdrop object is fine; this object just displays an image on the screen, but you are not able to program it in the event editor. The picture object is useful for displaying an image but not really that useful when you want to display many smaller images in the case of a hexagon. The active object is used when you might want to animate an object. In many of the war games you want to make, you may want to change the look of a hexagon object throughout the game. An example of this is that you might want to display aerial bomb damage or seasonal weather effects. When changing the look of a tile (and this is also appropriate to a unit square), using an active object is the best option to select.

We are now going to import an image into an active object to show you how to bring your own graphic assets into MMF2.

1. Ensure that you are running MMF2 and have no game files currently open.

2. Click on the New button or, alternatively, use the shortcut CTRL+N.

3. Double click on the Frame 1 text in the workspace toolbar, or click on the number 1 in the storyboard editor to display the frame editor.

4. Right click on the blank frame, and when the pop-up menu appears, select Insert Object.

5. The Create new object dialog box appears; select the Active object and then click on OK. The mouse cursor will change to a crosshair; left click anywhere on the frame to place the active object.

At the moment, the active object is represented by a green diamond, so now it's time to replace this with a hexagon graphic.

6. Double click on the green diamond, and it will enter the Picture Editor for that object.

7. Click on the first icon in the top left corner. This is the Clear button and will remove the current graphic from the canvas. Alternatively, you can use the shortcut CTRL+N. You will now have your blank canvas as shown in Figure 5.21.

8. You now need to import a graphic, so select the second icon in the top left corner of the picture editor, which is the Import button. You can also use the shortcut CTRL+O. The Open dialog box will appear, navigate to the CD-ROM drive that has the CD from this book loaded and navigate to the Import folder as shown in Figure 5.22.

9. By clicking on either graphic, you will be able to see a small thumbnail of each graphic. This is very useful when you have many images in one folder and want to get a better idea of what the image looks like before importing it. Select either PNG graphic and click on the Open button.

10. The Import Options dialog box now appears as shown in Figure 5.23. This dialog box is very useful when importing many images at once. When only importing a single image, as in this case, the main item to check is the

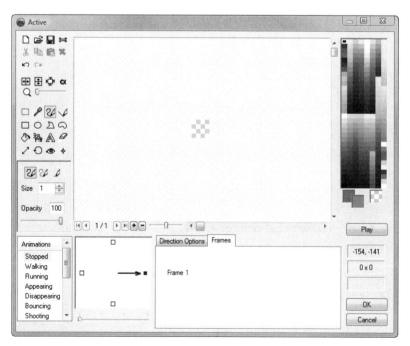

Figure 5.21
The blank canvas awaiting an image.

Figure 5.22
The Open dialog box that will import your image.

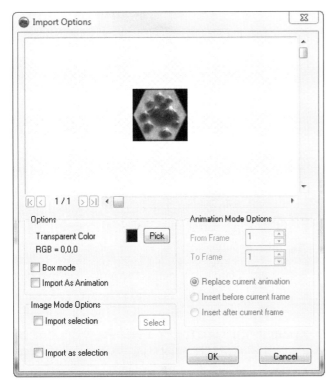

Figure 5.23
The Import Options dialog box.

transparent color. In this case, it has put the transparent color as black around the object, and it is the same within the Options dialog box. This means when it is placed on the frame the black area will disappear and become transparent. This is what we require, so click on the OK button.

11. You will now see the image on the canvas. At this stage, you have not saved the image to the frame editor because we do not want to make any further changes at the moment. Click on OK.

12. You will now see a single hexagon object on the frame.

Placing Units

Placing your units is a similar process to placing your hexagon map tiles. You can create a library of units and drag and drop them onto the frame, or you can import them to the frame using a default active object. You can move them manually into position or create the relevant actions in the event editor to move them at runtime.

The most important thing to take into consideration when creating your units is that they fit correctly onto the hexagon tiles that you would use for your map.

In Figure 5.24 you can see an example of a plane unit placed on an example set of tiles that we placed earlier.

To view this example file, you can access it off the CD-ROM provided with this book. The file is called example4.mfa and is located in the Examples folder.

Duplicating and Cloning

We previously discussed that when you drag items from the Library Toolbar onto the frame, they are duplicated. Duplication is one way of creating multiple objects that are either similar graphically or have similar properties.

Duplicate is very good for creating multiple tiles that have the same properties and size. They are used in many cases in maps or for bricks and other surfaces in a bat and ball game. If you create ten duplicates of the same tile, they all have the same name and will only appear as a single object in the event editor. This is great from a programming point of view because you only need to see one object in the event editor rather than say 10, 50, 100, or even more. Through the event editor you can also tell the program to make changes to a particular duplicate object,

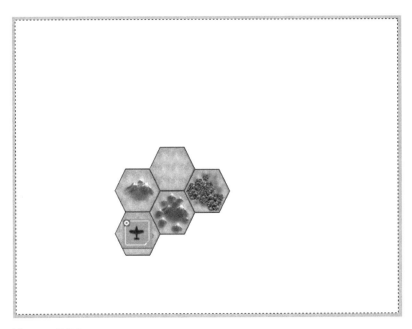

Figure 5.24
A plane unit on one of the hexagon tiles.

which will not affect any of the others. The downside to duplicates is that if you change the size or properties of any object through the frame editor, it will amend all other objects with the same name.

Another way of creating objects is by cloning. This is useful if you want an item to look the same and initially have the same property settings (because when you clone it to the new object it will retain the same properties) but wish to access it through a different object in the event editor. You may also want to change the size of the object, and a clone object will not affect any other objects. When you clone an object, it is given the same name, but the name will include a number at the end. So if your first object is called Trees, your next cloned object will be called Trees2.

It is not always clear when you might select duplication rather than cloning, and most of the time it will depend on the number of objects within one frame that are graphically the same. The main issue that you will come across in making games using duplicates or clones is that in the event editor only clones are able to have different values placed within their properties. Duplicates can have different values assigned to them, but this can only be done in the event editor. Cloning will require more objects to be configured separately in the frame editor but will make things easier to work with for our war game later on in the book. The next few examples all use a combination of cloning and duplication so that you can see how they are used. In Chapter 7 we move to a cloned hexagon tile map, which is easier for us to program.

Duplicating in the Frame Editor

As well as duplicating an object by dragging and dropping off the Library Toolbar, you can duplicate using the mouse button.

1. Ensure that all MMF2 applications are closed.

2. Create a new application within MMF2.

3. Ensure that you are on the blank frame editor, and using the Library Toolbar, select Tile Graphics and then Tile_Set1.

4. Drag and drop one hexagon object onto the frame. In this example we are going to drop Trees_1 onto the frame.

5. Right click on the Trees_1 object that you placed on the frame, and a pop-up menu will appear as shown in Figure 5.25.

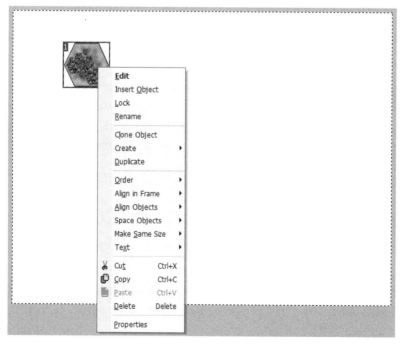

Figure 5.25
The pop-up menu when right clicking on an object on the frame editor.

6. From the pop-up menu choose duplicate.

7. The Duplicate Object dialog box appears with a number of entry boxes. This allows you to make numerous copies of an object and place them on screen in rows and columns. Type in 4 for the rows and 4 for the columns, with a 1 for row spacing and 1 for column spacing. Figure 5.26, shows these numbers already typed in.

8. Click on the OK button.

9. You now have a set of tiles that all look the same as shown in Figure 5.27. You can now manually move these tiles around the screen.

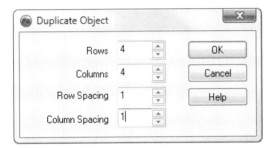

Figure 5.26
The Duplicate Object dialog box.

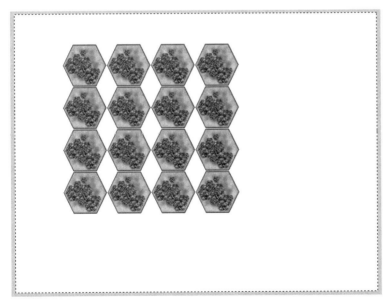

Figure 5.27
The items placed on the frame ready for you to position them.

You can see the tiles in an example file called Example5.mfa in the Examples folder on the CD-ROM provided with this book.

Cloning in the Frame Editor

Cloning is a very similar process to duplicating and will leave you with a number of tiles on the frame editor that look the same. The steps required to clone an object are as follows:

1. Ensure that all MMF2 applications are closed.

2. Create a new application in MMF2.

3. Ensure that you are on the blank frame editor, and using the Library Toolbar, select Tile Graphics and then Tile_Set1.

4. Drag and drop one hexagon object onto the frame. In this example we are going to drop Trees_1 onto the frame.

5. Right click on the Trees_1 object that you placed on the frame, and a pop-up menu will appear. From the pop-up menu, choose clone object.

6. The Clone Object dialog box appears with a number of entry boxes. This is the same type of box you would see when using the Duplicate option.

7. Type in 4 for the rows and 4 for the columns, with a 1 for row spacing and 1 for column spacing.

8. Click on the OK button.

This will create the same layout you created in the duplicate example, but each tile will be a separate entity.

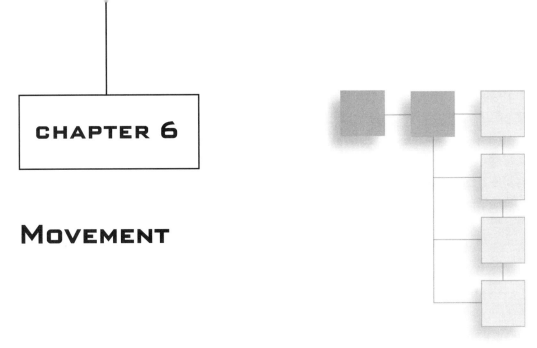

CHAPTER 6

MOVEMENT

In this chapter you will learn some of the various ways you can introduce movement of your units in the game. Unit movement is one of the key aspects of game play in a computer war game and is essential for any game you make. In this chapter you will learn about player movement and how you can begin to write your code to check movement points and move a unit on the screen. Computer controlled movement will be covered in Chapter 9.

Assigning Movement Points

When you create a war game, you will place several units, to which you will need to assign values, on your map. These values represent certain aspects of your unit's configuration, such as strength, morale, movement, and potentially many more. The game needs these values to be able to make decisions about whether a unit can move, what attack strength it has, and more.

To give an army unit a set of values that is able to change, you can use MMF2's alterable value system. This is a set of values, which you can access through the event editor, that can change as the game is played. The only real downside to using an alterable value is that they are internal to each object and you will not see the value while you are testing the game. To make testing your games easier and to make sure that when you move a unit that it removes the correct number of movement points, you can place an object called a counter onto the frame.

Throughout this book, we will use both alterable values and counters to show how the code is working.

Before you begin, we have created a simple MFA file that has a small set of tiles and a unit object ready to be worked on.

1. Open MMF2 and click on the Open button. Browse the CD-ROM provided with this book and within the Examples folder select Movement1.mfa.

2. You will see a few terrain tiles and a single plane unit, like that shown in Figure 6.1.

First you should place a counter on the frame so you can display the number of movement points you have left for your unit. You need to store the maximum movement points and the current movement value in alterable values. You can then place the current value into the counter so you can see its value. When the player presses the cursor keys, that tells MMF2 to move the unit and deduct a single movement point. Initially, we will just deduct a single movement point, but you can also begin to put together a way to remove multiple points, depending on the terrain.

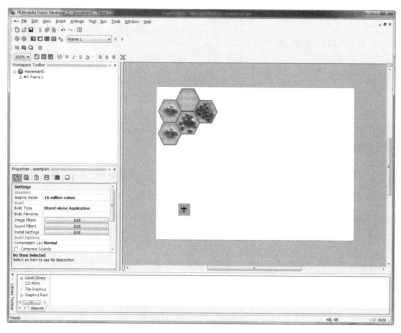

Figure 6.1
Our starting map with a single unit.

Adding a Counter

We will now add a counter onto the frame; this counter will be used to test whether your code is working.

To add a counter onto the Example4.mfa that is already loaded you will need to:

1. Ensure that you are on the frame editor and can see the tiles and the plane counter as shown in Figure 6.1.

2. Select Insert|New Object.

3. From the object list, find the Counter object, select it, and click on OK. The cursor will change to a crosshair. Click anywhere on the frame to place the counter.

4. You will now have a counter that is set to zero on the frame, as shown in Figure 6.2.

To begin with, we are going to keep with the default settings of the counter, which means by default it is set to zero. We will place values in the counter once we have configured the object's movement points.

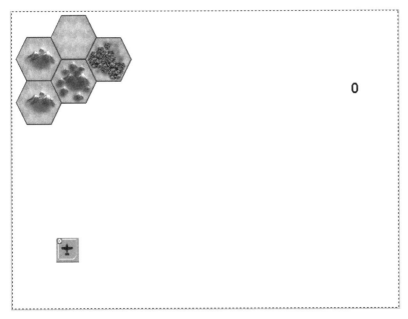

Figure 6.2
The map and counter on the frame with the newly added counter.

Note

In your games you might have multiple uses for a counter object. You could place one on screen for testing purposes, which would display the movement points that the unit has left. This would allow you to see it countdown as you move the unit on screen, allowing you to make sure you coded the movement and terrain modifiers correctly. You might also have a dialog box or graphical interface that displays information about the unit including the movement points that it has left. In the examples in this book, we will be using counters to test whether we have coded the game correctly and provide visual feedback.

Assigning Alterable Values

You are going to configure your plane unit with a set of values that you can use to calculate how many movement points the object has left. In Chapter 2, we discussed that there is a movement phase where a unit can use its movement points. When its movement has completed and all of the other phases have taken place, the object will be able to move that number of movement points again.

If you decide that your unit has five movement points each round, there are two things you need to consider in your game.

Maximum Movement Points: This is the maximum number of points that the unit will move each phase. This starting figure will never change; it is placed within the alterable values so that you can use it to reset the movement figure each round. You need to do this because after you get to the end of movement, the current movement points will be zero and will need to be reset.

Current Movement Points: Every time you move a unit on the map, you need to keep track of how many movement points that particular unit has left. You need to keep track of this so you know when the object has no movement points left, but you also need to keep track so you can compare the current movement points with the tiles terrain movement points figure. If a unit has one movement point left and it is going to attempt to cross a river, which costs three points, it cannot move.

It is very important to have an alterable value slot that contains the original value because this means you can refer to it, and use it to set other values that do change.

We are now going to assign two alterable values to our plane unit.

1. Ensure that you are on the frame editor for the movement1.mfa file that you previously added the counter object to. If you have reloaded the file, you need to re-read the previous section "Adding a Counter".

2. Left click on the plane object that is called active. This reveals the object properties; to access the alterable values, click on the values tab in the properties window. The values icon is shown in Figure 6.3.

3. After you click on the values tab, you see the default window as shown in Figure 6.4.

4. You want to create two new alterable values, so click on the New button for Alterable values twice. You can see the two values that have been created in Figure 6.5.

5. The identifiable name that each item is given is Alterable Value Letter because you added two alterable values, A and B. By default, all alterable values are given the starting value of 0.

Figure 6.3
The values tab in the object properties.

Figure 6.4
The Values tab window.

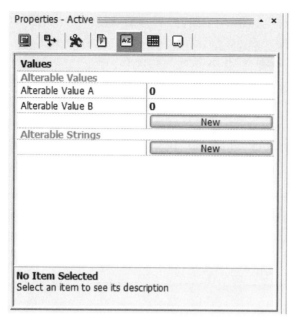

Figure 6.5
The two alterable values added to the Values tab.

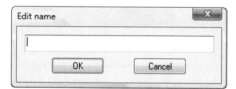

Figure 6.6
The dialog box that allows you to amend the name of the alterable values.

The names of both alterable values are not very descriptive and when you are programming in the event editor, you may forget which value is associated with which particular item. When your games are much larger and you have a large number of alterable values, this problem is magnified, so it is sensible to change the names of these values at the beginning of development. For this example, you are going to call alterable value A Starting Movement Value and alterable value B Current Movement Value. To do this:

1. Double click on the text Alterable Value A. A dialog box appears as shown in Figure 6.6. Enter the name Starting Movement Value.

2. Click on the OK button.

Figure 6.7
The completed changes to the Values tab for the Active object.

3. Double click on the text Alterable Value B, and when the dialog box appears, type in the name Current Movement Value.

4. Click on the OK button.

5. You have now changed the text name for both of these alterable values.

6. You need to edit the Starting Movement Value so that the object has an initial value. This value will not change. Click on the 0 opposite the Starting Movement Value line and then type in the number 5 and press Return. Your properties window should now look like the one shown in Figure 6.7.

Note

You may find that you cannot see the entire alterable values text name in the properties window. Using the mouse, you can drag the window so that the area is larger. You can make the value area smaller and the name area larger by holding the mouse over the dividing line and then holding down the mouse button and dragging the mouse left or right.

Note

You can have a maximum of 26 alterable values per object. If you need more than this, you should find other ways of storing information, such as the array object.

Basic Movement Point Calculation

Now that you have assigned an object with its starting point value, it is time to do a basic set of calculations so that when the player presses a particular key, the movement points will reduce.

Following are the things you need to do:

- Set the Current Movement Value to the same value as the starting movement value.

- Set the Current starting value to the counter object. This allows you to keep a real-time view of the movement points decreasing.

- Check for when the keyboard is pressed and reduce the current movement value by 1.

- To ensure that the counter is correct at all times, you must create a condition that sets the counter to the current value when a specific key is pressed.

Setting the Value

At the beginning of each game phase you need to set the current movement value of all objects back to the starting movement value. This allows you to restart the movement phase of your game with all your units back to their original starting movement and allows the player to move the units.

You do this by coding it in the event editor. In this example, you should set the starting value at the start of the game by using the start of frame condition because the program is just an example of how the coding works. In an actual game you would set this code in a code group and only run it when the new movement phase was about to begin.

1. If you still have the file Movement1.mfa open with the two alterable values added, you can continue to use that file. If not, you can open the file mcode1.mfa, which is located in the Examples folder on the CD-ROM that accompanies this book.

2. Ensure that you are on the frame editor for frame1 and click on the event editor button.

3. You will be in the event editor; and there are no events on screen at the moment.

4. Click on the New Condition text, right click on the Storyboard Controls icon, and select Start of Frame.

5. You now have a single event Start of Frame on event line 1.

6. You need to set the Starting Movement Value to match the Current Movement Value. This means you should set the Current Movement Value to 5. Because these alterable values are under your Active object, you need to select that object. Move across from event line one until you are directly under the Active plane object. Right click and select Alterable Values|Set. This brings up the Expression Evaluator with two options: a drop down box with the heading Choose Value and an Enter expression text entry box with a zero in it. The drop down box represents the object where you want to place the data, so change this to Current Movement Value.

7. Now you need to specify which object or data you want to retrieve. MMF2 is very powerful and can specify an object from which to get data. Ensure that you delete the 0 from the box, and then click on the Retrieve data from an object button; the New expression dialog box appears. You want to get the value from the Active object for the Starting Movement Value, so right click on the Active plane object. Select Values|Values A to M | Retrieve Starting Movement Value as shown in Figure 6.8.

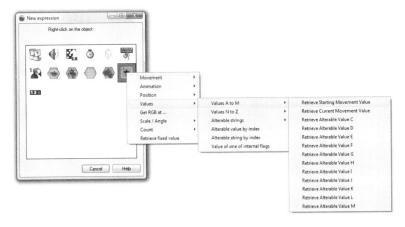

Figure 6.8
Retrieving alterable values.

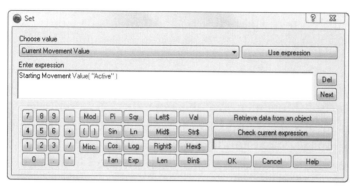

Figure 6.9
Expression evaluator with the Data to set and where it should be placed.

8. You will now see the expression evaluator updated, as shown in Figure 6.9. This shows that you will be setting the Current Movement Value to the Starting Movement Value. To save the information to the event editor, click on the OK button.

Note

In more complex games, you may want to do some additional calculations to reduce the starting value, for example, if the unit has taken too much damage or its morale has been reduced.

Setting the Counter

If you ran the program at this stage, you would see all of your objects on screen, but you would not know that the Starting Movement Value has been placed into the current value. You should now set the Current Movement Value into the counter at the start of the frame to show you that the action you previously created is working correctly.

In the event editor, use the first Start of frame event line to set the value of Current Movement Value to the counter.

1. Move across to the right until you are directly under the counter object, right click, and select Set Counter. A different style Expression evaluator appears, but it works in the same way as any of the other evaluators that appear in MMF2. We want to set the counter's value to that of the alterable value. Click on the Retrieve data from an object button and right click on the Active plane object, then select Values|Values A to M|Retrieve Current Movement Value. Your expression evaluator will now look like Figure 6.10.

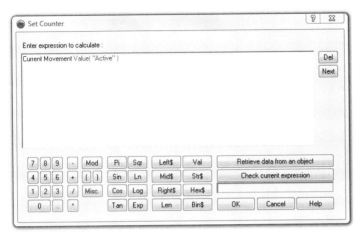

Figure 6.10
The expression evaluator for setting a counter.

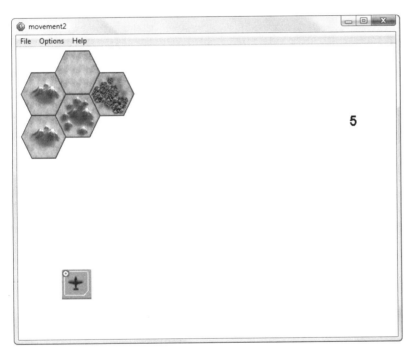

Figure 6.11
The counter has been set to the current movement value of 5.

2. Click on OK to save the information to the event editor.

3. If you now run your game by pressing F8, you will see that your counter has been set to a value of 5 as shown in Figure 6.11.

Reducing Current Movement Value on a Key Press

When the player presses a key, you want the unit to move and its movement points to be reduced. You will deal with moving the unit shortly; in this example, you will reduce the movement points by 1 each time the player presses a key.

In your own games, you would use the arrow keys or some other key combination to check for when to reduce the movement points. You will learn to use the arrow keys later on in this chapter when we move the unit on screen, but for now you will use the spacebar.

1. Ensure that you are in the event editor. Click on the New condition text.

2. Right click on the Mouse Pointer and Keyboard object, select The Keyboard|Upon Pressing a Key. A small dialog box appears prompting you to press a key on the keyboard. Press the spacebar.

3. You now have a condition on event line 2, and you need to add an action that will subtract 1 from the Current Movement Value alterable value. Move across until you are directly under the Active plane object. Right click and select Alterable Values|Subtract From. The Expression evaluator appears. Ensure that the drop down box says Current Movement Value and enter 1 in the text area as shown in Figure 6.12.

4. Click on the OK button to save the information to the event editor.

If you run the program now by pressing F8, you will see the starting value in the counter. When you press the spacebar, the counter will stay the same, but in the

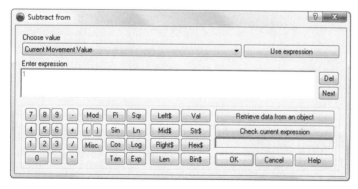

Figure 6.12
Subtracting a number from the alterable value.

background the Current Movement Value will be reduced by 1. Now you need to update the counter to show the current state of the alterable value.

You now have an event that checks for when the spacebar is pressed, which reduces the Current Movement Value. You can also use this same event line to pass the value to the counter.

1. Move across from event line 2 until you are directly under the counter object. Right click and select Set Counter.

2. The Expression evaluator dialog box appears. You want to retrieve the alterable value, Current movement value, so click on Retrieve data from an object. Right click on the Active object and select Values|Values A to M|Retrieve Current Movement Value.

3. You will now be back at the Expression evaluator box. Click on the OK button to save the information to the Event editor.

Now run the program by pressing F8, and when you press the spacebar the counter should reduce by 1.

Negative Alterable Value

In the previous example, we set the spacebar to reduce the movement value by 1 each time it was pressed. If you keep on pressing the spacebar, you will notice that the value on the counter decreases to a negative number. This means that the alterable value is now a negative value. We need to prevent this alterable value from going below 0 to prevent unexpected results and so that we can do checks within MMF2 to see when the value equals 0. You can set a minimum and maximum value for a counter, but as the value of the counter is retrieved from the alterable value, this would only prevent the counter from becoming negative and not the original value that it takes its data from. So now you need to prevent the alterable value going below 0, which in turn means that the counter will also show the correct value.

At the moment, the alterable value is subtracted when the player presses the spacebar. The easiest way to prevent the alterable value from going too low is to add an additional condition to check the current if the value has reached 0. This means that when the player presses the spacebar and the alterable value is greater than or equal to 1, it will run the relevant actions. Once the movement value has reached 0, it will no longer reduce the alterable value or the counter value.

1. In the event editor you will see two events; the second event is Upon pressing Space Bar. Right click on this condition to display the pop-up menu; then select Insert. The New condition dialog box appears. You want to compare two numbers, the value of the alterable value and a general value which you can test it against. Right click on the Special object and choose Compare two general values.

2. The expression evaluator appears. Highlight the 0 in the top edit box and then click on Retrieve data from an object, right click on the Active plane object, then choose Values|Values A to M|Retrieve current movement value. In the drop down box, change this to Greater or equal. Finally, in the lower edit box replace the 0 with a 1. Your Expression evaluator appears as shown in Figure 6.13.

3. Click on the OK button to save this information to the event editor. You can see the condition in Figure 6.14.

4. Run the program now and press the spacebar to see that the counter only gets to zero.

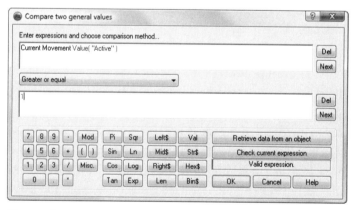

Figure 6.13
Comparing two values in the expression evaluator.

Figure 6.14
Two conditions in one event.

When MMF2 runs, it will check to see if the user has pressed the spacebar *and* that the Current Movement Value is equal to or greater than 1. This means that when it reaches 1, it will run one more time the actions on the right, thereby changing the value to 0. The next time it comes back around, the value is no longer equal or greater than 1 and so the event line is ignored.

Moving Your Units Onscreen

Now that you have a simple example of how you can check the number of movement points a unit has, the next stage is to make a unit move on screen. When working out unit movement, you first have to think about the map tiles size and how far your unit will need to move across them to stay in the center of each tile.

You can see in Figure 6.15 an example of the working out for our map tiles and unit sizes.

The unit can move in one of six directions from its original starting position. The six directions are the maximum number of directions it can move in. Some directions may be the edge of the screen or terrain tiles that the unit cannot move to. You can see an example of the unit and the directions it can move in Figure 6.16.

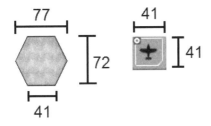

Figure 6.15
The tile and the unit size.

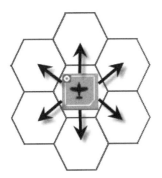

Figure 6.16
The unit's possible directions.

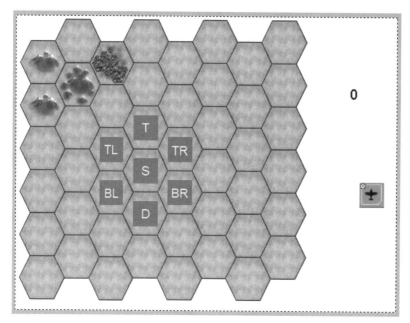

Figure 6.17
The possible directions a unit might move in from its initial starting position.

If you cannot work out the distance that an object would need to move on the terrain by using the sizes, another way is to place the unit on a set of tiles and move its position manually, making a note of its X, Y position and then doing a simple calculation to find the distance it needs to move in a particular direction to be in the correct place on the tile. Another method is to find the exact center of a hexagon tile and draw where the unit should be placed on a tile. Using this method, you can place temporary hexagons on your map, and this will allow you to move your unit and make a note of its position. You can see an example of the hexagons that have had the center of their tile colored differently in Figure 6.17.

Each of the positions that the unit could move is labeled. So the starting position of the unit is S and each of the other directions are also marked. Once the unit has moved from S to another location, for example D which is down, this position is then its starting position.

So if your unit's current X, Y position is 199, 232, and you want to move it up one tile, its new position (by moving it manually within the frame editor) is 199, 162. This means to make a unit move upwards, you need to change its Y position by −70.

Using the same process, you can work out what you need to do for the other five directions:

- Direction letter D—move down, increase Y by 70.

- Direction letter TL—move top left, decrease X by 58 and Y decreases by 35.

- Direction letter TR—move top right, X increases by 58 and Y decreases by 35.

- Direction letter BL—move bottom left, X decreases by 58, and Y increases by 35

- Direction letter BR—move bottom right, X increases by 58 and Y increases by 35.

Note

If an object is moving up the screen, its Y position will decrease; if an object moves down the screen, its Y position will increase. For the X coordinate, if the object moves to the left, its X position will decrease, and if it moves to the right, its X position will increase.

Programming Movement

The next operation is to make the unit move on the screen. The example file used in this section has the code to reduce the movement points to zero and display them within a counter already coded. You will add some additional code to prevent it from moving once its current movement points equal zero.

The file is called unitmovement1.mfa, and it is located in the Examples folder. This file already has a set of terrain tiles on screen and has the counter, which counts down when the spacebar has been pressed. Make sure you open the file before the next step.

Checking the Key Press

We will be changing this example to reduce the movement when the correct direction is pressed and then move the unit at the same time.

1. Double click on the frame 1 text in the workspace toolbar to display the grid and the single plane unit.

2. Click on the event editor button to access the event editor. You will recognize the code that we used in a previous example.

3. We need to create six keyboard checks for each of the movement directions. In this case, we are going to use the numpad keys because these work nicely with the directions the unit has to move. In your own games, you can use other keys if you want.

4. Click on the New condition text. Right click on the Mouse pointer and keyboard object, and then from the popup menu select The Keyboard|Upon pressing a key. When the dialog box appears, press the number 7 key on the numpad.

5. We now want to create a second condition on line 3, one that is the same as the second condition on line 2. This is to check whether the current movement value of the active object is greater than or equal to 1. You can do this manually, but a quicker way is to drag and drop the condition from line 2 onto the event line to create a second condition. To do this, hold down the left mouse button on the condition and drag and drop it over the number 3 on the event line as shown in Figure 6.18.

6. You will now see your new event in Figure 6.19.

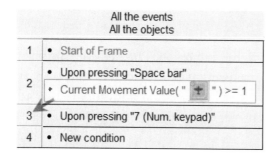

Figure 6.18
Dragging and dropping a condition onto the event line number adds it to that event line.

	All the events All the objects
1	• Start of Frame
2	• Upon pressing "Space bar" • Current Movement Value(" ➕ ") >= 1
3	• Upon pressing "7 (Num. keypad)" • Current Movement Value(" ➕ ") >= 1
4	• New condition

Figure 6.19
The two condition event.

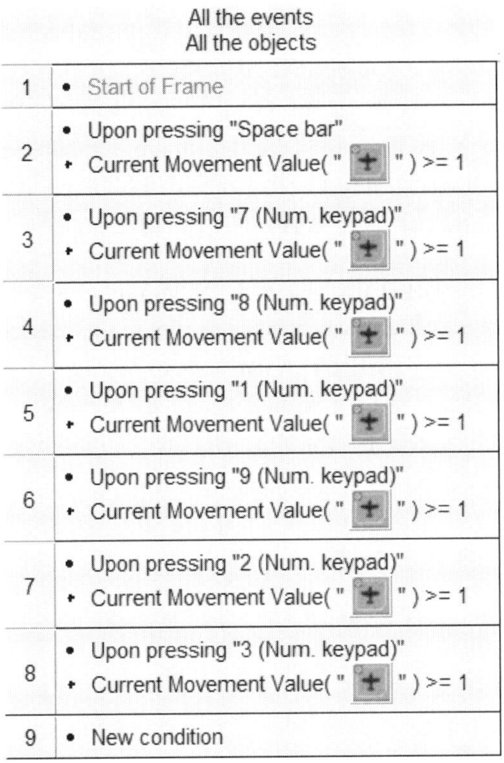

Figure 6.20
The events for all our key presses.

7. You now need to complete the same process of adding a key press using the numpad and adding the second condition to check if the value is greater than or equal to 1. You will then have a total of eight events as shown in Figure 6.20.

Note

It is very important that you drop the condition over the event line number; if you drop it over any condition in an event, it will replace that condition.

Setting the Unit's New Position

Now that you have your events in place to check when the player presses the numpad, you need to move your unit in the right direction and reduce the movement points by 1. The movement of the unit is very straightforward because in MMF2 there is an option to move the position of an object relative to its current position.

1. Move across on line three until you are directly under the Active plane object. Right click on the action box and then select Position|Select position. The Select Position dialog box appears. You using this dialog box to specify an actual X and Y coordinate or to specify a distance from a particular object. Click on the Relative to radio button. This bring ups the Choose an object dialog box. Select the Active plane object, and click on OK.

2. This will take you back to the Select Position dialog box. Now you need to put in the X and Y coordinate changes that you detailed earlier, so in this example you are programming event line 3, which is for the key 7 on the numpad. This moves the unit to the top left on the hex map, so for the X coordinate type in −58 and for the Y coordinate type in −35. You will see a dotted line and box move as you type in the coordinates, and you can see that it moves the active object to the left. You can see the Select Position dialog box with the correct settings in Figure 6.21.

3. Click on OK to save the action to the event editor.

4. Now you need to subtract one from the alterable value so that it removes a movement point. So right click on the action box where you created your position action (this is on event line three and directly under the Active object).

5. Right click and select Alterable Values|Subtract from; then when the expression evaluator appears, change the drop down box to read Current Movement Value and enter the number 1 in the Enter expression box.

6. Click on OK to save to the event editor.

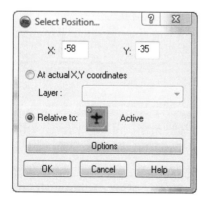

Figure 6.21
The relative position to the object.

7. Finally, move across from event line three until you are directly under the Counter object. In the event line above it, you will see an action. Drag and drop that action to event line three because you want the same action to apply. This means that the counter updates to the current movement value when the key is pressed. Hold down the left mouse button on the action under the counter on event line two and drag and drop to the blank action box directly below it.

8. You then see the current event line and its actions as shown in Figure 6.22.

9. You now need to follow the same procedure for the actions for event lines 4 through 8, Table 6.1 displays the relative X and Y coordinate positions for each direction.

10. After you complete the actions for the other events, you can delete event line two, which reduces the movement points by one on pressing the spacebar. This is no longer required because all of the code is now placed under movement keys.

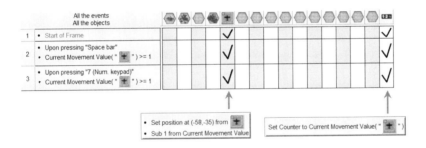

Figure 6.22
The actions for event line 3.

Table 6.1 The Relative Position of the Numpad Directions

Key	X coordinate	Y coordinate
7	−58	−35
8	0	−70
1	−58	35
9	58	−35
2	0	70
3	58	35

11. You can see the completed code in the file unitmovement2.mfa that is located in the Examples folder.

12. Run the game by pressing F8 and use the numpad keys to move the unit around the map. You will notice that you can only move the unit while its movement points are above 0.

Multiple Unit Movement

Creating movement for a single unit is straightforward, but in all computer war games the player will be looking after anything from half a dozen units to maybe 50 or even 100. The problem then exists how you handle movement for so many units. Even though the code to make one unit move is basically the same as moving a second unit, some additional code is needed to keep track of which unit is currently being moved. Most of the code is repetition of code you have already used, and as you become more experienced in MMF2, you will be able to copy and paste sections of code between tasks, and this will speed up the overall coding time.

In this section of the chapter, you will be moving two units on a hexagon map, so you need:

- Two units on a hexagon grid

- A piece of text that can display Unit 1 or Unit 2

- A counter that keeps track of the current movement points

- A counter that keeps track of which unit is currently selected

- A button to select the next unit

- To create a new alterable value that stores the unit's unique ID

- To create a qualifier group

- To use groups within the event editor to section the code

Rather than place all of the items on screen, we created a file that you can download with the text, button, and counters already in place. You can load this file from the CD-ROM provided with this book; the file is called multipleunits.mfa and can be found in the Examples folder. After you load the file and

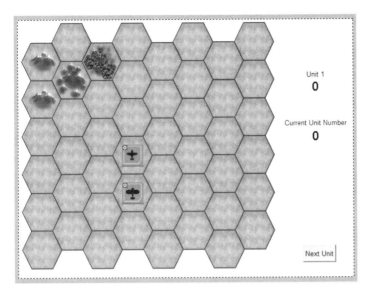

Figure 6.23
The frame of the multipleunits.mfa file.

double click on the frame name in the workspace toolbar you should see the frame editor, as shown in Figure 6.23.

Unit ID Alterable Value

So that you can identify the unit being moved, you need to give each unit an identifiable number. Each unit's number must be unique and it must start from 1 and count upwards. Using numbers is an easy way to scroll through your units in order when you need to move them one at a time. In this file, we have two plane units, one called plane1 and the other called plane2.

You need to add an extra alterable value in each object's properties sheet, in the values tab as shown in Figure 6.24 for the Plane1 object. Plane2 has the same line entry, but its value is set to 2.

Text Feedback

When you are making your own war games, it is sensible to provide some form of feedback to the player about her units, the map, and perhaps even the weather. For this example, we have created a string object that will change text to show which unit is currently available for movement. In the example file, the string object has already been placed on the frame, and in the Object Settings tab

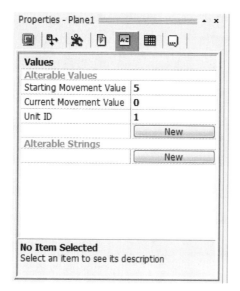

Figure 6.24
The Unit ID entry for Plane1.

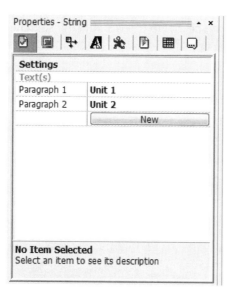

Figure 6.25
The String properties, the Settings tab.

(Properties window), two text paragraphs have been created for unit 1 and unit 2. You can see these two paragraphs in Figure 6.25. By default, paragraph 1 is displayed first, and you need to create some code in the Event Editor to display paragraph 2 when required.

Coding Multiple Movement

The next step is to create the event programming for multiple movements. This example allows you to move multiple units on the screen, one after another. We have not taken into account moving back through the units or what happens if the player wishes to move a unit over a couple of hexagon tiles and then go back to that unit at a later stage, this will be covered later in this chapter.

1. Ensure that you have the multipleunits.mfa file loaded; this is in the Examples folder.

2. Ensure that you are on the frame editor, and then click on the event editor. You can now begin to populate the editor with your code.

The first bit of code you need is to set the counter to the same number as the first unit object's ID, which is 1. You will use the counter to keep track of which unit is currently selected because you need this to enable and disable some code groups. These code groups contain specific movement instructions for our units, and it is better for this code to be grouped together. Having the code grouped together makes it easier to read, and ensures that we only run that section of code when required, which in this case is only when a particular unit is selected.

1. Click on the New condition text in the event editor. When the New Condition dialog box appears, select the Storyboard Controls icon and select Start of Frame. You created your first event. This event will run only at the beginning of the frame, and you use it to initialize (set-up) any starting values.

2. Move across from this event until you are directly under Counter2, right click the action box, and select Set Counter. Now enter the number 1 in the expression evaluator and click on OK.

You will come back to this event line shortly, but first you need to create a new event that checks when the Counter2 object equals 2.

1. Click on New condition, then select Counter2 and Compare the counter to a value when the expression evaluator appears, leave the drop down box as Equal. Replace the 0 with a 2, and click on OK. The actions required for this event are enabling and disabling two groups, but because you haven't created these groups yet, you cannot create the actions, so just continue to make your events and go back to these actions shortly.

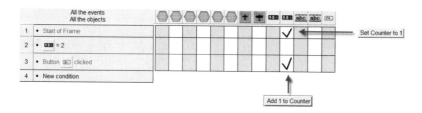

Figure 6.26
The first three events and actions.

Now you need an event that will check when the Button object has been clicked; this is your visual cue to let the player move to the next unit. From a programming perspective, you could also use a key press or an animated graphic that the user presses.

1. Click on the New Condition text and select the Button object from the New Condition dialog box. From the pop-up menu, choose Button Clicked?

2. The only action that the button click runs is to add one to the Counter2 object. This is what you use to keep track of which unit is currently selected.

3. From event line three, move across until you are under the Counter2 object, right click and select Add to Counter, then type in 1 in the Expression evaluator and click on OK. Your events and actions are shown in Figure 6.26.

Creating Two Groups

You need two groups to contain your code for each plane. At first, both groups will be disabled and you need to tell the program when to run each group. This allows you to specify when to run a particular set of code and, in this case, when it will move each plane object.

To create two groups:

1. Right click on the number 4 in the event editor, and from the pop-up menu select Insert|Group of events.

2. In the title of the group, type **Plane 1**, ensure that the Active when frame starts is unchecked and then click on OK. You now need to collapse the group, so double click on the group "Plane 1", this will hide the "New condition" that is tabbed under it. This will leave a single "New condition" line on event line 5 below it.

	All the events All the objects	⬡	⬡	⬡	⬡	⬡	⬡	✚	✚	🔢	🔢	abc	abc	⧉
1	• Start of Frame								✓					
2	• 🔢 = 2													
3	• Button ⧉ clicked								✓					
4	Plane 1													
5	Plane 2													
6	• New condition													

Figure 6.27
The two groups added to the event editor.

3. Right click on event number 5, and from the pop-up menu, select Insert|Group of events.

4. In the title of the group, type in **Plane 2**. Again, ensure that Active when frame starts is unchecked and then click on OK. You will see your two groups, which are currently disabled, in Figure 6.27.

Enabling and Disabling the Groups

Now that you have created two groups, you can create actions that will enable and disable them when required. For this, you need to create these actions on previous events. You do this because you cannot program enabling and disabling of groups unless the groups are already created.

1. Enable the Plane 1 group at the start of the frame.

2. Move across from the first event, which is the Start of Frame condition. Stop under the first object, which is the Special Conditions object. Right click and select Group of Events|Activate.

3. An Activate dialog box appears and displays the two groups that you created, as shown in Figure 6.28. The first group is selected by default, and this is the group that you need to enable, so click on OK.

Earlier on event line 2, we programmed a condition to check when the counter was set to 2. This number changes when the player presses the button to move to the next unit. At this point, you want to move to the second plane. For this, you need to disable the Plane 1 group because you don't want this code to continue running. After you disable the Plane 1 group, activate the second group, Plane 2.

Figure 6.28
The groups that we are using in this example.

It is always sensible to deactivate a group that is no longer needed before activating a group that is required; otherwise, you may get unexpected results as your code swaps over the groups.

1. Move across from the second event line. Under Special Conditions, again select Group of Events, but this time, select Deactivate. When the Deactivate dialog box appears, you want to deactivate the group Plane 1, which is selected, so click on OK.

2. You want to add a second action to the same event, so move across from the second event line, and under Special Conditions select Group of Events|Activate. When the dialog box appears, choose Plane 2 and click on OK.

Now you should have two actions for the second event under the special conditions object, the first to deactivate Plane 1 and the second to activate Plane 2.

Coding Group Plane 1

Now that the groups are enabled and disabled outside the groups, we now need to program the code within each of the two groups to make our planes move. You will recognize some of the code from one of the previous examples, where we only allow the unit to move if it still has available movement points.

1. Ensure that the Plane 1 group is open and that you can see the New condition event line under it, as shown in Figure 6.29.

All the events / All the objects	⬡	⬡	⬡	⬡	⬡	✚	⬆	123	123	abc	abc	n→
1 • Start of Frame							✓					
2 • 123 = 2												
3 • Button 🔲 clicked							✓					
4 Plane 1												
5 • New condition												
6 Plane 2												
7 • New condition												

Figure 6.29
The Plane 1 group expanded to show the New condition event line under it.

Run Once Condition and Its Actions

At the start of the group, configure the movement points. You need to do this to ensure that when you move from unit 1 to unit 2, the new set of movement points is placed in the Current Movement Value alterable value. You also need to place the current movement points into the counter that you are using on screen to show you how many movement points the unit has left to make. You only need to run this event once, and so MMF2 has a condition that you can select which will limit the number of times a condition is able to run within the life of the game.

1. Click on the New condition text on event line 5.

2. Select the Special object from the New condition dialog box and then choose Limit Conditions|Run this event once. While the group is enabled, it will only run this line and its corresponding actions once.

You now need to set the actions for this event, setting the values into the alterable values slot and the counter.

1. To set the Starting movement value to the Current movement value, move across from event line five until you are directly under the Plane 1 object. Right click and select Alterable Values|Set. This will bring up the Expression Evaluator with two options: a drop down box with the heading Choose Value and an Enter expression text entry box with a zero in it. The drop down box represents the object you want to place data into, so change this to Current Movement Value.

2. Now you need to specify which object or data you want to retrieve. Ensure that you delete the 0 from the box, and then click on the Retrieve data from

an object button. The New expression dialog box appears. You want to get the value from the Plane1 object for the Starting Movement Value, so right click on the Plane 1. Select Values|Values A to M|Retrieve Starting Movement Value.

3. To save the information to the event editor, click on the OK button.

Now that you have set the Starting Movement Value to current value, the plane will begin with 5 movement points. You must now set the value of the Current Movement Value alterable value to the counter. Remember all the counter does is provide a visual note to the player how many movement points are left.

1. Move across from event line 5 until you are under the Counter object.

2. Right click and select Set Counter, the Expression evaluator will appear, remove the 0 from the box and then click on the Retrieve data from an object button.

3. Select the Plane 1 object from the New expression dialog box and then from the pop-up choose Values|Values A to M|Retrieve Current Movement Value. Click on the OK button to save the information to the event editor.

Always

Rather than creating a number of actions each time the player presses a key to update the counter, you can use the Always condition. This always runs while it is in the main program code or within a group that is enabled. Always is a good way of ensuring that a counter or value is always up to date. Use the Always condition to update the display counter; whenever you amend the Current Movement Value alterable value, the counter is updated to display the same amount.

1. Click on the New condition text on event line 6.

2. Select the Special object and click on Always.

3. Right click on the Counter action box and select Set Counter. The Expression evaluator appears. Remove the 0 from the box and click on Retrieve data from an object button.

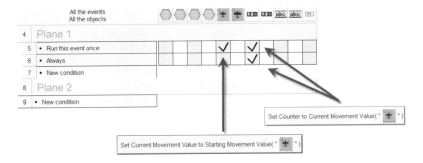

Figure 6.30
The Run once and Always conditions.

4. Select the Plane 1 object from the New expression dialog box and then from the pop-up choose Values|Values A to M|Retrieve Current Movement Value. Click on the OK button to save the information to the event editor.

5. You can see the conditions and actions in Figure 6.30.

N o t e

When you have actions that are going to be the same in other action boxes (for example, in the Counter, the action box on event line 5 is the same as the action on event line 6), you can drag and drop this action to the action box on another event line. This can save you a lot of time and effort if you have several actions that are the same. You can quickly copy and paste them rather than going through the menu options each time.

N o t e

For small updates such as a counter, using Always is a very sensible way of cutting down your code. Be aware, though, that if you are using Always with a lot of actions or actions that do a lot of mathematical calculations, your game may have performance issues.

Creating Plane 1 Movement

The planes movement is the same as the movement you did in a previous example. The first movement is described in the following list and in Table 6.2.

1. Click on the New condition text on event line 7. Right click on the Mouse pointer and keyboard object, and then from the pop-up menu select The Keyboard|Upon pressing a key. When the dialog box appears, press the number 7 key on the numpad.

2. To create a second condition on line 7, which will check to see if the current movement value of the active object is greater than or equal to 1, right

Table 6.2 The Relative Position of the Numpad Directions

Key	X coordinate	Y coordinate
7	−58	−35
8	0	−70
1	−58	35
9	58	−35
2	0	70
3	58	35

click on the condition you already entered on event line 7 and select Insert. From the pop-up menu, select the Special object and then Compare two general Values.

3. The Expression evaluator appears. Highlight the 0 in the top edit box and click on Retrieve data from an object. Right click on the Plane 1 object, and choose Values|Values A to M|Retrieve current movement value. In the drop down box, change this to Greater or equal. Finally, in the lower edit box replace the 0 with a 1. Click on the OK button to save the second condition.

Now you need to move the unit in the correct direction. Because the top left button has been pressed, the unit needs to move in a northwesterly direction.

1. Move across on event line 7 until you are directly under the Plane 1 object. Right click on the action box and select Position|Select position. The Select Position dialog box appears. Click on the Relative to radio button. The Choose an object dialog box appears. Select the Plane 1 object, and click on OK.

2. This takes you back to the Select Position dialog box. Type in the X and Y coordinates; for the X coordinate type in −58, and for the Y coordinate type in −35.

3. Click on OK to save the action to the event editor.

4. Now you need to subtract one from the alterable value so that it removes a movement point. So right click on the action box where you just created your position action (this is on event line 7 and directly under the Plane 1 object).

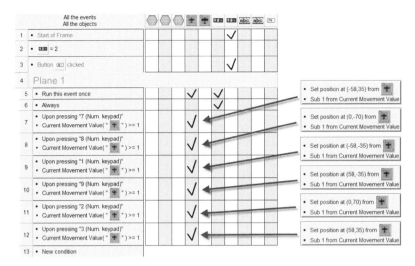

Figure 6.31
The conditions and actions for moving Plane 1.

5. Right click and select Alterable Values|Subtract from. When the Expression evaluator appears, change the drop down box to read Current Movement Value and enter the number 1 in the enter expression box.

6. Click on OK to save to the event editor.

Now you need to do the same events and actions for the other five directions. Table 6.2 contains the set of events and actions that match the screen shown in Figure 6.31.

Setting Counter to 0 and Disabling the Group

The final event required for this group is to check when the Current Movement Value of Plane 1 equals zero. Then reset the Counter object to the Current Movement Value and disable the group. Even though you are already using the Always event further up in the group, it will not update the counter when it gets to this event. This is because at this point you disable the group, and this means that the Always event cannot run to set the movement to 0. So as a manual process, you can set the counter to 0. You disable the group at this stage because no further movement points are available to this unit. You don't need this block of code running anymore, and it is more efficient and sensible to disable any groups of code that are no longer needed.

1. Click on the New condition text on event line 13.

2. Select the Plane 1 object, and choose Alterable Values|Compare to one of the alterable values.

3. The expression evaluator appears. Ensure that the choose value equals Current Movement Value and that the comparison method is Equal and the enter expression is 0. Click on OK to save to the event editor.

For the first action, set the counter to the current movement value.

1. Move across from event line 13 until you are under the Counter object.

2. Right click the action box and select Set Counter. The Expression evaluator appears. Remove the 0 from the box and then click on the Retrieve data from an object button.

3. Select the Plane 1 object from the New expression dialog box, and from the pop-up box that appears, choose Values|Values A to M|Retrieve Current Movement Value. Click on the OK button to save the information to the event editor.

4. To deactivate the group, move across from the event line 13 and under Special Conditions, select Group of Events; then select Deactivate. When the Deactivate dialog box appears, click on OK to deactivate the group Plane 1, which is selected.

Creating Plane 2 Movement

Now you have created all of the code you need to move Plane 1. The code for Plane 2 is similar to the code that was used in Plane 1. You could spend a lot of time creating all of the code from scratch, or as mentioned previously, you can copy and paste the events and change certain aspects of the code. For example, the object in event line 7 for the second condition is checking Plane 1. Once you have copied and pasted to a new event, you then need to change the object instance from Plane 1 to Plane 2.

To make things easier, we will detail how to make the code for Plane 2. Throughout the book you will be changing code by copying and pasting code and then making small changes to it.

Ensure that the Plane 2 group has been collapsed and the Plane 1 group is open and that you can see the New condition event line under it.

Note

If you do not collapse the Plane 1 group, the event line numbers will be different from those suggested in the following example.

Run Once Condition and Its Actions

As you did for the first group, you need to create a Run this event once condition and place the Starting Movement Value to the Current Movement Value. You also need to set the Counter to display the correct movement value, and you need to change the text that is your visual cue to text that represents the next available unit.

1. Click on the New condition text on event line 6.

2. Select the Special object from the New condition dialog box and then choose Limit Conditions|Run this event once. While the group is enabled, it will only run this line and its corresponding actions once.

You now need to set the actions for this event, and set the values into the alterable values slot and the counter.

1. To set the Starting Movement Value to the Current Movement Value, move across from event line 6 until you are directly under the Plane 2 object. Right click and select Alterable Values|Set. This brings up the Expression Evaluator with two options: a drop down box with the heading Choose Value and an Enter expression text entry box with a zero in it. The drop down box represents the object you want to place data in, so change this to Current Movement value.

2. You need to specify the object or data you want to retrieve. Ensure that you delete the 0 from the box, and then click on the Retrieve data from an object button. The New expression dialog box appears. We want to get the value from the Plane2 object for the Starting Movement Value, so right click on the Plane2. Select Values|Values A to M|Retrieve Starting Movement Value.

3. To save the information to the event editor, click on the OK button.

Now that you have set the Starting Movement Value to Current Value, the plane begins with five movement points. Now you must set the value of the Current Movement Value alterable value to the counter. Remember, all the counter does is provide a visual note to the player telling him how many movement points are left.

1. Move across from event line 6 (in the Plane 2 group) until you are under the Counter object.

2. Right click and select Set Counter. The Expression evaluator appears. Remove the 0 from the box and click on the Retrieve data from an object button.

3. Select the Plane2 object from the New expression dialog box and then from the pop-up choose Values|Values A to M|Retrieve Current Movement Value. Click on the OK button to save the information to the event editor.

4. One small change from the Plane 1 group is that you need to change the text in the String object that currently displays "Unit 1" when you run the program so that it displays "Unit 2".

5. Still on event line 6 right click on the action box under the String object and select Next Paragraph.

Always

Now you need to create the Always condition, as you did for the first group. This updates the counter to display the current number of movement points available.

1. Click on the New condition text on event line 7.

2. Select the Special object and then click on Always.

3. Right click on the Counter action box and select Set Counter. The Expression evaluator appears. Remove the 0 from the box and click on the Retrieve data from an object button.

4. Select the Plane1 object from the New expression dialog box. From the pop-up menu, choose Values|Values A to M|Retrieve Current Movement Value. Click on the OK button to save the information to the event editor.

Creating Plane 2's Movement

The same process for moving Plane1 can be used for moving Plane2. Follow these steps to configure the first movement direction when the user presses the number 7 key on the number pad:

1. Click on the New condition text on event line 8. Right click on the Mouse pointer and keyboard object. From the pop-up menu, select The Keyboard|Upon pressing a key. When the dialog box appears, press the number 7 key on the numpad.

2. To create a second condition on line 7, which checks to see if the Current Movement Value of the active object is greater than or equal to 1, right click on the condition already entered on event line 8 and select Insert. From the pop-up menu, select the Special object and then Compare two general Values.

3. The expression evaluator appears. Highlight the 0 in the top edit box and click on Retrieve data from an object. Right click on the Plane 2 object, then choose Values|Values A to M|Retrieve current movement value. In the drop down box, change this to Greater or equal. Finally, in the lower edit box replace the 0 with a 1. Click on the OK button to save the second condition.

4. Now you need to move the unit in the correct direction. Because this is the top left button that has been pressed, the unit needs to move in a north-westerly direction.

5. Move across on event line 8 until you are directly under the Plane 2 object. Right click on the action box and then select Position|Select position. This brings up the Select Position dialog box. Click on the Relative to radio button. This brings up the Choose an object dialog box. Select the Plane 2 object, and click on OK.

6. This takes you back to the Select Position dialog where you can type in the X and Y coordinates. For the X coordinate type in × 58, and for the Y co-ordinate type in × 35.

7. Click on OK to save the action to the event editor.

8. Now you need to subtract one from the alterable value so that it removes a movement point. Right click on the action box where you just created your position action (this is on event line 7 and directly under the Plane 2 object.

9. Right click and select Alterable Values|Subtract from. When the expression evaluator appears, change the drop down box to read Current Movement Value and enter the number 1 in the Enter expression box.

10. Click on OK to save to the event editor.

As you can see, moving Plane 2 is exactly the same as Plane 1 except any reference to the plane needs to be updated to point to the correct plane object. Using Table 6.2 as the reference point, create the other movement directions 8, 1, 9, 2, and 3.

Setting Counter to 0 and Disabling the Group

Again, you need to set the movement counter to 0 to ensure that it updates correctly, and deactivate the group to ensure that no code is still run when you don't require it.

1. Click on the New condition text on event line 14.

2. Select the Plane 2 object, and then choose Alterable Values|Compare to one of the alterable values.

3. The Expression evaluator appears. Ensure that the choose value equals Current Movement Value, and that the comparison method is Equal and the Enter expression is 0. Click on OK to save to the event editor.

For the first action, set the counter to the Current Movement Value.

1. Move across from event line 14 until you are under the Counter object.

2. Right click the action box and select Set Counter. The Expression evaluator appears. Remove the 0 from the box and then click on the Retrieve data from an object button.

3. Select the Plane 2 object from the New expression dialog box, and from the pop-up choose Values|Values A to M|Retrieve Current Movement Value. Click on the OK button to save the information to the event editor.

4. Move across from event line 14, and under Special Conditions, select Group of Events. Then select Deactivate. When the Deactivate dialog box appears, you want to deactivate the Plane 2 group, so select it and click on OK.

If you now run the application by pressing the F8 key, you will be able to control the first plane, and by pressing the Next Unit button, you will be able to control the second plane. Using this same code, you are able to create the ability to move multiple planes quite easily.

You can see the completed example on the CD-ROM, in the Examples folder in the multipleunits-final.mfa file.

Preventing Units from Leaving the Screen

If you run the multipleunits-final.mfa file that is located in the Examples folder, you will notice that you are able to move your units off the tiles and onto the white background area. You want to prevent your units from leaving the screen, and you can stop this from happening by checking to see if the tile is an edge hexagon. The main issue with preventing movement from the tiles is that there are different edge tiles and directions that an object can move safely once it has reached this edge tile. You can see this issue demonstrated in Figure 6.32.

Item 1 in Figure 6.32 is an edge tile and should prevent the unit from moving in direction 7 (NW) and direction 1 (SW), while the tile marked as item 2 should prevent movement in directions 7 (NW), 8 (N), and 9 (NE).

When you prevent movement from an edge tile, you have to ensure that you don't prevent its moving back along the path it came from or even onto another connecting tile.

You have already seen one potential way of figuring out this programming puzzle. Previously, you placed alterable values in the plane units to detail how

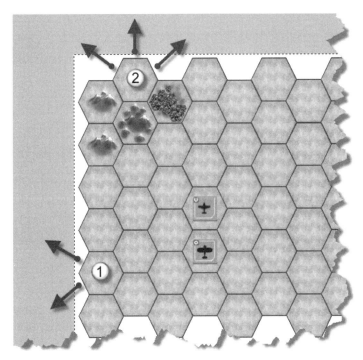

Figure 6.32
Edge movement directions.

many movement points each unit had left. You can also use alterable values to place numbers in your hexagon tiles to provide you with a way of doing calculations to see which directions a unit can move while on the tile. These alterable value slots represent all the directions that a unit can move (1, 2, 3, 7, 8, and 9 on the numpad), and there would be a choice between two values that appear, for example, a 1 or a 0. If the number is a 0, the object can move, and if the value is a 1, the number cannot move in that direction. You will use a similar method to prevent or restrict movement when you look at terrain types in Chapter 7.

You need to add several things to your program to prevent the units from leaving the screen:

- Configure the edge tiles with alterable values that tell MMF2 which direction a unit can move to.

- Configure the units with alterable values that you will use to do movement calculations.

- Add all tiles to a qualifier group.

- Add the units to a qualifier group.

- Replace certain tiles to ensure that they are unique.

- Check to see when a unit is overlapping a qualifier group and set that tile's values to the unit so you can do a check to see if the unit is okay to move.

Before you continue with your game programming, we will look at merging two MMF files into a single MFA file. The Examples folder contains two files: the multipleunits-final.mfa file, which contains the code you previously entered that will move two units on the screen, and alterablehex.mfa file, which has no code but contains changes to the terrain tiles that will be used shortly in this chapter.

In the course of game development, you might have multiple files with different bits of code that you want to reuse. To save time re-entering code you might have previously entered, it is possible to open a number of files in MMF2 and copy the required objects or events to another file. In the following example, you will take two files and copy and paste the events from one war game and place them within another.

1. Ensure that MMF2 is loaded and no game files are currently open.

2. Click on the File|Open menu option and browse to the CD-ROM provided with this book.

3. Navigate to the Examples folder and select the alterablehex.mfa file and click on open.

4. Click on the File|Open menu option again; the Examples folder should appear; choose the multipleunits-final.mfa file.

In the workspace toolbar, you will now see that the two files are loaded. You need to copy the events from the multipleunits-final.mfa file to the alterablehex.mfa file. It is important to ensure that you have the right game editor displayed for the correct application when looking at the Frame and Event Editor; otherwise, you could accidentally copy the wrong information to your newly combined file. You can double click on the application name or frame in the Workspace Toolbar for the application you are copying or pasting.

1. You should see that the multipleunits-final.mfa file is expanded in the Workspace toolbar. To ensure that this file is loaded, double click on the text Frame 1 from under the application name in the workspace toolbar.

2. Click on the Event Editor button.

3. You will see the Event Editor and all of the events. Click on event number 1 to select this event line. Hold down the Shift key and click on the last event line with contents. If both groups are collapsed, this will be event line 5. Do not select the last new condition line because this would not be copied from MMF applications.

4. Now that all of the events are highlighted, hold down the CTRL key and press the C key to copy.

5. Now that the events are copied into the computer's memory, we will copy them to our other MFA file.

6. Double click on the text alterablehex in the Workspace toolbar; this brings up the Storyboard Editor for that application. Click on the number 1 in the Storyboard Editor to open the Frame Editor.

7. Now click on the Event Editor button.

8. You should be presented with a blank event editor. Click on event line 1, hold down the CTRL key, and press the V key to paste the events.

The events are now copied and you can close the multipleunits-final.mfa file because it is no longer needed. You can close it by right clicking on the file name in the Workspace toolbar and selecting Close. We will now continue to work in the alterablehex.mfa file.

Note

If you intend to do your own copying and pasting, you need to ensure that the same Frame objects appear in both applications. MMF2 allows you to copy events from one application to another, but if you have an object in the original file that is not in the destination file, you will receive a message, and a temporary placeholder object graphic is created in the Event Editor. You will need to replace this placeholder with an object of the same type with the same name for MMF2 to use these events in the new application.

Replacing Tiles to Ensure That They Are Unique

Before you begin programming the code for stopping the unit going off the tiles, it is important to understand the copying or cloning of hexagon tiles in your game and how it would affect the use of alterable values. If the object to which you are adding your values is a duplicate (copy), then all tiles of the same type will inherit the same properties. So if your map has 50 grass-based tiles, and they are all duplicated (so they display as a single object in the event editor), when you add an alterable value to one of the edge tiles, all other tiles will also get that value. While working in the frame editor, all of these duplicate objects contain the same information, and you need to create additional code to give them different values at the start of the frame. You need to do this because the game would not be able to distinguish between an edge tile and a middle tile, and it would not be able to understand the difference between an edge tile on the left and an edge tile on the right. This can keep your units from moving. An example of the duplicate and cloning of hexagon tiles can be seen in Figure 6.33.

In Figure 6.33, you can see a set of tiles; some tiles look the same while others are graphically different. The tiles numbered 1 are all the same grass tile object; they are all duplicates, and therefore they share the same information and name and only appear once in the event editor. This is fine because any information you put into alterable values of one of the tiles is the same for all three tiles. The reason they can and should be the same is that if the unit is on any of these tiles, it can

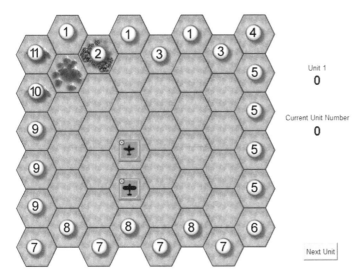

Figure 6.33
The different edge tiles in use.

only move in the same direction from each of the tiles. The tile numbered 4 is a grass tile and looks the same as tile 1, but it is a clone of the original grass object, and so it has its own name and its own alterable values. This is required because object 4 is different from object 1 because the player is not able to move in the southeast direction. In Figure 6.33, you can get an idea of which tiles are duplicates and which are individual tiles.

Note

You don't want to add the alterable values slots for every single tile when you start to create your hexagon map because this could take a long time. The easiest way to reduce the amount of work involved is when you are creating your initial tiles, you can place alterable values in to each object so when you clone or copy the tiles the information is copied across to the new tile.

It is also possible to have all tiles as duplicates, but as previously mentioned, you cannot put different values into the tiles/units in the frame editor. You are, however, able to set different values in the event editor.

Note

Throughout this book, you will generally use cloned map tiles for ease of programming, although you can use duplicates in your own programs if required.

Configuring Alterable Values for Tiles

Adding alterable values to the hexagon tiles is the same process that you followed for adding them to each of the units.

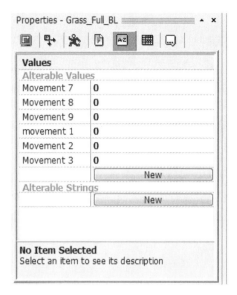

Figure 6.34
The alterable value slots and the default value of 0.

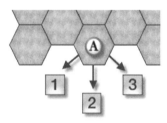

Figure 6.35
The directions a unit cannot move when on a particular hexagon tile.

In Figure 6.34 you can see the alterable slots we created for all unique edge tiles. We renamed the A to F slots to the movement direction.

We mentioned earlier that we were going to use a 0 or 1 in the values slot for each alterable value to tell MMF2 if a unit can move in a particular direction. If you look at Figure 6.35, you can see that if a unit was on the tile marked as A, then it should not allow movement when the player presses the 1, 2, or 3 keys on the numpad. It should still allow movement if they press 7, 8, or 9.

Using the 0 and 1 rule, we have configured slots 1, 2, and 3 with the value of 1, as shown in Figure 6.36. In MMF2, you can then do a calculation and check to see if the value for a particular direction exists and program MMF to not move in that direction.

Figure 6.36
Amended edge tile values.

Configuring Alterable Values for the Units

In your code you are going to check for a collision between the unit and an edge tile and then copy the contents of that particular tile's alterable values into the plane unit. It is important to update these values regularly; otherwise, your program may contain incorrect information, which would allow the unit to leave the screen.

If you are going to place the values of the tile into the unit object, you must also create a set of slots in the object's alterable value tab. You can see these slots in Figure 6.37. This needs to be added to all units in your game.

N o t e

If you look at the alterable slots for the tiles, the first item is called Movement 7. This is actually still classified as alterable value A to MMF; the next is B, and so on. If you look at the unit alterable values, the Movement slots do not start until Alterable value D because A, B, and C are taken by Starting movement, current movement, and unit ID. This is important to remember when in the event editor because sometimes you can reference using the name you have given the alterable value slot, and other times it will be referenced by A, B, and so on.

Qualifier Groups

When you are programming in the event editor, you occasionally may want to configure a condition or action that applies to a specific group of objects or pick a particular object from a group that meets certain criteria. For this, you can use Qualifier groups, and in doing so you can reduce your code drastically. This is

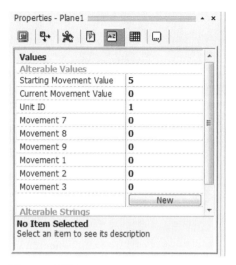

Figure 6.37
The alterable values in our plane units.

because rather than creating lots of conditions or actions for each individual object, you can specify a group.

Qualifier groups are accessed via the object properties. For this example, we have set qualifiers for both the plane units and all of the tiles. If you click on one of the plane objects or an edge tile and then click on the Events tab in the object properties, you will see the qualifiers option already configured, as shown in Figure 6.38. In this tab, you will see the image of an apple. This is just an image that identifies a particular group, and in this case the group is called good. For the example file, we have added all tiles to the group good and the player's plane units to the group called player, which has a joystick icon. When programming in the event editor, you see an apple and a joystick along the top row of action buttons, and you also see these icons in the New condition dialog box.

Programming the Event Editor

Now that we have detailed all of the configurations required for stopping the items leaving the screen, it is time to program this in the event editor. The code to do this is quite small; this is mainly because we have used Qualifier groups to reduce the amount of coding we require.

For the programming, you need to do the following:

- Create a condition event in the Plane 1 and 2 groups that checks to see if the plane is overlapping the tiles in the qualifier group that is associated

Figure 6.38
The qualifier group assigned to a tile object.

with all of the tiles. Set the plane's alterable values for the direction using the group good.

- Create an additional condition in all of your key presses to check to see if the alterable value of the plane's movement direction equals zero.

Collision Overlap Event for the Plane 1 Group

You need to ensure that the Plane 1 group is expanded; if not, double click on it to see all of the events contained within it.

Next you will add an event between other events, rather than at the bottom of the current set in the Plane 1 group. MMF2 reads the events from top to bottom, so it is important to ensure that events are in a logical order.

1. Right click on event line 6 in the Plane 1 group. This allows you to insert a new event line under event line 6.

2. Select Insert|New Event.

3. The New condition dialog box appears. Look for the Plane 1 graphic, and from the pop-up menu choose Collisions|Overlapping another object. Then select the apple graphic, which is the qualifier group called Group.Good. Click on OK.

You have now created the event to check for the collision overlap between the unit and a tile. When a unit is on any tile, it runs this event and its actions every time. Now it is time to create the actions that will set the unit's alterable value slot to contain the value contained in the hexagon's alterable value.

1. Move across from this event until you are under the Plane 1 object.

2. Right click the blank action box and select Alterable values|Set.

3. The expression evaluator appears. Click on the Choose value drop down menu and select the first movement direction, which is movement 7. Click on the Enter expression box and remove the 0. Then click on Retrieve data from an object. You need to retrieve the information from the hexagon tile.

4. Because you are using groups, select the Group.Good object and choose Values|Values A to M|Retrieve Alterable value A. This places the information into the expression evaluator. Click on the OK button to save the details to the event editor.

You now need to follow the same process and add the same actions for the 8, 9, 1, 2, and 3 slots. After you finish, your actions will look like those shown in Figure 6.39.

Note

Because you are using groups, MMF2 works out behind the scenes which object are currently overlapping with the plane and uses this information to find the correct hexagon. MMF2 will find the correct Group.Good object and place the information from that tile into the unit's alterable values slot.

Adding an Extra Movement Check

Now that you have written the value of the hexagon direction values (0 or 1) into the plane alterable values, you can add an extra condition to all of our movement

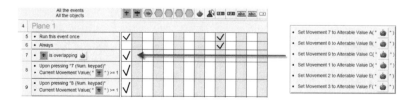

Figure 6.39
All of the actions for placing the values into the Plane1 object.

key presses. Remember that if one condition in an event is not true, then that event will not execute the actions to the right of it. So on each of the movement key presses (when you press a key to move a unit), it will now need to do an extra check to see if the direction you have asked it to move in is linked by another hexagon. You can do this very easily by using the compare an alterable values option. If the value equals 0, then, based on what you did previously, you know that the unit can move in that direction.

1. Right click on the last condition that is within event line number 8 and select Insert. This ensures that the new condition is placed last in the event.

2. Find the Plane1 object, right click on it, and select Alterable values|Compare to one of the Alterable values.

3. In the drop down box, select Movement 7. The comparison method is already Equal and the enter expression is 0. These two default values are fine, as shown in Figure 6.40. Click on OK to save the information to the event editor. You can see how this will look for event line 8 in Figure 6.41.

You need to add the same movement checks for the other five directions, which you can see in Figure 6.42. You can press F7 to test whether it works for the first unit, and then if you try it for the second unit, you will see that it still moves off screen. You need to add the same collision event/actions and the conditions to prevent movement in the Plane 2 group. You can see the completed code in the file alterablehex-complete.mfa, which is contained within the Examples folder.

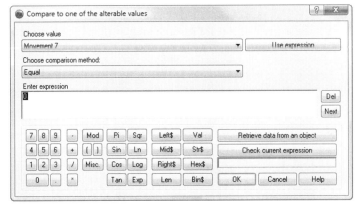

Figure 6.40
The comparing of the alterable value to a value.

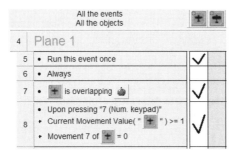

Figure 6.41
The condition added to the event line.

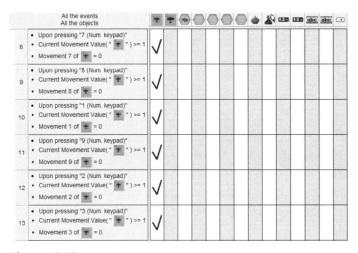

Figure 6.42
The extra conditions in all of the movement checks for the Plane 1 group.

Skipping Units

The player might not want to move a unit at a particular time, but might want to come back to it after she has moved a few others first. This might be because the units are all too close together or she wants to move other units into place for strategic reasons. For example, if you have created a dungeon game where the units are characters, the player may want to place them in an order which suits the type of characters in the game. It would be more sensible to place a warrior, which has good defense and attack skills, at the front rather than a wizard who wouldn't be able to handle hand-to-hand combat.

At the moment, you are able to skip a unit, but once you are at the last unit, when you click on the next unit button, it will continue to count upwards. In the example you have been working on, it will change the current unit number to 3 and still allow you to move unit 2 around the screen if it has any movement points still available. You need to stop it from counting any higher and then put some code in place for it to revert back to the first unit.

You can prevent the unit counter from counting past a particular number because all counters have a minimum and maximum number range. You might initially think that you can set the counter's maximum value to 2 because there are only 2 units, but actually from a programming point of view, setting it at 3 is better. This is because when you are on unit 1 and click on the next unit button, the counter will be 2 at that point. This can cause issues with your program if you start running code when the counter has hit 2 while you are still moving a unit on screen.

Close any game files that you are currently working on, making sure to save your progress before continuing.

1. Open the file skipping.mfa in the examples folder.

2. Ensure that you have double clicked on the Frame 1 text and can see the frame editor, which will display your two units on the hexagon map.

3. Under the text object, which displays the text Current Unit Number, click on the counter object to display its properties sheet.

4. If the Settings tab is not selected in the properties sheet, click on it.

5. You will see maximum and minimum values, which are currently at −999999999 and 999999999. In the minimum value, type in 1, and in the maximum value, type in 3. These values now look like those shown in Figure 6.43.

Now we need to add an event that will check to see when the counter reaches 3, which is when no further objects will be moved, and then reset the counter back to 1. It should also enable the Plane 1 group so you can continue to move the original unit.

1. Collapse both the Plane 1 and Plane 2 groups, if they are not already closed.

2. Click on the New condition text line.

3. Select the Counter2 object and choose Compare the counter to a value.

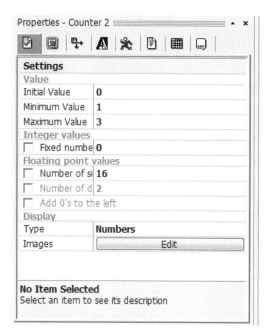

Figure 6.43
The minimum and maximum values.

4. The expression evaluator appears. Leave the comparison at Equal, type in the value of 3 into the expression area, and then click on OK.

There are a few actions that you will need to create, first setting the current unit counter back to 1, then changing the current unit text to paragraph 1. Then finally, you need to disable group 2 and enable group 1. You disable group 2 because in our original codethe group is only disabled once the movement points reach zero, so if you still have some movement points available and want to skip through the units, disabling group 2 ensures that multiple units do not move at the same time on the map.

1. Move to the right until you are under the Counter2 object. Right click the blank action box and select Set Counter. In the expression evaluator, type in the value of 1 and click on OK.

2. On the same event line, move under the String object, right click, and select Set Paragraph; a dialog box appears with all of the possible paragraphs that can be displayed. Choose paragraph one, which is selected by default, and click on OK.

Finally, you need to disable the group Plane 2 and enable the group Plane 1.

1. Still on the same event line, move under the Special Conditions object, right click on the blank action box, and select Group of events|Activate. When the dialog box appears, select the item called (1) – Plane 1 and click on Ok.

2. Under the special conditions box, there will now be a check mark. Right click on this and then select Group of events|Deactivate; select the item called (2) – Plane 2 and click on OK.

Run the program by pressing F8 and check to see if the program allows you to skip each unit after a few moves and then go back to that unit later.

End Turn

In a full war game, you will have several different phases; one of these is the End of turn. When you have moved all of your units, you tell the game that you have completed all of your moves, and the program then runs the other phases in the game. These other phases could be enemy movement, attack phases, and so forth.

In a normal game you would have these additional phases running after the end of turn phase of your game. You can, however, create it now because the same process could be used in a larger game.

The end of turn code is very simple and is all about resetting the values that are available to your units. In the following example, you will be resetting the movement points, but in a larger game it could also be increasing or decreasing values such as morale, unit size, the weather, and so on.

The easiest way to program your end of turn is to create a button that the player can press to signal the end of the turn, and then within the code create a new group that can be used to reset the movement values.

1. An example file, called endofturn.mfa, with the extra button already added is located in the Examples folder. Open the file and double click on the Frame 1 text to view the frame editor.

2. Click on the event editor button. Ensure that both the Plane 1 and Plane 2 groups are collapsed because you don't need them for this section of the code.

3. Click on the new condition text, select Button 2, and select Button Clicked.

When the button has been clicked, you activate the End of Turn group. Now that you have created the event, you need to create the group before you add the action to the button event line.

Note

Remember you can't activate and deactivate groups unless you have created them first.

1. Right click on the New condition number, which should be event line 8. Select Insert|A group of events.

2. The Group Events dialog box appears. Type in the title of the group to be End of Turn, also deselect Active when frame starts, because you want this group to only run after the player makes all of his initial moves.

3. Click on the OK button.

Now you can go back to event line 7 and enable the group. The group will be enabled when the player presses the End Turn button.

On event line 7, move across until you are under the Special Conditions object and select Group of Events|Activate. When the dialog box appears, choose the End of Turn option and click on OK.

Your event, action, and group will look like those shown in Figure 6.44.

End of Turn Group

Now that you have your code in place to enable the group, you can create your events. Ensure that the End of Turn group is expanded, and you can see the New condition option under it.

Note

Two New condition text entries should be displayed on the screen, one for the End of turn group and another which is always present at the end of the event editor.

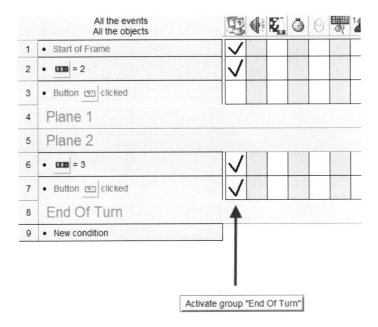

Figure 6.44
The action for the button 2 clicked event.

We are going to create two Always events. These normally run for as long as the program frame is available. When you place them in a group and disable the group at the end, they will only run once, but unlike the run only once option, when the group is re-enabled, these events will run again.

We will create the first Always event, which will contain the actions to reset the movement points for our plane units, reset the counters and text.

1. Click on the New condition text under the End of Turn group.

2. From the New condition dialog box, choose the Special conditions object and then the Always condition.

To set the starting values to both the planes:

1. Move across to the right from the Always event line, until you are directly under the Plane1 object.

2. Right click the blank action box and select Alterable values|Set.

3. The set expression evaluator dialog box appears. Ensure that the choose value drop down box displays Current Movement Value, and then delete

the 0 from the enter expression area. Click on the Retrieve data from an object button. Find and right click on the Plane1 object. From the pop-up menu, choose Values|Values A to M|Retrieve Starting Movement Value.

4. Click on the OK button to save the information to the event editor.

Now that you have reset the Plane1 information, it's time to apply the same process to Plane2.

1. Still on the Always event line, move directly under the Plane2 object.

2. Right click the blank action box and select Alterable values|Set.

3. The set expression evaluator dialog box appears. Ensure that the choose value drop down box displays Current Movement Value and then delete the 0 from the enter expression area. Click on the Retrieve data from an object button. Find and right click on the Plane2 object, and, from the pop-up menu, choose Values|Values A to M|Retrieve Starting Movement value.

4. Click on the OK button to save the information to the event editor.

Resetting the first counter object displays each unit's current movement points. You are going back to the first unit, so you need to set the counter to that unit's currently available movement points.

1. Move under the counter object, right click the action box, and select Set counter. In the expression evaluator dialog box, delete the 0 and click on the Retrieve data from an object button. From the new expression dialog box, right click the Plane1 object and select Values|Values A to M|Retrieve current movement value. Then click on OK to close the expression evaluator.

2. Now set Counter2 to 1; this counter is used to display which unit is currently selected, and also used in the code to keep track of which unit is being moved.

3. Move under the Counter2 object, right click, and select Set counter. In the expression evaluator, type in the number 1 and click on OK.

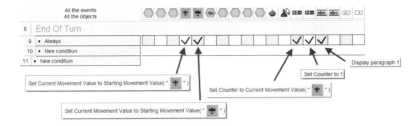

Figure 6.45
The first Always event in the End of Turn group.

4. Finally, for this event line, set the paragraph text back to the original first paragraph, which will tell the user that he is now on unit 1.

5. Move under the String object, right click, and select Set Paragraph. When the dialog box appears, the first item is selected by default; because you want the unit 1 text, click on the OK button.

6. You can see the event line and its actions in Figure 6.45.

Activating and Deactivating Groups

The last event you need is another Always condition, and then two actions to enable your Plane 1 group so that you can move these units, and disable the end of turn group; otherwise, it will keep resetting your units. We will also deactivate the Plane 2 group, in order to ensure that both Plane 1 and Plane 2 groups are not enabled at the same time.

1. Click on the New condition text in the End of Turn group. Select the Special object and then select Always.

2. Move to the right of this event and right click on the Special conditions object. Select Group of events|Activate. When the dialog box appears, choose the Plane 1 group.

3. You will now see a check mark on the special conditions action box. You need a second action here, so right click on the check mark, and select Group of events|Deactivate. From the dialog box, choose End of Turn group.

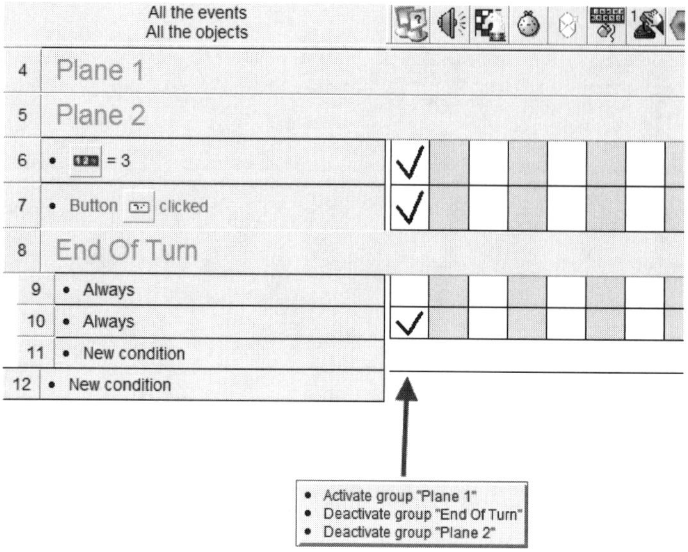

Figure 6.46
The second Always event with the enabling and disabling of groups.

1. On the same action box, right click then select Group of events|Deactivate, then from the dialog box, choose Plane 2.

4. You can see the event and its actions in Figure 6.46.

Congratulations! You have now completed a basic multiple unit movement system, with features such as skipping and ending the turn.

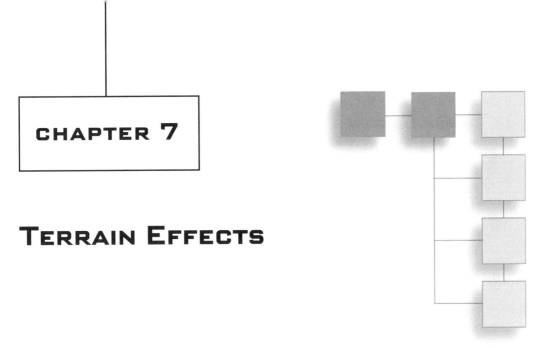

CHAPTER 7

TERRAIN EFFECTS

In this chapter, you will learn how the terrain can affect the movement of your units. An example of this could be a boat or ship unit that can't move on land, or a tank that, in most cases, could not move on water. There are some tanks that can actually move across rivers, and you may decide that in your game you want certain unit types to move on different terrain types, which they might not be able to do in real life. You are the game's creator, and it is your decision to configure your game as you see fit. Of course, if you are making a historical game, this would not be a good idea, but if you are making an unusual or science fiction game, you have more freedom to break the rules.

Creating Terrain Modifiers

In Chapter 4 we discussed a template for the war game engine. That chapter detailed all of the design aspects that you want your engine to achieve and the different rules and regulations required for it to run properly. If you are making your own engine, then you have already created your own unit tables, movement points, and movement effects tables. You can change the example files covered in this chapter to meet your own game requirements.

For this example, we are going to make a set of three dinosaurs move across a landscape, but one of the creature units will only be able to move on water, while the other two will not be able to move across mountains. All units will not be able to leave the hexagon maps as we will be using code that you used in the previous

Table 7.1 Terrain Movement Table for Three Dinosaur Units

Dinosaur	Water	Grass	Small Mountain	Large Mountain	Forest
Dino-1	0	NA	NA	NA	NA
Dino-2	NA	0	1	NA	1
Dino-3	NA	0	1	NA	1

chapter. You can see in Table 7.1 the movement effects table for the three dinosaurs.

As you can see, only one unit will be able to move on water, and this unit will not be able to move on land. The other two units can move on land but will have additional movement points removed if they try to move across a small mountain or forest tile. No units will be able to move across the mountain hexagon tile. This is a very simple example of how to restrict a small number of tiles on a hexagon map; you can also use the same process to restrict movement for a larger number of tiles.

Because MMF2 is very flexible, there are several ways of creating the logic for this part of the movement system. We could use the same system that was used in Chapter 6, where we used alterable values for each hexagon and each unit. The main downside to this is that the amount of work involved for each unit would be quite large; you would need to replicate all the different values in every single tile. Each of the tiles on the map would need to know what the corresponding connected tiles are to ensure that MMF would know which tiles those units can move over.

You still need to find a solution to check what a connecting tile is so you can do a comparison to see whether a unit is allowed to move on to it. You also need to use a new object to store some information about your game. This information will contain the terrain movement data shown in Table 7.1; the object that will store this information is called the Array object.

What Is an Array?

The Array object is a very efficient way of storing information (data), and each array can store either numbers or text. The object is placed on the frame as are all other objects, but it does not display anything; all data and information is accessed through the event editor only.

The main configuration required for the array to be ready to store data is the dimension. There are three types of dimensions that are configurable; these are:

- Single Dimension array

- Two-Dimensional array

- Three-Dimensional array

These dimensions are represented in the array object properties using the letters, X, Y, and Z, with each letter being given a number. These numbers within the object properties identify the size and type of array. An array with the details of X=10, Y=10, and Z=1 is a two-dimensional array. An array with the details of X=10, Y=1, and Z=1 is a single dimension array. To have an array on your game, you need to be on the frame editor, and right click and select Insert Object. When the Object dialog box appears, find and select the Array object. To view its properties, click on the Array object graphic. You can see the array properties in Figure 7.1.

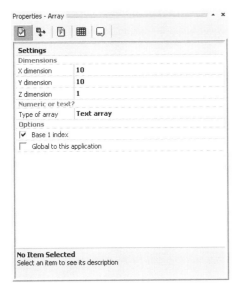

Figure 7.1
Array properties worksheet.

You will notice in Figure 7.1 that there is a drop down list next to the words Type of array. This is where you configure the array to accept either text or numbers. You cannot have both types of data stored in an array. You might think this is a bit of a problem, but actually it doesn't cause too many issues when creating programs, because you can just create an additional array object and configure it to be a numeric or text array. You should think about your array and what data is going to be saved and loaded before you jump straight in because the way you structure your array may change. For example, you may initially create an array that will only store three numbers. You may find later in development that you need more numbers or may need another array to store text. The way you program your game may then need to be overhauled and the events changed to take these changes in to account. This could slow down the development of your war game.

Single Dimension Array

For a single dimension array, you only need to use one dimension letter; in this case, we will use X. You can think of a single array as very much like a single column in a spreadsheet or a folder in a filing cabinet. The only place you can store information is in a single area, one on top of each other. You can see an example of some text data stored in a single array in Figure 7.2. In theory, this is what it looks like, but in practice, you can't actually see the data stored in an array, so this is just to show you conceptually how the dimensions differ.

	X
1	Hello
2	This
3	Is
4	Some
5	Text
6	In
7	A
8	Single
9	Dimension
10	Array

Figure 7.2
A single dimension array with data.

When you want to access data in the single array, you can identify the array's dimension letter, which in this case is X, and the data location number. If you want to read the data at X and position 4 on the X array, the actual data found would be the word "Some" as shown in Figure 7.2.

Two-Dimensional Array

For a two-dimensional array, you need to use two dimension letters and the array's location number, so we would use X and Y for the axis direction. You can think of a two-dimensional array as a spreadsheet, where you have rows and columns. Another way of thinking about it is to think of a bookshelf where you might have books going up and down as well as left and right. You can see an example of a two-dimensional array in Figure 7.3.

When you want to access data in the two-dimensional array, you need to identify the dimension letter and the data location number. If you want to read the data at the X axis position 4 and the Y axis position 7, the actual data found would be the text Contain as shown in Figure 7.3.

Three-Dimensional Array

Finally, the last type of array is three-dimensional; in this case, we use three axes of X, Y, and Z, and a position number for each one. You can think of a three-dimensional array as a set of packing boxes, stacked on top of each other, with boxes stacked to the right and left, and from front to back, as shown in Figure 7.4. A three-dimensional array is a bit more difficult to visualize, but it can store lots of information that you might need to save.

Figure 7.3
A two-dimensional array with data.

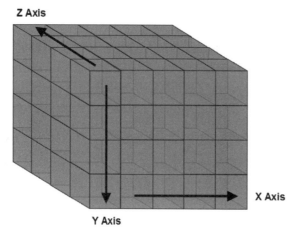

Figure 7.4
The three-dimensional array.

When you want to access data in a three-dimensional array, you must identify its letter axis and the number. So using X would move you across from left to right of the boxes, Y would move you up and down, and finally, the Z axis would move you forward and back.

Using the Array for Your Movement Table

You can add as many arrays to the frame as you need to use for storing text or numeric information. You cannot mix text and numbers in the same array. The other important thing to remember about arrays is that you can fill an array at runtime via the event editor, and then reference it in the game. Once the game is closed and restarted, the information is reset, so if you want to change array information throughout the game and allow this updated information to be used after a game is restarted, you also need to save the array. You can save an array to a file and load it back at any point in your game.

Using Table 7.1 as a reference, you can build an idea of the restrictions you need to place within your game. You could create an array that contains every unit, or, alternatively, you could use the unit type, such as vehicles or soldiers, to identify which groups cannot move on water or are affected by the terrain.

You might be wondering how you are going to reference the objects by name in a numeric array. Rather than thinking of Dino-1, Dino-2, and so forth, you can think logically that Dino-1's ID is 1, Dino-2's is 2, and so on.

If you create an array, you can use Table 7.1 as a reference point, Dino-1 does not lose any movement points in water, so it will reduce by the standard one movement point on each tile. You can use the other numbers to detail how many additional points to remove, and finally you need to pick another number to tell MMF2 that a unit cannot move at all on a tile (this is the NA in Table 7.1). For this, it is best to pick a number that is not within the range of other movement modifiers, so we will use 99.

To create the terrain movement engine code, you need to do the following:

- Create an array object that will store what units can move on what tiles and what movement point deduction will take place if a unit is moving on a tile that costs more movement points.

- Use the number 99 in your array to signify that a unit cannot move on that particular tile.

- Find out what the connecting tiles are around the currently selected unit.

- Do some number checks and comparisons to see if the unit can move or will have extra movement points removed from its movement value.

- Add a Tile Type alterable value to every tile to show what type of terrain it is.

Dinosaur Terrain Example File

We have already created the basis of the file that you will be using for restricting movement on certain types of terrain. This file can be found in the Examples folder on the CD-ROM provided with this book. The file is called terrainmod. mfa. The code is the same as the examples in Chapter 6, except for a few minor changes to take into account that there are three units on the screen now rather than two.

Load the file into MMF2 and double click on the text Frame 1 to display the frame editor. You will be able to see the frame, which contains a number of tiles, three dinosaur units, and some red directional units currently placed off the frame. You can see this in Figure 7.5.

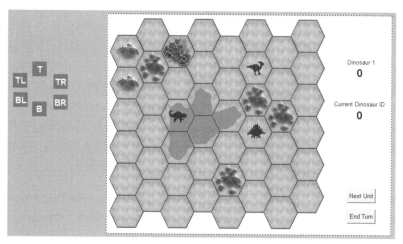

Figure 7.5
The frame editor containing the map and dinosaur units.

Movement Units

In the previous examples, we placed in values for all the edge tiles so that the unit knew which direction to move in. Because a unit could potentially move in up to six directions on any of the tiles (including those that are not on the edge), filling in the direction details for each tile would be a lot of work.

You can find a quick and easy solution to prevent units from moving on other units, and as mentioned previously one solution is to use an array. Another solution is to add six placeholder units that follow the currently selected unit around and check the connecting tiles. You can see an image of the six place-holder units in Figure 7.6.

These six units are not visible to the user playing the game, but while testing your war game, it is useful to display them to ensure that your coding is working correctly. You can see in Figure 7.6 that each placeholder unit also has a letter on it to describe the position tile that it will be placed on. This will be useful when programming in the event editor.

Note

You only need six placeholder units because once the user presses the next unit button, the six placeholder items are then placed around the next unit.

Each of the placeholder units also has a single alterable slot of Tile Type. This is used to get the tile type from the hexagon tile and place it in the placeholder so that you can use it for checks within our code. You can see this in Figure 7.7.

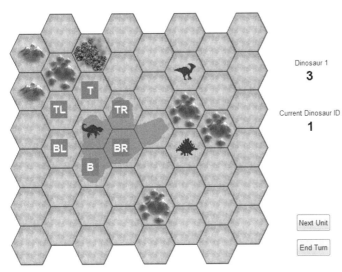

Figure 7.6
Six placeholder units moving with the Dino-1 unit.

Figure 7.7
The alterable value slot Tile Type in each of the placeholder units.

Alterable Values on Tiles

We have added a new item into the alterable values slot of each tile; this item is called Tile Type. This slot represents the type of terrain for that tile, you can see what each value will be associated with in Table 7.2.

The properties sheet for a small mountain tile is shown in Figure 7.8. Using Table 7.2, you can see that this tile has a value of 3.

Adding and Configuring the Array

Now that we have detailed some of the extra alterable values that have been added to the example file, you need to add the array object to the frame. This allows you to store the information required to do calculations on which unit can move on which tile.

Table 7.2 Unit IDs

Unit ID Value	Unit Type
1	Water
2	Grass
3	Small Mountain
4	Large Mountain
5	Forest

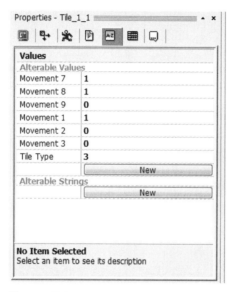

Figure 7.8
The properties sheet for a small mountain tile.

1. Ensure that you have the terrainmod.mfa file loaded from the Examples folder on the CD-ROM.

2. You should be on the Frame 1 frame editor; if not, double click on the text Frame 1.

3. Right click anywhere on the frame, and from the pop-up menu, select Insert Object. You will then see the Create new object dialog box. Find and select the Array object icon, as shown in Figure 7.9, and click on the OK button. Left click outside the white frame area to place the array object icon within the frame editor.

Array

Figure 7.9
The array object icon.

Figure 7.10
The array settings tab.

4. Click on the array object icon to display the object properties. Currently, the array settings are 10, 10, and 1; this means that it is set up as a two-dimensional array. To change the dimensions of the array to match the table size, change the X dimension to 5, the Y dimension to 3, and leave the Z dimension set at 1.

5. You also need to change the array from a text array, which would store text strings, to a numeric array, so click on the text array option and change it to a number array. Your array properties sheet will now look like that shown in Figure 7.10.

Coding Terrain Movement

Everything is now in place, ready for you to program the logic in the event editor. Click on the event editor button to see the events that have already been

Dinosaur	Water (1)	Grass (2)	Small Mountain (3)	Large Mountain (4)	Forest (5)
Dino-1 (1)	0	99	99	99	99
Dino-2 (2)	99	0	1	99	1
Dino-3 (3)	99	0	1	99	1

Figure 7.11
The new structure for your array.

programmed. Everything should look familiar to you, with three dinosaur groups, which have replaced the two plane groups we had previously for the plane units. This is because we are using three units in this example rather than two.

If you run the application now, you will see that the three dinosaurs move across the map in the same way that the planes did. The only difference is that the first dinosaur has only three movement points, while the other two dinosaurs have five. The reason for this is that we want the first unit to only have three movement points because it can only move in water, and the water is only a small number of terrain tiles.

Setting Up the Array Entries

You have added the array object and set its boundaries. Now you need to write information to the array in the event editor. The information you will write to the array is the values in Table 7.1, but where Table 7.1 states NA, place the value 99. See Figure 7.11 to see the structure.

You will notice that we have put a value in brackets after each tile type and the dinosaur unit. We will use that as the basis for where we will store the information about a particular tile and unit. For the array, across the top is the X coordinate (tile types) and going down is the Y coordinate (dinosaur unit). So when you want to find the value of unit 2 and learn whether it can move on a large mountain, look at X coordinate of 4 and Y coordinate of 2. This gives you a value of 99, which means that this unit would not be able to move on that type of terrain. Wherever the value is 0, there is no additional movement point deduction required, and any other number means that on top of the normal deduction of a single movement point, this value will be added as well. If unit 2 moves on to a small mountain, it will cost two movement points rather than the normal single movement point.

Follow these steps to clear the array and place a value in each of the slots that represent the table in Figure 7.11.

1. Ensure you are in the event editor for the terrainmod.mfa file.

2. On the first event line, you will see the Start of Frame event; this runs only at the start of the frame, and is the perfect place to set-up the array before the game starts.

3. Move across to the right of this event until you are directly under the array object. Right click on the action box and select Clear array.

A check mark will now be within that action box, but we require additional actions on the same event/object, so right click on the check mark to add an action to the same action box.

4. Right click and select Write|Write Value to XY. The expression evaluator appears, asking you to enter the value to write. We are adding a value for the table value 1,1. So according to our table, this value should be 0. The expression evaluator already has 0 as a default value, so click on the OK button.

5. The expression evaluator appears, and now it asks you to enter the X index, replace the 0 with a 1, and click on OK.

6. Now enter the Y index value, which is 1, and click on OK.

Continue to enter the values of each tile and its corresponding unit; once complete, the actions should look like those shown in Figure 7.12.

Update Code

In this part of the code, you need to create a group that will be used for updating the values that you will use in your game. You did something similar in the previous examples where we would update certain values so that we could do calculations on

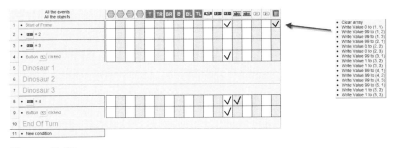

Figure 7.12
The array settings for our example file.

them. For this file we need to check when one of the six placeholder objects is overlapping a terrain tile. We need to do this as we will get the terrain ID from the tile and write it into the alterable value of the placeholder unit so that we can then compare it to the array to see if a unit can or cannot move in that direction.

Note

Because the program runs code from the top of the event editor to the bottom and then loops back around again, it is very important to ensure that the values are up to date. If they aren't up to date and a value is checked that has not been updated recently, this could cause strange effects in your game.

Because you want to ensure that the terrain ID is updated into the placeholder units, you need to run this update before the user presses a key to move the unit. This ensures that the correct information can be checked before the key press. So to ensure that this works correctly, we will add the group before the three dinosaur movement groups.

1. Right click on the number 5 in the event editor list. From the pop-up select Insert|A group of events.

2. The group of events dialog box appears. Type the title of the group which will be Update. You want this group to be active all the time, so click on OK.

We need six events that will check when one of the six placeholder units is over a tile to grab information from the tile they are overlapping. Because we have already created a Group.Good in the previous examples for each tile, we can use that to check against. We also need to place an Always condition on the event so that it will always update this information. Let's now create our six events, and then we can move on to the actions.

1. Click on the New condition text on event line 6 that is under the Update group.

2. When the New condition dialog box appears, right click on the first of the placeholder units, which is called Top, is red, and contains the letter T. From the pop-up menu that appears, choose Collisions|Overlapping another object. The Test a collision dialog box appears next. Find and select the Group.Good object, which is an apple graphic, and click on OK.

3. Now you need to add the always condition to the same event.

4. Right click on the condition text that you just added to event line six, and then select Insert. Right click the Special object and pick Always.

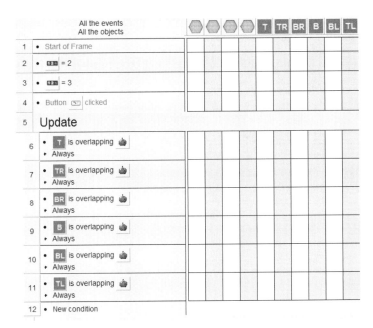

Figure 7.13
The six placeholder events.

You now have completed the first event, and you will need to complete the same process for the other five placeholder graphics. Once you have done that your events should look the same as those shown in Figure 7.13.

Now you need to add actions to each event. This is pretty straightforward; what you want to do is get the tile type from the currently overlapped tile and place it into the placeholder units (the red units that contain letters). This allows you to do calculations on them to see if a unit should move in that direction.

1. From event line 6, move across until you are directly under the Top object, right click, and select Alterable Values|Set.

2. The expression evaluator is displayed and has the value of Tile Type; this is the value required for the drop down box. Click on the Enter expression box and delete the 0; then click on Retrieve data from an object.

3. The New expression dialog box appears, so find the Group.Good object, right click on it, and select Values|Values A to M|Retrieve Alterable Value G. Then click on OK.

Figure 7.14
Dragging and dropping this action in to each of the corresponding boxes is quicker than manually adding the action.

The other events lines contain the same actions, so you can either follow the same process and under each relevant object add those events, or you can drag and drop the actions into each action box as shown in Figure 7.14.

All of the actions will be the same as that shown in Figure 7.15.

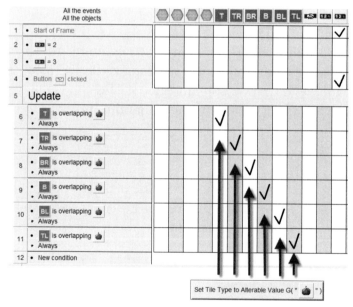

Figure 7.15
The action that will be in each of the six events.

You can now collapse the group; you have finished with this particular section of code.

Updating Dinosaur Movement

Now that you have the values being updated before the user presses any movement keys, it is time to add the code needed for each dinosaur.

We need to complete the following steps:

1. Set the position of the six placeholder units so that they follow the unit when it moves. This means that when you press a key to move a unit, it automatically updates the position of the units.

2. Amend the key press conditions, adding a new condition that checks the array object to see if the array position is greater or less than 99.

3. When there are no movement points left, ensure that the placeholder units are correctly positioned around the dinosaur unit.

Setting the Position of the Placeholder Units

The placeholder units are the six red unit squares that you will use to obtain the value ID of the hex that it is positioned over. This allows you to check to see if the dinosaur unit will be able to move in that direction. At the moment, if you run the game, no red unit boxes move with the dinosaur, so the first bit of code will be to always position the red units in different locations around the current dinosaur.

N o t e

> For simplicity, we will put code for the six placeholder units in each of the three dinosaur groups. MMF2 is very powerful, and there are many ways to program the same end effect. You could have created a single group containing the code and then position the current dinosaur relative to that unit. In your own games, consider the different ways you could program an aspect of your war game and think about how this would have an impact on a larger game or a game where you decide to add more features.

To have the red units at certain places, we are going to place them relative to the current dinosaur. We can easily select the dinosaur that we need because we will be programming it on a per group basis, so that when we are working on the group Dinosaur 1 we know that we need to be working with Dino-1, and so on.

The positions will not be totally precise, but as long as the red units are over-lapping the correct tile and not touching any others, the code will work perfectly fine.

We already have a condition that we can place our code against. We will use the Always event that already exists in each dinosaur group. In theory, you could add another event line, and it won't make any difference to the way the game works. But if you can use an event line that contains very few actions that is a good way to keep the number of events down and improve the overall readability.

1. Ensure that Dinosaur 1 group is expanded and you can see the events within it.

2. Locate the Always event line; this will be event line 8 if the Update group is collapsed or a higher number if that group is expanded. Move across to the right until you are directly under the Top object; this is the object that is a red unit square containing the letter T.

3. Right click on the action box and select Position|Select Position. When the Select position dialog box appears, click on the Relative to radio button, and when the Choose an object dialog box appears, select Dino-1 and click on OK. You will now see that the image of the dinosaur appears in the Select Position box; in the X coordinate box type **0** and in the Y coordinate box type **-70**. This puts the dashed box directly above the dinosaur on the next tile. Click on the OK button to save this information to the event editor.

You need to do the same process for the other dinosaurs but at different X and Y coordinates. A quick way of doing this is to drag and drop the action check mark across the other red units, right click on each action box in turn, and select Edit. You can then enter the information in Figure 7.16 for the coordinates.

Your actions will look like those shown in Figure 7.17.

Dino-1	Top	Top Right	Bottom Right	Bottom	Bottom Left	Top Left
X Coordinate	0	58	58	0	-58	-58
Y Coordinate	-70	-35	35	70	35	-35

Figure 7.16
The coordinates of all of the red placeholder units.

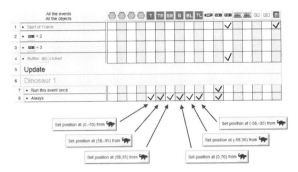

Figure 7.17
The actions for placing the red placeholder units.

Now that you have completed placing all of those coordinates you will need to place them in one other location in the Dinosaur-1 group. In one of our previous examples, you may remember that the counter didn't update properly when the current movement value was 0. This was due to the order of events, and so to fix this, we put in a condition of Current movement value of Dino-1 = 0, and then we reset the counter. We also need to ensure that the placeholder units are repositioned correctly one more time or they will not move on the units final movement step. Before we add those actions, run the game, and you will see that you can move Dino-1 and the placeholder units follow it. When the movement value gets to 1 and you press a key to move Dino-1, the red units do not move with it.

To fix this issue, find event line 16, which is the last event in the Dinosaur-1 group, and move across and place the same actions for the placeholder units that you did in the Always event line. You can do this quickly and easily by dragging each action down from the Always line and placing it in the correct corre sponding action box on line 16.

Preventing or Allowing Movement on Terrain

To start making the player movement smarter, you need to do two things. First you need to restrict movement if the player wants to move a unit onto a terrain tile that they shouldn't be able to move to, and second, you need to make a change to the reduction of movement points if the terrain tile the player wants to move onto costs more in points.

Restricting Movement

You already have a number of events in the Dinosaur 1 group that prevent the dinosaur from moving in a particular direction. You may remember this code from Chapter 6, where it only moves the unit if there are movement points available. This code also can be slightly amended to allow you to add another check condition, and in this case, we will check to see if the value in the array that we created is not equal to 99.

We created a table of movements in the Start of Frame event, where the array contains an X coordinate that stores the terrain type ID and the Y coordinate contains the terrain unit type. Using this table, you can easily look up the values in the table and then by checking to ensure that if the value doesn't equal 99 the unit can still move.

If you look at your Dinosaur 1 group, which should be expanded, you will see the movement code in events 10 to 15. The X and Y coordinates of an array are numbers, so you can tell it to look in a particular array position by using values from other objects. In this case, you will find the X coordinate by getting the ID value from the current dinosaur. This ensures that you are checking in the correct X row. You will also be using the value stored in the direction placeholder unit. In the case of moving directly to the top left, this would be the Top_Left object. The value in the placeholder unit is the value that is obtained from the tile directly under it; using this method, you can look up the unit and tile in your array and return a value to be checked.

Let's add our new condition on event line 10, which is the same event as pressing the 7 key on the number pad:

1. Right click on the last condition in event line 10. Remember it will only be event line 10 if the Update group is collapsed. Select Insert from the pop-up menu.

2. Select the Special object and then choose Compare two general values. The dialog box will then appear.

3. We need to change the first entry box, which contains a 0, to contain our array position (which contains a single value).

4. Select the 0 in the top box, delete it, and then click on the button Retrieve data from an object. Find the array object and right click on it to display the pop-up menu. Select Read Value from XY position.

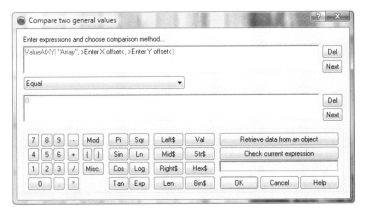

Figure 7.18
The incomplete array position information entered into the Expression evaluator.

A value will now be entered into the expression evaluator as shown in Figure 7.18.

The information in the expression evaluator is incomplete, so you need to specify the X and Y coordinate to read the value from. You may notice that the Enter X offset is already selected. For this game, you need to get the value of the X and Y offset (coordinate) from the objects previously discussed.

While >Enter X offset< is selected, click on the Retrieve data from an object button, so we will get a value from another object.

The X coordinate is the tile type. This is stored in the tile, and on every loop of the program it is pushed into the placeholder alterable value. You can obtain this value from the correct red placeholder unit. In this case, you are getting the value for the tile that is represented by pressing the 7 key on the number pad key. So the correct placeholder tile is Top_Left.

1. In the New Expression dialog box, right click on the Top_Left unit, and select Values|Values A to M|Retrieve Tile Type.

2. This information will be placed into the compare two values expression evaluator. We now need to change the Y offset with the correct information.

3. Highlight the text >Enter Y offset< and then click on the Retrieve data from an object button. The New expression dialog box appears.

4. We need to retrieve the ID of the unit type, and in this case, you know you are working with Dino-1, so you can get this value from the dinosaur's alterable value.

5. Right click on Dino-1 and select Values|Values A to M|Retrieve Unit ID.

You haven't finished in the expression evaluator yet; you still have two changes to make. The first change is that we want to allow the unit to move when the value isn't 99. Remember that 99 means no movement is allowed on that terrain tile.

1. Click on the Equal drop down box in the expression evaluator and select Different.

2. Finally, you need to ensure that the last edit box in the expression evaluator displays 99, so remove the 0 and type **99**. Your expression evaluator should now look like the one shown in Figure 7.19.

The next stage is to drag this condition from event line 10 and then drop it on event line 11 number. This places it as the last condition on event line 11. Please be careful because if you try to drop it on top of the actual conditions, it will replace them. You can see an example of what event line 11 will look like once you drag and drop the condition in Figure 7.20.

The great thing with MMF2 is that you can quickly change certain aspects of an event, and in this case the object that is being checked. We don't want the object Top_Left to be the object that the array is getting the value from because this

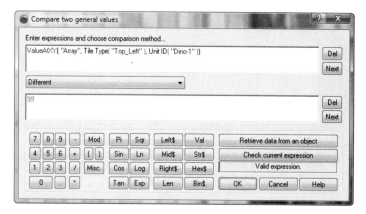

Figure 7.19
The finished condition within the movement event for pressing the 7 numlock key.

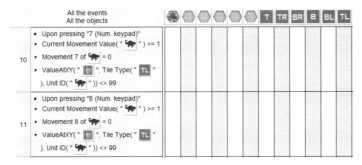

Figure 7.20
The condition dragged onto event line 11.

would be incorrect for the different directions. By double clicking on the object icon in the event line, you can bring up the object selection box and change the object.

On event line 11, double click on the Top_Left object icon.

The What do you want to test? dialog box appears, asking you to select an object. Event line 11 is associated with the 8 numpad key, and that means moving directly upwards, so find the Top object, select it, and click on OK.

The icon graphic in the event line now has changed to a T image, as can be seen in Figure 7.21.

Change the other four event lines, which contain an incorrect placeholder object. This means that all of the events are correct, but more importantly, you have been able to add and change events very quickly rather than manually adding them one by one for each event line. Your six events will now look like those shown in Figure 7.22.

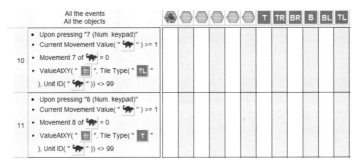

Figure 7.21
The object has changed in event line 11.

Figure 7.22
The six events with the correct placeholder icons.

If you run the game, you will notice that Dino-1 can only now move on water while the other two dinosaurs can move on any tile. You need to apply the changes you made on Dino-1 to the other two dinosaurs. To save some time, you can access a file with these changes already implemented. The file is located in the Examples folder and is called terrainmod-dinos-done.mfa.

Reducing Movement Points

Now you have the terrainmod-dinos-done.mfa file loaded, so if you run the file, you will notice that your dinosaurs are now restricted as to what tiles they can move on. If you move Dino-2 or Dino-3 onto a forest tile or a small mountain tile, you will notice at the moment they are only losing 1 movement point; in fact, they should be losing additional points.

In the previous chapter when the event for pressing a movement key was successful, we reduced the movement points by 1. We can do quite complex calculations within the expression evaluator, whereby we can have additional items reducing the movement. For example, at the moment it will say something like Sub 1. 1 will be the value in the expression evaluator, but by adding a + sign we can say subtract 1 and another number. This number will be retrieved from the array you created, so if the unit loses no movement points for moving on a certain type of terrain, the value in the array will be 0. So subtracting $1 + 0$ means that it will only cost a single movement point.

To do this, you need to edit the actions that you have already entered for each dinosaur.

1. Ensure that the groups Dinosaur 2 and Dinosaur 3 are collapsed, and ensure that the group Dinosaur 1 is expanded.

2. You may need to move your events toolbar that is on the bottom of the screen to the left or the right until you can see the Dino-1 action box.

3. If you move your mouse over the action box for event line 10, you will see that there are currently two actions in the box, which you added in Chapter 6. The first is setting the position of the dinosaur, and the second is subtracting 1.

4. Right click on the action box for event line 10 that contains these two actions and select Edit|Sub 1 from Current Movement Value as shown in Figure 7.23.

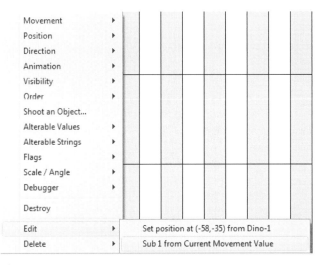

Figure 7.23
The editing of an action.

5. The expression evaluator now appears, and you will see that it is reducing the current movement value alterable value by 1. Click with the mouse after the number one in the Enter expression box and then type a + sign.

6. You will have 1+ in the enter expression box (without the quotes), and now we need to read the value that you have stored in your array, which will be added to the value of 1. Click on the Retrieve data from an object button, select the array object, and choose Read value from XY position.

7. The >Enter X offset< will be highlighted, so click on the Retrieve data from an object button again. Find the object Top_Left, right click on it, and choose Values|Values A to M|Retrieve tile type.

8. Now highlight the text >Enter Y offset< in the expression evaluator and again click on the Retrieve data from an object button. Now find Dino-1, right click, and select Values|Values A to M |Retrieve Unit ID.

9. You should now be back at the expression evaluator, as shown in Figure 7.24. Click on the OK button to save this information to the event editor.

Now when the user presses the 7 numpad key, it will subtract a 1 and the value that is stored in the tile type for that dinosaur. This value will either be a 0, or a 1; it won't contain 99 because the condition prevents the action from running if the value is 99. In your own games, you could have other values stored within the array for other types of units and terrain.

You need to replicate this change of action to the other five events within the Dinosaur 1 group. The quickest way to do this is:

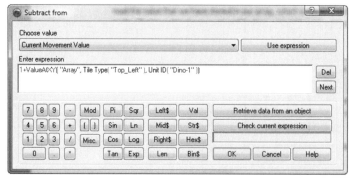

Figure 7.24
The expression for adding a value, which is retrieved from the array.

1. Re-edit the action you just amended on event line 10, and when in the expression evaluator, select all of the text and then use CTRL-C to copy the expression.

2. Click on Cancel on the expression evaluator to close the dialog box, then edit the subtract 1 from Current movement value action on event line 11; when the expression evaluator appears, delete the text in the box, and paste the text from the clipboard using the CTRL-V keys.

3. The problem with the text you just pasted is that it is linking to the Top_Left unit and Dino-1 unit. For this group, the Dino-1 text is correct, but you need to delete the text Top_Left and replace it with Top for event line 11, and the appropriate object name for the other events.

Note

When copying the text from the expression evaluator into the other actions for Dino-2 and Dino-3, you also need to change the text that relates to the dinosaur. For example, if you copy the text into the action for the Dinosaur 2 group, you will notice that it still says Dino-1 within the expression; you need to change this to Dino-2.

Do this for all of the subtract actions in the Dinosaur 1 group and also for the other two groups.

Note

You may notice that when using some shortcuts in MMF2, it is useful to ensure that the names of objects are easy to remember so that you can quickly type them in when needed. If you try to type the name of an object that does not exist in the expression evaluator, it will bring up an error dialog box.

Engine Issues

There are a couple of issues that you might see when running the test example. The most serious issue is that even with a single point left the unit could still move onto a terrain tile that would cost two points. This is a serious problem because it ignores the movement point system that we have worked on until now. The second issue is less of an issue and more about the design of your war game; the example files still allow you to move your unit onto a terrain tile that already contains another unit. In your game, you may actually allow units to move on to the same terrain tile, and so you may not require any changes to the game.

Terrain Type Issue

We need to have an event that checks to see how many movement points a player has and then compares it to the cost of moving onto the tile in a particular direction. The easiest way to do this is to add a condition to the existing code that checks for movement when a particular key has been pressed.

The code is similar to other code we have implemented in this chapter; first we can do a comparison of the available movement points left in the unit's alterable value slot for current movement points, and then we can check the number of points that the unit has left. If this number is equal to or more than the unit, then the unit can still move.

1. Load the file terrainmod-complete.mfa that is located in the Examples folder.

2. Click on the text Frame 1 in the workspace toolbar to display the frame, and then click on the Event editor. Ensure the group Dinosaur 1 is expanded.

3. Right click on the last condition in event line 10; this event will be for when the user presses the numpad 7 key. Select Insert.

4. When the New condition dialog box appears, choose the Special object and from the pop-up menu, select Compare two general values.

5. The expression evaluator appears with two edit boxes that will allow you to type in values. Select and delete the 0 in the first value box and then click on the Retrieve data from an object button. Find Dino-1, right click, and choose Values|Values A to M|Retrieve current movement value.

Remember that we only want the unit to move onto the tile if the correct number of points is available, so this means that it can be equal to or more than. In other words, if the player has 2 movement points left and the tile she wants to move on has a 2 movement point cost, then it is equal to. Of course, the unit may have many more points than the cost of the tile, so this is why you need to make a change to the comparison method.

1. Click on the drop down box that contains the value of Equal and change it to Greater or equal.

2. Select the bottom value box and delete the 0. Click on the Retrieve data from an object button. Find the array object, and Read value from XY position. The >Enter X offset< section will be highlighted, so click on the Retrieve

data from object button. Find the Top_Left object, right click on it, and choose Values|Values A to M|Retrieve Tile Type.

3. Highlight the >Enter Y offset< section of the text and click on the Retrieve data from an object; when the new expression dialog box appears, right click on Dino-1, then Values|Values A to M|Retrieve Unit ID. We have not finished with the expression evaluator yet, so do not click on any buttons.

This second expression has read the value from the hexagon, but there is a problem; all this is doing is reading in the additional value that the computer needs to remove from the player's movement points. We have to make one more change to make this work correctly; by default, the user is using a single movement point for each move, so we need to add this to the value that is retrieved from the hexagon. An example of this is that the player is going to move on to a forest tile. This incurs an extra movement point cost, and we add the normal single point value to it to make a total movement cost of 2. If we do not amend our code, the unit will still be able to move because though the unit will be charged two points to move onto the terrain, the comparison will only check if the unit has a single point available.

1. At the end of the second expression type in **+1**. Your expression evaluator should read as shown in Figure 7.25.

2. Click on the OK button to save to the event editor.

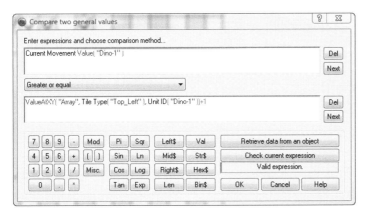

Figure 7.25
The expression evaluator with the additional +1 added to the expression.

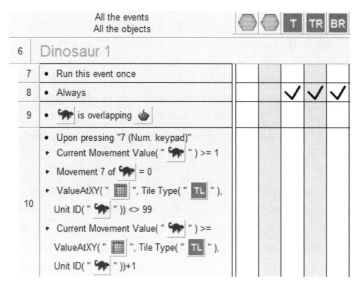

Figure 7.26
The condition preventing movement if not enough movement points are available.

Dinosaur Dino-1 is a water-based unit, so the actual code will not make any difference to this unit because it cannot move on land at all. It is still important to ensure that all units are using the same code to ensure that no problems exist in your game. Later on you may decide to change the movement from just water based to land and water, or any other combination.

You can see the condition, saved on the event line in Figure 7.26.

Now you need to copy this event to all of the other movement directions for Dino-1 and then also do the same for Dino-2 and Dino-3. You can give this a try if you feel that you need to practice more, or you can take a look at the example called engine-issue-complete1.mfa, which is located in the Examples folder.

Preventing Multiple Units on the Same Terrain Tile

You may want to prevent your units from moving onto the same terrain tile as another unit. This can be achieved quite easily by checking to see if a unit is on the tile in a particular direction. To do this, we will add to the code, which we have already written, that decides if a unit can move in a particular direction. We will check to see if the placeholder unit is not currently overlapping another unit.

1. Load the file called engine-issue-complete1.mfa from the Examples folder; this will contain all of the code you have been working on up till now.

2. Ensure that you are on the Event editor and that the Dinosaur 1 group is expanded.

3. Right click on the last condition on the event line 10 and select Insert.

4. As event line 10 is dealing with the numpad 7 key, find the Top_Left object, right click, and select Collisions|Overlapping another object. When the Test a collision dialog box appears, find the Group.Player group; this is a joystick image with a hand. Select it and click on OK.

Note

The Group.Player group represents all of the units and was created in the same way as creating the Group.Good group.

You now have a condition in event line 10 that says Top_Left is overlapping Group.Good. This is not correct because this allows the unit to move if there is another unit overlapping.

We need to change the meaning of this condition so that it means that the Top_Left is *not* overlapping. We can do that using the negate option.

Right click on the condition that you just added and from the pop-up menu select Negate.

You will now see that the condition has a big red cross in front of it; this means that it is now the opposite meaning to the statement, so that Top_Left is Not overlapping. You can see this event in Figure 7.27.

You need to do this for all of the other movements and dinosaurs, but remember to change the placeholder unit object that it references. You can see an example of the final code in the Examples folder with the file called engine-issue-complete2.mfa.

Making the Placeholder Objects Disappear

You might be thinking that you do not want to keep having the red placeholder units following the dinosaur units around the map. If you were creating a game that you were going to release, then of course, you would hide them from the

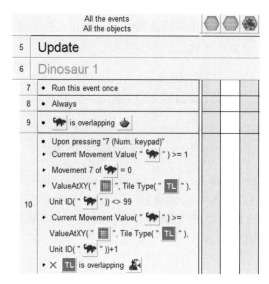

Figure 7.27
The negate option used to check when an object is not overlapping a group object.

player. Throughout this book, we will leave items such as this visible so that you are able to test the code that you enter to ensure that it is working correctly, but also it allows you to see the code working in a game.

Hiding the items that you don't need to see does not affect the running of the game, the items are still in the correct position, but you cannot see them.

There are two ways of making the units hidden. The first is to unselect Visible at start in the object properties. The alternative way is to hide them in the event editor.

To hide them in the event editor you would normally put the actions under a Start of Frame event, so that at the very beginning of the frame, the units are not visible to the player. Making the objects invisible is as simple as accessing the object's action box, for example, the Top_Left object, right clicking on the action box, and selecting Visibility|Make Object Invisible. You can make this change to your code if you want, but remember that it will mean you cannot see the placeholder items in the future and you would need to remove those actions if you want to see if that particular aspect of your game is working correctly.

CHAPTER 8

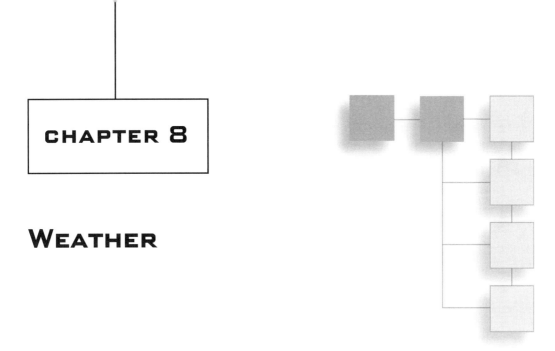

WEATHER

Weather can play an important role in the outcome of a battle. In history, many battles have been won or lost because of weather, and it is something that you should seriously consider for your own war games.

An example of weather having a possible major effect in a conflict is in sea battles in which mist and fog allow an outnumbered ship to hide and then escape from the enemy or to spring a surprise attack. The same might be said for land battles where one army moves to a position outflanking another army before its generals have time to set up a counterattack.

Weather such as rain or snow can severely affect movement and the effectiveness of a fighting force. In World War II, when invading Russia, Germany made massive territorial gains early on before the armies were brought to a halt because of the extreme cold and snow, which gave the Russian forces time to regroup. The Germans didn't have the right clothing for their soldiers, because they thought the battle would be over before winter hit. Also, low temperatures made fuel and equipment useless.

In this chapter, you will look at how to implement different tiles for land weather effects. You will use snow-based tiles, but you could use the same process for different effects if required.

Implementing Multiple Terrain Effects

You can implement a changing terrain-based weather effect system in at least four ways:

- **Animation Frames**: You can use animation frames—for example, similar to how multiple animation frames might be used to show a spaceship tilting to the left or right. You can use the same process for displaying different tiles at different times. The one consideration for animation frames is that, by default, they are set to play the frames automatically. So, if you have one animation for summer and another for snow, it will skip all of the animation frames and display the last frame, which in this example would be the snow image.

- **Animation Directions**: Every animation you create can have a set of directions. You will generally use these directions for setting animations for particular movements. If you have a medieval soldier that moves left and right, each direction is played depending on the direction that the character is moving in.

- **Multiple Animations**: You could create a different animation set for each tile. This is quite easy to do but is not as straightforward as the two other options.

- **Replacing the Tile**: You could store many tiles off-screen and then replace a specific tile with one that is out of frame. The main issue with this method is that you would need to store more objects in the file, and place more complex code in the event editor to handle precise movement of tiles. This movement, especially for a large number of tiles could also have a performance hit on your game.

You can use any of the four options mentioned, but here you will be using animation directions to change a hexagon tile from one type of weather effect to another.

Adding Another Tile Type

You can get your various weathered terrain tiles into your game in two ways. You can drag and drop your tiles from a Library, or you can store them on your hard disk as PNG or BMP files.

Copying a Tile Image

If you already have your different tiles in an MMF file (see an example in Figure 8.1), you can place them quickly into the corresponding weather effect tile. In Figure 8.1, you can see the normal terrain that is used in the previous chapter. A number of snow-based versions of these tiles are also outside the frame.

1. In the following process, you will take one of the snow-based tiles and place it within another tile so that it can be used when you decide that the weather has changed. Open the file called weather.mfa, which is located on the CD-ROM in the TileSets folder.

   In this example, you change the far-right water tile, Tile_5_3 (which has a small amount of grass on it), with the tile Water_Snow5.

2. First you need to store the image that you want to appear in the clipboard so that you can paste it into the Tile_5_3 tile. Double-click on the Water_Snow5 tile to open the object in the picture editor.

3. Click on the Selection tool; you can also press the B key. Your mouse cursor will change to a crosshair. Outside of the picture, press and hold the left mouse button and then drag across the whole image of the tile, which puts a dotted line around your image as shown in Figure 8.2.

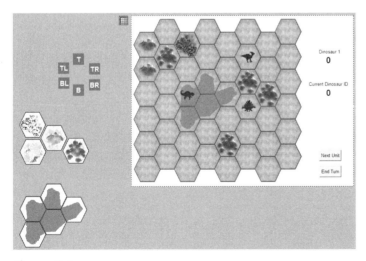

Figure 8.1
All of the terrain tiles within the frame.

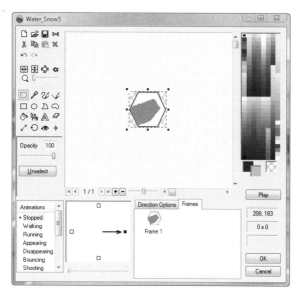

Figure 8.2
The current tile image selected.

4. Now you need to copy this image to the clipboard. The clipboard is a temporary place that you can store an image or some text, so use the Ctrl and C key to copy, or press the copy icon within the picture editor.

Note

You will know if the copy worked as the paste icon in the picture editor will then become enabled. You can also test what you have in the clipboard by opening up the Windows Paint program and pasting the contents using the Ctrl and V key to paste.

5. You can now click on the Cancel button for the Water_Snow5 picture editor because you don't need to make any changes to the image.

Now you need to place this image in the normal water tile.

6. Double-click on the right-most water tile called Tile_5_3; the picture editor for this image opens. You see the water and green grass tile, and also the current direction arrow pointing to the right. Click on the box on the left side; a blank checkerboard appears.

7. Click on the Paste button in the picture editor toolbox on the upper-left side. This pastes the snow-based tile into the same object but for a different direction. You can see an example of this in Figure 8.3.

8. Click on the OK button to save this image to the active object.

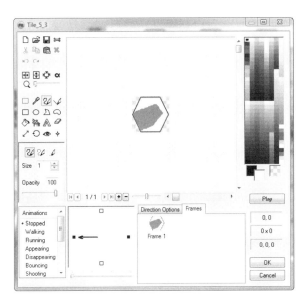

Figure 8.3
The snow tile pasted into the grass and water-based tile for the left direction.

You will now be back at the frame editor, and you will see that the image on screen is still the water and grass tile. Now you need to code a time for the tile to change to snow. In this example, you simply press a key to force the tile to update, but in your own game, you might use a random time or a time of year. You will find more about these items later in this chapter.

9. Click on the event editor icon on the toolbar to access the events. You will see all of the code that you created in the previous chapter.

   Make sure that all groups are collapsed, and you should see the New Condition text at event line 12. You need a key press that will initiate the change of the active objects' direction to snow; for this, you use the spacebar.

10. Click on the New condition text. Select The Mouse Pointer and keyboard object, then the Keyboard, and finally Upon pressing a key. When the dialog box appears press the spacebar.

11. Now the action will be created, so move across until you are directly under the Tile_5_3 file. Right-click the blank action box and select Direction | Select Direction. The Direction dialog box appears; click on the left square (identified as item 16) to create an arrow pointing in that direction. Click on the square labelled 0 to unselect the right-pointing arrow. This configures the dialog box as shown in Figure 8.4.

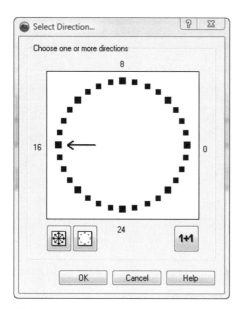

Figure 8.4
The active object will display the left direction.

If you now run the frame and then press the spacebar, you will see your tile change from water and grass to water and snow.

Importing a Tile

In the last example, the tiles were already on the frame, but if you are dealing with a large number of tiles, this may become a little unwieldy. Another option is to have all of your tiles stored as BMP or PMG graphics, and then import them into the tile rather than copy and paste.

The process for importing a tile is quite straightforward; the following is a brief explanation of how to import an image into an active object that's already created.

1. Open up the file weather-1.mfa, which is located in the TileSets folder on the CD-ROM; be certain you are on the frame editor screen.

2. Double-click on the far-right water tile (Tile_5_3) on the map. This will open up the object within the picture editor.

3. First you need to create a new place to import the image; otherwise, you will overwrite the current tiles. Click on the white top square in the Direction dialog box (this is the box that currently has the two directions of left and right assigned to an image).

4. By clicking on the top box, you will create a new image slot, and you will see the checkerboard.

5. Click on the Import button in the picture editor toolbar, this is the second icon from the top left.

6. In the Browse dialog box, browse to your image files; you can find some single tiles in the Import folder on the CD. Select an image and click the Open button.

7. You will now see an Import Options box. There are a number of options as shown in Figure 8.5, but for now you don't need to worry about them; click on the OK button.

8. The image has now been imported into the tile, and to save this information to that particular tile, you need to click on the OK button.

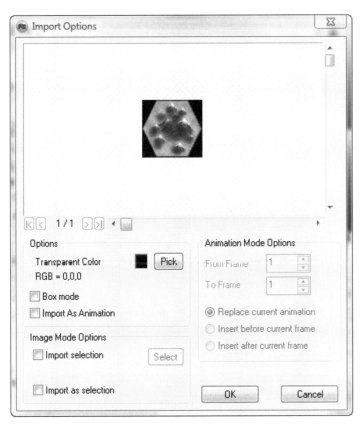

Figure 8.5
The Import dialog box.

More About Weather

You can use two types of weather within your war games. The first one I covered was changing the look of a tile, and I used snow as an example previously. There are only two types of weather you need to consider for changing the tiles, mud and snow. Mud would be caused by too much rainfall, while snow would occur depending on the timeframe of your game.

The second type of weather you need to consider is one that will not update a tile but that will have an effect on a tile. This means you can have a weather system of rain, sun, snow, or fog attached to certain tiles without actually changing the look of the tiles. In this case, you can then add certain modifiers to units depending on the type of weather on each tile.

You will find it useful to think about the weather in real life and how to apply it to your own games. Even though weather can be unpredictable, most of the time, certain types of weather can be placed at certain times of the year. For example, in the summer, you might get large amounts of sun and intermittent storms. In winter, there is a good chance you will have lots of rain, cold weather, and some snow. Of course, the types of weather you get in your own country may differ quite a lot from the weather of a person living in another part of the world. You need to consider this when applying weather to a certain battle or war in a particular part of the world. There is also a chance of freak weather or unusual weather—for example, snow late in the year or a summer that has unusually high rainfall.

Game Timeframes

You may remember the End Turn button from the previous examples. In many war games, each turn has a timeframe; this could be a day, week, month, or year. The type of game you are making determines the amount of time that passes when you press the button.

In a game where you have individual units, each turn can equal a few minutes or an hour. Where you have units of large number of soldiers on a campaign map level, each turn could be hours, days, or years.

Placing a date/time feature on the game interface helps the player see time progressing. You can do this in a couple of ways, depending on which timeframe you decide to choose for your game. You can choose a text or a numeric display.

Test Display

Start by adding a text date display that shows the current month that will change when the user presses the End Turn button.

1. Load the file called timeframe.mfa located in the Examples folder on the CD-ROM. This file contains three units with the British Royal Air Force insignia as the unit graphic.

   Make sure that you can see the frame, where you will see your map and units. You now need to add a text object that will contain all of the months.

2. Right-click on the frame, select Insert Object, and then select the String object. Click anywhere on the frame. Make sure that the string object is selected and then click on the Size/Position tab.

3. Change the X coordinate to 485 and the Y coordinate to 8.

4. Click on the Settings tab for the String object.

   You will see a single paragraph entry which currently contains the word Text. You need another 11 entries so that you have 12 for each month of the year.

5. In the object properties window, click on the New button for the String object 11 times. Your Properties window will look like Figure 8.6.

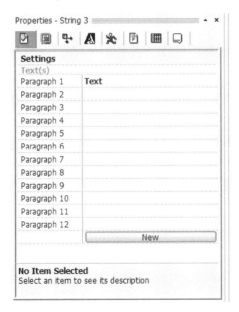

Figure 8.6
The 12 paragraph slots ready for your text.

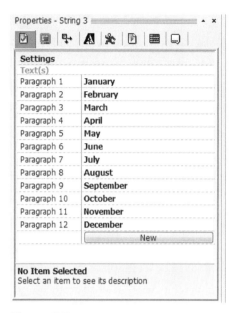

Figure 8.7
The 12 months of the year.

6. Enter the days of the month in each of the 12 slots; you will then have the string properties looking like Figure 8.7.

    You will see in the upper-right corner of the frame that the text now says January. I suggest centering the text.

7. Make sure that the string object is selected and the properties appear. Click on the Text Options tab and then change the drop-down entry for Horizontal to Center.

    Now you will need to code the logic to handle changing the months of the year. You are going to move the date every time the turn ends, so you can attach this action to the button being pressed. Click on the Event Editor button to see the code that is already present in the example file. Before you start adding code, make sure that all groups are collapsed.

8. You will see that event line 10 is the condition that checks for the End of Turn button; you can use this event line to change the month.

9. Move across from event line 10, which should be the button clicked condition, until you are directly under the String 3 object.

10. Right-click the blank action box and select Next Paragraph.

Run the program now and press the End Turn button. You will see that the month now changes to February. If you continue to do this, the text will get as far as December, and, as this is the last paragraph, the text will stay at December. Now you need to tell it to go back to January once it is already December and the player clicks on the End Turn button.

11. Make sure that you are in the event editor and all groups are collapsed.

12. Click on the New condition text on the last event line.

13. Select the Button 2 object, and select Button Clicked.

Now you need to add another condition on the same event line.

14. Right-click the condition on event line 13, select Insert, select the Special object, and choose the Compare two general values option.

The expression evaluator appears, which will allow you to do a comparison between two values. You need to check that the current paragraph number equals 12; this will provide the basis of setting the text back to the first paragraph.

15. Highlight the zero value in the first box and then click on Retrieve data from an object. When the New Expression dialog box appears, find the String 3 object and then right-click on it to reveal the pop-up menu. Select Current number of paragraph displayed. This will place an expression within the first box.

16. Select the zero in the second box and replace it with the number 12. Your expression evaluator will look like Figure 8.8. Click on the OK button to save this information to the event editor.

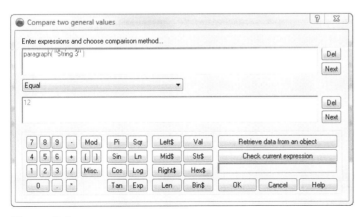

Figure 8.8
Comparing the paragraph currently displayed with the value 12.

At the moment, you don't have any actions, but if you did, there would be a problem with this code, because if it were to get to December, the paragraph value would equal 12 and the event would then run any actions straight away. This would mean that the month of December would effectively disappear off the screen very quickly. You can prevent these things happening by adding a flag. A flag can be switched on or off at particular times and can prevent a line of code running due to the event editor repeating the event lines too quickly.

The majority of objects have flags; unfortunately, the string object does not. So you will add a flag to the Button 2 object. It doesn't matter which object you add a flag to as long as you can remember which object you applied the flag to.

17. Right-click on the Paragraph <abc> = 12 object and select Insert. Find the Button 2 object then choose Alterable Values | Flags | Is a Flag on? The expression evaluator will appear, asking you to enter the flag number; in this case, the 0 is fine for the flag you wish to check. Click on OK.

    Now it's time to add the action to set the text paragraph back to January.

18. Move across from this event line until you are directly under the String 3 object, right-click, and select Set Paragraph; a dialog box will appear, as shown in Figure 8.9. January will already be selected, so click on the OK button.

    Now you need to set the flag to off; this ensures that it is ready for the next time it goes around to December.

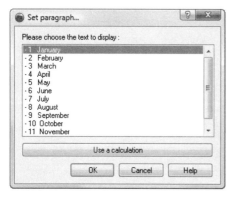

Figure 8.9
Setting the paragraph back to January.

19. Move under the Button 2 object, right-click the action box, and select Flags | Set off; the expression evaluator will appear, and it automatically contains the value 0. This is the flag you want, so click on the OK button to save the information.

You now need one more event to check that the paragraph equals December and that will switch the flag to on.

Click on the New condition text on event line 14.

20. Select the Special object and then choose the Compare two general values option.

21. Highlight the zero value in the first box and then click on the Retrieve data from an object. When the New Expression dialog box appears, find the String 3 object and then right-click on it to reveal the pop-up menu. Select Current number of paragraph displayed. This places an expression within the first box.

22. Select the zero in the second box and replace it with the number 12. Click on the OK button to save this information to the event editor.

Now you just have to apply the flag on the Button2 object to be switched on.

23. Move across from event line 14, right-click on the action box under Button 2, select Flags | Set off. The expression evaluator contains the value 0, so click on the OK button to save the information.

You can see an example of these two event lines in Figure 8.10.

Run the program now and keep clicking on the End of Turn button and see that the program goes through all 12 months. You can compare your coding with the example called timeframe-month.mfa on the CD-ROM.

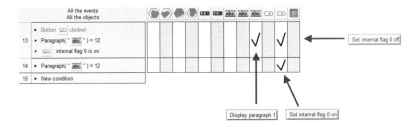

Figure 8.10
The two additional event lines added to handle the changing of the month back to January.

Number Year Display

You might decide to have a year displayed as well as a month. This is especially useful when making games that are played at the campaign level. You can achieve this two ways. You could use a counter object to display a number. Counters are very easy to use and will be perfect for a year; the only downside is they don't always look graphically pleasing. Another way is to use a text string object. You might be wondering how you will get a number to be displayed into an object that is meant to display text. MMF2 has an option to convert a number to text. The benefit of using a text-based object is that it has more font options and graphically can look better with the style of game you are making.

Year Display Using the Counter Object   In the following example, you will add a year that increments every time the month loops around to January, using the counter object.

1. Open the file Counter-start.mfa from the Examples folder.

2. Be sure you can see all of the tiles on the frame editor.

   First you will need to add a counter onto the screen to display the year.

3. Right-click anywhere on the frame and select Insert Object.

4. Find and select the Counter object, and click on the OK button.

5. The mouse cursor will change to a crosshair. Click anywhere on the frame where there is no other object. This will place the counter onto the screen.

6. Be sure that the new counter object has been selected and you can see its properties.

   You can see that you have a number of options you can configure to ensure that the range of your counter is configured correctly. Change the initial and minimum value to 1939, and the maximum value to 1945 as shown in Figure 8.11.

7. Click on the Size/Position tab to access the properties for the counters position on screen.

8. Change the X position value to 586 and the Y coordinate to 60, which will place the year just under the month text.

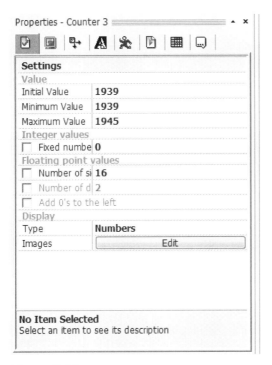

Figure 8.11
The initial values of the counter configure for the years 1939 to 1945.

Run the example file, and you will see the month and the year. Now, you need to create an event that will change the year by 1 each time January appears. The great thing is that you already have an event for this, because you programmed an event to check for when the month was December and the user had pressed the End Turn button.

9. Click on the Event Editor button.

10. Make sure all groups are collapsed and scroll down to event line 13, which should contain the code you created in the previous example that handles the looping of the month from December to January. Move across to the right of this event until you are under the year counter, which in this case is called Counter 3. Right-click on the action box and select Add to counter. When the expression evaluator appears, type the number **1** and click on OK.

This value adds 1 year every time the month goes from December to January. Run the program to test it and make sure that your code works.

Note

You may notice that the year counter only goes as far as 1945; this is because you set a higher limit to the counter. If you are creating a game that is within a set time period, you could do a comparison check on a particular date and then end the game.

Year Display Using the String Object   To have a string object display the year, you still need a counter to keep track of the current year. You need to place this value into a static text object. You cannot place a number directly into a string type object, and you cannot place text within a counter. You can convert a number into text and then display the result of that.

1. Load the file stringyear.mfa from the Examples folder on the CD-ROM.

2. Make sure you are on the frame editor; right-click on the frame and select Insert Object.

3. Select the Static text object and click on the OK button.

4. Click anywhere on the frame to place the object.

5. Make sure that the object properties are displayed; if they are not, left-click on the object.

6. Change the Text Alignment to Center.

7. Click on the Size/Position tab; change the width to 62 and the height to 22.

8. Change the X position to 535 and the Y position to 67.

   Now that the configuration of the box has been completed, you need to go into the event editor to configure the year into the text box.

9. Click the Event Editor button.

   The first thing you have to do is to make sure that, at the start of the frame, the initial year is set to the text box.

10. Move across from event line 1, which is the Start of Frame event, until you are under the Static Text object.

11. Right-click on the action box and select Set Text, which loads the Expression evaluator.

   You will see a set of quotation marks in this box. The marks indicate that text is expected, and, if you were to delete these and type a number, MMF2

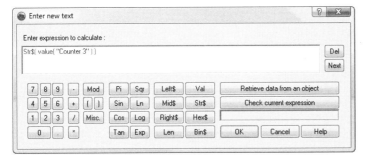

Figure 8.12
The expression to convert a number to a string.

would display an error message. You need to tell MMF that you want to display a number as text, which you can do using the Str$ option.

12. Click on the Str$ button on the expression evaluator, which replaces the quotation marks with an expression. In the middle, it will say >Enter number here<. Make sure that >Enter number here< is selected and then click on the Retrieve data from an object button.

You will now retrieve a value from the year counter.

13. Find Counter 3, which is the year counter, and then right-click on it. From the pop-up menu choose Current Value. Your expression evaluator will look like Figure 8.12. Click on the OK button to save the information to the event editor.

You will also need this action in the event on line 13, which is the event line that checks for the month being December and for whether the user has pressed the button to move to January. Once December changes to January you will want to update the text object with the next year date.

14. Left-click and hold the left mouse button on the action tick for the string conversion that you just added in event line 1 and drag it down to the Static text box on event line 13. This step ensures that your text object is kept updated.

If you run the program now, you can see that the year is set to 1939 and automatically changes in January. Notice that the quality of the text in the Static object is much better than in the Counter object, because the counter object is actually displaying an image.

Days of the Month

You may want your game to run on a day by day basis. This adds a little more complexity to your war game for a couple of reasons: the different number of days in February for certain years and the differences in the number of days among the months.

Using a day system does require more effort, but it is still relatively straight-forward. You may need to search the Internet or use your computer calendar to see the number of days within a particular month and year.

As the code for implementing this is very similar to code/methods you've already used, I will discuss only how to implement the system.

First, you need a counter to store the total number of days for any particular month. You will then need a second counter that will store the current day. The total number of days counted will change based on the current month.

Using a comparison condition, you can check the current month and year and then set the total number of days in the month. You could also set this value as the maximum counter value. Then using the current day counter for each end turn button pressed, add 1 to the value of the counter.

N o t e

Please note that when you use the term "days of the month," you are specifying a day as the actual number, for example the 23rd of July and not Wednesday. The reason for this is that specifying the actual day adds another level of complexity.

A calendar object is available from the clickteams website at www.clickteam.com (this calendar object works only with the full version of MMF2) that will allow you to check the actual day if you decide you want your game to return a day as well as the day number. Using the calendar object is the easiest way to implement this system without using a lot of events and effort.

N o t e

By using days, months, and years, you can easily set up a set of conditions that compare to when a specific timeframe has been met. This way, if you are trying to make a historically correct battle, you can simulate the weather of the time.

Random Weather

You can apply what you now know about having a day, month, or year system within your game to setting up weather. If you have a game that runs on a monthly basis, you might decide that when it reaches November, a certain type of weather, such as snow, will start to encroach onto the map; whereas in April, when there is no chance of snow, you can remove snow-based tiles.

Changing Random Tiles

Earlier in this chapter, I showed you how to change a single tile using the spacebar. The next stage is to change random tiles on the map when a certain date is met. This change allows you to see how you can implement date-based and season-based weather on your maps. Because the previous example is using months, you set the snow weather to hit random tiles from November, and then in April all tiles change back to the original green tiles.

1. Load the file snow-random.mfa from the Examples folder. This file has all of the code previously written, and every tile has a snow tile set in the left direction of each object.

2. You don't need to configure anything on the frame editor, so click on the Event Editor button to view the code.

   To make the random code work, you need to do the following tasks:

   ■ Check for when the month is November; then enable a group.

   ■ Check for when the month is April; then enable a group.

   ■ Within the Snow on group, randomly pick some tiles to change their direction.

   ■ Within the Snow off group, change all tiles back to the non snow version.

   First, you will need to create two events that will check when the month is November or April. You can use the standard comparison option. Each paragraph in the string object that stores the months has a number assigned to it, so 1 is January and 12 is December. So, you can compare when the number of the paragraph equals either 11 or 4.

   You can see the event editor, and it currently has 14 lines of code.

3. The first new event is to check when the paragraph of the string object equals 11. You could do this manually, but as the condition on event line 13 is very similar, you can drag and drop this condition on the New Condition

15	• Paragraph(" abc ") = 11
16	• Paragraph(" abc ") = 4
17	• New condition

Figure 8.13
The two new events created by dragging and dropping already created events and changing the contents.

text and then edit the new condition. When you edit the condition, the expression evaluator will appear; replace the 12 with the number **11**.

4. Drag and drop the condition on event line 15 to the New condition text, and then edit the condition on event line 16 and change the number 11 to the number 4. Your two new events will look like Figure 8.13.

You cannot add any actions to these two events yet because you have not created the weather on and off groups. These two groups will be used to handle switching on and off the weather. It is important to put your code into groups because you can easily change certain aspects of how the code works and you can find it more easily. You will add two groups, one called Snow ON and the second one called Snow OFF.

5. Right-click on the event line number of 17 (which has the New condition text on it) and select Insert Group of Events.

6. The Group Events dialog box will appear. Type **Snow ON** as the title of the group; then make sure that Active when frame starts is unchecked so that the group will be switched on when you need it. Click on the OK button to save this to the event editor.

Make sure you collapse the group Snow ON before continuing.

7. Right-click on the event line number 18, which is the last line in the event editor. Type the title **Snow OFF** and deselect Active when frame starts. You should have two groups as shown in Figure 8.14.

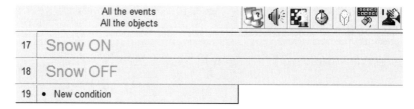

Figure 8.14
Two groups which are disabled.

Now go back to events 15 and 16 and add an action to enable the two groups you have just created. Event line 11 relates to November and designates when you require the snow to fall, and 4 is April when all the snow has melted away.

8. Move across from event line 15, and under the Special Conditions object. Select Group of Events | Activate. When the Activate dialog box appears, select the item number (6) Snow ON.

9. Move across from event line 16, and under Special Conditions, select Group of Events | Activate. From the dialog box choose item (7) Snow OFF.

Programming the Snow ON   You are ready to expand the Snow ON group and program the code to turn on a selection of snow tiles. You are not going to turn all the tiles on, which, in fact, is very simple to do; instead, you will select a number at random. In the following example, you select 10 tiles and turn them into snow-based tiles.

The first thing you need to do is add an event that will repeat a process 10 times. Check that the tiles selected are those that haven't already been changed to snow and then pick one at random. The reason you check whether the tile hasn't already been changed is that the Pick condition you are going to use doesn't have any way of knowing if it has already selected a particular tile.

Make sure that the group Snow ON is expanded.

1. Click on the New condition text in the Snow ON group.

2. First, you need to create a condition that allows a process to be repeated 10 times; this is the number of tiles that you will change. If you want more or fewer, you can change the number in the following condition.

3. Select the Special object from the New condition dialog box. Select the option Limit | Repeat; the expression evaluator appears. Type the number 10 and click on OK.

4. Now, you need to add a second condition to this event, so right-click on the Repeat 10 times condition and select Insert.

5. From the New condition dialog box, right-click on the Group.Good object, which is the apple icon. Then select Direction | Compare Direction of Group.Good. The Direction dialog box appears; it has an arrow pointing to 0 on the right. This is fine because you want to check that tiles the program

selects are currently displaying that direction, which means it is showing the grass tile. Click on the OK button.

You need to add one more condition; this condition will pick one of the tiles in the Group.Good, which will have all actions applied to it.

6. Right-click on the condition you just added, which will be Group.Good (apple) is facing a direction of right and select insert.

7. Right-click on the Group.Good object (the apple icon), and select Pick or Count | Pick Group.Good at random.

8. Move across from the event until you are directly under the Group.Good object. Right-click the action box and select Direction | Set direction. When the Direction dialog box appears, remove the arrow pointing to the right and make sure there is an arrow pointing to the left (direction 16). Click on the OK button to close the dialog box.

The code you just added will repeat the process 10 times selecting only objects that have no snow on them and will pick one at random. It will then change the animation direction of the single object to snow.

You now need to add an event to close the group. This will ensure that this code doesn't keep running.

9. Click on the New Condition text on event line 19, select the Special object, and then select the Always condition.

10. Move across and away from this event until you are under the Special Conditions object, choose Group of events | Deactivate, and select Snow ON.

You have completed the code for the Snow ON group. You can now collapse the group before you move on to turning the snow off.

Programming the Snow to OFF   Now that you have completed the events for turning the snow on, you need to be able to turn the snow off in April, which will be an easy process because you have used qualifier groups.

1. Make sure that the Snow ON group is collapsed, and then expand the Snow OFF group.

2. Click on the New condition text under the Snow Off group. Select the Special object and then choose Always.

3. Move across from this event until you are under the Group.Good object, right-click the action box, and select Direction | Select Direction. When the Direction dialog box appears, the arrow will already be pointing to the right; this is the direction you need to change the snow tiles back to normal grass tiles, so click on the OK button.

You now need to add one more event that will close this group; otherwise, it will always change the tiles to non-snow tiles. Turning off any groups of code you no longer need is important, or else strange results may occur in your game.

4. Click on the New condition text under the Snow OFF group, choose the Special object, and then choose Always.

5. Move to the right of this event until you are under the Special Conditions object, right-click the action box, choose Group of events | Deactivate, and select Snow OFF.

You have now completed the code for turning snow on and off within your game. You can easily change this code to be time-based or date-based using the same process. You can see the completed code in the Examples folder in a file called snow-random-complete.mfa. You can also see the new events that you added in Figure 8.15.

Figure 8.15
The new events used to turn the snow on and off.

Reducing Movement Based on Weather

If you decide to restrict movement or use additional movement points in bad weather you will need to modify the movement points system you put in place in Chapter 7.

In Chapter 7, you modified each unit's movement first by a single point, and then, within the same expression, you retrieved a value from the array that checked the tile the unit were overlapping to find the additional movement points cost.

The easiest way to do this change is to use the same method that was used in Chapter 7, and that is to create a weather-based movement table in an array. Create a new alterable value for each tile that will store the weather value, so, for example, a 0 for no weather and a 1 for snow, a 2 for mud, and so on.

Before all the movement key presses, you will need to check the tile state based on its direction, so in the previous examples in this chapter, the left direction was for snow. You can use up to 32 different animation directions, which should be enough for your weather tiles. Store this value in the alterable value.

You need to add an additional condition for the directional key press—to check whether, with this additional tile effect, the unit still has enough movement points. If so and all of the other conditions are correct, MMF2 would then run the actions of moving the unit and reducing its movement points.

To complete the process, you can read the value stored in the array and subtract it from the current movement points. If there are no additional movement points, it will just add a 0 to the end of the calculation and have no effect.

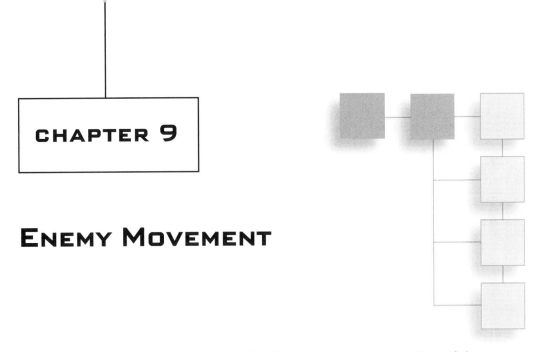

CHAPTER 9

ENEMY MOVEMENT

One of the most complex aspects of making any war game is that of the enemy player and its AI. AI stands for Artificial Intelligence, and within your game, it is associated with the computer-controlled player moving its pieces, commanding attacks, and giving the human player differing levels of game difficulty.

In this chapter, you will primarily look at enemy movement on the map and how to accomplish computer movement by using smaller projects that build up to a more complicated movement engine.

Basic Enemy Movement

Many of the configurations you place on the players' movement involve the automated computer-controlled movement. Computer units are controlled using the same rules that you implemented for the player.

In this example, you have a set of four enemy units to move along a predefined path. Even though this exercise doesn't use computer intelligence, it does allow you to configure many of the options that the unit needs before creating a more complicated example.

For basic enemy movement, you need to do the following:

- **Message:** Create a message to advise the player that the enemy is moving. It is important to let players know when something is happening that they cannot control.

- **Trigger Computer Movement**: You need to consider when you particularly want the computer to move its units. For the games you're creating now, you use the End Turn button to signal the next game phase, which is the phase that enables the computer to move the units before giving control back to the player.

- **Disable Player Movement**: If you implement computer-controlled movement, with the current code, the player will still be able to move because the code is still enabled. When the computer is moving its units, you need to disable all player movement to prevent any problems with your game.

- **Handle Computer Movement**: For this example, you move the computer units in a particular direction on the screen, based on their current location. This means that the code will be correct for only one movement turn; otherwise, you would need to program many events to handle each turn's movements. You won't configure extra movement because, in later examples, you will get the player to make decisions on where to move.

- **Enable Player Movement:** Once the computer has completed its movement, you need to give the player his ability to move again. You also need to consider resetting the values for the computer units and then disabling the computer-controlled movement group until the player enables it again by pressing the End Turn button.

Message

The first part of configuring the enemy movement is to display a message when the user clicks on the End Turn button. The message makes the user aware that it's the computer's turn to move.

MMF2 allows you to program a message a number of ways. First, you can display some text on screen. You will need to configure an interface window to display the text message. Another way that requires a little more work to the set-up is by using the Sub Application. The Sub Application is a special object that allows you to display another frame from either the same MMF2 file or another application within a selected frame.

In this example, you want a message appearing in Frame 1, which is the game frame.

1. You will now load up the file that contains all the player movements and the four enemy units from the file enemymovements.mfa located in the

Examples folder on the CD-ROM. Also notice on this map that you have added a city tile. In this example, the city tile acts very much like a grass tile and does not reduce the player's movement any further.

The first thing you need to do is to create a new frame that contains a message advising the user that the computer is taking its turn.

2. Click on the Storyboard Editor button or press Ctrl+B to access the Storyboard Editor. You will then see that you have a single frame in the game. Click on the number 2 in the storyboard list to create a second frame.

   The size of this frame is 640 by 480, which is too big for the message. You want a small dialog box to appear that doesn't take up the entire screen so that the user can see the enemy units moving on the map.

3. On the Storyboard Editor, you will see a small monitor icon on the second frame storyboard; next to it you will see the text 640 by 480. You can click on each number and change it, so change it to 200 by 80. Your storyboard frame will look like Figure 9.1.

   If you click on the number 2 in the storyboard screen, you will be taken to frame two of your game. You will notice that it is pretty small as shown in Figure 9.2, perfect for a pop-up message box.

   You now add two bits of text to the second frame, and also change the color of the background, which is currently displayed as white.

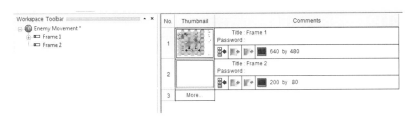

Figure 9.1
The configured storyboard with two frames.

Figure 9.2
The small window for the message.

4. Click on the text Frame 2 in the Workspace toolbar to access the Frame Properties window.

5. Click on the Background color option. When the color palette appears, select the second color block from the bottom right; this is the item to the left of the color white. This updates the frame color and also displays RGB as 230, 230, 250.

   You now need to add two lines of text.

6. Right click anywhere on the frame on Frame 2. Select Insert Object, choose the String object, and click on OK. The cursor changes to a crosshair, so click anywhere to place the object.

7. Right click again and insert another string object and place it on the frame. Move each text string so that it is within the frame playfield and so that one is above the other.

8. Double-click on the first of the two text objects and an edit box appears. Delete the Text that is currently displayed and then type the words **Enemy Movement Phase**.

9. Double-click on the second of the two objects. This time type the text **Please Wait**.

10. Use the text options in the toolbar to change the font size, type, alignment, and color of each text object. You can see an example of what it will look like in Figure 9.3.

    You have finished the frame. You can, of course, spend more time if you like adding an animation or graphics to make the text look more interesting, but for now it has enough information to tell the player what is happening in the game.

Figure 9.3
The frame with two lines of text.

11. Double-click on the text Frame 1 in the workspace editor to display your game frame; this frame shows the player and enemy units on the hex map.

    Using the Sub-Application object, you can display any frame on Frame 1.

12. Right click on the frame editor and select Insert Object; then choose the Sub-Application object and click on OK.

13. Click anywhere on the frame to place the object. You may notice that the object properties have an option called Source; at the moment, the Source option is set to Other-application. You could access the frame with another MMF2 application, but in this case, you have the display information on Frame 2.

14. Click on the Other application text in the Sub-Application properties and select Frame from this application.

    Automatically, MMF2 will select Frame 1 as the object to insert. Notice that the border for the Sub-Application object is now resized to 640 by 480, because this is the size of Frame 1.

15. Click on the number 1 in the object properties, and change the 1 to **2**. MMF2 now displays the enemy movement text that you created in Frame 2. Make sure that the message dialog box is off the current frame play area as shown in Figure 9.4.

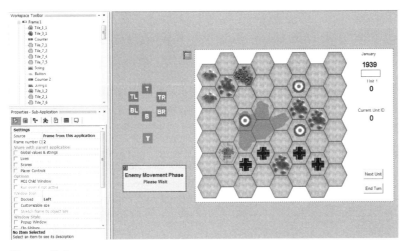

Figure 9.4
The Sub-Application object displaying the frame from Frame 2.

You have now configured all aspects of the sub-application and frame, so it is now time to program the logic.

You should be on the frame editor for Frame 1. Click on the event editor button.

You will see a large set of events that handle the player movement (covered in the previous chapters). You want the message dialog box to display when the user clicks on the End Turn button. If you have an object off-screen that you want to display on the frame at a particular point, it is usually best to make sure it is invisible. Move the object to the exact place that you want to display it and then make the object visible again. This step ensures that, if the game slows down, no strange display issues are created as the object is moved across the screen. So, the first thing to do is make the Sub-Application object invisible. You already have a Start of Frame event, so you can go and add the action to this line.

16. From event line 1 move across to the right until you are directly under the Sub-Application object. Right click on the action box and select Visibility|Hide.

You already have an event in the code that checks for when the player presses the End Turn button; MMF2 then runs the End of Turn group. You need to modify the code in order to make the following changes:

■ User presses the End Turn button; which will enable a group called Computer Move.

■ The Computer Move group has an event that displays a message "Enemy Movement Phase".

■ The last event in the Computer Move group disables that group and then enables the End of Turn group so that all the player values are reset.

These changes also allow you to get ready to make further changes to the code as described at the start of the Basic Enemy Movement section.

Creating a New Group

First, you need to create a group that will contain all of the enemy player movement code. You should already have the event editor open with the first frame of the example file displayed. Make sure that all groups are collapsed before continuing.

1. On the last line of the event editor, which is line 15, right click on the line number and select Insert|A group of events.

2. When the Group Events dialog box appears, type **Computer Move** as the name of the group, and also unselect the Active when frame starts option. Click on the OK button to save the information to the event editor.

Amending the Update Button Code

At the moment, if you run the game and press the End Turn button, the game will continue to rotate between the players' units. You need to remove a small bit of code to make sure the game doesn't run; then you can add some code to the new Computer Move group.

The End Turn text button is called Button 2. On event line 10, you will find the code related to when this button is pressed. Make sure the action scroll bar is all the way to the left so that you can see the Special Conditions object. If you hold the mouse over the action check mark, you will see four events: three that disable groups and one, the last one, which enables the End of Turn group. You need to delete this last action because you will enable it once the computer player moves.

1. Right click on the action box, which is directly under the Special Conditions object for event line 10, and select Delete|Activate group End of Turn.

   In the action box in which you just deleted an action, add a new one to enable the new group.

2. Right click on the action box under the Special Conditions object on event line 10, select Group of Events|Activate, and from the dialog box, select (6) Computer Move and click on OK.

Displaying the Message

You now need to display the message. You center it at the bottom of the screen. You will need to move it and then make it visible so that the player can see it.

Expand the group Computer Move so that you can see the New condition text.

1. Click on the New condition text. In the New condition dialog box, choose the Special object and then choose Limit Conditions|Only one action when event loops.

2. Move across from this event until you are directly under the Sub-Application object. Right click on the action box and select Position|Select Position. When the dialog box appears, type **220** for the X coordinate and **394** for the Y coordinate.

3. On the same action box, right click and choose Visibility|Show.

If you run the program now and press the End Turn button, the Enemy Movement Phase message box will appear.

Disabling Buttons

You need to disable the End Turn and Next Unit buttons to prevent the user from pressing them while the enemy units are moving. In all the games you make, disable anything the user can press or change while the enemy units are moving. This way, the user will not interrupt the game code and change any values while movement is taking place. Any interruptions to your game code could cause your game to have unexpected problems.

1. Under the Computer Move group, which should be expanded, move across from event line 16 to directly under Button 1, right click the action box, and select Disable.

2. On the same event line, move across and then under Button 2 and select Disable.

If you were to run your game now, you would see that when you click on the End Turn button (Button 2), the buttons become gray, which means they will not respond to clicks from the player.

Making the Enemy Move

You now need to move the enemy into a particular set of tiles; using a pre-defined path, and no computer AI is being used at this point.

In Figure 9.5, you see the different locations in which you want the units to move, and in Figure 9.6, you see the different direction coordinates needed to move the units precisely.

Note

At this stage, you are not worrying about where the player's units are, or how many unit points are required for the enemy to move. You are setting up all the code to make sure enemy movement works, and then you can add additional code into the Computer Movement group. This means you can be sure the simple code works with all the other systems before adding more complexity, in which case, you might have trouble figuring out where the problem is originating.

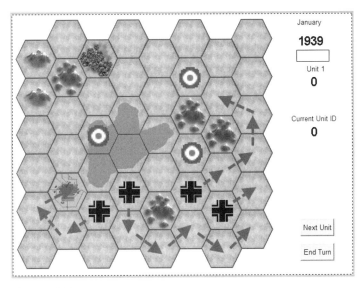

Figure 9.5
The different directions the enemy units will move in.

Unit Name	Dir 1	Dir 2	Dir 3	Dir 4	Dir 5
Enemy_Unit1	(-58,35)	(-58,-35)	(58,-35)	-	-
Enemy_Unit2	(0,70)	(58,35)	(58,-35)	(58,35)	(58,-35)
Enemy_Unit3	(58,-35)	(58,-35)	(0,-70)	(-58,-35)	-
Enemy_Unit4	(58,-35)	-	-	-	-

Figure 9.6
The direction movements each unit needs.

You are going to separate each unit into its own group so that you can apply code for that unit only, which will make the whole process of moving and testing a particular unit much easier. MMF2 makes the process of separating sections of code in groups easier because, you can place groups within groups.

1. On event line 17, right click on the event line number and select Insert|A Group of events.

2. When the Group Events dialog box appears, type **Enemy Unit 1** as the title of the group and unselect Active when frame starts; then click on OK.

3. Within the Computer Move group, create three more groups called Enemy Unit 2, Enemy Unit 3, and Enemy Unit 4; ensure each group is not active when the frame starts.

   The Computer Move group is enabled when the user presses the End Turn button; then one after another, each unit group will be enabled, and there will be code within each group that will move the enemy units. This

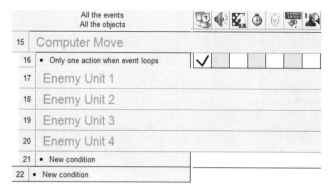

Figure 9.7
The Computer Move group with four unit groups within it.

ensures that only one enemy unit is moved at a time and allows you to step through the units in order.

You now need to start the process of enemy movement by enabling the first group.

4. On event line 16 (which should display Only one action when event loops) in the Computer Move group move across until you are under the Special Conditions object and right click Group of events|Activate. When the Activate dialog box appears, choose (7) – Enemy Unit 1 and click on OK. Your groups will now look like Figure 9.7.

Check to be sure that each group is activated and set a timer to 0 seconds. Using the timer, every second you move the unit to a different hexagon using the coordinates you set in Figure 9.6. You use different ranges of time to move each set of units.

5. Make sure that the Enemy Unit 1 group is expanded.

6. Click on the New condition text under the Enemy Unit 1 group. Select the Special group and choose Group of events|On group activation. Move across from this event and right click under the Timer object. Select Set timer, and when the Set Timer dialog box appears, make sure that the time in seconds is set to 0 and then click on OK.

When the group is activated and MMF2 gets to the first event in the group, MMF2 will set the program timer to 0 and automatically start counting forward. Now add four timed events; the first three will be to move the unit and the fourth will be to enable the next group.

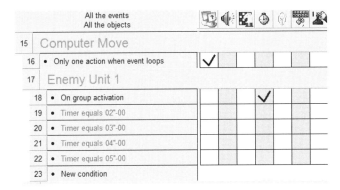

Figure 9.8
The events in the Enemy Unit 1 group.

7. Click on the New condition text on event line 19, select the Timer object, and then Is the timer equal to a certain value? When the Set Timer dialog box appears, change the seconds to 2 and click on OK.

8. Create the three other events, but for 3, 4, and 5 seconds, as shown in Figure 9.8.

   For Enemy Unit 1, you want it to move three hex tiles, based on the movements shown in Figure 9.6.

9. Move across from event line 19—where the timer equals two seconds—until you are directly under the Enemy_Unit1 object. Right click on the action box and select Position|Select Position. The Select Position dialog box appears. Click on the Relative to radio button, select the Enemy_Unit1 object, and click on OK. This step takes you back to the Select Position dialog box. Type the X coordinate **-58** and the Y coordinate **35**.

10. Follow the same process for when the timer equals 3 seconds, but this time type the coordinates **-58** and **-35**.

11. Finally, do the same process across from 4 seconds and set the position of the object (remember to make it relative to) at **58** and **-35**.

    You have now configured all the movements for this object, so it's time to enable the Enemy Unit 2 group so that Enemy Unit 2 can be moved.

12. Move across from event line 22, where the timer equals 5 seconds, until you are directly under the Special Conditions object, right click on the action box, select Group of Events|Activate, and then choose (8) Enemy Unit 2.

    Your events and actions will look like those in Figure 9.9.

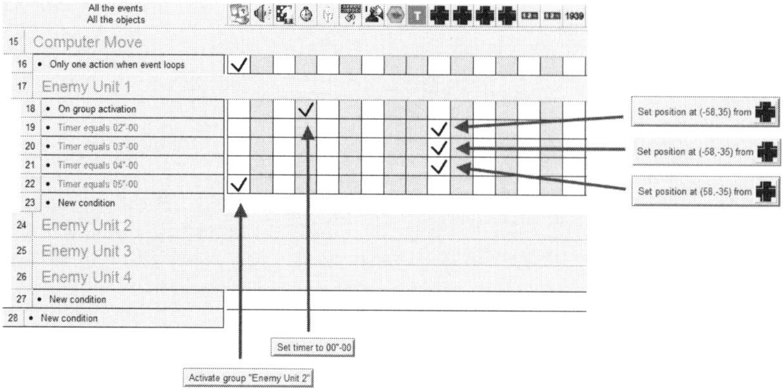

Figure 9.9
The events and actions for the Enemy Unit 1 group.

N o t e

The order of the objects in Figure 9.9 has been rearranged to show you all of the objects' actions that you've been working on; you don't need to rearrange them, as the order shown was only for the purpose of the screenshot.

Now that you have created the movement for the first unit, you need to follow the same process for Enemy Units 2, 3, and 4. You can see the events for this in Figure 9.10.

Remember that you need to add the timer that is set on group activation to the code. Set it to one second before the first group time. For example, in the Enemy Unit 4 group, the first enemy unit is moved at 30 seconds. So, on group activation, set the timer to 29 seconds. There will be a 1-second delay before MMF2 begins to move the unit.

■ You still need to add an additional event on to the end of the Enemy Unit 4 group to deactivate all of the groups and enable the End of Turn group that you removed when the user pressed the End of Turn button earlier.

■ Set the movement for the unit as shown in the Figure 9.6. Each column represents each of the timer seconds.

■ Make sure that you enable the next enemy groups in the Enemy Unit groups for 2 and 3. This should be the last event in each group.

■ Create the code for these other units; if you are having trouble or would rather just open a pre-created file, open the file enemybasic.mfa contained within the Examples folder.

	All the events All the objects							

17 Enemy Unit 1

18	• On group activation				✓			
19	• Timer equals 02"-00							
20	• Timer equals 03"-00							
21	• Timer equals 04"-00							
22	• Timer equals 05"-00	✓						
23	• New condition							

24 Enemy Unit 2

25	• On group activation				✓			
26	• Timer equals 10"-00							
27	• Timer equals 11"-00							
28	• Timer equals 12"-00							
29	• Timer equals 13"-00							
30	• Timer equals 14"-00							
31	• Timer equals 15"-00	✓						
32	• New condition							

33 Enemy Unit 3

34	• On group activation				✓			
35	• Timer equals 20"-00							
36	• Timer equals 21"-00							
37	• Timer equals 22"-00							
38	• Timer equals 23"-00							
39	• Timer equals 24"-00	✓						
40	• New condition							

41 Enemy Unit 4

42	• On group activation				✓			
43	• Timer equals 30"-00							
44	• Timer equals 31"-00							
45	• New condition							

Figure 9.10
The events for all four units.

The final event line for the Enemy Unit 4 group is needed to re enable the buttons that you disabled, hide the computer movement message, and disable the enemy movement code.

1. Make sure all groups are collapsed, except for the Enemy Unit 4 group.

2. Click on the New condition text on event line 24. Select the Timer object and then select Is the timer equal to a certain value? When the Set Timer dialog box appears type **32 seconds** and click on OK.

3. Move across from this event until you are directly under the Sub-Application object and then right click the action box and select Visibility | Hide.

4. On the same event line, move directly under Button 1 and select Enable. Do the same again and enable Button 2.

Lastly, you will need to deactivate all of the enemy movement groups, enable the End of Turn group so that movement points can be reapplied, and then disable the Computer Move group.

5. Move across from event line 24 until you are under the Special Conditions object; right click the action box and select Group of Events | Deactivate. Select the (7) Enemy Unit 1 option and click on OK.

6. On the same action box, select Group of Events | Deactivate and select (8) Enemy Unit 2.

7. Follow the same process again and deactivate groups Enemy Unit 3 and Enemy Unit 4.

8. Again on the same action box, this time select Group of Events | Activate; from the Special Conditions action, select End of Turn and click on OK.

9. Lastly, on the same action box, select Group of Events | Deactivate, select Computer Move, and click on OK. You can see the actions in Figure 9.11.

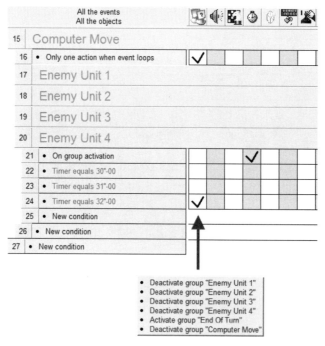

Figure 9.11
The disabling and enabling of specific groups.

If you run the program, now you will see that you can move, and when you click on the End Turn button, the message appears and the enemies begin to move. Once they have moved on their path, the buttons become enabled and the message disappears. You can actually click the End Turn button again, and the units will continue to move around the screen. Of course, because you have pre-programmed the directions, they will actually move off the map. The computer units will move off screen, for this example because the code you have written has shown you some of the key items you need for enemy movement. For a working engine, you will need to stop the units moving off the screen and put in place a number of other checks.

Advancing Enemy Movement

In some war games, the enemy units may not actually move at all, and the challenge is for the player to attack the enemy stronghold. Using this method does make for a much easier game creation because you have fewer things to worry about. It is very easy to make a war game of this type because no code is required for the enemy movement, and you need to concentrate only on player movement and any other rules that you require, such as attack and defense. There is no problem if you make a war game of this type, but generally a game with no enemy movement is used only in simple war games.

The basic movement example provides some of the components that a war game creator must address when creating computer-controlled movement. The movement was set up on a predefined path, which is fine if you want to create a simple illusion of movement. The main issue with that movement type is that it requires a large amount of programming to make it look like the computer is moving intelligently. The basic movement example is useful for very short bits of movement, but is not enough for war games where you want the computer to look like it "has a brain" and is "using its brain."

To give the computer player a level of intelligence, you need to think about the following concepts and rules:

- **Movement Points**: The enemy units have the same issues with regard to movement as the player units do, which means they are also tied into a movement points system. Using an array table and the same type of system that is in place for the player, you can take into account the tiles they move on and the number of points required when moving.

- **Moving Off the Map**: It wouldn't be very good if the enemy units could move off the map—this would be considered a bug. Utilizing the system you used for the player, you can prevent the computer from moving off the terrain tiles.

- **Moving Over Other units**: You want to prevent a computer-controlled unit moving over other units.

- **Moving Over Specific Tiles**: Once you configure the enemy movement table in an array, you can check whether a unit is allowed to move over a particular type of tile. Additional checks are needed to see whether the computer has enough movement points to move over the tiles.

- **Targets**: Does the unit have a particular target that it needs? In the simplest form, this would be moving from one particular place on the map to another position on the map.

- **Orders**: Taking the concept of targets to the next level, does the unit need to defend or attack a particular location or unit? To give the computer units an aim is the first stage in giving the computer a level of intelligence. It has to make decisions based on what it has been instructed to follow, just like units in war. The player would not know what these orders are and so would have to second guess what is going to happen.

- **Path Finding**: Probably the most complex thing that you need to implement for enemy movement is the requirement to get the computer to figure out the best path through a map to get to the destination. Moving from one point to another on the map and ensuring the best path or the most cost-effective one with regard to movement points require the most work in a war game.

Note

Many of the rules that you need for enemy intelligence are similar to ones that you had to apply to the player movement to make sure they stayed on the screen map or didn't move on tiles they were not able to.

In Figure 9.12, you can see an example of the war game map; this map shows the unit's starting location and the "T" displays its ending location. This unit is not able to cross water or travel over mountains, so the two shortest routes are around the water or around the mountains. By going in the lower route, the total

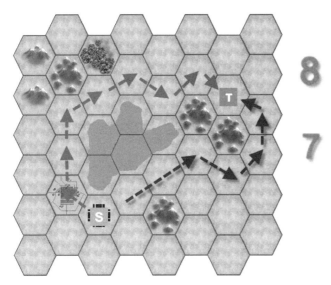

Figure 9.12
Movement costs on different paths.

movement cost if all grass units were a single movement point would be 7, while the alternative direction would cost 8 movement points.

Traditional programming languages provide many ways of writing code to make a unit find the best path. One of these systems is called A* (you can find out more about this by typing **A* War game movement** in Wikipedia). Using cost calculations, the A* algorithm will find the best path to a final location while taking into consideration which tiles it cannot cross.

Implementing A* movement in MMF2 is no easy task, even for the more experienced MMF2 user. Chapters 2 and 3 introduced MMF2. You may remember that anything you add to the frame editor is an object. You get a number of objects with the demo version of MMF2 that can do things such as adding text, playing video, adding counter, and displaying scores and a number of other features. The full version has a number of other objects that you can download for free from third parties, and, in many cases, these objects will be perfect for adding more functionality to your games and applications. None are perfectly suited to making A* movement, unfortunately. So, for this book, we have made a specific object that can easily deal with A* movement, which you can then easily program using events. This takes away many of the problems with writing lots of complex code to a specific task, because you can get the object to do much of the work for you.

Note

If you have knowledge of C++, you can also make your own objects using the software development kit. Even though in this case you made a special object to handle A* movement, you can do many other things in MMF2 by using either the extensions that come with the product or additional ones that have been released by Clickteam or third-party users since the product's release. For more information, visit www.clickteam.com.

Wargame Map Object

To make A* movement a much easier prospect for the MMF2 programmer, you create a new object to handle the calculation of the best path for a unit to take on a map. This object is called the Wargame Map Object.

This object can be found in the object list. To insert it, follow these steps:

1. Open MMF2 and create a new file.

2. Make sure you are on the frame editor.

3. Right click on the frame and select Insert Object.

4. Find and locate the Wargame Map Object; the icon is shown in Figure 9.13.

   The cursor changes to a crosshair. Click anywhere on the frame to place the object.

The object doesn't need to be placed on the frame, and because it doesn't interact with the frame, you should move it off the frame's play area. Because this object plays an important role with the creation of the war games, you detailed all of the conditions, actions, and expressions that are available for you to use.

Wargame Map Object Properties

If you click on the Wargame Map Object, you can access the object's properties. You do most of the configuration of the object through the event editor.

Wargame Map
Object

Figure 9.13
The Wargame Map Object icon.

Under the object settings tab, you have these three options:

- **Map Width:** This is the total width of the map. In the examples so far, the width of the map has been 8 tiles.

- **Map Height:** This is the total number of tiles that make up the height of the map. In the example files so far, the height has been 6 tiles high.

- **Even Columns High**: This sets the state of the first column; are the even columns higher or lower than the odd columns? In all of the examples so far, the selection is set so that the even columns (2, 4, and 6) are higher than the odd columns (1, 3, and 5).

You can see the three main Wargame Map Object properties in Figure 9.14. These settings are the only settings that need to be configured within the properties that have a bearing on the movement of enemy units.

Wargame Map Object Conditions

You use a condition when you want to check when a particular event has happened. A number of useful conditions are available for you to use with the Wargame Map Object, as shown here:

- **Compare to cost of movement for a tile:** Allows you to compare the cost of movement at a particular tile.

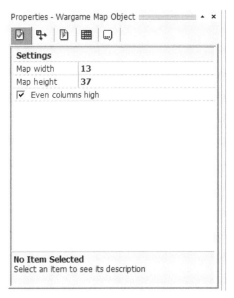

Figure 9.14
The three main configuration properties of the Wargame Map Object.

- **Is tile impassable**: Two types of impassable tiles are in the war games. The first is a terrain tile that the unit cannot move on, for example, water. You are also considering a tile as impassable if another unit is currently located on it. You will need to enter the X and Y coordinates to check whether or not a tile is passable.

- **Does a valid path exist**: Is there currently a valid path? The wargame map object allows you to check whether there is a path and, if so, to run any particular action.

- **Compare to the total cost of the entire path**: Compare the total cost of each movement point in a path to the total cost of the entire path. For example, if you have two tiles, and tile one costs two movement points and the other tile costs one, the total is three movement points. You can then check to see whether the movement cost is equal, more than, and so on.

- **Compare to the total cost from the beginning to a specified movement**: Compare the total cost of a movement in a path from the start to a specified movement location.

- **Compare to the total cost from the beginning to the current movement**: Compare the total cost of a movement from the beginning to the current movement location (index).

- **Compare to the number of movements in the path**: You can compare a number to the number of movements in the path.

- **Compare to the direction of a specified movement**: Check the direction of a particular movement. This allows you to pick a movement index; for example, you could check move four out of a five-movement path.

- **Compare to the direction of the current movement**: Compare the current movement path with a particular direction.

- **End of path reached**: Has the end of the movement path been reached for the current unit? The end of the path is based on the target tile that the programmer specifies for that unit.

Wargame Map Object Actions

You can use a number of actions in the Wargame object, as shown here:

- **Set Map Width**: What is the number of terrain tiles for the map width?

- **Set Map Height**: What is the number of terrain tiles for the map height?

- **Set the cost of movement for a tile**: Allows you to enter a number for the cost of moving on a particular tile.

- **Calculate a path**: Allows you to set the starting point and destination.

- **Next movement in path**: Move to the next movement item so that you can return information about it.

- **Previous movement in path**: Allows you to access information regarding a previous movement in the path.

- **Reset movement to start of path**: If you have been moving through a movement, you can reset the index of the path back to the start.

- **Debugger | Add object to debugger**: The debugger is used to check for programming errors or to check details such as values of an alterable value or counter, and so on. Adding the object to the debugger allows you to check information stored within the object when you are running the application.

- **Destroy**: Destroy the object, which will also destroy the data stored within the object.

Wargame Map Object Expressions

The final set of information that you can obtain from the Wargame Map Object contains the details that you can place into expressions (calculations). This information is basically the information you can retrieve from the object. This information is as follows:

- **Map Properties | Map Width**: Get the map's width value.

- **Map Properties | Map Height**: Get the map's height value.

- **Map Properties | Cost of Movement for a Tile**: Get the cost value from a particular tile.

- **Total Cost | of Entire Path:** Get the cost for the entire path.

- **Total Cost | from Beginning to a Specified Movement:** Get the total movement cost from the start of the movement path to a selected tile.

- **Total Cost | from Beginning to Current Movement:** Get the total movement cost from the start of the movement path to the current movement item.

- **Number of Movements in the Path:** Return the number of movements in the path.

- **Current Movement | Index:** Returns the current movement item index number.

- **Current Movement | Direction:** Returns the current movement item's direction.

- **Current Movement | X Coordinate:** Returns the X coordinate value of the current movement.

- **Current Movement | Y Coordinate:** Returns the Y coordinate value of the current movement.

- **Current Movement | Cost of Movement:** Gets the cost of the current movement.

- **Specified Movement | Direction:** Returns the direction of a specific movement item.

- **Specified Movement | X Coordinate:** Returns the X coordinate of a particular movement.

- **Specified Movement | Y Coordinate:** Returns the Y coordinate of a particular movement.

- **Specified Movement | Cost of Movement:** Gets the cost of movement for a specific tile.

- **Start and Destination Tiles | X Coordinate of Starting Point:** Returns the X coordinate of the starting point.

- **Start and Destination Tiles | Y Coordinate of Starting Point:** Returns the Y coordinate of the starting point.

- **Start and Destination Tiles | X Coordinate of Destination Point**: Returns the X coordinate of the destination.

- **Start and Destination Tiles | Y Coordinate of Destination Point**: Returns the Y coordinate of the destination point.

- **Count | Number of Objects**: The number of objects of this type on the current frame. You aren't likely to have more than 1 in most cases.

- **Retrieve a Fixed Value**: This can be ignored because it is not used within this extension.

More Information about the Wargame Map Object

You need to consider many things in order for the Wargame Map Object to function, and these directly relate to how you use the object.

- First, the object needs to be able to calculate the most cost-effective route. To do so, it needs to know the size of map it is dealing with. You need to tell the object the height and width of the map, which it then uses to create an array. You can work out the size of the map by counting the number of tiles in one row and the number of tiles in one column. The size options are set up within the Wargame Map Object.

- Each tile will have a movement cost associated with it. You must assign a value for the tile each time your own units move to prevent a unit from moving on or over an impassable tile. There may also be another unit placed on a particular tile and the player unit should not move over that tile. For the player movement, you create an array table of the different types of units and the movement effects table. You configure this using an array object.

- The tile movement cost needs to be taken from the array and placed into the Wargame Map Object array. The map has a numbering system that identifies the tiles in a column and row so that data can be stored in the array, such as the movement costs, and then retrieved later in the game. Figure 9.15 shows a snapshot of part of a map; each tile is numbered. These numbers relate to the array slot that will be required when you place movement costs from the standard array.

- You need to tell the Wargame Map Object which tiles the unit cannot move over. You do this by placing a value of 99 for all impassable tiles—for

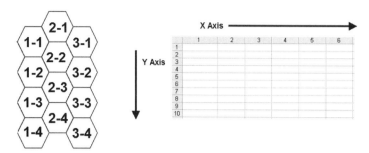

Figure 9.15
The terrain tiles mapping to an array to store information about a particular tile.

example, a tank cannot move over water. You also add a new option that will check for other units. If there is a unit on a tile, you use the value 100.

- At each turn, a unit requires start and destination points. These points allow the Wargame Map Object to figure out the best route. You identify the starting grid, which is where the enemy player is currently placed and its target destination. You do this by using the map numbering system, so a starting tile could be 2-3 and its destination might be 5-6.

- The Wargame Map Object will need to be told to calculate the path. Once that happens, the Wargame Map Object will work out the best route on the map, moving around any tiles that are impassable. Once the Wargame Map Object completes this process, the object will store each move into a memory slot, storing a value of 1, 2, 3, 7, 8, or 9 into the memory slot. The number relates to the direction that the unit has to move to reach its final destination. These numbers directly relate to the NUM pad keys and the direction related to the keys. For example, if you have a three-movement path stored in memory and the values within these slots are 2, 2, and 1, the object's first move will be downward, its second move will be downward, and its final move will be in a downward, left direction.

- You can then scroll through these different path slots to tell the enemy unit to move in the correct direction without needing to worry about the correct path.

- You need to check for when a unit has no more movement points available, and at this point, you are ready to move onto the next unit. Before you move onto the next unit, you need to reload the information about the tiles for the new unit. This is because different units may have different tiles that they can move on.

Enemy Movement Example

In this section of the book, you are going to create the first enemy movement that uses the Wargame Map Object rather than using a set path. You will use a simple map with only one enemy unit, which will reduce the overall number of events that you have to program. You will also have three player units on screen that you can move around to test whether the wargame object is recalculating its path to an object each turn.

Before you load up a premade map with the objects already placed on the frame, you may notice that the code is now becoming larger and taking up more space, and it's becoming harder to read and remember what each bit of code achieves. In your own games, you should definitely consider putting code comments into the event editor to make your code more readable. You can even put blank comment lines in to make your code more readable.

To follow this example, you need to load the file called compute-ai1.mfa, found in the Examples folder on the CD-ROM. You can see an example of this map in Figure 9.16. On this map, you have three player units and one computer-controlled unit; the aim of the computer unit is to reach the city, which is located in tile 2-5.

In the compute-ai1.mfa file, you have already deleted the conditions that automatically move the enemy units; this is so you can replace it with movement

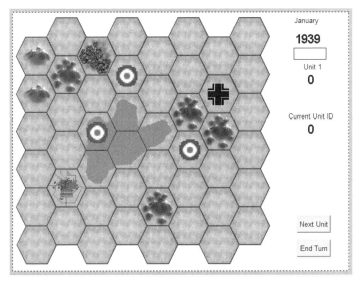

Figure 9.16
The example terrain and unit positions for the movement example.

using the wargame object. So, if you expand the Computer Move group, no code is contained within the group.

Note

> You have hidden the red placeholder markers around the player's units as they are currently not required to be visible. You did this by making the object invisible in the Start of frame condition. You have also removed the enemy movement phase message and the disabling of the two buttons, which makes it easier to ensure that you have a working skeleton of the program before you begin to make the enemy movement.

Pre-Configured Items

To speed up the development of this example, you have already configured additional items in the compute-ai1.mfa file. You should have the example file loaded up and ready to configure player movement; if not, upload the file from the Examples folder on the CD-ROM.

Each tile has been given an ID number; this identifier contains a number value from 1 to 48. If you count all the tiles on the board, you will find 48 in total. These tile ID's are applied from the upper-left going down and then back to the top on the second line, and so on. This value can then be used within conditions to identify a particular tile. When creating the war game with the Wargame Map Object, you need to get the type of tile (Tile Type) and compare this to the computer movement terrain table. With this information, you can retrieve the movement cost, which you need to store in the Wargame Map Object array.

The Wargame Map Object stores the movement cost of a particular tile for each movement turn and is refreshed each time a unit is about to move. This ensures that, if any other unit has moved in-between the time of those units' last turn, it can recalculate the movement path. The Wargame Map Object calculates the movement by using the X and Y number of each tile. This means you have to get the correct X, Y tile to retrieve the data from. To achieve this, two additional alterable value slots for each tile that stores the X and Y number have been pre-configured. These two new alterable values are X Coord and Y Coord. These are already programmed in with the value positions. You can see these new alterable values by clicking any of the terrain tiles. If you click on the upper-left terrain tile, you can see an example of the new pre-configured items as in Figure 9.17.

Three additional objects have been added onto the frame, outside the white play area (top left), an additional array object and the Wargame Map object. The array object stores the computer-controlled terrain movement table. This table contains

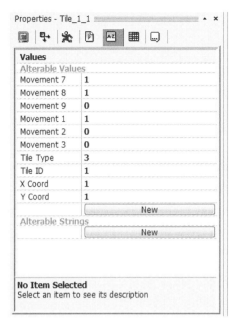

Figure 9.17
The three additional alterable values for each terrain tile.

the cost of moving over certain tiles. The Wargame Map Object will contain various information to work out the A* movement path. Finally, you added a counter that will keep track of which computer player you are currently moving; this enables MMF2 to know what information to retrieve from the movement array.

Setting the Size of the Terrain Map

The first thing you need to do with the computer movement is to tell MMF2, or more precisely the Wargame Map Object, the size of the map that it is dealing with. The Wargame Map Object requires this information to do its movement calculations. As the size of the map isn't going to change throughout the game, you need to set this information only once, and using the Start of Frame condition, which is already programmed in, is the perfect place to enter the actions.

Click on the event editor button to display the code that you have worked on over the last few chapters. As mentioned earlier in this chapter, you have added a number of text comments to the code so that it is easier to understand what each bit of code means.

1. On event line 2, move across until you are directly under the Wargame Map Object.

2. Right click on the action box and select Set map width; when the expression evaluator appears, type the number **8** and click on OK.

3. Right click on the same action box and select Set map height, enter the value of **6** in the expression evaluator, and click on OK.

Setting Up the Computer Movement Array Table

Now that you have set up the size of the map, it's time to configure the effect that the terrain has on the computer units. This table will be stored in the new array, called Computer Table, that has been added to the frame. You can see the computer terrain table in Figure 9.18. In the player movement, where some tiles had a cost of 0, you added a value of 1 to make sure a single move has a cost. In the example, we take into account the normal movement cost for each tile, which is why, in Figure 9.18, moving across grass costs a single movement point. Using a single movement point for all terrain before additional cost modifiers reduces the complexity of your code a little bit and means one less thing to worry about. You could amend the player's movement to use the same system so that you do not have to add a single value for each movement.

Though you have only one unit on the screen at the moment, you have created an effects table that can take into account additional units at a later stage. This capability makes designing your game easier if you find that you need more items before adding the information to MMF2. As you can see in Figure 9.18, Unit 1 will move on most tiles but cannot move on water or large mountains.

To set up the array, you will need to be on the event editor, and you will need to create the movement array at the start of the game. So, again, you can use the Start of Frame event that is already in place.

1. Move across from event line 2 until you are directly under the second array object called Computer table. Right click on the action box and select Clear array.

Unit	Water (1)	Grass (2)	Small Mountain (3)	Large Mountain (4)	Forest (5)
1	99	1	2	99	2
2	99	1	2	99	2
3	99	1	2	99	3
4	99	1	99	99	3

Figure 9.18
The effects movement table for the computer units.

- Clear array
- Write Value 99 to (1, 1)
- Write Value 99 to (1, 2)
- Write Value 99 to (1, 3)
- Write Value 99 to (1, 4)
- Write Value 1 to (2, 1)
- Write Value 1 to (2, 2)
- Write Value 1 to (2, 3)
- Write Value 1 to (2, 4)
- Write Value 2 to (3, 1)
- Write Value 2 to (3, 2)
- Write Value 2 to (3, 3)
- Write Value 99 to (3, 4)
- Write Value 99 to (4, 1)
- Write Value 99 to (4, 2)
- Write Value 99 to (4, 3)
- Write Value 99 to (4, 4)
- Write Value 2 to (5, 1)
- Write Value 2 to (5, 2)
- Write Value 3 to (5, 3)
- Write Value 3 to (5, 4)

Figure 9.19
The array information displayed in the action box for the Computer Table.

2. Now that you've made sure the array doesn't contain any information, you need to write each of the values in Figure 9.18 into the array, so array position 1, 1 would have the value of 99.

3. Right click on the action box for the Computer Table array again and select Write | Write value to XY. The expression evaluator appears. Type the value **99** and click on OK. Then enter the X index, which is **1** and click on OK. Type the Y index value, which is **1** also and click on OK.

   You have saved the first entry in the table in Figure 9.18 in the array. You will now need to add all of the other values, starting with the X index of **1** and Y index of **2**. The completed array table is in Figure 9.19.

Which Computer Unit?

In this example, you have only a single computer-controlled unit, but thinking ahead for larger games requires some way of keeping track of which unit is being moved. This will become clearer when you need to transfer values from various units into the Wargame Map Object. You have the counter, called Enemy Unit Selected, in place already, and for now you need to configure it for a single unit.

1. Click on the Event editor button.

   You need to set the maximum number, which will store the maximum number of computer-controlled units on screen, in this case it's 1.

2. On event line 2, move across until you are directly under the Enemy Unit Selected counter. Right click on the action box, choose Set maximum value, enter 1 in the expression evaluator, and click on OK.

3. On the same action box, choose Set counter, and then in the expression evaluator type the value of 1 and click on the OK button.

You must change these values if you want your game to contain more than one computer-controlled unit.

Creating the Code

In this part of the book, you create the code that will be used to move the computer-controlled players. A number of events are required to move the single unit you have placed on the screen, but the code is very much reduced because you are using the Wargame Map Object. If you get stuck at any stage, you can also look at the completed example called computer-ai1-complete.mfa, which is on the CD-ROM in the Examples folder.

Adding the Unit 1 Movement Group

Before you begin writing the code, you need to make sure that all the required groups for the computer movement are already set up. At the moment, in the example file, you will find a group called Computer Move. This is the main group for handling the set up of the computer-controlled movement, which at the moment is blank. You also have another group under Computer Move called Enemy Unit 1 (expand the Computer Move group to see this additional group). This group is required to set up any code-specific initialization code to Unit 1. Finally, you need to create another group under the Enemy Unit 1 group that will handle the actual screen moves. Keeping the code in different groups makes the code easier to manage, and because it runs from top down, make sure that code can be switched off when required so that it doesn't run when it's not supposed to.

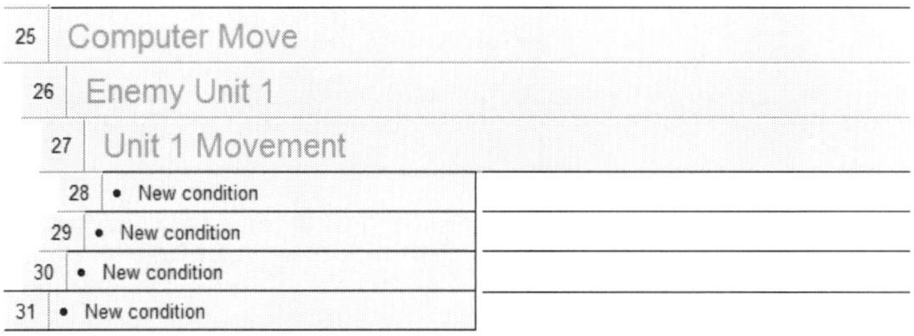

25	Computer Move
26	Enemy Unit 1
27	Unit 1 Movement
28	• New condition
29	• New condition
30	• New condition
31	• New condition

Figure 9.20
The groups you need for computer movement.

Now you are ready to create the new group:

1. Make sure that the group Computer Move is expanded and that you can see the Enemy Unit 1 group.

2. Make sure the Enemy Unit 1 group is expanded so that you can see the New condition text for that group.

3. Right click on the number 27, which should be under the Enemy Unit 1 group (remember this number may be different if other groups are expanded). Select Insert | A group of events.

4. When the Group Events dialog box appears, type **Unit 1 Movement** as the name of the group. Unselect Active when frame starts and click on the OK button. Your three groups should now look like Figure 9.20.

Coding the Computer Move Group

Before the computer can figure out the best movement, you need to load the movement cost into the Wargame Map Object array for each tile. To handle this, in theory, you would have to write 48 different events with an action in each one, which could end up being a lot of work to complete a simple logic task.

To drastically reduce the amount of code you need to write, saving time and making the code easier to read, you can use loops to complete a task that is repetitive. A loop is a task that requires you to do a similar process over and over again for a certain amount of time. In this case, you need to create a loop that will run 48 times; this loop is required to get information from every hexagon terrain tile and compare the Tile Type with the unit you are currently interested in. The loop returns a movement value for the unit type moving over the particular tile. You then need to place this information in the correct X, Y slot of the Wargame Map Object, which then stores the movement cost for each tile.

Using a loop will reduce the code required for this process down to two events rather than the original 48 that could have been used. Hopefully, you can see how useful a loop is in reducing the amount of code in your programs.

When creating a loop, you need to complete two things. First, you need to create a condition that starts the loop, a start of frame condition, for example. For the action, you need to tell MMF2 the array that you are going to start and how many loops you require. You then need another event that tells MMF2 which loop to select and the actions to run 48 times. As you are going to run this process 48 times, one for each tile, you can also place different information in each loop. MMF2 keeps track of the current loop by using a loop index; this is a value that is the current loop number.

You are actually going to create two loops in the Computer Move group, the first to place the tile movement cost into the Wargame Map Object, the second array to write the value of 100 into any tile that has a player unit located on it.

You also need to create a single event that will enable the Enemy Unit 1 group, which will handle calculating a path for the computer unit.

Note

The values 99 and 100 signify to the Wargame Map Object that a tile is impassable.

Note

The loop index is the number used to keep track of the current number that the loop is on. For example, you might say you want a process to run five times, and each time it runs (looping), the index increases. The loop index in MMF2 begins at zero, so when setting up a loop to fill particular data, you need to be careful that you run it enough times. In this example, you want to fill 48 tiles with information; setting the loop to run 48 times will only fill 47 items because the loop begins from 0. You can rectify this within the code though so that setting it to 48 loops will begin from one rather than zero.

Setting Up the Loops   First, you will need to configure the tile array, which needs to run 48 times. You can run this event when the group is activated, and using the On group activation condition is useful when you want something to run only once every time the group is enabled.

1. Right click on event line number 26, which is the Enemy Unit 1 group, and select Insert | A new event. Then Click on the Special object and choose Group of events | On group activation. This creates the event directly under the Computer Move group.

Now you need to create the action that configures how many times the loop will run and its required name.

2. Move across from the new condition on event line 26 until you are under the Special Conditions object, right click on the action box, and select Fast Loops | Start Loop. The expression evaluator appears, two quote marks are in the edit box; within this box, type the name of the loop, which in this case is **ArrayFill**. Click on OK, type the number **48**, and click on OK.

You are now ready to create the second loop. The second loop will handle checking of all player units and placing the value 100 into the Wargame Map array so that the program knows not to move onto that terrain tile.

3. Right click on the event number 27 and Insert | A new event. Then Click on the Special object and choose Group of events | On group activation. You will now have two events before the Enemy Unit 1 group.

4. Move across to the Special Conditions object and select Fast Loops | Start. In the expression evaluator, type Player as the name of the loop, click on OK, and when MMF2 asks for the number of loops, type the number **3** and click on OK.

You know only three player units are on screen, so it is a simple process to work that out. In your own games, you would need to change this value to the number of units on screen.

The next event is the first of the two loops running. This runs the actions to place information into the Wargame Map Object. For the event, you need two conditions, the first being the condition to see if the loop ArrayFill has started, which is what you did in event line 26. The second condition checks the alterable value stored in H of the Good.Group (all of the tiles). The condition then checks when the value equals the loop index, which starts from 0 to 47, and you add a value of **1** onto the end so that the loop will include all 48 tiles. The H alterable value is the tile ID number; all tiles have a unique ID. This means the loop will go through each tile in turn; the actions then apply to the tile that is currently equal to the loop index.

5. Right click on the event number 28, which is the Enemy Unit 1 group. Select Insert | A new event. Select the Special object from the pop-up menu and choose On Loop. Enter the name of the loop that you wish to check is running, which in this case is ArrayFill. Click on OK.

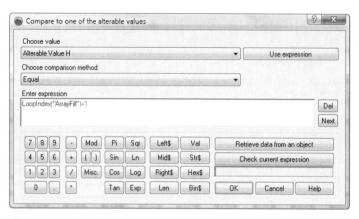

Figure 9.21
The expression evaluator with the comparison of an alterable value.

6. Right click on the condition you just created on event line 28, which is On Loop ArrayFill and select Insert. Right click on the Good.Group and select Values | Compare to one of the alterable values. The expression evaluator appears; in the drop-down box, select Alterable value H. Leave the comparison method as Equal and, in the Enter expression box, click on Retrieve data from an object. The New Expression dialog box appears.

7. Click on the Special object and select Fast Loops | Get Loop Index. An expression will fill the bottom edit box the expression evaluator, and within the expression, it will ask for the name of the loop. Highlight <Enter name of the loop> and replace it with **"ArrayFill"**, including the surrounding quotes. You need to add the value **+1** onto the end of this expression. You can see how it should look in Figure 9.21. Click on OK to save the information to the event editor.

Now you have set the event to run a loop based on the Group.Good alterable value of H, (the Tile ID range 1 to 48) which is equal to the loop index +1. You now need to create the actions. The event will run these actions on the object that is returned as being true from the two conditions, so in each turn, it will apply the action to each of the 48 terrain tiles.

You need the Wargame Map Object to work out a movement path through the tiles; to do this, you have to specify an X and a Y value, these being the grid values (for example, 1-1 being the top left of the map). The Wargame Map Object then requires the cost to move on that tile. Using this information, the Wargame Map Object can then create a path of the best route.

You will take the X and Y from the Good.Group, because each terrain tile has two alterable values that store their X and Y values; the alterable values are I and J. You can get this value because the event will step through each of the 48 tiles in turn retrieving all of the different values stored in that alterable value's slot. Once you have placed that information into the Wargame Map Object, you need to find the cost of the tile. You can do that only if you know the unit movement cost for that tile, which is stored in the Computer table array. Remember, this array has an X and Y set of values; the first is the tile type, and the second set of values is the unit number. The table created earlier has a row that contains the values for each unit's movement cost on a different set of tiles. The Wargame Map Object can retrieve the X and Y values from the array. The X relates to the tile type value from the alterable value, while the Y is taken from the counter that currently has a value of 1, which is the only computer unit you have on screen.

I hope this makes sense because it can seem a little complex when taking a set of values from one object and placing them in another. This gives MMF2 a lot of power because you can retrieve data from most objects. If you are still not sure about obtaining and setting value, hopefully, as you walk through adding the data, what the process is doing will become apparent. Remember to refer to Figures 9.15 and 9.16 for the map tiles X and Y and the computer movement table X and Y information.

1. Move across to the right of event line 28, until you are directly under the Wargame Map Object, right click, and select Set the cost of movement for a tile.

2. The expression evaluator appears asking for the X tile coordinate. As you are looping, you want it to specify a different value each time, and this value is from Group.Good, which is a group of objects rather than a constant single value. Select the expression box, click on Retrieve data from an object, choose the Group.Good object, choose Values | Values A to M | Retrieve Value I, and click on OK.

3. You are now asked for the Y coordinate. You need the Good.Group alterable value that represents this value in the terrain tiles, which is the J value. Click on the Retrieve data from object button, click on the Group.Good object, choose Values | Values A to M | Retrieve Value J, and then click on OK.

4. Lastly, you are asked for the movement cost for this tile. Click on the Retrieve data from an object button, select the Computer table array, and choose Read value from XY position.

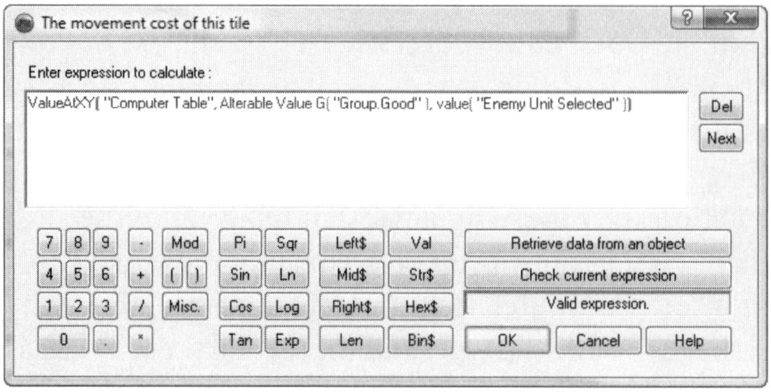

Figure 9.22
The Movement cost of the tile expression.

The expression will be automatically entered, but you will need to replace the placeholders in the expression for the X and Y offset. These two values will return a single movement value from the array.

5. Select the >Enter X offset< in the expression and then click on Retrieve data from an object. Right click on the Good.Group and select Values I Values A to M I Retrieve Value G (G is the tile ID alterable value).

6. You will be back at the expression evaluator; highlight the >Enter Y offset< and click on Retrieve data from an object. Find the Enemy Unit Selected object and click on Current Value. You will return to the expression evaluator. You can see the expression which is shown in Figure 9.22. Click on the OK button to save this information to the event editor.

Now, you need to work on the second loop, which uses the Player loop. This works out which tiles have a player unit overlapping them, and if they do, MMF2 stores the value of 100 into the movement slot for that tile in the Wargame Map Object. You have already set the general movement cost on the tiles, but if there is currently a unit on the tile, MMF2 will overwrite that value with 100. Storing 100 in the Wargame Map Object allows you to indentify another tile that the unit cannot move on. You will use the stored value for the A* path movement calculation.

7. Right click on the event line number 29, select Insert I A new event. Click on the Special object and select On loop; then, in the expression evaluator type **"Player"** and click on the OK button.

Now you need to add the second condition to the same event. This process is similar to what you did in the previous loop example. You will be checking the alterable value of C against the loop index of the Player loop. This will loop through all three player units checking which tile they are on and use an action to set the value to the Wargame Map Object.

8. Right click on the condition that is on event line 29, which should be On loop Player and select Insert. Click on the Group.Player object and choose Alterable Values | Compare to one of the Alterable values. The expression evaluator appears. In the first drop-down box, select Alterable Value C. Leave the second drop-down box as Equal. In the Enter expression box, click on the Retrieve data from an object button.

9. Now, select the Special object and then Fast Loops | Get loop index. The edit box will be filled with an expression, but it will not be complete because it is asking for the name of the loop. So, select the >Enter name of the loop< text and type **"Player"** including the quotes. At the end of the expression, type **+1** to add one onto the loop index, because the loop starts from 0. Your expression will now look like Figure 9.23. Click on the OK button to save this information to the event editor.

Note

Alterable value C is the player's unit ID. This is a unique number from 1 to 3. If any additional units were added, these new units would become 4, 5, and so on.

You still have one more condition to add to the event, and this is to check whether an object from the Group.Player group is overlapping any of the

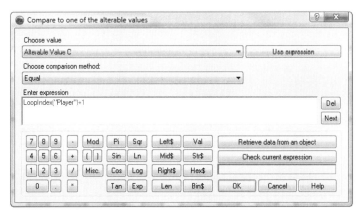

Figure 9.23
The expression for comparing alterable value C.

Group.Good terrain tiles. This is the condition that will pick the correct Group.Good object and allow you to write information into the Wargame Map Object using each of the selected terrain tiles in turn. Without this condition, this whole event will not work because it will not know which terrain object it's storing information about.

10. Right click on the alterable value comparison with the loop index condition on event line 29. Then select the Insert option, right click the Group.Player group, and then Collisions | Overlapping another object. When the Test a Collision dialog box appears, choose the Group.Good object and click on OK.

You have completed all of the conditions for this event, and it is time to add the action. The action will set the movement cost of a particular tile to 100; this is the value you are using to specify that a player unit is on a particular tile. Because you are using a loop that is stepping through each of the tiles one by one, the loop checks the terrain tile the object is on and then can use that as a reference to which tile the Wargame Map Object is asking for.

1. Move across to the right of this event, right click the action box under the Wargame Map Object and select Set the cost of movement for a tile.

   The expression evaluator appears asking for the X coordinate of the slot that you want to fill in the Wargame Map Object. You get this information from the Group.Good object that is being overlapped by the player unit.

2. Click on the Retrieve data from an object button, select the Group.Good object, and choose Values | Values A to M | Retrieve Alterable Value I. Click on the OK button.

   Now, you need to enter the Y coordinate for the data slot in the Wargame Map Object.

3. Click on the Retrieve data from an object button, select the Group.Good object, and then select Values | Values A to M | Retrieve Alterable Value J. Click on the OK button.

   Last, you are asked to enter a value for this particular tile.

4. Enter the value of 100 and then click on OK to save this information to the event editor.

   You need one final event for the Computer Move group before you begin to program on the two groups specific to enemy unit 1. You use the On group activation event to run when the group is activated, and at this point, you set the position and visibility of the Computer Movement message box. Then you will enable the next group, which is Enemy Unit 1.

First, you need to create the new event line.

5. Right click on the event line number 30; then select Insert | A new event. The New condition dialog box appears. Then right click on the Special object. From the pop-up menu, select Group of events | On group activation.

Now, you need to add the actions for this event.

6. Move to the right of this new event until you are directly under the Sub-Application object. Right click on the action box and choose Position | Select position. The Select Position dialog box appears; type **220** for the X coordinate and **382** for the Y coordinate. Click on the OK button.

7. Right click on the same action box for the Sub-Application to add another action. Choose the Visibility | Show option.

8. Move directly under the Special Conditions object on the same event line (On group activation), right click the blank action box, and choose Group of events | Activate. The Activate dialog box appears, select (7) – Enemy Unit 1 and click on OK.

You can see these events and actions in Figure 9.24.

Coding the Enemy Unit 1 Group

You now need to begin coding for the Enemy Unit 1 group. This group handles a few initialization tasks before you start moving the actual computer unit on screen. Separating the initialization tasks from the actual movement is handy because you may need to do more global initialization tasks, maybe for all computer units; and placing it in a particular group could make your programming task harder to complete or even mean you are duplicating code.

Two events in this group handle whether the particular unit has reached its target. If the unit hasn't reached the destination tile, the events will still allow the unit to be moved each turn. You have a third event that doesn't need to be in this program, but it's there to help you test data being placed into the Wargame Map array. You will now look at each event in more detail and add its code to the event editor.

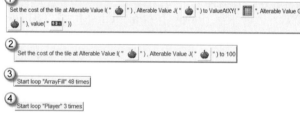

Figure 9.24
The Computer Move groups events.

The first event in the Enemy Unit 1 group has three conditions. The first condition checks for group activation, which, as previously mentioned, is great for controlling how often a set of actions will run. You then check to see if the Enemy_Unit1 object is overlapping the Group.Good object. The final condition checks whether the alterable value of H from the Good.Group, which represents the Tile ID, is not equal to 11. Remember that each terrain tile is numbered from 1 to 48; tile 11 is the destination tile for the computer-controlled unit. This means that you can check each turn if the unit is on the city tile; in this case, you are saying that it hasn't stopped on this tile.

Now, add the first condition for the new event.

Make sure the Enemy Unit 1 group is expanded so you can see the Unit 1 Movement group below it.

1. Right click on the event number 32, which will be the Unit 1 Movement group, because you want to place the event above it. Select Insert | A new event. Choose the Special Conditions object and then pick Group of events | On group activation.

2. Right click on the condition you just added and select Insert. Click on the Enemy_Unit1 object and select Collisions | Overlapping another object. When the Test a collision dialog box appears, pick the Group.Good object and click on Ok.

3. Right click on the condition you just added, select Insert, then select the Special Conditions object and Compare two general values. The expression evaluator appears. Select the first edit box and click on Retrieve data from an object. From the New Expression dialog box, right click the Group.Good object and then select Values | Values A to M | Retrieve Alterable Value H. Change the drop-down box that currently displays Equal to display Different. In the bottom box, replace the 0 value with the value of 11. Your expression evaluator box will look like Figure 9.25. Click on the OK button to save this information to the event editor.

   You have completed the event that checks that the computer unit hasn't reached its target. You will now add the actions that will display the next unit and End Turn buttons. You will calculate the path for the unit using the Wargame Map Object and then you will activate the Unit 1 Movement group so that you can initiate the unit's movement.

4. Move to the right of event line 32, where you just created your three-condition event, until you are directly under the Button object. Right click the action box and select Disable.

5. Move under Button 2 on the same event line and select Disable.

   Both buttons are disabled when you click on the End of Turn button when running the game.

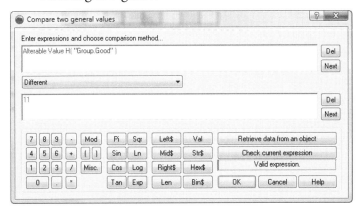

Figure 9.25
Checking that alterable value H does not equal 11.

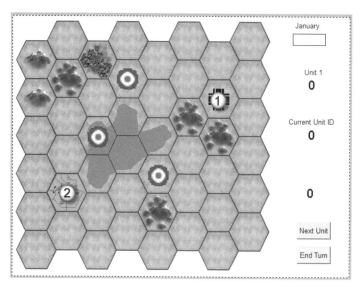

Figure 9.26
The starting location shown as 1, and the destination shown as 2.

You now need to tell the Wargame Map Object some information so that it can calculate the path that the unit will take to move from its starting position and arrive at its target location. You have only one unit, so you can use a manual process for a particular grid position.

If you look at Figure 9.26, you will see on the map that the computer unit is located on tile 7-2, and the destination tile is 2-5.

To calculate the path the unit will take:

1. Move across from event line 32 until you are under the Wargame Map Object. Right click on the action box and select Calculate a path. You now see the expression evaluator and are asked for the starting point's X coordinate. Type the value **7** and click on the OK button. You are then asked for the starting Y coordinate; enter the value **2** and click on OK.

2. You now need to create the next event, which has two conditions. The first checks whether the computer unit is overlapping a Group.Good object, which, of course, it will be. The second condition checks to see if the alterable value of H for the selected computer unit equals 11, which checks that the computer unit is overlapping the city terrain tile and has reached its final destination.

3. Right click on the event number 33 and select Insert | A new event. Select the Enemy_Unit1 object and then Collisions | Overlapping another object. The test a collision dialog box appears. Select the Group.Good object and click on the OK button.

4. Right click on the condition you just added and select Insert. Choose the Special Conditions object and Compare two general values. The expression evaluator appears. In the first edit box, make sure that the first edit box is highlighted and click on Retrieve data from an object. Then choose the Group.Good object and select Values | Values A to M | Retrieve Alterable Value H. The comparison drop-down can be left as Equal. Then type the value **11** in the bottom edit box and click on the OK button to save the information to the event editor.

   You have now added both conditions to the event line, so it is time to add the actions. This event checks when the computer unit has completed its moves. In this example, you have only one unit, so when it completes its move, the computer movement is complete. First, you need to enable both buttons, which ensures that the players can move their own units and end the turn again once they finish moving. You need to hide the Computer Moving message box, because it will not be moving the computer units. Since you only have one computer unit, you need to deactivate all of the groups involved in the computer movement—in this case, three different groups: Unit 1 Movement, Enemy Unit 1, and Computer Move.

5. Move across from event line 33 until you are under the Button object. Right click the action box and select Enable.

6. Follow the same process for the Button 2 object and enable it.

7. Move across until you are under the Sub-Application object; then from the action box, choose Visibility | hide.

8. Again, on the same event line, right click on the Special Conditions action box and choose Group of events | Deactivate. When the Deactivate dialog box appears, choose (8) – Unit 1 Movement and click on OK.

9. On the same action box (Special Conditions), select Group of events | Deactivate; then pick (7) – Enemy Unit 1 and click on OK.

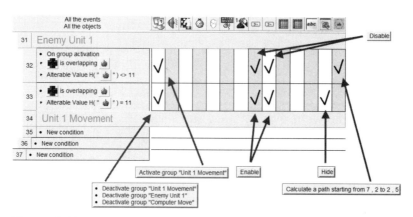

Figure 9.27
The Enemy Unit 1 group code.

10. Right clicking on the same action box again, select Group of events | Deactivate; then select (6) – Computer Move and click on OK.

You have now completed the code for the Enemy Unit 1 group, and you can see the code in Figure 9.27.

Coding the Unit 1 Movement Group

Everything is in place to begin programming the actual movement for the computer unit. You have already calculated the path the unit needs to make, and this information is stored within the Wargame Map Object.

If you look at Figure 9.26, you will see the starting position and the end position that the unit needs to move on. Taking into account that the unit cannot move over other player units or the mountain, the Wargame Map Object has two sensible routes to use. These routes are displayed in Figure 9.28.

Figure 9.28 shows the two routes available as being the shortest, most cost-effective routes; the top route takes nine movement points and eight steps, while the bottom route (route 2) costs nine movement points and nine steps. In many cases, the Wargame Map Object will be able to decide the best route based on the cost of the route; in a case where the cost is the same, the Wargame Map object will also take into account the number of tiles. For this example, the top route is more cost-effective because it takes only eight tile steps.

When the calculation of the route is created, the Wargame Map Object will store the direction of each step in a number of memory slots, which you can retrieve.

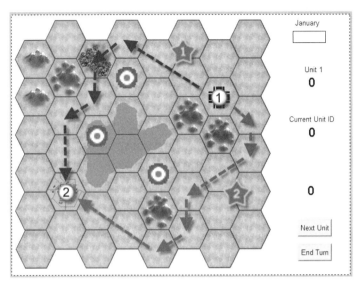

Figure 9.28
Two possible routes for the Wargame Map Object to select for the unit.

In the case of Figure 9.28, the Wargame Map Object will store the following direction numbers:

> 7, 7, 7, 1, 2, 1, 2, 2

You can then go through each movement and compare the numbers, and knowing what the number is, you can then make the unit move in that direction. This process is the same type of process you used to move the player's unit. You checked which key the player pressed, compared it to the number of movement points available, and then moved the unit in the right direction.

You need to add a number of events for the unit movement, and you need to do the following:

- Set up a condition that runs every second and that will then step through the Wargame Map Object's stored movement slots. You can then check for the direction of each movement slot.

- Set up a set of events that run for every 1 second, this means that the object doesn't automatically jump to the final position, but moves as though it were stepping one tile at a time. Within this event, you also check the current direction against the number pad keys. If the current direction equaled 2, for example, you would need to place an action to move the unit object down the screen.

■ Create an End of path reached condition that handles enabling the buttons, and disabling the groups because they are no longer needed.

First, you need to create the event that will run every second and then step through each of the movements stored in the movement path.

1. Make sure that the Unit 1 Movement group is expanded. Click on the New condition text on event line 35 under the Unit 1 Movement group. Select the Timer object and select Every. When the Every dialog box appears, it will already be configured by default for 1 second. This is exactly what you require, so click on the OK button to save this information to the event editor.

2. Move across to the right of this new event until you are under the Wargame Map object, right click on the action box, and select Next movement in path.

   Now you have set up the process for the program to step through each of the movements in turn. You now need to set up each of the six movement directions.

3. Click on the New condition text on event line 36. Select the Timer object and then choose Every; a timer based dialog box appears already configured with one second; this is what you require so click on the OK button.

4. You need to add another condition on the same event line. Right click on the condition on event line 36 and select Insert. Select the Special object and then choose Compare two general values. The expression evaluator appears. Select the first edit box and then click on Retrieve data from an object, find the Wargame Map Object, and then pick Current Movement | Direction. The drop-down box is set to Equal, which is fine. In the lower of the two edit boxes, type the value 1. Your expression evaluator will look like Figure 9.29. Click on OK to save it to the event editor.

   You will now set the only action for this event, which is to move the unit in a downward, left direction.

5. Move across from event line 36 until you are directly under the Enemy_ Unit1 object, right click the action box, and select Position | Select position. The Select Position dialog box appears. Click on the Relative to radio button;

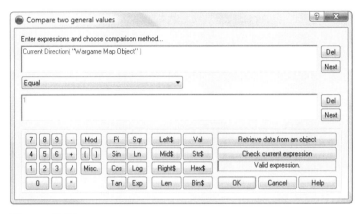

Figure 9.29
Comparing the current movement direction to a value.

then when asked to choose an object, find and select the Enemy_Unit1 object and click on OK. This takes you back to the Select Position dialog box. Type the values **-58** and **35** in to the X and Y coordinate boxes and click on OK.

Now, it is time to set up the second movement.

6. Click on the New condition text on event line 37. Select the Special Conditions object, choose Limit conditions | Restrict actions, and click on the OK button.

7. Right click on the condition on event line 37 and select Insert. Select the Special object and then choose Compare two general values. The expression evaluator appears. Select the first edit box and then click on Retrieve data from an object, find the Wargame Map Object, and then choose Current Movement | Direction. The drop-down box is set to Equal, which is fine. In the lower of the two edit boxes, type the value **2**. Click on the OK button.

8. Move across until you are directly under the Enemy_Unit1 object, right click the action box, and select Position | Select position. The Select Position dialog box appears. Click on the Relative to radio button, and then, the Choose an object dialog box appears. Find and select the Enemy_Unit1 object and click on OK. This takes you back to the Select Position dialog box. Type the values **0** and **70** in the X and Y coordinate boxes and click on OK.

Follow the same process for the event lines 38 to 41. When adding the condition for each event, make sure the next direction is 3, then 7, 8, and

Table 9.1 Movement Position for the Enemy_Unit1
for Event Lines 38, 39, 40, and 41

Event Line	X Position	Y Position
38	58	35
39	−58	−35
40	0	−70
41	58	−35

then 9. You should be used to the positions of the objects now, but, if not, you can refer to Table 9.1 to see how to configure them.

You now need to add one final event that checks to see if the end of the path has been reached and then to enable the buttons, hide the message, and disable the movement groups.

1. Click on the New condition text on event line 42. Select the Wargame Map Object and then End of path reached?

2. Move across from this event until you are under the Button object, right click the action box, and select Enable.

3. Move under the Button 2 object on the same event line and select Enable.

4. Move under the Sub-Application object and select Visibility|hide.

5. Move under the Special Conditions object and choose Group of events| Deactivate; then from the dialog box, choose (8) – Unit 1 Movement and click on OK.

6. Still under the Special Conditions object, choose Group of events| Deactivate; then from the Deactivate dialog box, choose (7) – Enemy Unit 1 and click on OK.

7. Again under the Special Conditions object, choose Group of events| Deactivate, select (6) – Computer Move, and click on the OK button.

   You have now completed the code for the basic movement using the Wargame Map Object. Run the program and click on the End Turn button. Watch the computer unit follow the route around the player through the forest and then down into the city.

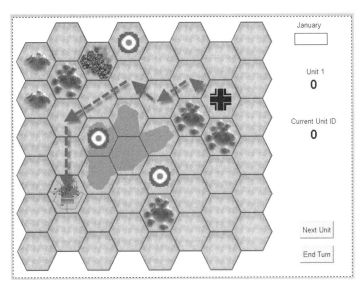

Figure 9.30
The new route for the computer unit if another unit moves out of the way.

If you want to see A* working its magic, move Unit2 before pressing the End Turn button to see the unit take a different route. For example, move Unit2 up one tile; then the computer unit will take the quicker route below it. You can see this new route in Figure 9.30.

Implementing Movement Points

You may have noticed in the previous example that the computer-controlled unit moved from the starting location to the end location in one turn. In many cases, it might have taken a few turns for the unit to reach its destination. At the moment, the code allows only one unit to move directly from a single point to the end point, which gives the computer an unfair advantage.

Each of the computer units has two alterable values for the starting movement and the current movement. This configuration is the same configuration as in the player units, so you will be implementing a similar system for the computer units. The main difference between the player movement and the computer movement is that you need to take the Wargame Map Object into account for aspects of moving a unit and the cost of moving onto the next tile. For the player movement, you had to use a number of placeholder objects around the unit that was moving as the player could move in any of the six directions.

To implement movement points for the computer, you need to do the following:

- Set the current movement value for the computer unit to the starting value. In this case, the unit has five movement points, and it will place the value into the alterable value B, which is used to count down the number of movement points available. These movement points need to be reset at each turn.

- Rather than program in a constant starting position for the computer unit, you set the current position of the unit to the new starting position. At the moment, the Wargame Map Object is told that the starting position for the unit is 7, 2. This is not a problem if you are setting up a single movement path from position A to position B. In larger games where you may want to give the unit a set of orders, always having its starting point as 7, 2 could cause the Wargame Map Object calculation problems. If the unit is somewhere else on the map, the Wargame Map Object will continue to calculate its path from 7, 2 regardless of its current position on screen. This means Wargame Map Object could calculate a different route from the route it may take if it is somewhere else. You can solve this problem quite easily by setting the starting position information for the Wargame Map Object to be the location at which the object is currently located.

- You will add some additional conditions into events in the Unit 1 Movement group to check the current movement value for the unit and compare it to the terrain tile it will move onto next. You will be able to take into account the number of movement points a unit is given at the start of each turn. Enemy_Unit1 has been given five movement points in its alterable Starting Movement point slot. You will also need to add an action to reduce the number of movement points available; this step ensures that the unit doesn't continue to move to the end location if it doesn't have enough points.

- You already have an End of path reached event, but you also need to take into account when the unit reaches the furthest point it can go on its movement point allocation, which may not be the end point. Once the unit's movement point is not higher than the points to move on to the next terrain tile, its movement turn has effectively ended. At this point, you need to reenable the buttons and remove the computer moving message.

■ Once these conditions and actions are complete, run the program. You will notice that the Enemy_Unit1 reacts to where your player units are located, but if you move your player units when you click on the End of Turn button, these units do not get their original movement points back. If you have used all of the unit's movement points, it will not be able to move again. The unit cannot move because you changed how the groups run in the previous examples to take into account the computer movement. You need to enable the End of Turn group, which resets the player unit's movement numbers.

Resetting Current Movement Points

You need to load a pre-programmed file from the CD-ROM, the file is located in the Examples folder and is called compute-ai2.mfa. This file contains the code you have been working on to get the Enemy_Unit1 moving from a starting point to a destination point.

Once you load the file, make sure all groups are collapsed before you begin any work, as this may change the line numbering used to highlight which line you need to make changes to.

1. Expand the Computer Move group. The Enemy_Unit1 alterable values are already configured, as shown in Figure 9.31. Figure 9.31 shows the only computer unit you have on the frame as having a starting movement of 5 in alterable value slot A, and a current movement value of 0 in alterable value slot B. When MMF2 enters the Computer Move group, it will be because the computer is starting a new move for the computer unit. Once you click on the End of Turn button, the computer movement will have all its available movement points. Once the computer completes the unit movement, that particular unit might have only a single or no movement points left. You need to reset the Current Movement Value to ensure that the unit can move again. You do this process at the start of the group. You copy the total number of points in the Starting Movement value slot to the Current Movement value. This process is the same one you used for the player unit.

2. Move across from event line 26, which is the first of the two On group activation events, until you are directly under the Enemy_Unit1 object.

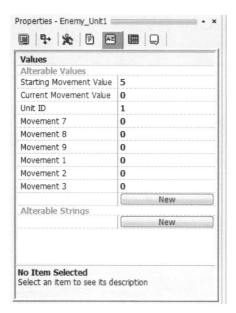

Figure 9.31
The alterable values of the Enemy_Unit1 object.

3. Right click on the action box and choose Alterable Values | Set. The expression evaluator appears. In the drop-down box, pick Current Movement Value, highlight the 0 in the expression box, and click on Retrieve data from an object. When the New Expression dialog box appears, find the Enemy_Unit1 object, right click on it, and select Values | Values A to M | Retrieve Starting Movement Value. When you are back at the expression evaluator, click on the OK button to save the information to the event editor.

Now, every time the Computer Move group is enabled, it will place the value 5 in to the Current Movement Value, which is the alterable value slot that you will use to calculate whether you have enough points to move on certain tiles, by subtracting each move from the total.

Changing the Starting Location Tile

At the moment, you have a "Set in stone" starting location of 7, 2. This means that every time the Computer Move group is enabled, which will be every time the player finishes moving and pressing the End Turn button. Of course, as discussed earlier, the problem in a proper war game is that units will have most likely moved from this starting location, which may cause the Wargame Map Object to calculate the best route incorrectly. You will also have the same problem with the end route at some point in the future with the game because you may want the unit to have different orders throughout the game; and at the moment the destination tile is set in stone. For now, you amend the starting location because it has the most impact in the game.

1. Make sure the group Enemy_Unit 1 is expanded.

2. Move to the right of event line 32, until you are directly under the Wargame Map Object. This is where the path for the wargame object is configured.

3. Right click on the action check mark that is already present and then select the Edit option. The expression evaluator appears with the X coordinate of the starting location, which is shown as 7.

   You want to get the current X coordinate location of the tile that the unit is currently overlapping. As you already have an overlapping condition on the Group.Good within the event, you can return the value from the tile that the unit is placed on.

4. Highlight the number 7 in the expression evaluator expression box and then click on Retrieve data from an object. Find the Good.Group object, right click on it, and from the menu choose Values | Values A to M | Retrieve Alterable Value I. Click on the OK button.

   You will now be asked for the Y coordinate starting location, which is currently set to the value of 2.

5. Highlight the value 2 in the expression box, click on the Retrieve data from an object button, right click on the Group.Good object, and select Values | Values A to M | Retrieve Alterable Value J. Click on the OK button.

6. You will now be asked the destination X coordinate; you don't want to change this right now, so click on the OK button. You will then be asked the Y coordinate destination; again, you don't want to amend this, so click on the OK button to complete editing the action.

   You can see the amended action in Figure 9.32.

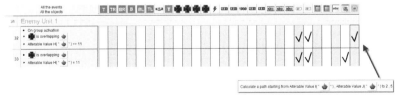

Figure 9.32
The updated action for the starting location for the path of the Wargame Map Object.

Unit 1 Movement Group Changes

The next part of the changes requires us to add some new conditions to the events, add a new event, and move one of the current events. You shall start with amending the current events.

You are going to amend events 36 to 41, which are the events that handle moving the unit based on the movement direction value from the Wargame Map Object. The first two conditions in each of these events are fine, and you will add a new single condition to each line. This new condition will check the current movement value alterable value of the Enemy_Unit1 object and compare it to the movement cost of the next tile. If the movement cost of the Current Movement alterable value is greater or equal to the cost of the next tile, then the event will still run. This means that the actions to move the unit will work only if the unit has enough points to move on the next tile. You are going to use the Compare two general values condition to check the values.

1. Right click on the last condition of event line 36 in the Unit 1 Movement group and select Insert.

2. The New Condition dialog box appears. Choose the Special object and then Compare two general values. The Compare two general values dialog box appears.

3. Select the first of the two expression boxes and click on Retrieve data from an object. You need to find the current movement value of Enemy_Unit1, so in the New Expression dialog, box find the Enemy_Unit1, right click on it, and select Values | Values A to M | Retrieve current movement value.

4. In the drop-down box, which currently is set to Equal, change Equal to Greater or Equal.

   You need to compare the current movement value with the movement cost for the tile that the unit will move onto. The easiest way to do this is find out the index of the current tile and then add one to it to get the index and its value of the next movement.

5. In the lower of the two expression boxes, highlight the 0 and click on Retrieve data from an object. Find and right click on the Wargame Map Object. Then from the pop-up menu, choose Specified movement | Cost of movement. The expression box will be filled, but MMF2 is now expecting the Index of the movement. Select the >Index of movement< text and then

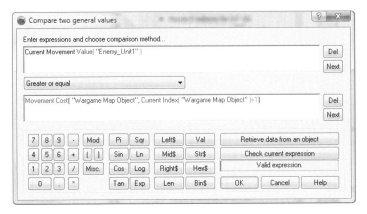

Figure 9.33
The expression to retrieve the next movement slot movement cost.

click on Retrieve data from an object. Right click on the Wargame Map Object in the Expression dialog box and choose Current movement | Index.

6. This expression gets the current movement index, when actually you need the next available one stored in the slot. So, in-between the two brackets at the end of the expression, type **+1**. You can see the full expression in Figure 9.33. Click on the OK button to save this to the event editor.

You can see the new condition in the event in Figure 9.34.

At the moment, when the event is true, the only action you have is to move the unit in the correct direction. To make accurate comparisons between the current movement points available and the cost of the movement for the next tile, you need to make sure that when the unit has moved, you reduce the current movement points by the tile cost they have just moved onto.

1. Move across from event line 36 where you just added the new condition, until you are directly under the Enemy_Unit1 object. An action is already in the action box, and now you add a second action. Right click on the action box and select Alterable values | Subtract from.

2. The expression evaluator appears. Change the Choose value drop-down box to read Current Movement Value. Select the Enter expression area and highlight the value 0; then click on the Retrieve data from an object button. Choose the Wargame Map Object and select Current movement | Cost of movement. Click on the OK button to save this information to the event editor. You can see the action in Figure 9.35.

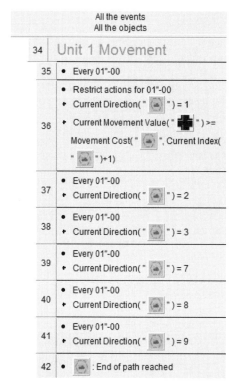

Figure 9.34
The additional condition to test whether the unit has enough movement points for the next terrain tile.

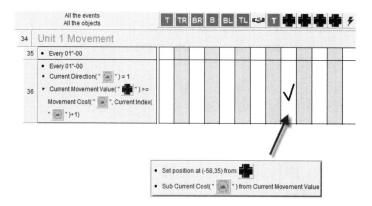

Figure 9.35
The additional action to remove the cost of the tile from the current movement value slot.

You now need to follow the same process for events 37 to 41, for adding both the new condition and the new action to subtract the movement cost from the current movement slot. You can add the conditions manually, or a quicker way is to drag the condition from event line 37 and drop it onto each

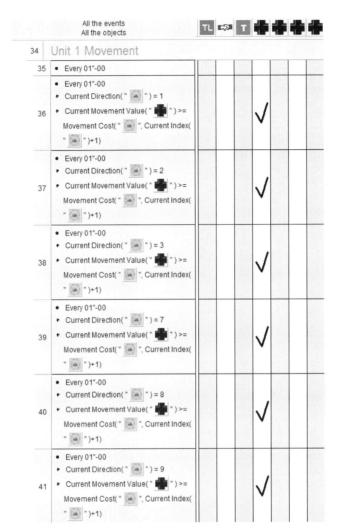

Figure 9.36
The movement value check for each event.

of the event line numbers, which makes it the last condition in each event. You need to add the action for each event line.

You can see all of the events amended in Figure 9.36.

If you run the program now, the computer unit will move and will have used all of its movement points up once it lands on the forest terrain. This is, of course, as long as you don't block its route so that then it calculates a different route to the city tile. If you leave the program running long enough, the computer movement message box will disappear, because every second you have told MMF2 to move to the next movement path in the Wargame Map Object. So, even though it is not moving the unit because none of the movement events are activated, the End of path reached event will still be run as the last path movement is activated.

The End of path reached event will enable the buttons, remove the message, and disable all of the computer movement groups. At the moment, this means that the player's units will not have any new movement points each turn, like they did in earlier chapters in the book. Originally, when the player moved all of her units, she would click on the End Turn button, which would activate the End of Turn group. The End of Turn group would reset all of the player values before allowing the player to continue moving the units. When you added the computer movement groups, you then had to take into account a new order for the groups to be run in, because the End of Turn group had to allow the computer to move first. You now need to put the action to run the End of Turn group after the computer movement groups are disabled.

3. Move across from event line 42, which is the End of path reached event.

4. Right click on the action for the Special Conditions object box, which already contains three actions to disable the different computer movement groups, and select Group of events|activate. When the Activate dialog box appears, choose (5) – End of Turn and then click on OK.

   You now need to create an event that will check whether the current movement value is less than the cost of the next movement tile cost. If so, you can enable the buttons, remove the message box, and disable and enable the correct groups when the computer movement has ended. This new event is needed to ensure that the game turn ends when the player doesn't have enough movement points, rather than waiting for the timer to get to the end of the path and run the previous event actions.

5. Click on the New condition text on event line 43; then select the Special Conditions object, and Compare two general values.

6. The expression evaluator appears. Make sure the first expression box is selected and click on the Retrieve data from an object button. Find and right click on the Enemy_Unit1 object and then Values|Values A to M|Retrieve Current Movement Value.

7. Still in the expression evaluator, change the comparison method from Equal to Lower.

8. In the bottom expression box, select and then click on the Retrieve data from an object button, right click on the Wargame Map Object and pick Current movement | Cost of movement.

   The event is added, so now you need to add all of the actions to enable the buttons and hide the Sub-Application message.

9. Move across from the event you just created on event line 43, until you are directly below the Button object. Select Enable in the action box.

10. Find the Button 2 object on the same event line and select Enable in the action box.

11. Find the Sub-Application object, right click the action box, and choose Visibility | Hide.

    As this event means the computer movement is over, you need to disable all of the movement groups and enable the End of Turn group.

12. On event line 43, move directly under the Special Conditions group and choose Group of events | Deactivate. From the Deactivate dialog box, select (8) – Unit 1 Movement.

13. On the same action box for the same event line, right click and again choose Group of events | Deactivate. From the dialog box, choose (7) – Enemy Unit 1 and click on OK.

14. Right click on the same action box, select Group of events | Deactivate; then select (6) – Computer Move and click on OK.

15. Right click on the same action box for a final time, select Group of events | activate, select (5) – End of Turn, and click on OK.

    Run the program now, and you will find that you can stop the computer-controlled player from moving the direct route to the city, and it will keep changing its route to the most cost-effective one.

    You can view the completed code in the file called compute-ai2-complete. mfa, located in the Examples folder on the CD-ROM.

Computer Unit Orders

In the previous example, you created a new starting point from where the unit was located, and the destination was a set location on the map. When making a larger game, you need to consider having a bigger map and many more units. Using this single A to B approach probably will not create a sufficiently complex computer AI, and the competing human player will quickly figure out the strategy of the computer, which will mean very little challenge for the player, especially in reply value.

To give a unit a set of orders, you need to store a list of possible destinations in memory that can be called at any point in the game. The order of these destinations won't matter because you may decide to specify a particular destination at a particular time in the game or when a certain tile has been captured by the player. You can use many different times or triggers to tell your units when to move to a tile. The most important thing is to have a system to store this information within your game so it can be recalled.

You can implement such a feature many different ways, such as using the INI file or list object to store the coordinates. You are going to use the array object because you already have some experience of it; also, it is very good for creating numeric lists as well as saving and loading at runtime.

You will create a simple numeric array that will contain the possible movement locations for four computer units. You can see an example of the destination tiles that each unit will have programmed into the array.

The array will be a three-dimensional array, but you will use the X coordinates number to specify which numbers relate to each unit. You will also use the Z coordinate to specify if it is the first value to be stored or the second. For example, if you have four units and you want to save 5 destination movements for each unit, you can say that the X coordinate of 1, 1, 1 represents unit 1. Then using the Z coordinate, you can say that 1, 1, 1 will store the X destination location, while 1, 1, 2 will store the Y destination location. In this way, you are using the actual array index as an identifier to which unit you want to store and access information about. You can see this in Figure 9.37, which details the X coordinate locations for the data. Remember that the coordinates such as 1,1 are single data slots, so you will be using the Z coordinate (which is not shown in Figure 9.37) to detail which piece of data you need access to.

As you currently have only one unit on screen, you will take the X column of Enemy_Unit1 and break it down into its five possible movements. You can see

Unit 1	Unit 2	Unit 3	Unit 4
1,1	2,1	3,1	4,1
1,2	2,2	3,2	4,2
1,3	2,3	3,3	4,3
1,4	2,4	3,4	4,4
1,5	2,5	3,5	4,5

Figure 9.37
Units associated with array slots and the X coordinate.

Array Coordinate	X Destination	Y Destination
1,1,1	2	-
1,1,2	-	5
1,2,1	3	-
1,2,2	-	1
1,3,1	8	-
1,3,2	-	1
1,4,1	5	-
1,4,2	-	4
1,5,1	1	-
1,5,2	-	2

Figure 9.38
The X 1 column broken down to show a list of destination orders.

the movement list in Figure 9.38. To store both the destination X and Y coordinates requires two storage slots in the array. So, when finding out the first movement for the Enemy_Unit1, you need to load both the array coordinates of 1, 1, 1 and 1, 1, 2, which stores the X and Y information.

On a bigger map, these locations may be towns, cities, the only route through to a location, or a strategic location allowing access to factories or other resources. In Figure 9.38, you have selected a number of different places on the map, including (2,5) which is the original city destination, (3,1) which is a forest, (8,1) upper-right corner of the map, (5,4) a location that holds a player unit, and (1,2) a small mountain terrain tile that is one of two ways of getting access to the upper-left terrain tile. On a larger map, you would design the terrain tiles in such a way to provide these strategic points. You can see these locations marked on the map in Figure 9.39.

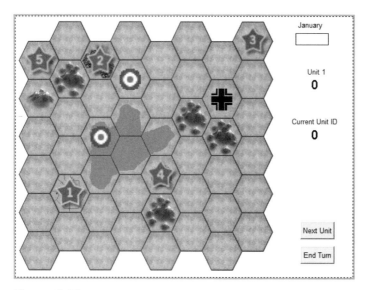

Figure 9.39
The order destinations for Enemy_Unit1.

Trigger Movement Orders

You have created a file that has the Enemy_Unit1 unit moving from its starting location and having its destination on the City terrain tile. You have also made a few modifications to this file to prepare for the programming of the unit orders system.

Locate and load the file called orders1.mfa, located in the Examples folder on the CD-ROM.

You will recognize the map and the units as they are the same ones you used in the previous examples. This time you are going to set up the movement list for this unit to go to different locations on the map at specified times. In this example, you will use the month and year as the deciding factors of when the tile should move to a particular location. This trigger can be anything you require it to be and will depend on the type of game you are making.

Some examples of when you could trigger the movement of units from one destination to another are:

- **Capture Point:** If a player unit takes over a particular terrain tile, you could trigger a particular unit or units to go and rescue that location.

- **Time Frame:** Perhaps the computer units are defending a stretch of land and you want them to attack in a specific time of year or month. This is very useful if you are making battles based on historic events.

- **Financial**: If you have a war game that includes factories and income, you may need to set up triggers that defend a particular tile based on its value. Without money, you cannot buy new equipment and provide food and additional armor for soldiers.

- **Retreat**: If a battle is going badly, you may want to specify a retreat destination for the units. If they lose so many units or the overall battle is going badly, the unit would then retreat to a particular tile, which helps create a more real realistic world.

- **General Orders**: Similar to capture point, the units have to take a number of locations on the map. The main difference is that this is triggered at the start of the game, and it makes no difference if the terrain unit has a player unit on it or not. Each unit has a starting order, either to hold a location that it is already on, or perhaps to move forward. You can copy history in the case of a game based on a realistic event.

Pre-Configured Items

In the file orders1.mfa, you have already set up and configured the main component of the computer unit orders system. This is the array object, which has been placed next to the two other array icons on the frame editor. You have renamed the array Orders and have changed the X, Y, and Z dimensions to 10, 10, and 10. You have changed it to a Number array so that it can store the tile destination locations.

Click on the array called Orders to see its properties as shown in Figure 9.40.

Setting up the Array Values

You are now ready to set up the array values. Much like with the other arrays, you need to clear the array first and then load the values in at runtime. These values are those specified in Figure 9.38.

1. Click on the event editor button to access the events that have already been written to handle player and computer movement.

2. Make sure all groups are collapsed because, for the moment, you do not need to worry about any groups.

3. Scroll to the top of the events.

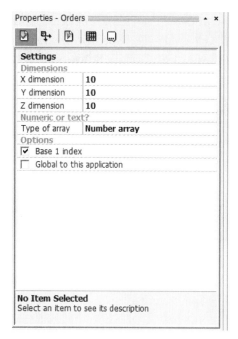

Figure 9.40
The Orders array properties.

You want to configure the array at the very start of the frame; this will be at the same time when it is configuring the other array files. You already have a Start of Frame event, so you can use this event line.

4. Move across from the event line 2 line until you are directly under the Order array.

5. Right click on the action box and select Clear array.

You now set up all of the destination movement locations for Enemy_Unit1. All of these actions will apply to the action box for the Orders array on event line 2.

6. Right click on the action box and select Write | Write value to XYZ. The expression evaluator appears. Enter the value that you want to write, which in this case will be the first destination coordinate of 2. Enter **2** in the expression evaluator and click on the OK button.

7. You will now be asked to enter the X index; type the value **1** and click on OK.

8. You will now be asked to enter the Y index; type the value **1** and click on OK.

9. You will be asked for the Z index, type in the value of **1** and then click on OK.

This information now is saved to the event editor. You have entered only the first part of the destination, so you need to enter another action to make sure you have both the X and Y destination coordinates saved in the array.

10. Right click on the Order array again and select Write | Write value to XYZ.

11. The expression evaluator appears asking for a value. The value will be the Y coordinate for the destination. This, as shown in Figure 9.38, is the value 5. Enter the number **5** and click on the OK button.

12. You will now be asked for the X index; this is the value 1. Enter this value and then click on OK.

13. You will now be asked for the Y index; this is also 1. Type **1** and click on OK.

14. Now you will be asked for the Z index; this is value 2, to show that this is the second destination coordinate. Type **2** and click on Ok.

If you look at the actions by holding the cursor over the action check mark, you see the current actions for this action box, as shown in Figure 9.41.

Follow the same process and enter the rest of the array entries for the computer unit. Once you finish, your array actions should look like Figure 9.42.

- Clear array
- Write Value 2 to (1, 1, 1)
- Write Value 5 to (1, 1, 2)

Figure 9.41
The actions completed for the current order array object.

- Clear array
- Write Value 2 to (1, 1, 1)
- Write Value 5 to (1, 1, 2)
- Write Value 3 to (1, 2, 1)
- Write Value 1 to (1, 2, 2)
- Write Value 8 to (1, 3, 1)
- Write Value 1 to (1, 3, 2)
- Write Value 5 to (1, 4, 1)
- Write Value 4 to (1, 4, 2)
- Write Value 1 to (1, 5, 1)
- Write Value 2 to (1, 5, 2)

Figure 9.42
The completed actions for the order array object.

Considering Different Locations

When you are writing the code, you need to consider what will happen when you add more units, where the best place to add the code might be, and how you might implement it. All of these things may help reduce the work that you might have to do later on when you add new units or features.

You have a list of destinations, and they currently apply to Enemy_Unit1. In the future, the array may have additional values to support more units. At the moment, you have a destination coordinate that is set manually in event line 32. You need a system where the value that is placed in the action in event line 32 can handle different values from the array at different times. Even though you can tell the action for the Wargame Map Object to look in the array, you are still reading in a manually placed static value. You need two values, the X and Y location from the array, to be read into another object, which means you can change the value in this other object whenever you want.

You have used alterable values within an object to set up values that can change throughout the life of the game, and, again, this approach is perfect for the task that you need to get working.

1. Click on the Enemy_Unit1 object on the frame editor. Make sure the Values tab is selected in the object properties. Under Alterable Values, click on the New button twice.

2. These two new values will be called J and K. You need to rename them to something more appropriate, so double-click on the Alterable Value J text and, in the edit box, type \"**Destination X** and click on OK.

3. Double-click on the Alterable Value K test and, in the edit box, type **Destination Y** and click on OK to save.

You now have somewhere to place the unit's final destination, which you can change at any point in the game using the array object.

Creating the Code

Now you have the array in place for the list of orders, and you have the alterable values in the unit you need to create the code that will handle this process.

You can set the destination path using the event and action that already exist. You can pass the Destination X and Y coordinates you created in the alterable values. Remember that at the moment those values contain 0. So, the Wargame

Map Object will not know which tile that value corresponds to, which will not matter for the moment because shortly you will set up a condition and action to place the correct data into the object.

1. Expand the Enemy_Unit 1 group.

2. Move across to the right of event line 32 and right click on the Wargame Map Object action box and select Edit.

3. The expression evaluator opens with the starting X coordinate for the Enemy_Unit1 object. You do not need to amend the starting X coordinate, so click on the OK button.

4. The Y coordinate appears; again, you do not need to amend this, so click on the OK button.

5. The destination X coordinate is displayed as the value 2; this is one of the hard-coded values that you need to change. Delete the value 2 in the edit box, and click on the Retrieve data from an object button. You need to get the value from the alterable value in the Enemy_Unit1 object, so find the Enemy_Unit1 object and select Values I Values A to M I Retrieve Destination X, which enters an expression in the edit box. Click on the OK button.

6. Now you will see the Y coordinate, which is hard coded with a 5. Delete the value 5, click on the Retrieve data from n object button, and select Values I Values A to M I Retrieve Destination Y. This creates an expression, and you can click on the OK button to complete the change to the action. You can see this new action in Figure 9.43.

   In Figure 9.43, you now see that the action retrieves the starting location from the current location of the unit, and the destination gets the X and Y values from the alterable values. The path movement is no longer hard-coded, and all you need to do is place values in to these alterable values to change the movement path.

In the event editor, you need to add some additional code related to the computer player moving on screen. You may have noticed this when amending the

Figure 9.43
The new action to retrieve data from the alterable values.

code for the destination action in event line 32. If you look at the conditions in event line 32 and 33, you are checking the alterable value of H, the Tile ID value. You used this to check that a unit had reached its destination and so that you could then continue to move the unit or close the movement groups.

You need to replace the tile number ID value with another value. This value needs to be set every time you set a new destination so that the computer knows it has a new destination to reach. If you do not change this value, once the unit reaches the terrain tile with the ID of 11, the computer movement may stop working because it believes it is already at the destination. MMF2 provides an easy way to store and retrieve values using global values. Global values are values that are available throughout the life of MMF2. When running a game with multiple frames, the information contained within that global value will still be available to the whole program, unlike a non-global value which is only available in a single frame. Even though you don't need the value over multiple frames, using global values is still an easy way to store information that you need to access. You also can use an alterable value within the unit object and set the destination tile ID. Each object has a maximum number of alterable values, which is set at 26. As you are limited to 26 alterable values, if the values you wish to make global aren't part of the core engine, you can use global values, counters, arrays, and other methods to save information that you need to retrieve at a later stage.

You now configure event lines 32 and 33 to use the global value A to check to see whether the unit has reached its destination. At the moment, the global value is blank, and you will need to configure it with a value later on.

1. Right click on the condition Alterable Value H (Group.Good) <>11—this is the third condition on event line 32—and select Edit.

2. The Compare two general values dialog box appears. Highlight the second of the two edit boxes, delete the value 11, and click on Retrieve data from an object.

3. Click on the Special object and select Retrieve a global value. The Retrieve a global value dialog box appears, as shown in Figure 9.44. Select Global Value A and click on the OK button.

4. You are taken back to the Compare two values expression evaluator. Click on the OK button to save the information to the event editor.

    You now need to follow the same process to change the value in event line 33.

Figure 9.44
The Retrieve a global value dialog box.

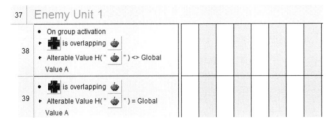

Figure 9.45
Two updated events that now use Global values.

5. Right click on the Alterable Value H (Group.Good)=11 condition in event line 33. Then select the Edit option.

6. The Compare two values expression evaluator appears. Highlight and delete the value 11 and click on the Retrieve data from an object button.

7. Click on the Special object, choose Retrieve a global value, select Global Value A, and click on OK.

8. Click on the OK button to save the information to the event editor.

    You can see the two amended events in Figure 9.45.

Creating a Destination Group

The Computer Move group will ultimately contain all of the computer units, and the configuration for the path is set up in the Enemy_Unit 1 group. You need to pass the current movement from the array into the alterable values for each unit. You could do this in the Computer Move group, but placing it in another group allows you to change when these values are amended, and also makes the code easier to understand what needs to be changed and where. Within this new group, you create any triggers that you want to move any particular units. Then in the future, if you decide to add more units or change the triggers, the information won't be scattered among a group that is used to move the units, but will be in its own dedicated group.

Make sure that the Computer Move group is collapsed.

1. Right click on the last event number, which has the New condition text next to it, and select Insert I A group of events.

2. The Group events dialog box appears. Type **Computer Destinations** as the title of the group and unselect the Active when frame starts option.

   This new group appears under the Computer Move group. Though you will be changing the order in which groups are enabled so that the code runs in the correct order, it is still better for this group to appear before the Computer Move group. Your code will be easier to understand if you order it in the order it generally runs. You will not be able to do this for all groups and code, but when you can, you will have a better sense of what is happening when.

3. To move the group, click and hold the left mouse button on the Computer Destinations group and drag the cursor over the event line number 25, which should be the collapsed Computer Move group. Release the mouse button, and the groups should be reordered. Your two groups should now look like Figure 9.46.

Computer Destinations Code

For the Computer Destinations group, you place code that manages the Enemy_ Unit1 movement with regard to where its final destination will be. This code does not handle the actual movement because that is still within the Computer

Figure 9.46
The two computer groups' order rearranged.

Move group. Without the code in the Computer Destinations group, the unit will not know what its final destination will be.

1. Expand the Computer Destinations group.

   The first bit of code you need to implement is to set the initial destination of the Enemy_Unit1 unit. You do so because you changed the code that dealt with the starting and destination points to take information from the unit's alterable values. At this point in time, no zero values are within these alterable values. You need to run this event only once when the group is enabled because this destination is just a starting destination, and you will give the unit other orders at other times in the game.

N o t e

If you don't want the unit to move at the start of the game, you can give its current starting location as a destination.

2. Make sure that the Computer Destinations group is expanded.

3. Click on the New condition text. Select the Special object and then Limit Conditions | Run this event once.

   Selecting Run this event once condition runs the event only once in the running of the program. Closing and restarting the program will allow it to run once again.

   You are going to fill the X and Y destination of the Enemy_Unit1 from the terrain tile it's currently placed on. You need a condition that will pick the object that the unit is currently located situated, for this, you use the overlapping condition.

4. Right click on the Run this event once condition you just added and select Insert. Then find the Enemy_Unit1 unit, right click on it, and choose Collisions | Overlapping another object. From the Test a collision dialog box, find and select the Good.Group object and click on OK.

5. Move across to the right until you are directly under the Enemy_Unit1 object, right click the action box, and select Alterable Values | Set.

6. The expression evaluator appears. Click on the Choose value drop-down box and select Destination X. Highlight the 0 value in the expression edit box and click on the Retrieve data from an object button. Right click on the

Group.Good object and select Values I Values A to M I Retrieve Alterable Value I. Click on the OK button to save this information to the event editor.

This action sets the destination alterable value slot to the value of the current tile that the unit is overlapping. You now need to configure the Y coordinate.

7. Right click on the Enemy_Unit1 action box where you just added the action and select Alterable Values I Set.

8. The expression evaluator appears. Click on the drop-down box, select Destination Y, highlight the 0 value in the expression evaluator's edit box, and click on Retrieve data from an object. Right click on the Group.Good object and select Values I Values A to M I Retrieve Alterable Value J. Click on the OK button.

You can see the completed event and its actions in Figure 9.47.

You are now going to add a text comment that explains what the two events after the comment will achieve. After the comment, you set two destinations based on the current month.

1. Right click on the event line number 27, which will be the New condition dialog box in the Computer Destinations group.

2. Select Insert I A comment. The Edit text dialog box appears. Type **Load Different Destination Targets at specific times**. You can change the font size and colors, if required. Click on the OK button to save this information to the event editor.

You now add two events that will move the destination point of a unit, using the months March and August. These months are represented by the string

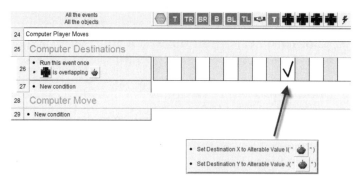

Figure 9.47
Setting the initial destination value for the unit.

objects, which have 12 text items, and each line represents a particular month. You can do a comparison of the current line number to find out which month it is.

3. Click on the New condition text in the Computer Destinations group.

4. Select the Special object and choose Compare two general values. The expression evaluator appears. Select the 0 in the first box and click on the Retrieve data from an object button. Find the String 3 object and select Current number of paragraph displayed. Leave the drop-down box as Equal, replace the 0 in the bottom box with a **3**, and click on OK.

   You now need to set the destination, and this time you use the Order array object to fill the information for the destination location.

5. Move across to the right of the event you just created on event line 28 until you are directly under the Enemy_Unit1 object. Right click on the action box and select Alterable Values | Set.

6. The expression evaluator appears. Change the Choose Value drop-down box to Destination X and click on the enter expression edit box to highlight the 0 value. Click on the Retrieve data from an object button and then pick the Orders array and then Read value from XYZ position.

7. The expression is now entered, but you need to replace three areas. The areas that you need to replace are detailed with a >text< tag. Select the first tag, which is >Enter X offset<, and type **1**. Select the Y offset tag and type **1**. Select the Z offset flag and type **1**. You can see this expression in Figure 9.48.

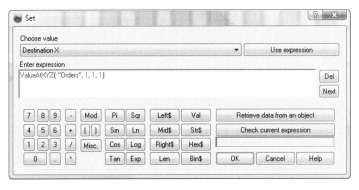

Figure 9.48
Placing the value from an array into the alterable value.

The expression now reads the value in 1, 1, 1 in the Orders array into the Destination X alterable value.

8. Right click on the same action box under the Enemy_Unit1 object on event line 28 and select Alterable Values | Set.

9. In the expression evaluator, change the Choose Value drop-down box to Destination Y. Highlight the 0 value. Click on the Retrieve data from an object button, and then pick the Orders array and Read value from XYZ position.

10. The expression is now entered. Replace the X tag with the value **1**. Replace the Y tag with the value **1** and then enter the Z tag with the value **2**.

Now, when the month is March in any year, this code will set the destination tile to be the value in 1, 1, 1 and 1, 1, 2 from the Orders array object. Even though this is hard-coded from the array, you can set up complex triggers and events that will fill the destination value when you require it.

You may remember that you created a global value to check when a unit reaches its destination. So, as well as setting the destination X and Y coordinates, you also need to set the tile ID into a global value so that the events in the "Enemy Unit 1" group know when to activate/deactivate.

11. From event line 28, move under the Special Conditions object, right click, and select Change a global value | Set.

12. Global Value A is already specified, which is correct. In the enter expression box, type the value 11 and click on OK.

You are now ready to create another event that will trigger the destination in August of any year.

1. Click on the New condition text on event line 29.

2. Select the Special object and choose Compare two general values. The expression evaluator appears. Select the 0 in the first box and click on the Retrieve data from an object button. Find the String 3 object and choose Current number of paragraph displayed. Leave the drop-down box as Equal, replace the 0 in the bottom box with **8**, and click on OK.

3. Move across to the right of the event you just created on event line 29, until you are directly under the Enemy_Unit1 object. Right click on the action box and select Alterable Values | Set.

4. In the expression evaluator, change the Choose Value drop-down box to Destination X. Highlight the 0 value. Click on the Retrieve data from an object button and then select the Orders array and Read value from XYZ position.

5. The expression is now entered. Replace the X tag with the value **1**. Replace the Y tag with the value **3** and enter the Z tag with the value **1**.

6. Right click on the same action box under the Enemy_Unit1 object on event line 29 and select Alterable Values | Set.

7. In the expression evaluator, change the Choose Value drop-down box to Destination Y. Highlight the 0 value. Click on the Retrieve data from an object button and then pick the Orders array and Read value from XYZ position.

8. The expression is now entered. Replace the X tag with the value **1**. Replace the Y tag with the value **3** and then enter the Z tag with value **2**.

   Now you need to add the tile ID, which for the map location is 43. This is because the array values of 1, 3, 1 and 1, 3, 2 point to the XY values of 8, 1. The tile Id for the tile in the upper-right corner of the map is 43.

9. Right click on the action box under the Special Conditions object on event line 29, select Change a global value | Set, enter the value **43**, and click on OK. You can see the events and actions in Figure 9.49.

You require one more event; this event will disable the Computer Destinations group. You haven't enabled it as yet, but because this is the last event you need in

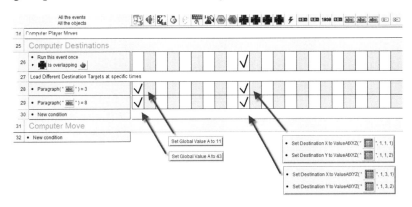

Figure 9.49
The two events that will change the destination based on a particular month.

the group, you will add it first. You will disable this group and enable the Computer Move group. You do so because the order will be rearranged so that when the player clicks on the End Turn button, this group will be enabled first to set any particular destination orders. Once these values are set, the group is disabled and the normal process of computer movement can take place.

1. Click on the New condition text on event line 30 and select the Special object and then Always.

2. Move directly under the Special Conditions object and select Group of events | Deactivate, choose (6) – Computer Destinations, and click on OK.

3. Right click on the Special Conditions object where you just placed the action, select Group of events | activate, choose (7)-Computer Move, and click on OK.

   You have now completed the code to set the destination, but you still have a small issue—when the player presses the End Turn button, it is already configured to activate the Computer Move group. The code does not activate the new group with the destination order. I suggest that you always check the order of your groups if you add additional ones as it is a likely source of coding mistakes in any game you make.

4. Ensure all groups are collapsed before starting. Find event line 17, which should be the Button 2 has been clicked event.

5. If you hold the mouse over the actions in the Special object, you will notice it disables three groups and enables the Computer Move group, which now isn't correct because you want it to activate the Computer Destinations group first.

6. Right click on the action box that contains these four actions and select Edit | Activate group Computer Move. The Activate dialog box appears. Select the (6)-Computer Destinations group and click on OK.

   The order of your groups is now changed.

   If you run the example file now, you will see that the computer unit moves from March to the city tile and then in August will move to the upper-right corner tile.

   If you want to compare your code with a working example of this program, you can view the orders1-complete.mfa file, located in the Examples folder on the CD-ROM.

Prevent Player Units Overlapping Computer Units

When you play the current movement examples, you will notice that you are still able to move your own units on top of those of the computer-controlled ones. The computer has this issue resolved because the Wargame Map Object stores a value of 100 in its array, which prevents moving onto a tile. You do not have this luxury for the player units and so have to add an additional event to prevent this from happening.

Each of the computer units has been assigned to a qualifier group called Enemies. You can view this by clicking on Enemy_Unit1 and in the properties window clicking on the Events tab. You can use this qualifier group to check that one of the placeholder objects is not overlapping the computer unit; if it is, you can prevent it from moving.

1. Load the file Player-stop.mfa, from the Examples folder on the CD-ROM.

   This example file has the entire computer unit's movement configured. Run the file and see if you can move your units over the single computer unit. You will notice that this is possible, so you will now make a small change to the code to prevent this from happening.

   You store all of the player movements in the Unit 1, Unit 2, and Unit 3 groups. If you expand the group Unit 1, on event lines 15, 16, and so on, you will see the code that handles the unit's movement. You have a similar piece of code already in place, which is when the TL is overlapping Group.Player. This event is negated saying that when it isn't overlapping another player object, the condition is still true and the actions will run.

2. Right click on the last condition in event line 15 in the Unit 1 group and then select Insert.

3. Select the Top Left object from the New condition dialog box and then Collisions | Overlapping another object. You now need to select the object to test the collision against. Find the Group.Enemies qualifier group and then click on OK.

4. This event current runs the actions if the object is overlapping, which means it will continue to move on top of the unit. So, right click on the TL is overlapping Group.Enemies object and select Negate. This step places a red cross in front of the condition, which means it will work when the event is opposite to the event text—in this case, when it is not overlapping.

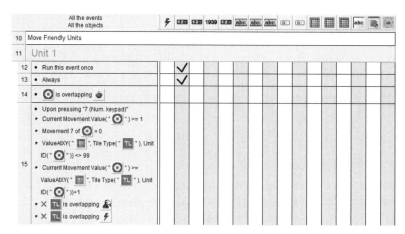

Figure 9.50
The new condition to prevent player units moving over computer-controlled units.

You can see the new condition in Figure 9.50. You will need to carry out this condition for all of the movements in each of the units. Once these additional conditions have been added to the program, run the program again and see if you can move any of your units over the Enemy_Unit1 object.

To see a completed version of this file, you can load the player-stop-complete.mfa file located in the Examples folder on the CD-ROM.

Multiple Computer Units Movement

The final aspect of computer movement that you deal with in this chapter is looking at the code that needs to be changed to handle multiple computer units moving around the screen.

Here is a list of things that you need to do to make sure the units move around the screen successfully:

■ Make sure all computer-controlled units have a qualifier group of Enemies.

■ Place them on the terrain map.

■ Configure the Array in the Start of Frame event on line 2, to contain the destination values for each unit.

■ Configure the triggers for the Computer Destinations group for each of the units, which includes setting up the default location of the unit based on its current location.

- Create a new group by copying and pasting the Computer Move group. When you paste it, it will automatically rename the new group.

- Make sure that all actions relating to the unit from the group you copied are changed to the new unit that it will represent. If you have only a single movement unit for Enemy_Unit1 and you copy the group to create one for Enemy_Unit2, all of the conditions will still refer to Enemy_Unit1 and will require you to change them.

- You need to change the group activations in Enemy Unit 1 to enable the next unit movement code, rather than just enabling the End of Turn group.

- In the last movement group, make sure you activate the End of Turn group.

You had to make some other changes to the code to reflect the fact that there are now more groups. In the following figures and notes, you examine changes that were made to allow to computer units to move on screen.

When you test your war game, you may find that placing units in different areas on the screen might trigger a bug or issue you didn't previously consider. One such problem you might encounter unless you set up the screen in a particular way is that the computer units could overlap each other. You will see this problem only if there is only one route through an area and another unit's computer unit is blocking the way. To fix this problem, you created another loop straight after the other two loops, which set the tiles value to 100. To call the loop you used an On group activation event and called the loop Computer. You can see the conditions for this event in Figure 9.51.

Because you added a second unit on screen, another issue was created that you might not notice when designing your engine. Having two units on screen and setting the computer units to 100 means that another piece of code will stop working. You may recall that at the end of the movement events, you checked the movement value and checked whether it is less than the current tile cost. This information was used to close the movement groups if there were no longer enough points available to move on the map. Unfortunately, because you set all computer unit tiles to 100, suddenly no unit was able to move because its initial moving value of 5 was never enough when compared to 100.

You have added an additional condition on the event to check that the value is less than 99 and the current movement value is less than the current movement tile. This means that if the tile ever has a movement cost of 100, the code will

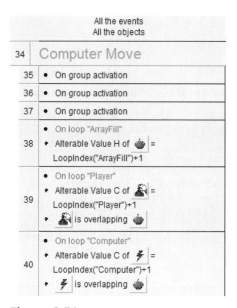

Figure 9.51
The additional loop to tell the computer about a tile on which unit cannot move.

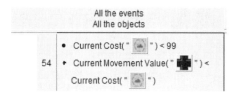

Figure 9.52
The additional condition check to prevent the movement group closing if the value is above 99.

never automatically close the group and prevent the unit from moving. A unit cannot move onto a tile that has a value of 100 because the Wargame Map Object prevents that from happening. If a unit is placed on a tile, the unit should not be able to move on, the unit can move off that tile as long as there is a valid adjacent tile. You can see this extra condition in Figure 9.52.

You can view the example file two-units.mfa that shows two computer units moving on the screen. The file is located in the Examples folder on the CD-ROM. Try moving the player pieces around the board to block the computer units to see how they react. Enemy_Unit1 will move between its starting point and tiles 2,5 and 8,1 in March and August, whereas Enemy_Unit2 will move from April, but once it's reached its destination it will stop.

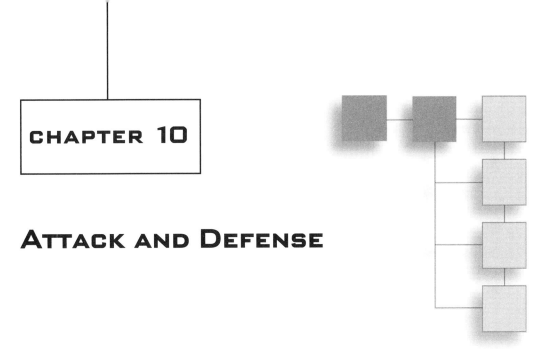

CHAPTER 10

ATTACK AND DEFENSE

Now that you have completed the player and computer movement, you are ready to begin on attack and defense. In this chapter you will learn how to implement a battle engine in your war games.

In this chapter you will learn how to implement an attack and defense phase between the movement sections of your game. After the player moves and is able to attack, the computer-controlled player will move its units and enter into its attack phase. This means you will have two separate attack engines running, one for the player and another for the computer. From a logical programming point of view, having these two separate phases is easier to work with than trying to get a single engine to control both player and computer player. You need to make some changes to the order of running for your groups as well as some changes in the code to accommodate the new code you'll be adding to handle units that have been defeated and need to be removed from the game.

The amount of complexity you need to put in to your game depends on the type of war game you are making.

The attack and defense table from Chapter 4 is shown in Figure 10.1. You can use this as the basis for different types of combat engines you might need. Here are two suggestions:

- **Simple Combat:** If you want to implement a simple combat engine, you can use just the Att and Def options. The attacking unit uses its Att value, and the defending unit uses its Def value. Behind the scenes, the computer rolls a random number, in this example from a value between 0 and 9. This value is added to the Att value, while the defending unit adds its own random number between 0 to 9 to its value. The one with the higher value wins. If the attacker wins, the defending unit is removed from the board; if the defending unit wins, no damage is taken.

- **Multiple Soldier Combat:** The removal of a unit if it fails in combat is one such system. You may decide that each unit consists of groups of soldiers rather than just a single soldier. You may not want to remove the whole unit at once because you want your game to be more representative of a longer battle and give units the chance to counterattack. In this case, we can use the Sze option from Figure 10.1 to reduce the forces by a set amount as well as decide when to remove the unit.

When implementing a combat engine, you should consider several items, such as:

- **When:** When is the player going to be able to initiate combat? Will she still be able to move once she has attacked a unit, or will her turn end?

- **How to begin**: How is the player going to initiate the combat routines? Will you use a button or an actual phase, like moving? Will it be automated, or will the player have full control of how she attacks?

- **How to select a unit:** How is the player going to select a unit to attack? Will she use the mouse or the keyboard and move a cursor?

- **How to end**: How does the player end the combat? This could be by using the current End Turn button or some other method. This all depends on how you implement the combat engine in your game.

We will answer these questions using the following example files. It is important to note that you could implement many of these features in different order or

Unit (ID)	Att	Def	Sze	FiD
1	3	2	5	2
2	4	4	5	3
3	7	8	8	6
4	8	1	20	12

Figure 10.1
The attack and defense table.

change the rules to a totally different system. It depends on what type of war game you are going to make because the type of game may determine the way your game works.

Basic Player Combat Example

In this section of the book, we are going to implement basic combat for the player. For the moment, we will not consider combat for the computer. In the following example, we will have two units on screen next to each other, and we will use a key press to initiate combat. This is a simple starting point of the combat engine so that you can understand how the basics work before implementing the engine in a more complex game.

Pre-Configured Items

In the following example file, we have already created a number of items ready for programming. We have a new button called Btn_Combat, which is used to initiate combat between the two units closest to each other. We have also placed a computer controlled unit right next to Unit2, which will be the attacking unit. We have also added a hit and miss graphic, which you can use to show the player the result of the battle. Finally, we added a new piece of text and a text box that can be used to tell the player what is happening in the game. This is useful not only for relaying data back to the player about combat, but they could also be used for other game system messages. You can see the new objects in Figure 10.2.

N o t e

The text box we added is of limited size, and you may find that it doesn't display enough text, even if you change the font size and type. You could increase the size of these boxes to accommodate the text, but the terrain map and other items on the frame take up most of the screen. In Chapter 13, we will be making the terrain map larger and the screen size of the application bigger. At this point it would be sensible to increase the size of any text boxes that are used to display information.

For each unit, we have added an attack and defense alterable value, as shown in Figure 10.3. This will be used to calculate the attack and defense scores of each unit.

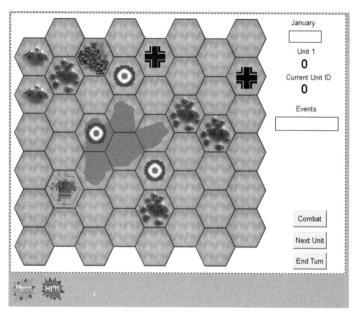

Figure 10.2
The new items and the moving of a computer unit ready for battle.

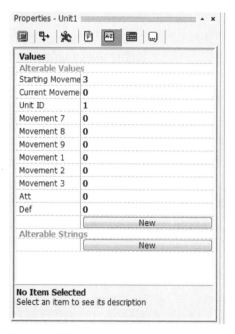

Figure 10.3
The Att and Def alterable values for each unit.

Coding Basic Combat

For this example, we are going to have combat work in a very specific way to show you how the calculations work and what to do when a unit is successfully destroyed. You will be able to initiate combat as soon as you launch the game because there are two units next to each other. To initiate combat, all you have to do is click on the Combat button.

We will use alterable values to work out our calculations; you can see the basic method we are going to use in Figure 10.4. In Figure 10.4, you can see the two units at the top; both have an attack and defense value. When one unit is attacking another, it will use its attack value, while the defending unit will take its defense value. Each value will be added to a random number out of 10, and this combined value of each unit will then be compared. If the attacker has a higher value, it wins the battle and the other unit is removed; if the defending unit wins, then no action is taken and the game continues.

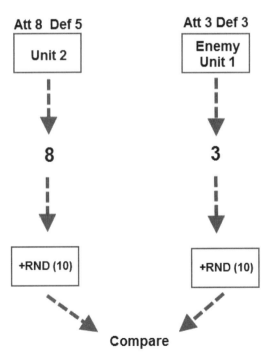

Figure 10.4
The basic combat method.

For this example we will need to do the following:

- **Combat button:** We need a button to tell MMF2 when the user has requested combat to begin. A button is already on screen, so we just need some simple code to tell the program to run a specific set of code once the button has been pressed.

- **Combat Group:** We will create a specific event group to handle the initial combat button being pressed. Within this group will be two additional groups that will handle when the attack has hit or missed the opposing player.

- **Computer Destinations Update:** We need to update the Computer Destinations group to check for when the computer controlled unit has either been destroyed or is still on screen. This is because the code runs from Computer Destinations to Computer Move to Computer Move 2. Computer Move is directly related to Enemy_Unit1, while Computer Move 2 is related to Enemy_Unit2. We do not want or need to run the code for the Enemy_Unit1 if it no longer exists on screen. This is because it is not required but also because the object no longer needs to be moved on screen. Some code relating to that unit may no longer work correctly and cause the game to stop working or to work incorrectly.

You can continue from the last completed file from Chapter 9, or you can load combat1.mfa from the Examples folder. Ensure that you have the file loaded and ready before continuing with the instructions.

Creating the Combat Group

Before we create the new group for combat, we will create a comment line to separate it from the code before it.

Right click on the very last event line number and select Insert | A comment and in the edit text box type Combat group code and press the OK button.

Next you need to create a combat group. This allows you to place your combat code in a specific group to keep it away from the main code. The group will be disabled to begin with because you only want the code to be activated when the user presses the button.

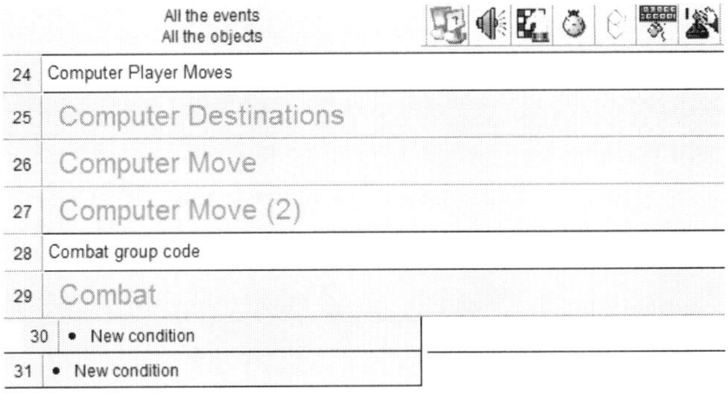

Figure 10.5
The new Combat group before entering any code.

1. Right click on the very last event line. Then select Insert I A group of events.

2. When the Group Events dialog box appears, enter the title of the group (Combat), deselect Active when frame starts, and click on the OK button.

You will see the group entered at the end of the movement groups as shown in Figure 10.5.

Initiating Combat via the Button

You need a way to enable the combat group; in this case, you will do this using a button. In your own games, you may make the process automatic when the user presses end turn. In this example, the player can continue to move his own units, can allow the computer to move its units, and once he is ready, can click on the Combat button to begin the battle between the two units.

To create a comment to break up the code between the combat group and the button press:

1. Right click on the event line number for the very last event line, and select Insert I A comment. In the edit text box type Combat button pressed, and then click on OK.

   Now you need to create the event that will check for the button being pressed.

2. Click on the New condition text on the very last event line. From the dialog box, select Btn_Combat and then Button clicked?

   This creates the event line; now it is time to create the action, which will activate the Combat group.

3. Right click the action box under the System object, and then choose Group of events ⏐ activate, and when the Activate dialog box appears, select the group (13) – Combat and then click on OK.

You now have the event to activate the Combat group. Now you need to create the code to manage the combat process.

Programming the Combat Group

The first event in the combat group is to set the unit's alterable values of Att and Def. In this example, we will use the manual process to show how the example works. For your own war game, you could also use a value saved in the actual alterable values or load in the values from an array. At the moment, all units have a zero value in their alterable value slots for Att and Def, so this is why you will set a value into both the Unit2 and Enemy_Unit1.

Note

Although loading the values from an array is a slightly longer process, if you are making several games and want to change various values, using an array can save lots of time. This is especially true if you use an editor to create and save an array file. That way you can view the information in another MMF2-created executable and configure your game without needing to amend the alterable values of many units.

You need to create the condition first, which will activate every time the combat group is enabled. You will use the group activation condition that you have used in previous examples.

1. Ensure that the Combat group is expanded and click on the New condition text.

2. When the New condition dialog box appears, select the Special object and then select Group of events ⏐ On group activation.

In Figure 10.4 you can see that you need to consider the Att value of Unit2, and the Def value of Enemy_Unit1. For this example, place the value of 8 into the Att value of Unit2, and 3 into the Def value of Enemy_Unit1. This means that in many attacks, the Unit2 object will most likely win the battle.

To set the value 8 for Unit2:

1. Move across to the right of the condition you just added until you are directly under the Unit2 object.

2. Right click on the action box and select Alterable values | Set. When the Expression Evaluator appears, in the Choose Value drop down box, select Att. In the expression box, type the value of 8 and click on OK.

3. On the same event line, move across until you are under the Enemy_Unit1 group. Right click and select Alterable values | Set. In the Expression Evaluator, choose Def in the drop down box, type 3 in the expression box, and click on OK.

As shown in Figure 10.4, we have to use these two values of 8 and 3 and add a random number to them. In MMF2, random numbers are specified in the event editor's Expression Evaluator as Random (10). The number in the brackets is the range of random numbers available for you to select from. MMF2 uses a zero index, so this means it will use one of up to ten random numbers from 0 to 9. For the condition, we will use the On group activation condition because it only needs to be run once when the group is enabled.

1. Click on the New condition text on the second event line in the combat group.

2. Select the special object and then Group of events | On group activation. The event line will now be added.

3. Move across until you are directly under the Unit2 object, right click the action box, and select Alterable values | Add to. This brings up the Expression Evaluator. Click on the drop down box for Choose Value and select Att. In the Expression edit box, type **Random(10)** and click on OK. You can see the expression in Figure 10.6.

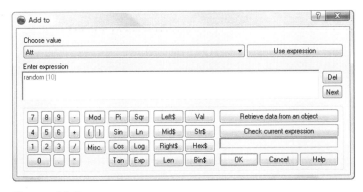

Figure 10.6
The random value between 0 and 9.

4. Move across from the same event line until you are under the Enemy_Unit1 object, right click, and select Alterable values | Add to. In the Expression Evaluator, select Deff on the drop down menu, type in **Random(10)**, and click on OK.

You have now told MMF2 that you will add a random number to the value that it has in the alterable values.

Note

After you complete the example, you can change the two values to change the odds of an attack being more or less successful. This is useful if you have a number of units that have better odds and you want to make sure that your code is working correctly for when an attack is not successful.

Checking the Attack Values Now you have your attack and defense values with a random number value added. We will now add two further events that check to see if the attack value is higher than the defense value and if the defense value is higher than the attack value. If the attack value is higher, we will enable a group called Hit, and if the defense value is higher, we will enable a group called Miss (these two groups have yet to be added).

Next we will add the first of our two events. This event will have three conditions: the first will check to see if the attack value of Unit2 is higher than the defense value of Enemy_Unit1. The next condition will restrict the actions in the event line to only happen once each event loop (when the code reads from top to bottom). Because MMF2 runs very quickly, if you do not have this condition, the actions will repeat on each event loop. In this example, we will play a sound when the unit attacks. Without the Only one action when event loops condition, the sound will play continuously rather than just one time. The final condition in the line will check to make sure that the number of Enemy_Unit1 units on screen equals 1. This ensures that this code only runs when the object exists; as if it has been killed in battle, it will be destroyed and you will not want to run the Hit or Miss code.

1. Click on the New condition code in the Combat group.

2. Select the Special object from the New condition dialog box. Then select Compare two general values.

3. The Expression Evaluator box appears. Click in the top box and then click on Retrieve data from an object. Find the Unit2 object and select Values | Values A to M | Retrieve Att. The top expression box will now have a value in it.

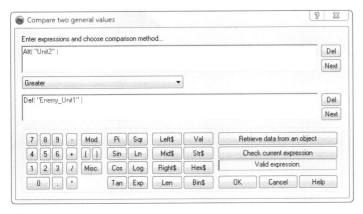

Figure 10.7
Comparing to see if the attacking value is greater than the defense value.

4. Change the Equal comparison method to Greater.

5. Click on the bottom expression box and click on Retrieve data from an object. Find the Enemy_Unit1 object, and select Values I Values A to M I Retrieve Def. An expression will appear in the bottom box. You can see the expression in Figure 10.7.

6. Click on the OK button to save the information to the event editor.

   We now need to add the next condition to the same event.

7. Right click on the condition that you just added, and select Insert.

8. Select the Special object and then choose Limit conditions I Only one action when event loops.

   We will now add the final condition to this event, which will check to see if there is a unit available.

9. Right click on the condition you just added, and select Insert.

10. When the dialog box appears, find the Enemy_Unit1 object and select Pick or Count I Compare to the number of Enemy_Unit1 objects. The Expression Evaluator appears. Leave the drop down comparison box as Equal, and type in the value of **1**. Click on the OK box to save this information to the Event Editor.

We need to add three actions: the first to create a hit graphic at the location of the object that is being attacked. This will show that the object has been hit by the attack; second, we will play a sample sound; and finally, we will activate a group.

We will not be able to activate the group just yet because we haven't created it yet, so we will need to come back to that shortly.

Use the Create Object action to create another version of an object, either an object on screen, or in this case, an object that is out of frame.

1. Move across from the event line you just created until you are under the Create new objects object. Right click the action box, and then select Create object.

2. The Create Object dialog box appears, and we need to select the object we want to create, so find and select the Active_Hit object and click on OK.

3. You will now get the Create Object dialog box, but with a set of coordinates. At the moment, it is using direct coordinates on the screen, but we want to display it relative to another object, so click on the Relative to radio button.

4. When the Create object dialog box appears, find the Enemy_Unit1 object and click on OK.

5. You will now be back at the Create Object dialog box. Type in a **0** for the X coordinate and a **0** for the Y coordinate. This means that the object that is created will be placed at 0, 0 from the Enemy_Unit1 object. Click on the OK button to save the information to the Event Editor.

   It is now time to add our second action to this event line, which will play a sound when the unit is hit:

6. Move right from the conditions line until you are under the Sound object. Right click the action box and select Samples | Play sample.

7. When the Play Sample dialog box appears, click on the Browse button opposite the From a file text.

8. Browse the CD-ROM drive and select the Sound folder, select the impact02 sound, and click on the Open button.

You have now added a sound when the attack is successful. We cannot add the third action until we have completed the next couple of events and the two new groups. The next event will check to see if the attack was unsuccessful.

1. Click on the New condition text in the last event line in the Combat group.

2. Select the Special object from the dialog box. Then select the Compare two general values option.

3. When the Expression Evaluator box appears, click in the top box and then click on Retrieve data from an object. Find the Unit2 object and select Values | Values A to M | Retrieve Att. The top expression box will now have a value in it.

4. Change the Equal comparison method to Lower or equal.

5. Click on the bottom expression box and click on Retrieve data from an object. Find the Enemy_Unit1 object and select Values | Values A to M | Retrieve Def. An expression will appear in the bottom box.

6. Click on the OK button to save the information to the event editor.

   We now need to add the next condition to the same event.

7. Right click on the condition that you just added, and select Insert.

8. Select the Special object and choose Limit conditions | Only one action when event loops.

   The final condition we will add to this event checks to see if there is a unit available.

9. Right click on the condition you just added, and select Insert.

10. When the New condition dialog box appears, find the Enemy_Unit1 object, and select Pick or Count | Compare to the number of Enemy_Unit1 objects. When the Expression Evaluator appears, leave the drop down comparison box as Equal and type in the value of **1**. Click on the OK box to save this information to the Event Editor.

We now need to create the two actions, the first to display the miss graphic and play a sound, which in this case is the same sound we used for a hit; in your own games, you might use different sounds.

1. Move across from the event line you just created until you are under the Create new objects object. Right click the action box and then select Create object.

2. The Create Object dialog box appears; we need to select the object we want to create, so find and select the Active_Miss object, and click on OK.

3. You will now get the Create Object dialog box; click on the Relative to radio button.

4. When the Choose an Object dialog box appears, find the Enemy_Unit1 object, and click on OK.

5. You will now be back at the Create Object dialog box; change the X and Y coordinate values to 0 and 0. Click on the OK button to save the information to the Event Editor.

Now we will add a sound, which will play when the attacking unit has done no damaged to the defending unit:

1. Move right from the conditions line until you are under the Sound object. Right click the action box, and select Samples | Play sample.

2. The Play Sample dialog box appears. Any sound you have previously added to the game is displayed in the Samples list. You should be able to see the impact02 text. select it, and click on OK.

End of Turn Check   We need a way of knowing when combat has completed, so in this case, we will check to see when the Btn_EndTurn has been clicked. If it has, it will close the combat group.

1. Click on the New condition text in the Combat group.

2. Find and select the Btn_EndTurn object, right click on it, and choose Button Clicked.

   The event will be added and now we will add the action to close the combat group.

3. Move across until you are under the Special conditions object, right click the action box, and choose Group of events | Deactivate. When the Deactivate dialog box appears, select (13)-Combat and click on OK.

We will add two further actions; these will be to reset our Att and Def values back to 0. In your own games, you may need to reset values; otherwise, MMF2 could return values that are incorrect or out of the range you are providing within your engine rules. The incorrect data that has not been reset could make your program work incorrectly or have unpredictable results.

1. Move across from the button clicked event until you are under the Unit2 object, right click the action box, and select Alterable values | Set. In the drop down box, choose Att and then leave the expression value as 0. Click on the OK button to save the information to the Event Editor.

2. Move across until you are under the Enemy_Unit1 object, right click, and select Alterable values | Set. Change the drop down box to Def and then click on the OK button.

Note

You may need to extensively test your code when making your games. In this example, if the end of turn button is pressed, it will deactivate the Combat group. Shortly we will be adding code to enable the Hit or Miss groups; while these groups are activated, the user could press the End Turn button, causing some issues with what happens on the screen. This is unlikely because they would have to be very quick to press the button before the code has finished running, but on occasions you may get issues if a group is still enabled and still running code and you allow the player another option they can select on screen. One way is to enable and disable options that you do not want the player to use while you are running certain processes. This is what we have done when the computer movement is taking place.

Adding Two New Groups   We need to add two new groups, which will contain code for what to do when a unit is hit or missed in combat.

1. Right click on the last event line number in the Combat group. This contains the New condition text. Select Insert | A group of events.

2. When the Group Events dialog box comes up, type the title **Hit**, deselect the Active when frame starts checkmark, and click on the OK button.

   We will now create the second group.

3. Right click on the last event line number in the Combat group. this contains the New condition text. Select Insert | A group of events.

4. When the Group Events dialog box comes up, type the title **Miss**, deselect the Active when frame starts checkmark, and click on the OK button.

Enabling the Correct Group   We now need to go back to the two events we created earlier and enable or disable the Hit and Miss groups, depending on the values of the attack and defense alterable values.

In the third event in the Combat group, we will only run the actions if the Att value is higher than the Def value. This means that the attack is successful, so in this case, we will enable the Hit group.

1. From the third event line in the Combat group, move across until you are under the Special Conditions group. Right click the action box and select Group of Events | Activate. When the Activate dialog box appears, select (14) – Hit, and click on OK.

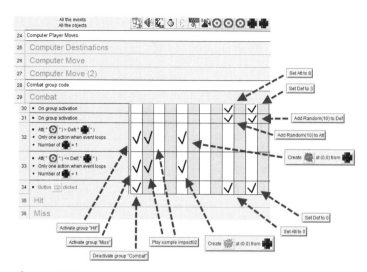

Figure 10.8
The events, actions, and groups in our Combat group. (We have removed some objects from the top list in this image so you can see all of the different actions in one image.)

To do the same for the event line when the Att value is equal or less than the Def value:

2. From the fourth event line in the Combat group, move across until you are under the Special Conditions group. Right click the action box and select Group of Events | Activate. When the Activate dialog box appears, select (15) – Miss, and click on OK.

You can see the events, actions, and groups created so far in Figure 10.8.

Programming the Hit Group   For the Hit group, we will want to make the Enemy_Unit1 object slowly disappear. We can do this using transparency, where we slowly change a value and make it fade away. When the transparency of the object equals 128, we will destroy the object. Transparency starts at 0 for fully visible and 128 for invisible. So we can do a comparison on the transparency value and if it equals 128, we can destroy the object. We need some way of knowing when to close the Hit group. If we check that the number of Enemy_Unit1 objects equals zero, we can then close the group. Once the Enemy_Unit1 has been destroyed, we can also destroy the Active_Hit object.

First, we will add a time-based event that will change the transparency value every quarter of a second.

1. Expand the Hit group to display the New condition text line.

2. Click on the New condition text. From the New condition dialog box, select the Timer object and choose Every. The Every timer dialog box appears; change the seconds dialog to **0**, then put **25** in the hundreds section. Click on the OK button.

   This will now add the event Every 00.25 event line.

3. Move across until you are under the Enemy_Unit1 object, right click the action box, and select Visibility | Set semi-transparency.

The Expression Evaluator appears, and asks for a number between 0 and 128. We want to retrieve the current value of the object (which initially is 0) and then we will add a value to this transparency number. This means that the next time the event is triggered it will retrieve the number that we previously added as well as adding the value we want on to it. This means that the object will slowly become invisible.

1. In the Expression Evaluator, select the 0 value and click on Retrieve data from an object.

2. Find the Enemy_Unit1 object, right click, and select Animation | Get semi transparency ratio. The expression will be added to the expression evaluator; at the end of the expression type **+25**. You can see the expression in Figure 10.9.

3. Click on the OK button to save the information to the Event Editor.

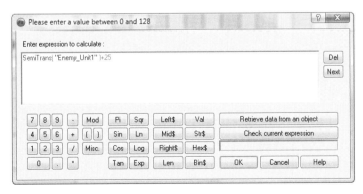

Figure 10.9
Getting the current transparency ratio and adding 25 to its value.

If you run the program now and hit the Combat button, as long as the alterable value of attack is more than the alterable value of defense, you will see the hit graphic appear, and slowly the enemy unit disappears. Even though the object has become invisible, it is still on screen, taking memory, so it is important to destroy any objects that you no longer need in the game. To do this, you need to check to make sure that the transparency value is equal to or above 128 and then destroy the object. The reason we use equal or greater is that if you are using calculations, such as adding 25, the transparency value may never be 128 exactly, and so the code would not run if we used that equation.

1. Click on the New condition text in the Hit group. This will form the basis of the second event in this group.

2. Select the Special object and choose Compare two general values. When the Expression Evaluator appears, select the first edit box, and click on Retrieve data from an object.

3. Locate and right click on the Enemy_Unit1 object, and choose Animation | Get semi transparency ratio. Change the drop down comparison method from Equal to Greater or Equal. Click on the lower edit text box and change the default zero value to 128. Click on the OK button.

    We now need to create two actions that will destroy both the enemy unit and the hit graphic that overlays it.

4. Move across from the event until you are under the Active_Hit object, right click, and select Destroy.

5. On the same event line, find the Enemy_Unit1 object, right click, and select Destroy.

If you run the program now and press the Combat button, the hit graphic appears. The enemy unit will disappear, and once the enemy unit has disappeared it will then be destroyed. Once it's invisible, the hit graphic will also be destroyed.

The next event confirms that the enemy unit has been destroyed; if so, we can then happily deactivate the group. When making your games, you need to consider what triggers you can use to help you decide when to close a group. In this case, we know that the aim of the group is to destroy the object, so checking to see if the object still exists on screen is the best way to consider when to close the group.

1. Click on the New condition text in the Hit group. Find and right click on the Enemy_Unit1 object, and select Pick or count | Compare to the number of Enemy_Unit1 objects.

2. The Expression Evaluator appears. Leave the comparison method as Equal and because we want to check to see if there are no objects left, leave the zero value, and click on the OK button.

3. Move across from this event and right click on the Special conditions action box, then choose Group of events | Deactivate. When the Deactivate dialog box appears, select (14)-Hit, and click on OK.

You have now completed the programming for the Hit group; you can see the events and conditions in Figure 10.10.

Programming the Miss Group   The Miss group will be programmed differently from the Hit group, mainly because we are not making any unit graphic disappear if it is missed in battle. For this group, we will use a group activation event to check the enabling of the group, and we will set the timer back to 0. The timer will then count to three seconds at which point another event will be triggered and destroy the Active_Miss object. We will again use an event to check the number of objects on screen; in this case, we will be checking to see if there are any Active_Miss objects on screen, and if not, we will close the group.

We will start with the group activation and the resetting of the timer.

1. Ensure that the Miss group is expanded.

2. Click on the New condition text in the Miss group. Select the Special object and choose Group of events | On group activation.

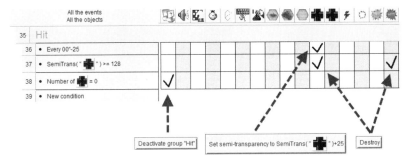

Figure 10.10
The Hit group conditions and actions.

3. Move across to the right of this event until you are under the Timer object, right click the action box, and select Set timer.

4. The set timer dialog box appears. Change the second's option to 0 and then click on OK.

This will reset the timer to 0 seconds where it will begin to count upwards again.

We now need to create an event that will check to see when this reset timer counts up to three seconds. When it does, we will destroy the Active_Miss object.

1. Click on the New condition text in the Miss group.

2. Select the Timer object, and then Is the timer equal to a certain value. When the timer based dialog box appears, change the seconds bar to three seconds and then click on OK.

3. Move across to the right of this event until you are directly under the Active_Miss object, right click, and select Destroy.

If you run the game now, you will probably have to reset the game each time (using the menu bar and selecting New) because the attacking unit has a much higher chance of winning. At some point, the defense value will be higher than or equal to the attack value. When it is, the green Active_Miss object will disappear after three seconds.

We need to create an event that will check to see when the Active_Miss object has disappeared, and then we will close this group.

1. Click on the New condition text in the Miss group.

2. Find the Active_Miss object, and choose Pick or count | Compare to the number of Active_Miss objects.

3. The Expression Evaluator appears, and all of the values are exactly as we need them, so click on the OK button.

4. Move across from this event until you are under the Special conditions object, right click the action box, and select Group of Events | Deactivate. From the deactivate dialog box choose (15) –Miss, and click on OK.

You can see the conditions and actions for this group in Figure 10.11.

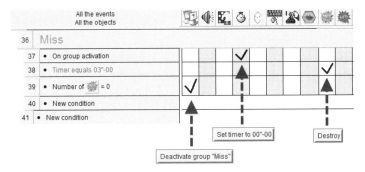

Figure 10.11
The Miss group code.

Making Some Changes   If you run the program now, you will have a simple combat example, which will work until the enemy object has been destroyed. By writing this code you have inadvertently caused another problem, and you should notice this when running the example. If you destroy the enemy unit, some code written earlier, which moves the object on screen, no longer runs. We now need to make a few small changes to the earlier code to ensure that it will still run.

The movement issue comes from the Computer Destinations group, because this is the code that sets the starting point and locations. It also tells MMF2 to enable Computer Move. If the unit is destroyed, it will still run this group and will continue to display the computer move message.

For now, we can change the code in Computer Destinations to fix this issue.

1. Expand the Computer Destinations group.

2. Select the Always event and then delete it.

    We will now create two new events that will check to determine if Enemy_Unit1 still exists.

3. Click on the New condition text in the Computer Destinations group.

4. Select the Enemy_Unit1 object, and Pick or Count | Compare to the number of Enemy_Unit1 objects.

5. The Expression Evaluator appears, and all of the values are perfect for our expression, so click on OK.

    This creates an event that checks to see if the number of enemy unit 1 on screen equals zero. If it does, this means that the enemy unit 1 was destroyed in battle, and there is no need to run the movement for this object.

6. Move across to the actions, right click under the Special conditions object, and choose Group of events | Deactivate.

7. When the Deactivate dialog box appears, choose the (6) – Computer Destinations group and click on OK.

8. On the same action box, right click and select Group of events | Activate; then choose (10)-Computer Move (2) and click on OK.

Now we need to create an event that checks to see if there is an enemy unit on screen and then enables the Computer Move group, which will move the first unit around the screen.

1. Click on the New condition text in the Computer Destinations group.

2. Select the Enemy_Unit1 object, and Pick or Count | Compare to the number of Enemy_Unit1 objects.

3. When the Expression Evaluator appears, change the zero value to a 1, and click on OK.

4. Move across to the actions, right click under the Special conditions object, and choose Group of events | Deactivate.

5. When the Deactivate dialog box appears, choose the (6) – Computer Destinations group, and click on OK.

6. On the same action box, right click and select Group of events | Activate; then choose (7)-Computer Move and click on OK.

You can see the code change in Figure 10.12.

You have now amended the code that allows the second computer unit to continue with movement if the Enemy_Unit1 has been destroyed.

Player Combat All Units

In this section, you will take the next step in creating a combat engine. This next example deals with how to implement combat from any of your player units and how to attack a single enemy unit. This enemy unit can only be on a surrounding hexagon around the attacking player.

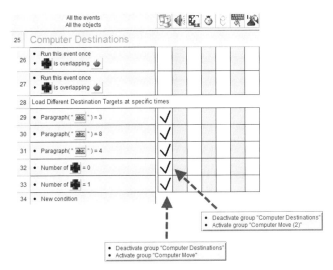

Figure 10.12
The conditions and actions for the changed code.

This involves a lot more work than the previous example and is certainly more complex. The complexity arises because of the need to pick an enemy object to attack. To choose this enemy object, start thinking about the Pick conditions in MMF2; these will allow you to choose the right enemy unit.

Even though some conditions and actions are still valid from the previous example, you need to change/add a fair bit of code to make the program select a specific object at a certain time, rather than picking one object in particular to attack. We have created a combat example file, which still has the combat group, as well as the Hit and Miss groups, but each group will contain no code.

We have also made a few changes to the Frame editor as follows:

- Added a counter called Ref_Player to store the current unit reference number.

- Added a counter called Ref_Computer to store the current computer unit's reference number.

- Both counters have a minimum value of × 2147483648 and a maximum value of 2147483647, as shown in Figure 10.13.

- Added two additional alterable values to each of the player and computer units. These two extra values store amended values for attack and defense.

Figure 10.13
The counter configuration.

You can see them in Figures 10.14 and 10.15. Notice how the alterable value positions of both values are different for the player units when compared to the computer units.

■ Attack and defense values for each unit have been entered.

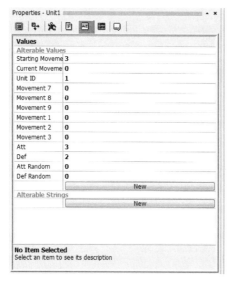

Figure 10.14
The two new alterable values for the player units.

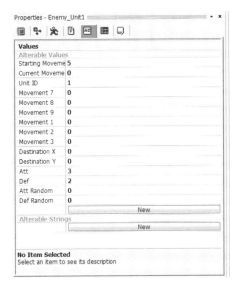

Figure 10.15
The two new alterable values for the computer units.

- Removed the code to make the placeholder units invisible. This is a temporary measure to allow for testing the file. In your own games, you would hide these placeholder units before giving the game to someone.

You can see all of these changes and begin to make changes, once you have loaded up the MMF2 file called combat2.mfa located in the Examples folder.

The code we will implement in this section can be broken down in the following ways:

- We will enable the combat group only when the button is pressed and when an enemy unit is overlapping the placeholder qualifier group. This prevents running the combat groups code when we don't need it.

- Every time the player moves a unit, we will check to see if the placeholder units are overlapping an enemy unit. If so, we will store the object's fixed value in one of the two new counters we have created. (You will learn more about fixed values shortly.)

- In the combat group, we will still have a Hit and Miss group, but accessing these two groups will be slightly different. We will need to pick the correct objects that will do battle using the fixed values and then checking to see if the alterable attack value is higher or lower than the defense value. The result will determine which group we need to enable.

■ In the Hit and Miss groups, we will use a timer event to check for the amount of time passing and then destroy the relevant objects off screen.

Amending the Button Clicked Event

The first change to our events is to prevent the Combat group code running when the user presses the Combat button. This is because when she presses the Btn_Combat object, it runs the code to check the attack and defense values and calculates the results immediately. The player might be in no position to attack the enemy, and so we wouldn't want it to run every time the player presses the button. We can prevent this for the moment by adding an additional condition that checks to see if any enemy units are within the one hexagon range of the player's unit. We can use the placeholder unit's qualifier group to see any objects overlapping it.

1. Ensure that the combat2.mfa file is loaded and you are on Frame 1's Event Editor.

2. Ensure that all groups are collapsed and move to the very last event. Right click on the event Button Btn_Combat clicked, and select Insert.

3. When the New Condition dialog box appears, select the Group.Friends object, right click, and choose Collisions | Overlapping another object. When the Test a collision dialog box appears, find and select the Group.Enemies object, and click on OK.

At the moment, because there is no code in the Combat group, pressing the button will have no effect.

Setting Objects Reference to a Counter

The easiest way for us to identify the correct enemy object and then reference it in actions is to find out its fixed value. Every object that is added to the frame has a value; this is its identifying value that MMF2 uses to internally know which object it is working with. You can retrieve this fixed value and use it to compare the value so you can select an object.

We have two additional counter objects on the frame; these are for testing only, to see that the values are being set. We will set the internal value of two objects in to each of the counters. First, we will get the fixed value of the player's currently selected object and place it in to the Ref_Player object. Then we will set the fixed value of the computer's unit that is overlapping any placeholder units.

Note

We will only retrieve one fixed value for the computer units, so if you have three enemy units surrounding the player's unit we only retrieve one value. This is because the unit can attack only one enemy unit at a time.

Note

In Figure 10.13 the counter minimum and maximum values are quite large because when an object is created with a value, the value could be anywhere within this range. To ensure that the counter can display this figure, we need to change its range.

We need to put some extra actions and events in the Player's movement groups; this ensures that the fixed value is updated every time you move a unit. First, we will add an action to an already created event.

1. Expand the group Unit 1. You will see that the first event in that group is checking to see when a unit is overlapping a terrain tile.

   This is a perfect condition for us. We can use it to obtain the fixed value of Unit1 and then place that value in the counter Ref_Player.

2. Move across to the right of the Unit1 is overlapping Group.Good event until you are directly under the Ref_Player counter object. Right click on the action box and choose Set counter.

3. When the Set Counter Expression Evaluator box appears, click on Retrieve data from an object. Find the Group.Player object, and select Retrieve fixed value. Click on the OK button to save the information to the Event Editor.

Now you need to add a new event to check for when the Enemy Group is overlapping the Friends group. This will check to see if any object from the qualifier group Enemies (all of the enemy units) are overlapping any unit from the Friends qualifier group (the placeholder units).

We now need to get the fixed value for Unit1 and place it in the Ref_Player object.

1. Right click on the Event Line number that represents Event Line 15. Then select Insert | A new event.

2. When the New condition dialog box appears, right click on the Group.Enemies object and choose Collisions | Overlapping another object. When the Test a collision dialog box appears, find the Group.Friends object, select it, and click on OK.

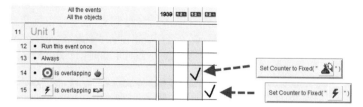

Figure 10.16
The new action and new event for getting the fixed value into a counter.

3. Move across to the right of this event until you are directly under the Ref_Computer object. Right click on the action box and choose Set counter.

4. When the Set Counter Expression Evaluator box appears, click on Retrieve data from an object. Find the Group.Enemies object, and select Retrieve fixed value. Click on the OK button to save the information to the Event Editor.

You need to add the same action and new event to both the Unit 2 and Unit 3 groups. You can see the events and their actions for the Unit 1 group in Figure 10.16.

After you add the action and the new event to the Unit 2 and Unit 3 groups, run the game and click on the next unit button. You will notice that the counter we added to the frame to display the values changes for each unit. The bottom counter is set when you move to the second unit because it overlaps the place-holder units. You will notice that there is still a value in the counter once we have moved the placeholder units off any enemy unit, but because we only enable the Combat group to run when a unit is overlapping it, this will not cause us any problems.

You can find the file called combat2fixed.mfa, which contains these changes, in the Examples folder on the CD-ROM.

Combat Group Code

The combat group consists of three parts: the code that falls directly under the combat group, the code for the Hit group, and the code for the Miss group.

For the code directly under the combat group we need to do the following:

On Group Activation: We will disable the combat button so the user cannot click on it twice. We will then set the default alterable values Att and Def values to the Att Random and Def Random alterable values, for both the player and the computer units. This is where we can work out a new attack and defense value each turn and still leave the original value intact.

On Group Activation: We will create a second On group activation event. This will take the original copied values in the Att Random and Def Random slots and add a random number from 0 to 9 to the value.

Comparison Event – Attack Successful: We will create an event that picks the attacking and defending units based on their fixed values. It will also compare the values in the Att Random of the attacking unit with the Def Random value in the defending unit. If the attacking value is larger, it will run a set of actions to set up the hit and enable the Hit Group.

Comparison Event – Attack Failed: We will create another pick event, but this time it will check for when the defense value of the defending unit is equal to or higher than the attacking unit, and if so, it will run a set of actions to display a miss icon and enable the Miss group.

Note

Remember that the alterable value letter assigned to the players Att, Def, Att Random, and Def Random value slots are different from the computer values. This is important to remember so that you don't end up putting the wrong values in to the wrong slots. It is useful to print out the properties list of the alterable values for any objects that are configured differently; this will ensure that you make fewer mistakes.

Combat Group – Setting the Initial Values

We can now start coding the initial combat events. We will begin with a group activation event. This event will take the starting attack and defense values from all units and place them in another alterable value slot. The reason for doing this is that it will leave the original value intact so that we can use it again to reset the value each turn. We can also amend the other slot and do calculations on it at runtime.

To create the On group activation condition:

1. Expand the Combat group. You will see that there are no events in this group, but there are two additional groups, the Hit and Miss groups.

    We need to add the event above the Hit group, so that it is part of the Combat groups code routine.

2. Right click on the Event Line number for the Hit group, then select Insert | A New Event.

3. Select the Special object and choose Group of events I On group activation.

   Now that you have your new event, you need to disable the Btn_Combat to prevent the player from pressing it when he shouldn't.

4. Move across from this new event until you are directly under the Btn_Combat object, right click, and pick Disable.

   Now we will copy the values in the alterable values slot, which stores the attack and defense values, and copy them in to the random alterable values, which will be amended in the next event.

5. On the same event line, move across until you are directly under the Group.Player object. Right click the blank action box and choose Alterable Values I Set. The Expression Evaluator appears; in the drop down box, choose Alterable Value L, and in the edit area of the Expression Evaluator, click to highlight the 0. Next click on Retrieve data from an object. When the New Expression dialog box appears, find the Group.Player object and choose Values I Values A to M I Retrieve Alterable Value J. Click on OK to save the information to the Event Editor.

6. On the same event line, find the Group.Enemies object, right click on the action box, and choose Alterable Values I Set. In the Expression Evaluator change the drop down box to Alterable Value O, then select the edit area, and click on Retrieve data from an object. Find the Group.Enemies object, select Values I Values A to M I Retrieve Alterable Value M, and click on the OK button.

You have completed the first event of this group and its three actions; you can see the code in Figure 10.17. Some items have been removed from the image to make it easier to see all of the different actions.

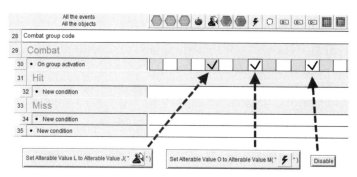

Figure 10.17
The event to move alterable values to our working alterable value slots.

Combat Group—Setting the Random Values

The next event uses the group activation event again, but this time we will add a random number between 0 and 9 to both the Att random alterable value for the player and the random Def alterable value of the computer units. This is using the same concept that we used in the simple combat example.

1. Right click on the event number for the Hit group line.

2. Select Insert | A new event. When the New condition dialog box appears, select the Special object and then Group of Events | On group activation.

   Now that the event is added, you need to add a random number of between 0 and 9 to both the Group.Player object for the Alterable value of L.

3. Move across from this new event until you are under the Group.Player object, right click on the action box, and pick Alterable values | Add to.

4. Change the drop down box to Alterable Value L and select the edit box. Type in the text **Random(10)**, and click on OK.

   Now you need to repeat steps 1 through 4 for Alterable value O for the Group.Enemies object.

5. Move across from the second event in the Combat group until you are under the Group.Enemies object, right click the action box, and select Alterable values | Add to.

6. Change the drop down box to Alterable Value O, select the edit box, type in **Random(10)**, and click on the OK button.

You can see the actions for this event in Figure 10.18. We have removed some objects from the picture to display the actions on the same page.

Combat Group—Picking Objects for Successful Hit

Now you have set-up the alterable values you need to create the next event in the Combat group. This event will have four conditions, which will do the following:

- Pick the attacking object based on its fixed value. (This value is obtained from the counter that we stored it in earlier.) The attacking unit in this case is the player and the value would be stored in the Ref_Player counter.

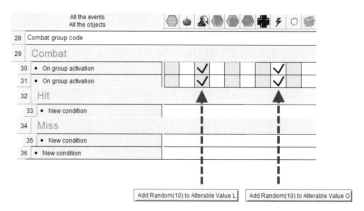

Figure 10.18
The actions to add a random number from 0 to 9 to the alterable values.

- Pick the defending object based on its fixed value. (This value was stored earlier in a counter.) The defending unit in this case is the computer unit and the value would be stored in the Ref_Player counter.

- Compare the alterable value for the attacking object with the defending unit's alterable value.

- Run the event once per loop to limit it.

To create the new event:

1. Right click on the event number for the Hit group, and select Insert | A new event.

2. Select the New objects object, and choose Pick objects with reference to their value | Fixed.

3. When the Expression Evaluator appears, highlight the 0, and click on the Retrieve data from an object button.

4. When the New expression dialog box appears, find the Ref_Player counter object, right click on it, and select Current Value. The expression will now be entered, so click on the OK button to save it to the Event Editor.

We now need to create the next condition for the event, which will pick an object with the fixed value equal to the Ref_Computer counter.

1. Right click on the condition we just added, and select Insert.

2. Select the New objects object, and choose Pick objects with reference to their value | Fixed.

3. When the Expression Evaluator appears, highlight the 0, and click on the Retrieve data from an object button.

4. When the New expression dialog box appears, find the Ref_Computer counter object, right click on it and select Current Value. The expression will now be entered, click on the OK button to save to the Event Editor.

Now that you have selected the two units, you need to compare two alterable values to see if the attack value (with its random value between 0 and 9) is greater than the defense alterable value from the enemy unit that has been picked.

1. Right click on the condition you just created and select Insert.

2. Select the Special object and choose Compare two general values. When the Expression Evaluator appears, select the first edit box, and click on the Retrieve data from an object button.

3. Find the Group.Player object, right click on it, and select Values | Values A to M | Retrieve alterable value L.

4. Change the drop down box to Greater.

5. Select the bottom edit box and click on the Retrieve data from an object button. Find the Group.Enemies group, and select Values | Values N to Z | Retrieve alterable value O.

6. Click on the OK button to save to the Event Editor.

We now need to create one more condition for this event; this tone will ensure that the event only runs once on a loop, which prevents it from running the actions multiple times in quick succession and causing problems with your game.

1. Right click on the condition you just created and select Insert.

2. Select the Special object, and choose Limit conditions | Only one action when event loops.

You have created the event shown in Figure 10.19.

You now need to create the actions, which will do the following things:

■ Create a hit graphic at the picked enemy unit.

■ Play a sample sound.

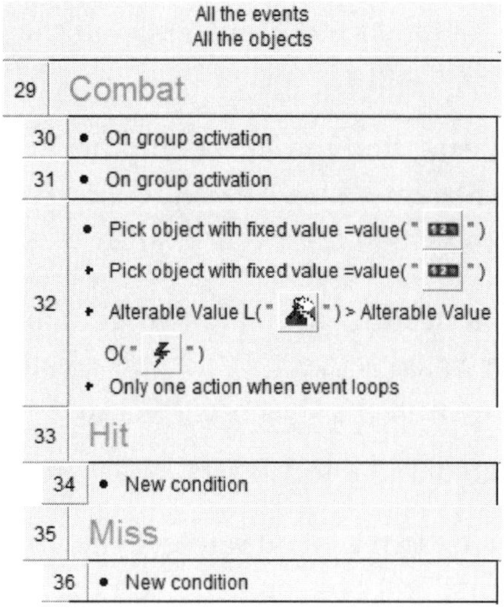

Figure 10.19
Four conditions that check for a successful attack.

- Destroy the enemy unit.

- Activate the Hit group.

Start by creating the hit graphic at the source of the computer controlled unit by completing these steps:

1. Move across from the event you just added until you are under the Create new objects object. Right click the action box and choose Create object. When the Create object dialog box appears, find the active_Hit object, select it, and click on OK.

2. Another Create Object dialog box appears; click on the Relative to button, and in the next dialog box, select the Group.Enemies object and click on OK to take you back to the previous dialog box.

3. In the X and Y coordinates boxes type **0** and **0**. Click on OK to save the information to the Event Editor.

You have now told MMF2 to create a hit graphic at 0,0 for the object that you selected from the Group.Enemies group.

Now you want to play a sound. In your own games, this could be the sound of battle; in this example, it is a simple impact sound.

1. On the same event line, move across until you are under the Sound object. Right click the action box and select Samples | Play Samples.

2. The Play Sample dialog box appears. You need to find the sound, so click on the Browse button opposite the From a file text.

3. Navigate to the CD-ROM that comes with this book, select the Sound folder, and click on the impact02.wav file and click on the Open button.

   Now we will destroy the computer unit that has been hit.

4. Move across the event until you are under the Group.Enemies object, right click, and select Destroy.

After the computer unit is destroyed, you need to destroy the hit graphic that you placed on screen. You can do this using another set of events in the Hit group, so you need to enable this group. We will program these events shortly.

Move directly under the Special Conditions object, right click the action box, and select Group of Events | Activate. When the Activate dialog box appears, click on (14)- Hit, and then click on the OK button.

If you have coded everything correctly, you can run the program now, and in most cases, the attack will be successful. Occasionally, the button will be disabled and nothing else will happen; this is because the attacking value is equal to or less than the defense value and so will not run any code. We will now add that event.

Combat Group—Picking Objects for Miss

You now need to code the event for a miss by the player unit. This next event will have four conditions and will be nearly identical to the attacking event except for the comparison method. It will do the following:

- Pick the attacking object based on its fixed value. (We stored this information earlier on a counter.)

- Pick the defending object based on its fixed value. (This value too was stored earlier in a counter.)

- Compare the alterable value for the attacking object to the defending unit's alterable value to see if it is equal to or less than that value.

- Run the event once per loop to limit it.

Let's create the new event.

1. Right click on the event number for the Hit group, then select Insert | A new event.

2. Select the New objects object, and choose Pick objects with reference to their value | Fixed.

3. When the Expression Evaluator appears, highlight the 0, and click on the Retrieve data from an object button.

4. When the New expression dialog box appears, find the Ref_Player counter object, right click on it, and select Current Value. The expression will now be entered; click on the OK button to save it to the Event Editor.

   You now need to create the next condition for the event, which will pick an object with the fixed value equal to the Ref_Computer counter.

5. Right click on the condition you just added, and select Insert.

6. Select the New objects object, and choose Pick objects with reference to their value | Fixed.

7. When the Expression Evaluator appears, highlight the 0 and click on the Retrieve data from an object button.

8. When the New expression dialog box appears, find the Ref_Computer counter object, right click on it, and select Current Value. The expression will now be entered, so click on the OK button to save to the Event Editor.

Now that you have selected your two units, you need to compare two alterable values to see if the attack value (with its random value of between 0 and 9) is equal to or less than the defense alterable value from the enemy unit that has been picked.

1. Right click on the condition you just created and select Insert.

2. Select the Special object and choose Compare two general values. When the Expression Evaluator appears, select the first edit box, and click on the Retrieve data from an object button.

3. Find the Group.Player object, right click on it, and select Values | Values A to M | Retrieve alterable value L.

4. Change the drop down box to Lower or Equal.

5. Select the bottom edit box and click on the Retrieve data from an object button. Find the Group.Enemies group and select Values | Values N to Z | Retrieve alterable value O.

6. Click on the OK button to save to the Event Editor.

   We now need to create one more condition for this event.

7. Right click on the condition you just created and select Insert.

8. Select the Special object and choose Limit conditions | Only one action when event loops.

You can see this event in Figure 10.20; compare it to Figure 10.19 to see the small difference between the two.

We need to create three actions for this event that will do the following:

- Create a miss graphic at the picked enemy unit.

- Play a sample sound.

- Activate the Miss group.

Create the miss graphic, which will appear on the computer unit, with the following steps:

1. Move across from the event you have just added until you are under the Create new objects object. Right click the action box and choose Create object. When the Create object dialog box appears, find the Active_Miss object, select it, and click on OK.

Figure 10.20
The four events that check for a failed attack from the player.

2. Another Create Object dialog box appears. Click on the Relative to button, and in the next dialog box, select the Group.Enemies object and click on OK to take you back to the previous dialog box.

3. In the X and Y coordinates boxes, type **0** and **0**. Click on OK to save the information to the Event Editor.

This will now display the miss graphic when the player's attack score meets the criteria. If the unit odds are weighted so that an unsuccessful attack is unlikely, you can temporarily change the alterable values to make sure that the code works.

To play a sound:

1. On the same event line, move across until you are under the Sound object. Right click the action box and select Samples | Play Samples.

2. The Play Sample dialog box appears. Because you added this sound earlier, it will be listed under the samples list, so select the impact02 file, and click on OK.

   Finally, you need to activate the Miss group.

3. Move under the Special conditions group, select the action box, and choose Group of events | Activate. From the dialog box, choose (15)-Miss and click on OK.

You have now completed the code for both successful and unsuccessful attacks. In Figures 10.21 and 10.22, you can see the actions for both events as displayed in the Event List Editor.

Figure 10.21
The successful attack actions.

Figure 10.22
The unsuccessful attack actions.

Combat Group—Programming the Hit Group

You created the code to identify when the enemy unit has been hit, and now you need to destroy the hit graphic from the screen. You also have a few other tidying up processes to set-up.

For the Hit group you need to do the following:

- Set a timer to 0; you will use this as the basis of destroying the hit graphic you placed on screen.

- Continue to disable the combat button to ensure that the user cannot press it at any stage of the attack routine.

- When the timer equals three seconds, destroy the hit graphic.

- Check for the number of hit graphics on screen, and if that number currently equals 0 all graphics (destroyed) close the combat groups and re-enable the combat button.

Start by setting the timer and disabling the combat button, for which you will use the group activation condition.

1. Ensure the Hit group is expanded.

2. Click on the New condition text in the Hit group.

3. In the New condition dialog box, select the Special object, and then select Group of events | On group activation.

4. Move across from this event until you are under the Timer object, right click the action box, and select Set timer. When the timer dialog box appears, change the time to 0 seconds, and click on OK.

   Now for the button disabling:

5. Move across until you are under Btn_Combat, right click, and select Disable. Now we need to set up an event that will check to see when the timer equals 03"-00 seconds.

6. Click on the New condition text in the Hit group.

7. Select the Timer object, and then select Is the timer equal to a certain value. When the dialog box appears, change the timer to 03"-00 seconds.

   Now you need to create an action to destroy the hit graphic.

8. Move to the right of this event until you are directly under the Active_Hit object, right click the action box, and select Destroy.

   The final event in the Hit group is to check to see if the Active_Hit object has been destroyed.

9. Click on the New condition text in the Hit group.

10. Select the Active_Hit object and choose Pick or Count | Compare to the number of Active_Hit objects.

11. When the Expression Evaluator appears, leave the drop down method at equal. While you are checking to see if there are no objects left, you can also leave the 0 in the expression edit box. Click on OK to save the information to the Event Editor.

   You need to ensure that all combat based groups are closed and re-enable the button.

12. Move across until you are under the Special Conditions object, right click, and select Group of events | Deactivate. Then from the dialog box select (14)-Hit and click on OK.

13. On the same action box, right click and select Group of events | Deactivate. From the dialog box, choose (13)-Combat and click on the OK button.

14. Move across until you are under the Btn_Combat object, right click the action box, and select Enable.

You have now completed the code for the Hit group, which you can see in Figure 10.23. We have removed a number of objects on screen so that you can see all of the actions together.

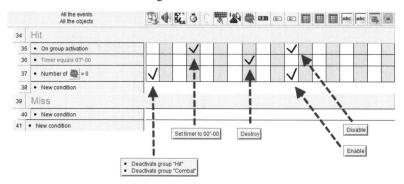

Figure 10.23
The Hit group code.

Combat Group—Programming the Miss Group

You created the code to identify when the enemy unit has been missed in combat, and now you need to destroy the miss graphic from screen.

For the Miss group you need to do the following:

- You need to set a timer to 22 seconds because will be using the time as the basis for destroying the miss graphic we placed on screen.

- Continue to disable the combat button to ensure that the user cannot press it at any stage of the attack routine.

- When the timer equals 25 seconds, the miss graphic will be destroyed and the combat groups will be disabled.

Start with the group activation event, which will set the timer to 22 seconds and disable the combat button.

1. Ensure that the Miss group is expanded.

2. Click on the New condition text in the Miss group.

3. In the New condition dialog box, select the Special object, then Group of events | On group activation.

4. Move across from this event until you are under the Timer object, right click the action box, and select Set timer. When the timer dialog box appears, change the time to 22 seconds and click on OK.

5. Move across to the Btn_Combat object, right click the action box, and select Disable.

Now check to see when the timer equals 25 seconds and run several actions to complete the group code.

Now you need to set up an event that will check to see when the timer equals 03"-00 seconds.

1. Click on the New condition text in the Miss group.

2. Select the Timer object, and then select Is the timer equal to a certain value. When the dialog box appears, change the timer to 25 seconds.

    Now you need to create an action to destroy the miss graphic.

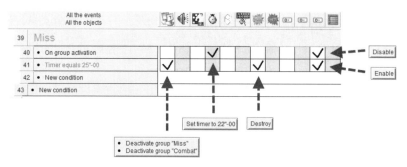

Figure 10.24
The Miss group code.

3. Move to the right of this event until you are directly under the Active_Miss object, right click the action box, and select Destroy.

   Next you must enable the combat button to allow the player to continue with her game.

4. Move across to the Btn_Combat object, right click the action box, and select Enable.

   Now you need to disable two groups to ensure that the combat code does not run.

5. Move across until you are under the Special Conditions object, right click, and select Group of events | Deactivate. From the dialog box, select (15)-Miss, and click on OK.

6. On the same action box, right click and select Group of events | Deactivate. From the dialog box, choose (13)-Combat, and click on the OK button.

You have now completed the code for the Miss group, and you can see the conditions and actions in Figure 10.24. This code should now allow you to initiate combat from any of your three units as long as it is one unit away from an enemy unit.

Computer Combat

Now that you have programmed the player's attacks, it is time to program the computer attack code. This is slightly more complicated than the player's attack code because it means the computer needs to find out which unit is selected, which unit it should attack. It will also need to find out the results of the attack and play them out on screen.

Note

Because many aspects of the code is reused, we will only be covering the combat aspect in detail; for any changes to other aspects of the code, we will provide a quick overview of what has changed.

First you need to open the file that we have already created with all the previous changes implemented and our other changes. The file is called Combat3.mfa and can be found in the Examples folder on the CD-ROM. Ensure that you load this in to your MMF2 demo software and ensure that the Frame Editor is displayed.

Note

There is a small coding error in this example file which prevents enemy combat taking place. You can download a slightly modified version from the following url : www.computerwargames.co.uk/ combat3.mfa.

New Objects and Screen Size

We have made some changes to the previous examples by adding some new objects and changing the screen size. You can see these changes in Figure 10.25.

Following is a list of these items and changes, with an explanation of why we changed them:

Screen size: The previous example's screen size was fine for the number of items we needed on screen, but we now need to display more objects, so it is essential to increase the screen size. The screen size is now 800×600, which is smaller than

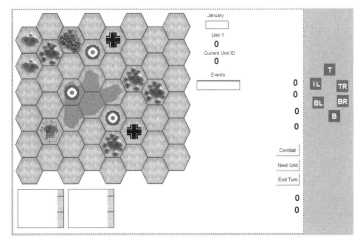

Figure 10.25
The Frame Editor, displaying some new objects and a change of screen size.

the normal screen size resolution of 1024×768. We are keeping the screen small to ensure that it fits on to the majority of computer resolutions available.

Computer placeholder units: These are a set of purple placeholder units that surround the current computer unit in much the same way that the player's current unit is surrounded by red placeholder units. These purple units will help us with the combat code by identifying whether any player units are overlapping the placeholder units and so are available for attack. These units are members of the qualifier group Group.Bad.

Two list boxes: These list objects are called List_Computer and List_Player. The list object is a great way to store temporary information and retrieve it when required. Even though the List object is used for storing text, you can use the conversion expression in the Expression Evaluator to convert from a number to text and back again. These two list boxes are used to store the object fixed values. The List_Computer stores all of the computer units' reference numbers, while the second list box stores the current overlapped fixed value. We will only be placing one value in this list for the Player objects, so even if the computer's placeholder units are overlapping two or more player units, it will only take the reference of one. This is because one unit can only have one attack per round.

Additional counters: We have added some additional counters to keep track of fixed values, as we need to load the current values into these counters to access them from the conditions.

You will notice that the static text object called Sttxt_Messages is also present from the previous example, although it wasn't used. In this example, we will use the Sttxt_Messages object to display simple messages of what is going on in our game. In a completed game, you would use a larger display and would probably place it in a nice interface.

Order of Running

Before you begin looking at the new code for your computer combat, it is important to understand how this code works. Whenever you add new code and groups, it is important to remember to update any links between groups, for example, enabling and disabling groups. If you do not do this or do it incorrectly, then you can have problems with your code that may take many days of checking and double checking until you find the problem.

Where possible, keep your groups in the order in which they will be run in the event editor. You could also flag with a note any code that enables or disables a group. In this example, our code runs in the following group order:

- Player Movement

- Player Combat (if initiated)

- Computer units initialization

- Computer Unit 1 movement

- Computer Unit 2 movement

- Enemy Combat

- End of turn initialization

Some of these processes (phases) may contain additional groups. The Enemy Combat process contains code for both the first and second units combat, these will be contained in separate groups.

Note

It can be very difficult to trap an error with groups not being closed at the correct time. More information about testing can be found in Chapter 15.

Enemy Combat Order

The main work needed for the following example is a code group to handle the enemy combat. The enemy combat group is a little more complicated than some of the other code. This is because the whole process is automated as soon as the player presses the End Turn button and so no interaction takes place between the player and computer. This means that we must give the computer more information (code) so that it can make the whole process work.

1. The combat group is initiated when the two units have no movement.

2. The combat group is initiated when the first unit has moved and the second unit has no movement.

3. The combat group is initiated when both units have moved.

Once the enemy combat group has been initiated, we have a set of code that handles combat for each unit. It handles it using a set of timed events. When adding your own timed events, it's important to ensure that the timer code does not overlap with other computer units because that may cause strange things to happen with your program. The enemy combat group is split into two key sections:

- **Initialization**: The initialization section sets up any variables or information needed for the combat group to function. It also handles timed events for both units, the first being initiated when the timer equals 3 seconds, while Enemy_Unit2 is initiated on 6 seconds. The very first thing to happen in both these timed events is to place the purple placeholder units around the correct computer unit; this is so that it can correctly check for overlapping items. The code will also check if there are no overlapping items and if this is true for the first unit, will close any corresponding groups, while if there are no overlapping items for the second unit, it enables the End Turn code.

- **Unit Combat groups**: Each unit has a Combat group, and within it a Hit and Miss group; this will handle the display of a hit and miss icon and its destruction after a set amount of time.

Note

You are able to change the timer within the code to speed up the process if needed in your own games. If you feel the combat takes too long, setting the timer lower will speed it up, while increasing the timer will slow the game calculations further.

Changes to the Original Code

We have made a few changes to the code in our previous examples. A quick summary of these changes are now discussed:

Start of Frame and Placeholder: In the Enemy combat group we move the purple placeholder units around the screen, depending on where the current unit is. At the start of the frame we want to place these placeholder units around the first unit. We will do this using a simple Start of Frame condition and a second condition which will pick Enemy_Unit1 using its fixed value. The action is simply to place the placeholder units around it using the same positions we have used for the red placeholder units. You can see this code in Figure 10.26.

Friends and Enemies: In each of the three player movement groups called Unit 1, Unit 2, and Unit 3, we added an additional action for the Unit is overlapping Group.Good. We place the fixed value of the player unit in the Ref_Player object. We also have an additional event and action that checks to see if the Enemies group is overlapping the friends group. This is the computer units overlapping the player's placeholder units. This creates an action to place the

Figure 10.26
The code to place the placeholder units around Enemy_Unit1.

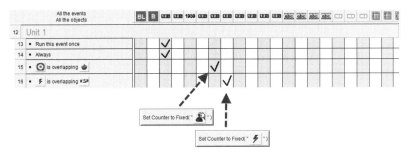

Figure 10.27
Additional action and additional event and action for fixed value information. This is replicated in all three player movement groups.

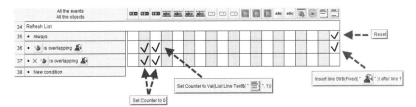

Figure 10.28
The resetting of values to ensure that only correct information is used within the groups.

fixed value in to the Ref_Computer object. This code allows you to update two counters with the fixed value information of units overlapping. You can see this in Figure 10.27.

List Refresh: When you are reading information in to a list that you use for other purposes (in this case, as the basis for which unit to attack), it is important to ensure that the information that you obtain is the latest data. The main problem with any programming language is that you fail to clear the original contents and then do any comparisons using this out of date data. In the core code, we will update the list and the two counters that contain the fixed references, and then we will clear them. For the refresh code, we will use the Always condition to reset both lists. We will use the conditions for one group overlapping another to fill the list and negated (not overlapped) to reset the list. You can see these events and conditions in Figure 10.28.

Note

Because the first list box only contains the entire computer unit's fixed values and does not change throughout the life of the program, we do not need to reset it and reload the values.

Note

You will notice in Figure 10.26 and some others in this chapter that the image does not look like the normal Event Editor. This is because to be able to show you all of the events and actions within a simple diagram, in some cases, we have decided to show you two different editors in one image. As usual, on the left side, you can see the relevant events, which are displayed in the Event Editor. In the part of the image where the arrow appears is a list of actions that is normally displayed in the Event List Editor. The list of events shows an icon, then a (), and then an expression. The graphic before the colon is the object that the action is assigned to.

Enemy Combat Group Code

The first set of events in our Combat Group contains two On group activation conditions. These will only run when the group is enabled, and they are used to:

- Disable the buttons so the user cannot select them while the computer is moving the units and performing combat calculations.

- Setting the alterable values of the defending player unit, and the alterable value of any computer unit to the appropriate alterable value slot. You may remember doing the same thing for the player combat, but this is just the opposite way around. So the computer unit stores its values in its Att Random slot, while the player's units store any values in their Def Random slot.

- Setting the Event's static text object box on the Frame Editor to contain the words Starting Combat.

- Resetting the timer back to 0 so we can begin the process of using the timer as the primary method for activating some of the other events.

For the second On group activation event we only have two actions:

- Adding a random number of up to 10 to the alterable value M for all the units in the Player group.

- Adding a random number of up to 10 to the alterable value N slot for all the units in the Enemies group.

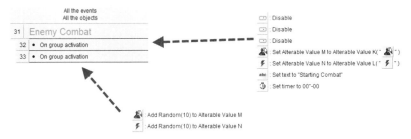

Figure 10.29
The initialization of the Enemy combat group.

This gives the units a total value that we will use for combat calculations. You can see the events and the associated actions in an event list in Figure 10.29.

The next set of code is split into two parts; the first is code for the first computer unit, and the second set of code is for the second computer unit. In order of code, we do the following for Enemy_Unit1:

- For the first event, when the timer equals 3 seconds, we pick the object with a fixed value equal to unit 1. This ensures that any actions will relate to this particular object. We will then place the purple placeholder objects around Enemy_Unit1.

- The second event occurs when the timer is equal to 3 seconds and the Bad group is overlapping the Player group, this event runs the actions when the placeholder objects are touching a player unit. It runs the single action to place the fixed reference of this object in the Ref_Fixed_Attack1 counter. This counter is used to store the fixed value for the Enemy_Unit1 code only.

- The third event, timer equals 3 seconds, and the Ref_Fixed_Attack1 counter does not equal 0. This means that there is a player unit overlapping the placeholder units. In this case, you would want to run some additional code to check for combat success or failure. If there is a unit overlapping the placeholder unit it would then run the relevant combat code group, which in the case of the first unit would be a group called Enemy 1 Combat. We will also disable the buttons to ensure that the player cannot click on them while the calculations are taking place.

- The fourth and final event for unit 1 checks to see if the timer equals 3 seconds and the Ref_Fixed_Attack1 object equals 0. This means that there is no overlapping player unit for it to attack. The action is simply to close the

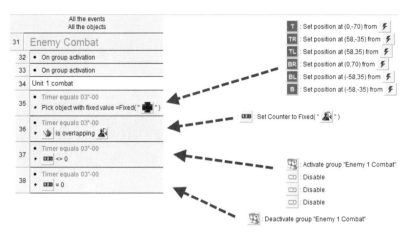

Figure 10.30
The initial code for the Enemy_Unit1 object.

Enemy 1 Combat group. It is sensible to close groups when they are no longer needed, as leaving a group open can cause your program to no longer work correctly.

The same code exists for Enemy_Unit2 except the timer events happen at 6 seconds, the reference counter is called Ref_Fixed_Attack2, and it closes both its own combat group and the primary Enemy Combat when there are no overlapping units. It no longer needs either group open because all combat code has run. You can see the events and actions for the first unit in Figure 10.30.

The Enemy Combat group has two additional groups, called Enemy 1 Combat and Enemy 2 Combat. These contain code for running attack and defense options for each unit. We will detail the Enemy 1 Combat group and its contents, but the code will be nearly identical.

The Enemy 1 Combat group has three sections; the first is two events, which are used to ensure that the Enemy_Unit1 and the player unit that is overlapping the placeholder objects are selected. This is so we can run specific combat values against only the objects we require. After MMF2 gets these values, it will run one of two groups: the Enemy 1 Hit if the hit is successful, and Enemy 1 Miss if the computer unit misses in the attack.

You can see the first two events and their respective actions in Figures 10.31 and 10.32.

Figure 10.31
Checking to see if the attacking unit has more attack points than the defending unit's defense points.

Figure 10.32
Checking to see if the attacking unit has equal or less than attack points than the defending unit's defense points.

The actions for the first of the two events, which will be if the unit has a successful attack, are as follows:

- Create the Active_Hit object at the location of the player unit.

- Play an impact sound.

- Activate the Enemy 1 Hit group.

- Destroy the player unit object.

- Set the text for the message box (under the Events text on the Frame Editor) to C1 Attack Successful.

The actions for the second of the two events, which will be if the attack is unsuccessful, are:

- Create an Active_Miss object at the location of the player unit.

- Play an impact sound.

- Activate the Enemy 1 Miss group.

- Set the text for Sttext_Messages to C1 Attack Failed.

Finally, we have the code for the Hit and Miss groups. For the Enemy 1 Hit group we have the following events and actions:

- **On Group Activation**: When the group starts, set the timer to 20 seconds. Disable all of the buttons.

- **Timer Equals 23 seconds**: Destroy the Active_Hit object; this removes the object from the screen after a pause of three seconds.

- **Number of Active_Hit objects equals 0**: Deactivate the groups for Enemy 1 Hit and Enemy 1 Combat. Set the timer back to four seconds, which ensures that the code we had at the start (which checks for items at three seconds) does not run, and then two seconds later the code for the six second timer events will run.

The conditions and actions for the Enemy 1 Miss group are as follows:

- **On Group Activation**: When the group activates, set the timer to 30 seconds. Disable all of the buttons.

- **Timer equals 33 seconds**: When the timer equals 33 seconds, which creates a three second pause, destroy the Active_Miss object, then disable the Enemy 1 Miss and Enemy 1 Combat groups. Reset the timer to four seconds so that the code for the second unit will run.

You can see the two groups and their actions in Figure 10.33.

This code is replicated in the second combat-specific group, the only difference being that the group activation in both the Enemy 2 Hit and Enemy 2 Miss enables the next group, which is the End of Turn group. All combat groups are disabled.

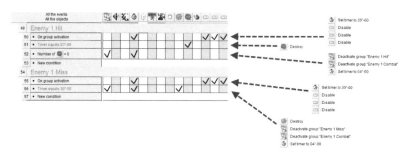

Figure 10.33
The Hit and Miss group's events and actions.

Additional Concepts

Now that you have a good idea of how to implement computer movement using code that you have already used in previous examples, it is time to think about what other things you might want to implement in your game. We have listed them here for completeness, along with some ideas for how to implement them if you feel that you would like them in your own game.

Line of Sight

Line of sight is very common in Real Time Strategy games, but it can also be useful in war games. Line of sight is the method of checking to see if one object has a clear view of another object. This is important in war games if you want to implement long range attacks. If a unit is behind a mountain, it does not have line of sight and would not be able to attack. You may decide that you want to change the combat from a one-tile system to allow combat on a larger area. After you changed the code, it would be a case of placing the range of each unit's weapons into an array so that you can calculate whether a unit can fire that distance. Otherwise, it is a missed attack. Once you have done this, you will need to calculate a line of sight path; fortunately, the Wargame Map object can do this for you.

Using the Wargame Map object, you would configure it in the following way:

- Calculate a path between two objects in the same way as calculating a path between the starting location and destination. You will be asked for the XY coordinates for both locations.

- Test to see if the path is valid. You can do this using Condition A valid path exists. This checks to see if there is a path between the two objects. Note that you must tell the Wargame Map object about any obstacles that may make this path invalid, such as any impassable terrain (mountains) or other friendly units perhaps, using the numbers 99 and 100.

You can see the line of site option in the Wargame Map object in Figure 10.34.

Morale & Retreat

When a unit is put under immense pressure, there is a likelihood it may crack as a unit, and retreat. Morale is an important aspect in any war game. More experienced units are more likely to fight while inexperienced units may turn and flee if they feel the tide of the battle is not with them.

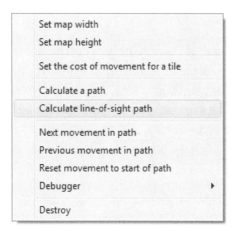

Figure 10.34
The Wargame Map object's prebuilt code for calculating a line of sight path.

In certain armies, retreating was not an option to take lightly, and they could be killed by their own side for doing so. In the Second World War, there were instances where armies were forced to fight with limited ammunition and not every soldier had a weapon against a heavily armed opposition.

If you want morale to play a part in your games, there are a few things to take in to account:

- **Basic Morale**: Every unit needs a basic morale indicator. This is an alterable value that you can increase or decrease when the need arises. Probably the easiest way to make a morale modifier is to use this basic value and then roll a random number against it. This is very much like the attack engine. You need to consider the range of morale used in your game, including any other possible values that you might add to get the maximum value of morale.

- **Officer Morale**: We will talk more about officers and generals in Chapter 11. If a unit has a particular officer attached, this may increase or decrease the morale modifier. A good officer may add a couple of additional morale points.

- **Fight to the death**: If a unit is cornered with nowhere to go, then regardless of morale, the unit has to, in most cases, fight to the death. If you want your game to be more complex in the battle engine side, this is a nice feature to add. This would involve checking around the unit to see if it has a possible escape route. If it does not, then you can ignore any morale considerations. If a unit is cornered, you may decide to add additional defensive points, and they are more likely going to fight harder than before because they have no choice.

- **Experience Counts**: As a unit has battles, it will become more experienced and have a reduced chance of losing morale, which will stop it from running away. You should consider a sliding scale, so that after each battle, this tally increases; once it reaches the next scale, it will add to their morale value. For example, after five battles, a unit will receive a +1 role on its morale tally.

- **Safe Surroundings**: If a unit is being attacked by a force superior in numbers, but has a tactical advantage such as defensive items like walls, buildings, or a town between them and the enemy, they may not feel as much threat from an enemy attack.

- **Dead and wounded**: If multiple soldiers are within a single unit object, you can scale your morale modifier by the percentage of soldiers still available to fight. If a single unit graphic contains 100 soldiers and 50 are dead or wounded, the morale would be reduced by a number of points.

- **Tired**: If a particular unit is fighting too often, it is likely to become battle weary. If it is always at the front line doing the fighting and never has the chance to rest, this is a recipe for morale being reduced further. You could have an alterable value for Battle Fatigue, again using a sliding scale to reduce morale once a unit has been in the fight for a set period of time. You could set a number of safe areas where the soldiers can begin to reduce this fatigue level.

After you set the rules in motion to dictate that a unit has lost its morale, then it should retreat as fast as it can from the battlefield, or from the immediate area of play. The keys to a retreating unit are where it can go, whether it will be immediately routed and removed from the game, or whether it will run in a particular direction off the field of play. If you decide to make the object run in a particular direction, then you could set a morale-based comparison so that when the morale hits a particular value, the Wargame Map object then sets the destination tile for that unit.

Multiple Soldiers in One Unit

In many of the examples we have completed so far, single graphic object represents either a single unit (a single plane), or a set of soldiers in a unit, such as a platoon. When an attack is successful on that unit, we automatically remove it from the battlefield. What if you wanted to have a unit take a bigger part in a battle, and place 50, 100, or even 1,000 soldiers in a unit graphic? This is possible and only requires a slight rethink of the code you have already created.

The things you will need include:

- **Total number of soldiers alterable value**: To store the starting number of soldiers within a unit, for example 250.

- **Current number of soldiers alterable value**: To store the current number of soldiers; this is useful because you may allow units to be resupplied with more troops if they are away from the battle area for a while. You will need a value slot that can change throughout the course of a battle. Having the original alterable value allows you to reset this variable value if required.

- **Display:** A method of telling the player the number of soldiers left in the unit. This could be a separate graphic in the interface, text, or an image of the actual unit itself.

- **Combat changes**: You will need to make a small change to the way your combat code works. Rather than destroying a unit, you need to reduce the alterable value that stores the current soldier value. You also need to check to see when the number of soldiers equals 0 and then remove the soldier unit from screen.

You have now completed the chapter on attack and defense. In the next chapter, we will be looking a little more closely at generals and officers and how they might have an impact on your games.

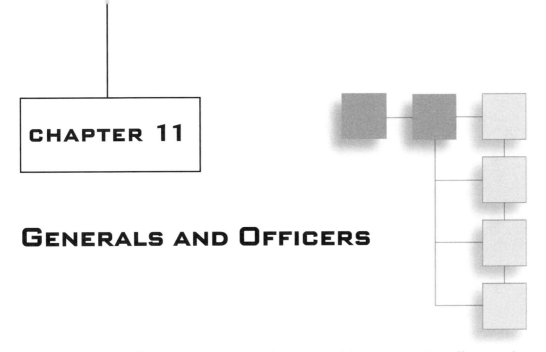

CHAPTER 11

GENERALS AND OFFICERS

Those in charge of a unit or army can have a positive or negative effect on the morale of a fighting force.

You can find many cases throughout history where a smaller, outnumbered army has won an unlikely battle against the odds.

In 1415, Henry V gave a stirring speech to the English forces at Agincourt in France. Though the English forces were outnumbered, the use of sound tactics, the large number of longbow men, the terrain, and the likelihood for the common soldiers that, if captured, they would be killed ensured that the English were successful. It could also be said that Henry as a person added to the overall morale and effect of his forces to bring about success that day.

You can find just as many cases throughout history where bad decisions sent many troops into battle either poorly equipped or unprepared. The First World War on many occasions sent troops "over the top" of the trenches, only to be cut down by machine gunfire. In a number of cases, the Allied troops bombarded the German trenches for hours or even days, but the German troops went underground and, for the most part, were safe from the bombardment. In a miscalculation, the Allied officers stopped the bombardment and told the troops to march slowly toward the German trenches, because they didn't expect resistance, which gave the German troops enough time to come up from the trenches and fire on the soldiers. You can also find cases where soldiers refused to fight because of the number of these poor judgments, and then were shot for treason.

You can see how good or bad decisions by generals or officers might have an effect on a unit's morale. In Chapter 10, I discussed how you can implement a simple morale system. You can add or remove morale points depending on the type of person who is in charge of a unit.

Here are some ideas for generals and officers in your games:

- Each unit could have a general, or perhaps only special units would contain one. High ranking officers would always have a set of guards to protect them in battle.

- You could add modifiers to the morale of a unit if it has a good or bad officer.

- You could create a game where each unit or officer has to be purchased. This way the player has to make a conscious decision about which officers they choose.

- If you decide to go for a system where the player purchases units and officers, then you would need to consider giving your officers more than one attribute. This allows you to have multi-layered officers where they may be weak in one or more areas but strong in another.

- A good officer could have an impact on the attacking values. So, rather than the attack value plus the random number, you could have an additional value on top. This would give the unit more chances for successful attacks, but only while that officer is attached to that unit.

Officer Attributes

I mentioned previously that your officers could have a number of attributes that might have different effects on a battle at various times. Here are some ideas that you might want to introduce into your own games:

- **Attack Modifier:** Give the unit additional attack modifiers for having the officer in the unit. It could also be the case that the officer reduces the attack modifier score.

- **Morale Modifier:** Morale makes a difference to whether a unit stands and fights or is reduced to a force running away from the field of battle. With the right type of officer in charge, this could increase the overall morale of the fighting unit.

- **Retreat Point/Rally Point**: When a unit retreats from battle, is it automatically removed, or does it have a set place on the map where it will regroup. Perhaps a unit will retreat to or rally near a particular officer.

- **Income**: Perhaps an officer is so popular (or hated) that that officer changes the amount of income a particular tile can generate.

- **Uprising**: If you have invaded a particular town or area, there is always a chance of the local populous rebelling and trying to take back their area. The officer may have an overall effect on the possibility of an uprising.

You can see an example of some attributes attached to two different army generals, Napoleon and Caesar, in Figures 11.1 and 11.2. You can have whatever attributes you require for your game, and these are just examples.

Identifying a Unit with an Officer

Once you have decided to implement officers within your army, you need some way of identifying them on the battlefield. Some possibilities are:

- **Officer's head is the unit graphic**: Rather than have a normal unit graphic for a unit (for example, tank, plane, or logo), you could have a particular

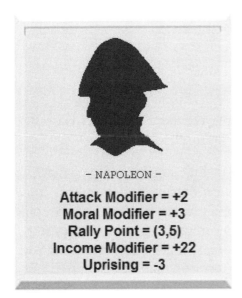

- NAPOLEON -

Attack Modifier = +2
Moral Modifier = +3
Rally Point = (3,5)
Income Modifier = +22
Uprising = -3

Figure 11.1
The officer attributes for Napoleon.

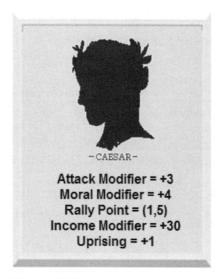

Figure 11.2
The officer attributes for Caesar.

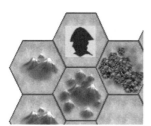

Figure 11.3
Officer represented on the unit.

officer's head silhouette. This shows the player where the officer is on the map. You can see an example of this in Figure 11.3.

- **Icon or other smaller graphic**: You could include some identifying mark on each of the units to show that it has an officer of value attached. This could be in the form of a smaller graphic icon or a text letter. A common graphic used in World War II games for American officers might be a set of star graphics. The more stars, the higher the officer attached to that unit. You can see an example of this in Figure 11.4.

- **Text**: Perhaps all units would have an officer attached to them, and you could identify them with a small amount of text under the unit graphic.

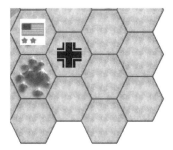

Figure 11.4
Officer represented on the unit as a graphical icon. In this figure, the number of stars represents the seniority of the officer attached to the unit.

- **Graphic separate from unit**: You could have a graphic menu bar on the side of your map that details information such as the weather, time, day, unit selected, and unit information.

Setting Up Officers

Whether to set up an officer for a unit depends on how many attributes you decide to place on an officer within the game. You need to seriously consider how you implement officers within units because, if you decide an officer has only one attribute (to increase or decrease an attack, for example) and later on you decide to change this so that an officer has many more attributes in the game, you may be doing significant reworking of your officer configuration and programming.

- **Single Attribute**: The easiest option for setting up a single attribute on an officer is to use the unit's alterable values slot. This option is the quickest and easiest way of storing information for a unit.

- **Multiple Attributes**: The best way to store multiple values for a particular unit is within an array. You can then have multiple attributes that you can call when you need them. In previous chapters, you used arrays for storing lots of information for tile data, for example. All this requires is setting up a numeric array and then assigning various values to each set of slots. Alternatively, you could set values at runtime using a condition such as Start of Frame.

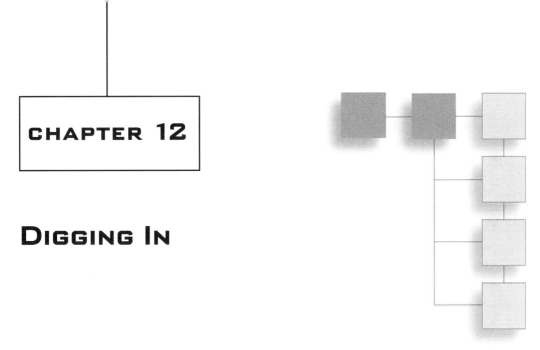

CHAPTER 12

Digging In

In many wars and battles, the type of terrain and any manmade features has changed the course of a battle from impossible to win to success. In Chapter 7, I talk about actual terrain such as hills, roads, and water. In this chapter, I will discuss how the armies themselves can change or use the terrain or other equipment to their advantage to provide additional protection.

In this chapter, you will find out about these manmade features and how they might affect or be introduced into your games.

Trench Warfare

Trenches were a common feature of the First World War and were a way of creating a holding line between two opposing forces. This created the stalemate that ensured that the First World War continued for much longer than it might have otherwise.

Creating a war game using trenches would be possible, but has its own issues, such as barbed wire to reduce speed of the soldiers, machine gun nests, and artillery units.

Here are some things to take into consideration:

- **Barbed wire**: The use of barbed wire was quite extensive in the First World War trench systems. Any soldier going over the top trying to take an enemy trench would most likely have to traverse a set of wire. Any way the enemy could slow down the attackers would give their own soldiers more time to man the machine gun nests, which could have devastating effects. A movement effect modifier should be used to reduce the speed of any soldiers moving over wire.

- **Craters:** The First World War also had extensive use of artillery units, where many shells would be fired at the enemy before an attack. In many cases, these artillery attacks were inaccurate, but also the constant shelling of a position had a serious effect on a unit's morale. Many of the trenches' no man's land (the land in-between the two opposing side's trenches) would be potted with craters from the artillery strikes. The craters were often filled with large amounts of water, creating a death trap for soldiers that were injured or wounded and fell into them. Ironically, the craters also provided shelter from machine gunfire for soldiers who needed cover. When using craters in a war game, you are better off selecting either a negative or positive effect in the first instance. So, for example, all trenches will provide cover for a unit adding +3 to their defense value. You can make this more complicated by using weather effects in addition to the tile type. If it has been raining, provide a negative effect to the number of units destroyed if they are successfully attacked.

- **Trenches:** You can certainly have a war game fought within a set of trenches, imitating, for example, those in the First World War. Creating a war game would be best at the single soldier per unit. You could also include a no man's land, but allow soldiers to cross over and fight within the trenches. Remember that soldiers in other wars also dug small trenches to provide cover. Small one- and two-man trenches provided additional defense for soldiers in wars such as the Second World War and the Vietnam War.

Outposts, Forts, and Castles

When particular countries' armies are expanding and taking land from other countries, it is useful to create outposts or bases for defense to protect the soldiers from attack. Leaving yourself without a way to defend against a local force would be very dangerous and could lead to large losses and defeat.

Roman armies were highly adept at creating defensive positions when marching in foreign lands. They created forts to protect them from attack. For makeshift bases, these forts were sometimes quite elaborate and impressive.

Some of the base types you might find throughout history include:

- **Forts**: Sometimes temporary in the case of marching armies, or more permanent places of residence. These forts were common in both ancient history and more recent American history. The forts, which often were made from local wood, were cheaper and easier to build and repair than stone-based fortifications, which were much more labor-intensive and difficult to transport. Forts can provide additional cover and defensive points against attackers in your games.

- **General Outpost**: This might consist of a few buildings, horses, and carts. The soldiers themselves might live in tents. An example of an outpost might be the one at Rorkes Drift. As the British army expanded its empire in parts of Africa, a small outpost of 150 soldiers defended an outpost against around 4,000 Zulu soldiers. Using the terrain, carts, and buildings as a defensive perimeter, they were able to survive wave after wave of attacks. An interesting idea for a war game is a small battle based around an outpost, either in a traditional war game setting or in the future. Additional defensive points would be used to give these soldiers less chance of being hit in an attack.

- **Castles**: As medieval armies forged mighty empires, it became apparent that to keep the local populace subjugated, a base of operations was required: a structure that would be positioned in an important crossing point or strategic location. After the Norman invasion of 1066, William the Conqueror set about a massive castle-building exercise across many parts of England and the borders between England, Wales, and Scotland. He took the designs and defenses that were already successful and popular in Europe and improved upon them. Castles provided an excellent place of defense against the weather and also against invading or attacking armies. They provided a location to handle both taxes and trade and so were a good source of revenue. In many cases, the only way to successfully defeat an army barricaded within a castle was to prevent anyone from entering or leaving. By creating a siege over many months, the inhabitants didn't have access to additional food and disease was rife. In your war games, being in a castle or on a castle tile will provide a bonus defense value. Later on in history with the advent of gunpowder, castles became less of a defensive structure and fell out of favor with armies.

Towns and Cities

I have already discussed some types of buildings, such as forts and castles, but battles taking place in a town or city took on a different type of warfare. This is very true of modern warfare, where such battles are called "street to street" or "street fighting."

Ever since they came into use, guns and gunshot have changed many aspects of war. They allowed forces to be more mobile but, at the same time, take full advantage of cover and the buildings around them. Wars in the Napoleon era used buildings as well as open warfare, allowing soldiers to fire but also take cover and hold a strategic area in the battle. Wars today are less about open warfare because of the high availability of technology that can quickly and easily destroy any units in open ground.

Chapter 6 covers movement over towns and cities, and even though they slow units down while moving on them, they can provide a large amount of protection from enemy fire.

The era that your war game will concentrate on depends on whether you decide to use a city as a single or a small number of hex tiles or use many hexagon files to display both the buildings and the streets around them. Regardless of which you decide to use, being located in a building or city should offer some protection and gain the unit additional defensive points. If you are working on a game whereby a single soldier will be represented by a single unit tile, your game may have additional complexities if enemy units can enter the same building that contains the opposing force's men. In this case, you will need to program the code to check for when a soldier is on a street tile or in a building.

Other Defenses

Your forces can get protection from enemy fire or attacks in other ways, including the following:

- **Pillboxes:** Pillboxes were generally concrete boxes that provided very good cover for soldiers and had heavy machine guns or artillery contained within them. In wars such as the Vietnam War, the pillboxes might also have been made from wood and camouflaged to prevent the opposing side from seeing them until it was too late. Pillboxes should give the side occupying them an increase in defensive points. Pillboxes were most susceptible to flame throwers or grenades if a unit could get behind them. In the Second World War, the Germans installed a large number of concrete pillboxes along the coast to give added protection from invading forces.

- **Sandbags**: Sandbags are very easy to create for an army; they just require a set of bags and something to fill them with. Because they are called sandbags, one component they can be filled with is sand, but they can also be filled with dirt. Sandbags provide limited protection from gunfire, so any force stationed behind sandbags should get a small increase in defense points.

- **Vehicles**: Certain heavy vehicles, such as armored tanks, can provide some protection from enemy fire. These tanks can provide cover inside and outside to foot soldiers. If an advancing tank unit had infantry units dispersed among it, when attacked, the soldiers could get behind the tanks for cover. They could also use the tanks as a way of advancing to an enemy position. This will be difficult to implement in your own games, though you can have units enter and exit a vehicle, if these units do not exceed the maximum capacity of the vehicle they are trying to enter. If a unit is behind a vehicle, you can give the soldiers an increase in defense value, but you might want to take into account that additional damage might be taken by the infantry if the vehicle unit in front of them is destroyed. It is likely that the vehicle carrying ammunition and fuel will explode.

- **Moats**: Many castles and settlements in medieval times were situated by water such as a river, sea, or near marsh land. Moats were ditches around a castle or settlement filled with water. The only way to get to the settlement was by way of a drawbridge (a bridge that could be raised or lowered to prevent access).

- **Manmade Hills**: Some of the manmade hill structures created in medieval times were extremely impressive. Tons of earth was moved to create a set of trenches around a hill at different levels. This meant that any force on top of the hill could throw missiles down at an army moving slowly up the hill. But the ditches were difficult for the soldiers to navigate and created killing zones, areas where they were most exposed to the attacks from above.

- **Walls**: Building a wall made with stone could not be done quickly, but such a wall could provide excellent cover for any force needing to protect its borders. Two such walls are the Great Wall in China and Hadrian's Wall, which was built by the Romans on the border between England and

Scotland. Using ditches on the attacking side of the wall, the Romans could gain an advantage over any attacking force.

Implementing

You can implement some of the items discussed in this chapter.

- **Engineer Unit**: You can create a special unit, such as an engineer unit that can build certain structures like pillboxes, barbed wire, and sandbags. A number of turns will be taken until the unit creates a particular item, and once the engineer unit has completed the structure, the terrain tile will be updated to show this new feature. You need to take into account any additional modifiers that need to be added to the tile once this new feature is added. Don't forget that you also need to create a unit graphic for the engineer unit or have a particular icon on the unit to show that it can make these items.

- **Cost**: Is there a cost to building these features? Building a fort or castle will cost in terms of time, manpower, and finances. A cost will be involved if the unit will gain defensively from creating such an item. In the case of sandbags, the only cost is in terms of time, but if you are creating a medieval war game, there is some financial cost to creating a castle; otherwise, the player could create castles everywhere and change the balance of the game, making it unwinnable for the computer or the second player.

- **Resources**: You might want to have a resource management aspect to your game so that if the player does not have the skills, money, or resources to build a fortification, the player will not be able to build one. Your game will have more depth because you can begin to give the player options for what is the most important aspect of the game. Is the game's aim to conquer units by using an aggressive style, or will the game provide more of an "attack only when needed, build up resources and money" type of game play?

- **Tiles**: You will need to create additional graphical frames to depict the change to the landscape for your game. So, for example, if a trench is created, it should be represented on your map tile.

When a unit is in the process of making defensive positions, it may be more susceptible to attack, or it may not gain the full advantage of the defenses it is making. You might want to consider the following options for showing the player on screen what is happening when the unit is building:

- **Icon or other smaller graphic**: You can include an identifying mark on each of the units to show that it is building. This mark could be in the form of a smaller graphic icon or a text letter.

- **Text**: You can just tag a unit with text to say it is an engineering unit.

- **Graphic separate from unit**: You can have a graphic menu bar on the side of your map that details information such as the weather, time, day, unit selected, and unit information. This might also include details of what any units are building and how much time they have left until the item is completed.

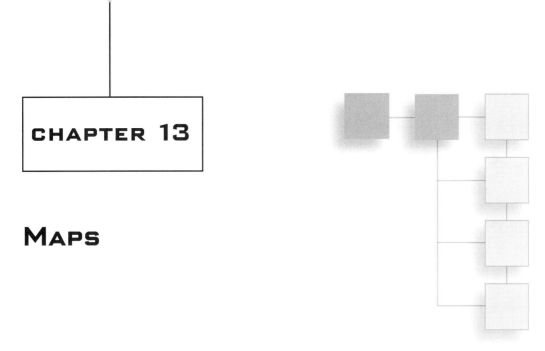

CHAPTER 13

MAPS

In the examples, you have kept the maps to a small area on the screen and at a low resolution, such as 800 × 600. In your own war games, you may want to have a really large battlefield. In this chapter, you will be looking at the size of the playing area, implementing a mini-map for larger games and when and why you implement Fog of War.

Note

Fog of War is a term used in many war games to describe the visibility of the battlefield. Rather than allowing the player to see all enemy units or the whole map, introducing Fog of War means the player can only see a certain distance around each unit.

Scrolling

If you decide to have a war game played over a large number of tiles, then you will want the screen to scroll around the map. In the following example, you will move around the screen using the cursor keys.

When you create a game with MMF2, you set the application size, which then filters down into the frame sizes. So, in some of your previous examples, you had an application and a frame size of 800 × 600. If you change the frame size to something larger than the application size, you will still retain the 800 × 600 application window, which is displayed as a dotted outline around the window. Now you will also have an off-the-frame area that you can move around in. The off-the-frame area is the basis of scrolling games in MMF2, but also an area for your war game map to be extended.

In the example later in this chapter, you will do the following to make your scrolling map:

- Create a placeholder graphic that will tell the current position on the map.

- Code a Start of Frame event to place this placeholder graphic in the center of the screen.

- Code an Always condition that will always set the center of the frame to be at 0,0 of the placeholder graphic.

- Configure a number of events that will check for the arrow keys being pressed and change the position of the placeholder graphic.

- Check the position of the placeholder graphic so that it does not move off the screen, and, additionally, so that it stays central to the window.

To begin, you will use a file that you have already created which has all of the player and computer movements as well as the attack and defense phases.

Open the file called Scrolling.mfa, which is located in the Examples folder on the CD-ROM.

Changing the Screen Size

The total screen size for the war game map frame will be 1600 × 1200, which doesn't mean that your monitor will resize the application to this size, but this is how large the frame will be in the application's 800 × 600 window. You will now change the screen size:

1. Select the Frame 1 text in the Workspace toolbar, and click on the Properties tab if it is not already selected in the Properties window.

2. In the Size option, select 1600 × 1200.

   You will notice that the frame now resizes, and you can see the dotted line around the application, as shown in Figure 13.1. This dotted line represents where the application window border will appear when you run the game. You will not see the rest of the white area outside the dotted line unless you scroll the screen or make the application window bigger.

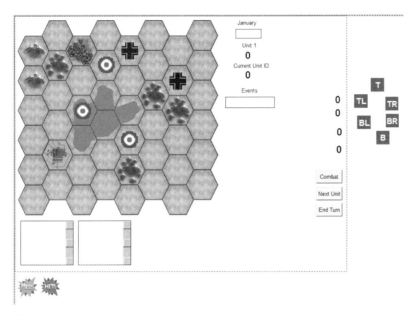

Figure 13.1
The resized frame with a dotted line around the application.

3. You will need to move the Active_Hit and Active_Miss objects back onto the gray area because they are currently on the play area, due to the change in the size of the frame. Drag both objects off to the left side.

Note

Things placed in the gray area are never displayed on the frame, though you can make an object move off the gray area and onto the playfield when required.

Creating a Placeholder Graphic

You will use a graphic on screen to help move the frame when the user presses the cursor keys. In your own games, you would make the object invisible, but for this example, the graphic will be left visible so that you can see it working.

1. Make sure you are on the frame editor.

2. Right-click anywhere on the frame and select Insert Object.

3. Find the Active object, select it, and click on OK.

4. Click somewhere off the frame on the gray area, maybe to the left of the frame where other off-frame objects have been placed. A new Active object will now be created.

5. Double-click on the object, delete the current contents, and fill it with a single color of your choice. Filling the active object with a single color will change the active object from a green diamond to a single colored square.

Note

When creating the placeholder graphic make sure you select a color that is not already present in the game background, which will make the placeholder graphic easier to see.

Coding the Screen Scrolling

You have now placed all of the components you require to configure the screen for scrolling; now, you need to create the programming logic that will make it move.

1. Click on the event editor button.

   You are now ready to add the code for your scrolling.

2. Scroll down to the bottom of the screen so that you are at the bottom of all of the events.

   First, you will add a comment to separate the code from the code that has already been programmed.

3. Right-click on the very last event line number; select Insert|A comment; in the Edit text box that appears, type **Screen Movement**; and click on OK.

   You will now create a start of frame event that will run some of the code straight away. This code places the new Active object in the middle of the screen. You know the frame is 800 × 600, so you will place the object at 400 × 300.

4. Click on the New condition text, select the Storyboard Controls object, and choose Start of Frame.

5. Move across from this object until you are directly under the placeholder Active object. Right-click on the action box and choose Position|Set X Coordinate. In the expression evaluator, type **400** and click on OK. Right-click on the same action box, choose Position|Set Y Coordinate, and in the expression box, type **300**. Click on OK.

You will now have an Always event that will always place the frame to center on the location of the Active placeholder object. This means that, as the object moves, the screen will always stay in the center. This forms the basis of a scrolling screen.

1. Click on the New condition text and select the Special object and then Always.

2. Move across to the Storyboard Controls object, right-click on the action box, and choose Scrollings|Center Window Position in Frame.

3. You will now see a dialog box asking you where on screen to position the frame—you want it to be based on a particular object. Click on the Relative to radio button. Find the placeholder Active object and click on OK. You will now be back at the dialog box. You want to change the coordinates from this object so that it is using its upper-left corner, so in the X and Y coordinates type **0** and click on OK.

You will now create some events to move the Active object either up or down left or right when the user presses a cursor key. You could use the single key-press condition, but you want the screen to keep moving if the user has kept her finger on the key. For this, you can use the Repeat option.

You will create the first event, and the process to create the rest is the same.

1. Click on the New condition text, select the Mouse pointer and Keyboard object, and choose The Keyboard|Repeat while key is pressed. A dialog box appears asking you to select which key to use; press the Down cursor key.

    When the player is pressing down, you want the Active object to move down the screen by 20 pixels. To implement, you can capture the current Y position and then add 20 onto it. If you want the object to move up the screen, you can reduce the value. For moving left and right, you are moving the X axis, to the left reduces the value, whereas moving to the right increases the value.

2. Move across until you are on the Active placeholder object. Right-click the action box and choose Position|Set Y coordinate.

3. The expression evaluator appears. You need to get the current object position before you amend it. So click on the Retrieve data from an object button. Find the Active object, select Position|Y Coordinate. You are still in the expression evaluator, and you need to amend the expression further. At the moment, you have retrieved its current location, so you are placing it

back in its original place. At the end of the expression, type **+20**. You can see this expression in Figure 13.2. Click on OK to save this to the event editor.

If you test the game now and then press the down arrow key, you will see the screen move in a downward direction.

4. Program the three other directions using the same method. Remember, you will need to program the up key to move along the Y axis and minus 20, moving to the left and right moves along the X axis; left is minus 20 and right +20.

Once you have programmed these events, you should have something that matches Figure 13.3.

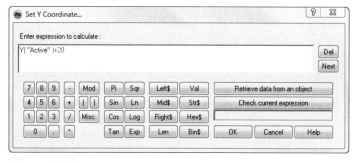

Figure 13.2
Expression to get the current location of the active object and then move it 20 pixels down its Y axis.

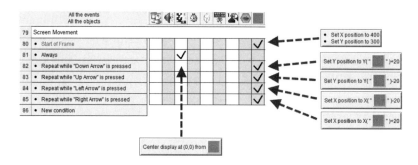

Figure 13.3
The events, actions, and conditions so far.

Once you have programmed the other three key directions, test the game. You will notice that you can move the screen in any of the directions and the screen will move. There is a problem—the placeholder active object can be moved so far in one direction that it will disappear off screen. You now need to create four events that will check the location of the placeholder active object on the frame. If it is at a specific location where it will be too far to the left, top, right, or bottom, MMF2 will replace the active object back to a specific location.

You can get MMF2 to check the position of the active object at specific points on the screen. These points will be on the Y coordinate 300 and less, or 900 and more. While on the X coordinate, you will be checking when it is more than 1200 or less than 400. If the object has gone past this position, you will place the object back to 300, 900, 1200, or 400, depending on where it is.

You will now add the first of these four events, which will check whether the position of the active object is equal to or less than 300 on the Y coordinate.

1. Click on the New condition text, find and select the Active object; from the list choose Position|Compare Y position to a value.

2. The expression evaluator appears. Change the drop-down box to Lower or Equal and then type the value **300** in the edit box and click on the OK button.

3. Move across to the right of this object until you are under the Active object, right-click the action box, and select Position|Set Y Coordinate. The expression evaluator appears. In the edit box, type the value **300** and click on OK.

If you run the game now, you will be able to move the cursor down and then back up, but will prevent the object moving up and off the top of the screen.

Do the next three events in the same way, and you should have it configured as shown in Figure 13.4.

If you run the program now, you should be able to move around the screen using a simple scrolling technique. You may notice one small issue though—when you move the screen, certain items move with the frame while others stay still. This causes the program some issues as you may want all items to move or all items to stay where they are. The reason you may want them to stay where they are on screen is that you may have created a user interface on the right side of the screen and want it to stay where it is. The text of the current month, which to begin with

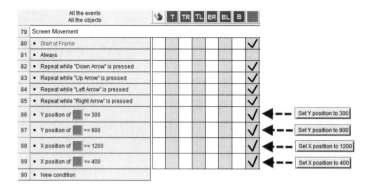

	All the events All the objects		T	TR	TL	BR	BL	B	
79	Screen Movement								
80	• Start of Frame							✓	
81	• Always								
82	• Repeat while "Down Arrow" is pressed							✓	
83	• Repeat while "Up Arrow" is pressed							✓	
84	• Repeat while "Left Arrow" is pressed							✓	
85	• Repeat while "Right Arrow" is pressed							✓	
86	• Y position of ▨ <= 300							✓	◀-- Set Y position to 300
87	• Y position of ▨ >= 900							✓	◀-- Set Y position to 900
88	• X position of ▨ >= 1200							✓	◀-- Set X position to 1200
89	• X position of ▨ <= 400							✓	◀-- Set X position to 400
90	• New condition								

Figure 13.4
Additional events to stop the screen placeholder active object from moving off the screen.

is January, is one of the items that stays where it is. I will now show you where this setting is, and you can turn it on or off as required.

1. Go to the frame editor and click on the Str_Months object, which is the object that currently displays January.

2. The properties will appear, click on the Runtime Options property tab. You will now see scrolling options.

3. Select or unselect Follow the Frame if you want the object to scroll as the window moves.

You can see this property window with the option selected in Figure 13.5.

Mini-Maps

You may have come across mini-maps in commercial games such as role-playing or strategy games. In a large map, it is very useful to show users a cut-down version of the map so that they can see what is happening when they are potentially on the other side of the map.

In this section of the chapter, you will re-create your main war game map as a smaller mini-map, which will give you enough information to tackle larger game maps.

Earlier, you created the file to begin programming; the file is mini-map.mfa in the Examples folder on the CD-ROM. Before beginning to program, I will take you through some of the items that were added to the program.

You can see the updated frame in Figure 13.6.

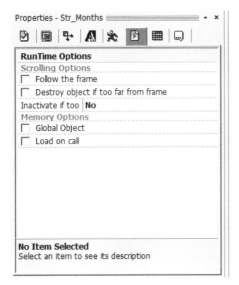

Figure 13.5
Scrolling options to prevent or allow the object to move within the window scrolling.

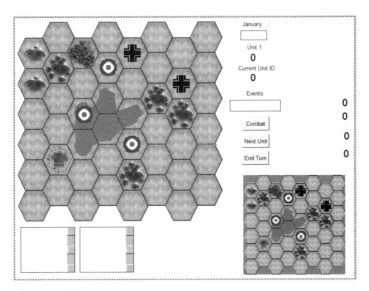

Figure 13.6
The updated frame with a new mini-map at the lower right.

You've already added the following:

■ A new frame called Frame 3 was added; it contains a mini-map of the real map. This map is 241 × 228 in size and is an exact copy of the original map, except for the size. The tiles are all present and are copies of tiles from the first frame, so these tile objects contain all of the alterable value slots. The units are copies but have been renamed, again they were copied and resized but retained the alterable value slots.

■ An additional array object called Array_TileID was added; it will keep track of all the units' locations on the map.

■ In each of the units, you added two new alterable value slots, one called MiniMap_ID and the other called TileID_Temp. The first is a sequential number that is assigned to each object, which enables you to loop through the units later. The second value will keep track of the tile id of the terrain these units are situated on. You may remember earlier in the book that each tile was given a tile ID number.

■ You added some global values, which will keep track of when an object is destroyed so it can be destroyed in the mini-map.

■ The Sub-Application object will display the mini-map. The properties of the Sub-Application were amended so that the internal values within the object are global, which means the Sub Application object can access any global information. You can see how the second Sub-Application object was configured to allow this communication with other global information in Figure 13.7.

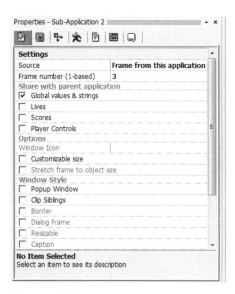

Figure 13.7
The second Sub-Application object, which displays the mini-map's configured global values.

- All units are now members of a new qualifier group called Arms, which is depicted with a pistol icon.

- You created some initial global value slots and renamed them. All of these global values were given the starting initial g_ followed by a piece of text to identify it.

You first need to program the information in Frame 1 which will then be used by Frame 3 to move its units to mimic those in the map. You will create the following code:

- Every one second, you will run a loop that loops through each of the five objects and places the value of the tile they are overlapped on into an array. You will then save this array.

- You will also need a set of code, which you place in a group, to check whether one of the five objects has been destroyed; if so, MMF2 will change a global value to 1. This will allow you to create the relevant conditions to check if a particular object has been destroyed and then you can create actions to destroy the mini-map objects on Frame 3.

Note

Because you will be using an array to save and load information to and from an array file, you need to copy the .mfa file that you will use for programming to your local hard disk. This way, when an array file is created in the same folder as the application file, you will not get errors. You will not be able to save an array file to the same location as the original file because that file is located on a read-only CD-ROM.

Programming the First Frame

You begin programming your first frame with a comment and two conditions, one that will run every second and will call a loop, while the second event will run the loop. You are using a timed event, such as every second, because your movement engine works on an every-second basis.

1. Make sure that you have copied the mini-map.mfa file to your hard disk and that it is open. Make sure you are in Frame 1's event editor.

2. Make sure all groups are collapsed and go to the very last line.

3. Right-click on the New condition event line number, which should be event line 38. Then select Insert|A Comment.

4. When the Edit Text box appears, type the text **Unit Placements** and click on OK.

5. Click on the New condition text, select the Timer object, and select Every. When the Every dialog box appears, it will already show 1 second, so click on OK.

6. Move to the right until you are under the Special Conditions object, right-click the action box, and select Fast loops|Start loops.

7. Type the word **Run** between the quotation marks in the expression evaluator and click on OK. You will be asked how many times to run the loop; because you have five units, you want to run it five times. So enter **5** and click on OK.

Now that you have called the loop, you need to set the configuration of the loop and its actions. You check the value of alterable value P for all units, which is the sequential number from one to five. When the alterable value P equals the index and the unit is overlapping the terrain, MMF2 will run the actions. You have added 1 onto the loop index because, as you remember, the loop index begins at zero.

1. Click on the New condition text. Select the Special object and then On Loop. When the expression evaluator appears, type the word **Run** in-between the quotation marks and click on the OK button.

2. Right-click on the condition you just added and select Insert; then select the Group.Arms group and choose Alterable Values|Compare to one of the Alterable Values. When the expression evaluator appears, change the value drop-down box to Alterable Value P, select the 0 value, and click on Retrieve data from an object button. Click on the Special object and choose Fast loops|Get loop index. The expression will be added but will require you to replace >Enter name of the loop< with Run. At the end of this expression, type **+1**. You can see this expression in Figure 13.8. Click on OK to save this to the event editor.

3. You need to add one more condition to this event, so right-click on the condition you just added and select Insert.

4. Select the Group.Arms object, select Collisions|Overlapping another object, select the Group.Good object, and click on OK.

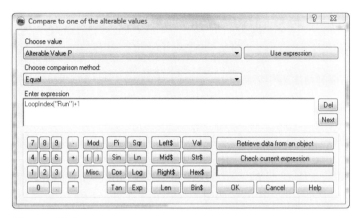

Figure 13.8
The expression to compare an alterable value to the loop index value.

You now add the three actions for the event. Each tile has an ID. You obtain the ID for any tile that is overlapping a unit which will be placed in that particular object's Q alterable value slot. You then write this information to the array. You use the sequential number from each unit to tell MMF2 which X coordinate to save the information in. So, Unit1 has a unit id of 1, and the information about the tile that is overlapping will be placed in X arrays coordinate of 1. The next unit will be placed in the X array slot of 2, and so on. Finally, you save the array to a file called array.arr.

1. Move across to the right until you are directly under the Group.Arms object, right-click the action box, and select Alterable Values|Set. The expression evaluator appears. In the drop-down box, choose Alterable value Q and, in the expression area, select and then click on Retrieve data from an object.

2. Find the Group.Good object and select Values|Values A to M|Retrieve Alterable Value H. Click on the OK button to save this information to the event editor.

   Now you will write values to your array object.

3. Move across until you are directly under the Array_TileID array object, right-click on the action box, and select Write|Write value to X.

   The expression evaluator appears. For the value to write, click on Retrieve data from an object, find the Group.Good, and select Values|Values A to M|Retrieve Alterable Value H. Click on the OK button to save this information to the event editor.

4. Click on the Retrieve data from an object button and select the Group.Good object and then Values|Values A to M|Retrieve alterable value H.

5. Click on the OK button in the expression evaluator to move to the next item.

   You now want to enter the X array locations. The X array will be taken from the alterable value P of the Group.Arms group.

6. When the expression evaluator asks for the X index, press the Retrieve data from an object button and select the Group.Arms object. Then select Values|N to Z|Retrieve alterable value P and click on OK.

   The last thing you need to do for this event is save the array file.

7. On the same event line, right-click on the action box you just added the array action to (for the Array_TileID object) and select Files|Save array to file. The Please select an array file dialog box appears. Click on the Expression button.

8. Click on the Retrieve data from an object button and select the Special object and then Filenames|Application pathname. Once the expression is added, type +**"array.arr"** (including the quotation marks) and click on the OK button.

You can see the events and actions for the unit placement and its loop in Figure 13.9.

Now that you have created the loop that is keeping track of each unit's position, you are ready to create a set of code in an activated group that will check whether any of the units are destroyed in battle.

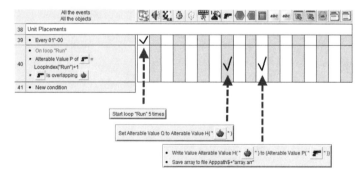

Figure 13.9
The conditions and actions to find out where the units are currently located.

1. Right-click on the last event number that has the New condition text associated with it. Select Insert|A comment. In the Edit box, type **Destroyed Flag** and then click on OK.

   You will now create an active group, which will run all the time. This group will check for the destruction of any of your units.

2. Right-click on the last event line number and select Insert|A group of events, type **Destroyed** as the title of the group, leave the group active, and click on OK.

   You need to create an event with a single condition in each event one of each of the five units: Unit1, Unit2, Unit3, enemy_Unit1, and enemy_Unit2. You create the first one and then the other four.

3. Click on the New condition text, select Unit1 and then Pick or Count|Have all Unit1 been destroyed.

   You can drag and drop the condition four times below the first event to create the additional events and then double-click on the icon within each event to change the unit.

   You need to set a global value when each unit has been destroyed. You've already configured these, and they are already set in the starting file for this section. You created a global value for each unit, so for Unit1, the global value is called g_Unit1.

4. Move across from the first event in the Destroyed group until you are under the Special Conditions object, right-click, and select Change a global value|Set.

5. The expression evaluator appears. In the drop-down box, you select the global value that relates to this unit, so change the drop-down box to g_Unit1. In the Expression area, type the value **1** and then click on OK to save this information to the event editor.

Once you create the next four events for the other four units, the events should look like Figure 13.10.

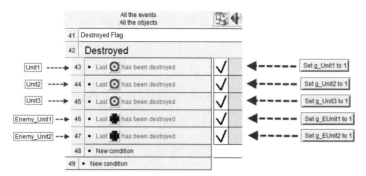

Figure 13.10
Have any of the units been destroyed? If so, set the global value that has been assigned to that object.

You have completed the code for the first frame. Now, you need to program the third frame to take the information in the array and within the global values which will then update the mini-map.

Programming the Mini-Map Frame

You are now going to program the third frame to handle the information from the array and then update the positions of the units on screen. The names of these units are slightly different to avoid confusion with the first frame objects. This is not generally a problem when all objects are individual, but if you select an object to be global, changing it in one screen will change the size and properties in another. So, even though they are not global units, you keep the names different to avoid the possibility of issues.

The code for this frame is split into the following:

- Always load the array file.

- Every tenth second start a loop.

- On the loop, fill in the current information about the tile that the unit is overlapping. Set the alterable values into the units based on their unit ID.

- Create a new loop that runs every $1/4$-second and that runs a loop to place the objects over all terrain tiles that have the correct tile ID.

- Create a set of events that check whether the global values equal 1; if so, delete the corresponding unit.

The first thing you always do is to load the array file, because the array file will always be updated, and you will always need to access it.

1. Make sure you are on the third frame and in the event editor.

2. Click on the New condition text, select the Special object, and then select Always.

3. Move across to the right of this event until you are directly under the Array_TileID object. Right-click on the action box and select Files|Load array from file. Click on the Expression button and then click on Retrieve data from an object. Select the Special object and then Filenames|Application pathname. The expression evaluator appears, type +"array.arr" and click on OK.

You now need to read in the values from your array. You need one comment line to break up the code, one event that starts a loop, and another event to fill the units with values.

First, you create your comment line.

1. Right-click on the event line number and select Insert|A comment. In the Edit text box, type **Read in Values** and click on OK.

2. Click on the New condition text. Select the Timer object and then Every. When the timer dialog box appears, remove the second option and change the 1/100 seconds option to **10**. Then click on the OK button.

3. Move across to the Special conditions object, right-click, and select Fast Loops|Start Loop. Enter **Fill** as the name of the loop, click on OK, enter the value **5**, and click on OK.

You now create the loop that will place the tile information into the alterable value Q of all the units on the screen.

1. Click on the New condition text. Select the Special object and then On Loop. When the expression evaluator appears, type the word **Fill** in-between the quotation marks and click on the OK button.

2. Right-click on the new condition you just added and select Insert, select the Group.Arms group, and choose Alterable Values|Compare to one of the Alterable Values. When the expression evaluator appears, change the value drop-down box to Alterable Value P, select the 0 value, and click on the

Retrieve data from an object button. Click on the Special object and choose Fast loops|Get loop index. The expression is added but will require you to replace the >Enter name of the loop< with **Fill**. At the end of this expression, type **+1**. Click on OK to save this to the event editor.

3. You need to add one more condition to this event, so right-click on the condition you just added and select Insert.

4. Select the Group.Arms object, select Collisions|Overlapping another object, select the Group.Good object, and click on OK.

Now for the action.

1. Move across to the right until you are directly under the Group.Arms object, right-click on the action box and select Alterable values|Set. Change the drop-down box to Alterable Value Q, and in the Enter Expression box, click on Retrieve data from an object.

2. Find the Array_TileID object and then Read value from X position; then the expression will be filled. Select the >Enter X offset< part of the expression and click on Retrieve data from an object. When the Object Selection dialog box appears, choose the Special object and then Fast Loops|Get loop index. Now, you are asked for the name of the loop; type **"Fill"** with the quotation marks. Before the final left, round bracket, type **+1** and click on OK to save the expression.

Your current events and actions will look like Figure 13.11.

The next three items comprise another comment to break up the code: a timed event, an event that will pick all your units and compare them, and the value in

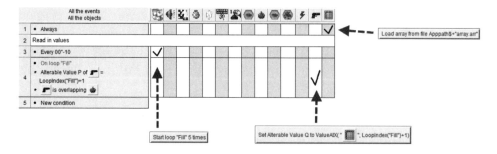

Figure 13.11
The current events and actions to read data into an array and place these values into the units.

the array with the tile's alterable value. MMF2 will then place each of these objects over the correct terrain tile with the matching terrain ID.

First, you create the comment line.

1. Right-click on the last event line number and select Insert|A comment. In the comment box, type **Placement of Objects**, and click on OK.

    You now add the timed event that will start the loop that will be used to place the units over the correct tiles.

2. Click on the New condition text and select the Timer object and then Every. When the timer dialog box appears, replace the seconds with 0 and change the 1/100 option with 25, click on OK.

3. Move across to the Special conditions object, right-click, and select Fast Loops|Start Loop. Enter **"Place"** as the name of the loop and click on OK; then enter the value **5** and click on OK.

Now, you are ready to place the units over the correct terrain tiles.

1. Click on the New condition text. Select the Special object and then On Loop. When the expression evaluator appears, type the word **"Place"** in-between the quotation marks and then click on the OK button.

2. Right-click on the new condition you just added and select Insert. Then select the Group.Arms group and choose Alterable Values|Compare to one of the Alterable Values. When the expression evaluator appears, change the value drop-down box to Alterable Value P, select the 0 value, and click on the Retrieve data from an object button. Click on the Special object and choose Fast loops|Get loop index. The expression is now added but will require you to replace >Enter name of the loop< with **Place**. At the end of this expression, type **+1**. Click on OK to save this to the event editor.

3. You need to add another condition to this event, so right-click on the condition you just added and select Insert. Then find the Group.Good object and select Alterable values|Compare to one of the alterable values.

    When the expression evaluator appears, in the drop-down box, select Alterable Value H. Make sure the comparison method is Equal.

4. In the Enter Expression area, click on the edit box and then click on the Retrieve data from an object button. Select the Array_TileID object and then

Read value at X position. The expression is now added but will require you to replace >Enter X offset< with the loop index. Make sure that the offset text is selected and then click on Retrieve data from an object. Select the Special object and then Fast Loops|Get loop index.

5. You are now asked for the name of the loop; type the name **"Place"** including quotation marks and then at the end of this expression type **+1**. Click on OK to save the information to the event editor.

   The action for this event is to place the object from the Group.Arms group into a position slightly across and down from the 0,0 position of the tile. The program will automatically know which object as it will select the object based on the objects ID.

6. Move across to the Group.Arms object, right-click the action box, and select Position|Select position. Click on the Relative to button and select the Group.Good object. Then within the X and Y coordinate boxes, type X as **7** and Y as **5** then click on OK.

   This places it seven pixels across and five pixels down from the Group.Good object, which will be from the terrain tile it has selected. You can see this code and its actions in Figure 13.12.

Your final bit of code is very straightforward. You will check whether the global value of each of the global values you set in Frame 1 equals the value of 1. If so, the object is destroyed, and you will then destroy the appropriate unit.

First, you will create a comment line to break up your code.

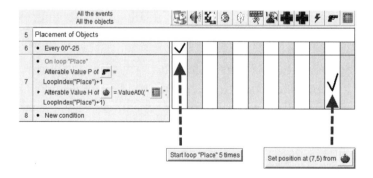

Figure 13.12
The code to place the unit over the correct terrain tiles.

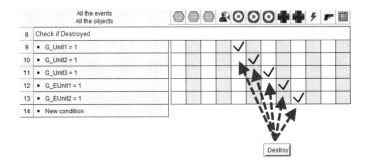

Figure 13.13
The five events to destroy the appropriate units.

1. Right-click on the last event line number and then select Insert|A comment. In the edit dialog box, type **Check if Destroyed** and click on OK.

   You will create the first of the next five events as they are very straightforward. You will check the value of each of the global values and see if it equals 1.

2. Click on the New condition text, select the Special object, and select Compare to a global value. The expression evaluator appears. In the Choose value drop-down box, choose g_Unit1. Leave the comparison at equal, enter the value **1** in the expression box, and click on OK.

3. Move across from this event until you are directly under the PUnit1 object. Right-click on the action box and select Destroy.

   You are now destroying object PUnit1, which is the mini-map version of Unit1. When Unit1 is destroyed in Frame 1, it will also destroy PUnit1 on the mini-map. You now need to construct the other four events for the other units. Once those events are complete, the events will look like Figure 13.13.

   You can access the completed version in the mini-map-complete.mfa file, which is in the Examples folder on the CD-ROM.

Fog of War

One further aspect that you might want to add to the maps is Fog of War, which has been used in many war games to simulate the potential aspects of poor weather, time of day, or of the environment masking the movements of soldiers on the battlefield. Using Fog of War, a unit might suddenly appear on the battlefield where you didn't expect it, which adds a level of surprise. It also requires the player to have more tactical skills to take into account where the enemy unit might be hiding.

You can implement Fog of War in several ways, and I've put together a few ideas on how it can be implemented quite easily. The book has covered many ways to do all aspects of the code, so you will not need an exacting "walk-through" at this point.

- **Using Multiple Animation Frames**: If you want an area to look like it hasn't been discovered yet or to look like it is covered in fog (for example, an area that can't be viewed), then you can have an additional covered animation frame. When a unit is within a particular distance, change the animation image for that terrain tile so that it is uncovered. The main issue is how to keep track of when to change the animation frame.

- **Have a Covering Tile**: You could cover every single tile with a graphic, and then make it visible or invisible depending on where the units are on the screen. You might have seen similar systems in very old dungeon games, where the dungeon is slowly revealed as the player's units move through the dungeon. The main problem with this system is that you could have many additional graphics on screen, which might cause the game to be much larger than it would be otherwise. You will also need some way of tracking when a tile should be hidden or made visible.

- **Hide the Units**: Rather than using the terrain, you can just make the units visible or invisible depending on the distance between the player and computer units, which will reduce the amount of programming and graphics required. You will still need a system for managing when to hide or unhide a unit.

Once you decide on a method, you need to decide how you intend to initiate the Fog of War around the player units. The easiest method is one that you have used extensively in this book, and that is the use of a placeholder graphic around the player units. Using the placeholder, you can check for any units overlapping any tiles and reveal any terrain or computer units. This option is probably the easiest one to implement. You could also use the Wargame Map Object and work out a distance between the player units and any other units surrounding it. This is perfect if you want to find the distance between units and then reveal them, but will not work so well if you are revealing terrain tiles. If you want to change the graphic state of a tile, you are better off using the overlapping placeholder graphic(s).

You have completed the chapter for utilizing maps and mini-maps. In the next chapter, look at how to build money and finance into your war games.

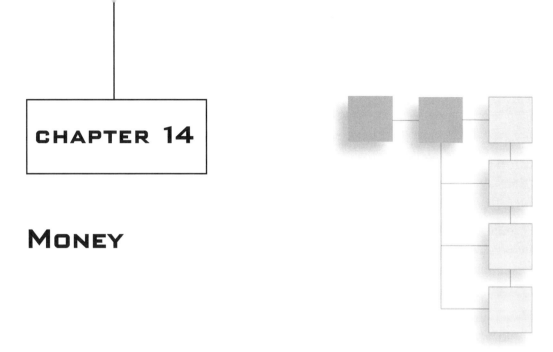

CHAPTER 14

MONEY

Without a source of income your army is unlikely to win the war. Money is essential to keep your army paid, motivated, fed, and equipped for the long campaign ahead.

Money is an essential item in a campaign level war game, where you have a number of armies moving over a large map. In a single war game battle, you may decide there is no need for money to be involved in the game. Money is used to make a war game more of a challenge; with the addition of money, you have to balance your finances, which means paying for the creation of new units and paying for the salaries of current units.

In games such as Total War, money is used as part of the game mechanics to balance which important areas on the map the player should consider capturing. It is also used for helping you decide whether to invest in new buildings within a capital city, which will provide different types of units or technologies. In many board and computer games, capturing a location or having a unit placed on a specific part of the map means that the player owns that location and will earn revenue. In the board game Risk, you gain extra units for owning the different locations on the map. Different places account for varying levels of reward, which makes capturing some areas important to winning the game.

Paying Income per Tile Location

Your map may be at the campaign level, and so you may want to pay income per location held. This could be a location with a unit sitting on a particular tile. We can pick a specific schedule for the money to be paid; this could be weekly, monthly, or yearly, depending on the timeframe that has been set in the game.

You can program this into your game in several ways: you could give every tile an income value based on its strategic location or resources. This could get quite involved if you have a few hundred terrain tiles and you want a value for each tile. You might specify the value of only a select number of tiles. This all depends on the type of game you are making and how you want to manage the games finances.

If you have enough available alterable value slots for the terrain tiles, then you could add an alterable value to store the income when you create your game; just because you add it doesn't mean you have to use it in the game (the default value would just be 0).

Preconfigured Items

We have created an example file that contains several preconfigured objects and items. The file is called money1.mfa, and it is located in the Examples folder.

On loading the file, if you access the Frame editor, you will see a number of new items. In Figure 14.1 you will see a new border graphic with the $ sign and a number 0. These

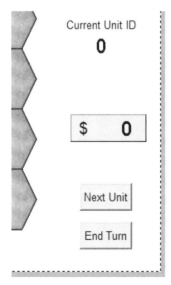

Figure 14.1
Three objects needed to display the total income amount.

are three separate objects that have been added to the frame to handle the finance module. We have also made changes to the alterable values list for each terrain tile. Details of these objects and the new alterable value are as follows:

- **Background System Box**: The background system box is an object that can be used to create backgrounds, menu bars, and buttons. It always appears in the background of any other items, so in this example, we have two other objects on top of the object. The background system box is a very powerful object that allows precise configuration of the box on the screen and has a large number of features. This makes the object quicker in many cases than using a graphic you have drawn yourself. You can double click on the object to access the object properties, which can be seen in Figure 14.2.

- **String object**: This is a standard string object that you have used within your game to display text. We have amended the font size and properties to match the size of the background system box.

- **Counter**: You have used counters before to detail which unit is currently selected and how many movement points it currently has. This counter

Figure 14.2
The background system box object properties.

keeps track of the total amount of money that the player has. The counter has been configured with a minimum value of 0, though in your own games, you may want to have a minus number. We have also set a maximum value of 5000 for this example. The figure you decide on depends on the type of game you are making and how important money is to the overall strategy of the game. You may also notice that there is a gap between the $ sign and the counter object. This is because the counter object works from right to left, based on its current location. At the moment, you can see in the Frame Editor that it has the value of 0. When this displays a value of 100, the 0 will still be in the same screen position, but the hundreds will take up space to the left. Without this gap, the money counter would overlap the $ sign. You can see the counter configuration in Figure 14.3.

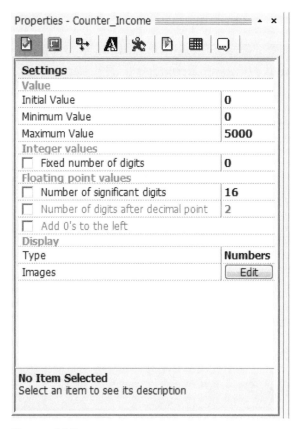

Figure 14.3
Properties for the counter object.

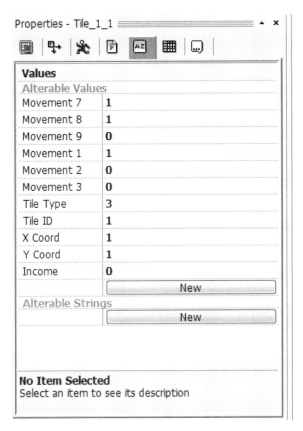

Figure 14.4
The new alterable value named income in the K slot.

- **Alterable Value K**: For each tile, we have created a new alterable value in slot K. We have renamed this slot to income and this will store the amount of revenue that a particular tile will give to the player at a designated point in the game. For the example, we will calculate all income in January of every year. Not every tile will have an income value, though in your own games, you may want to do this for certain games. You can see the new alterable value in Figure 14.4.

- **Qualifier Group Bonus**: In previous chapters we used Qualifier groups to select those items that are grouped together. In this case, we will use the qualifier group Bonus to identify which tiles are part of the income system.

Note

In many games the overall amount of money a country/player can have can go into negative numbers. Like governments today, countries and players can also borrow money they don't have. So you may want to have a negative financial figure, which you can use to trigger other events. In games such as Caesar IV and CivCity Rome, the player can go into negative financial figures for a set period of time, and this will then end the game. You may not want the game to finish, but you may want to punish the player by having units disband (because the player cannot afford to pay them) or people revolt against them.

Note

Qualifier groups are useful for identifying or picking groups of objects. In previous chapters we used qualifiers to select certain tiles from a large group.

Naming of Objects

The objects that we have added to this program have been renamed from the original names they were given when added to the frame. They are:

- DollarSign_Income

- Counter_Income

- BSB_Income

As you add more and more code, it becomes increasingly more difficult to identify the same type of objects in the event editor. If you have five string objects, by default, they will be named String 1, String 2, String 3, and so on. When you are working in the event editor, it is very difficult to remember which object applies to each task, and this means you then have to switch between the Frame Editor and Event Editor to ensure that you have the correct object. Where possible, you should give your objects names that you will be able to identify easily when programming in the event editor. You may even decide to come up with your own naming conventions for different objects. This is useful if you want to standardize your objects; for example, you can precede everything with a shortened version of the object name and then, after the underscore, a word that describes what it does. An example of this could be Act_player, the Act signifies that it is an active object, and the word player tells the programmer that it is the player's graphic.

We have renamed some of the other objects in the engine as follows:

- Next Unit button called Button is renamed to Btn_NextUnit.

- End Turn button called Button 2 is renamed to Btn_EndTurn.

- Text to display the year called Static Text is renamed to Stxt_Year.

- Counter to display current movement points called Counter is renamed to Ctr_CurMovPoints.

- Counter to display current player unit selected called Counter 2 is renamed to Ctr_CurPlayerUnit.

Configuring the Alterable Values

Now that we have detailed the different changes we have implemented in the example file, we are going to configure a number of tiles with an income value. This will be the value that they earn each year. We will calculate the total amount of value and add it to the Counter_Income counter. The player will only earn money for the tile if she has a unit placed on top of it.

In this example, the player will earn money for the tile locations shown in Table 14.1.

When creating a map, you will include some way for the player to be able to identify the resources that are on that tile and have a value. This could be done graphically, or the user could click on a tile to reveal details about it.

We now need to configure the values in each of the tile objects alterable value.

1. Ensure that you have the money1.mfa file loaded.

2. Ensure that you can see the map and units on the Frame Editor.

3. Click on the tile at X2, Y5; this will be the City tile.

4. Click on the Values tab in the object properties.

5. You should see the list of alterable values with the entry Income at the bottom. Click on the 0 and enter the value **120**. Press Enter to save the information to the value slot.

Table 14.1 The Tile that Activates Payment and Its Value

Tile X	Tile Y	Value	Comment
2	5	120	City tile
3	1	20	Forest Resource
5	3	10	Sea Resource tile

We will now do this for the other two tiles.

1. Click on the tile at X3, Y1; this is the forest tile.

2. The values tab is already selected.

3. Enter the value of **20** in to the Income alterable value slot.

4. Click on the tile at X5 and Y3; this will be the top right corner water tile.

5. Enter the value of **10** in to the Income alterable value slot.

You now have all the tiles with the values you require, and now you need to create the code that will handle making money when you have a unit placed on it in the month of January.

Coding the Income

The coding of a basic income system is very straightforward, and in fact, the hardest part is to ensure that the code sits nicely in all of the other code contained in the Event Editor. For this reason, we will use the group system to keep the income code in one place.

1. Click on the Event Editor button.

2. Ensure that all code groups are collapsed.

   We will now add a new group to contain the income code.

3. Right click on the last event line number, then select Insert|A group of events. In the dialog box type the title to be **Income** and ensure that the Active when frame starts is unselected. Click on the OK button.

The group now exists and we need to populate it with code to handle getting the information about which tiles have a unit on them and then calculate the total income from that, then add that to the current income that the player has.

First we are going to create a loop that goes through each of the player units to see if they are on the Bonus tiles. These tiles being those that we have manually added to the Bonus qualifier group.

1. Click on the New condition text in the Income group.

2. From the New condition dialog box choose the Special object then Group of Events|On group activation.

3. Move across from this event until you are under the Special Conditions object and select Fast Loops|Start Loop, the Expression Evaluator will appear with quote marks. Within the quotes type in the text **Money**. Click on the OK button. Enter the value of 3, as we have three player units to loop through and then click on the OK button.

Our next event will create the loop and loop through each of the player units. It will only run the event if the unit is overlapping the Bonus qualifier tile.

1. Click on the New condition text on event line 30 in the Income group.

2. Select the Special object and then pick On Loop. Enter the name of the loop as **Money** and click on OK.

3. Right click on the loop condition you have just created on event line 30, and select Insert, then choose the Group.Player object and Alterable values|Compare to one of the alterable values.

4. The Expression Evaluator will appear, in the drop down box select Alterable Value C, leave the comparison method as Equal and then select the 0 in the expression edit box and click on Retrieve data from an object.

5. The New expression dialog box appears, select the Special object and then Fast Loops|Get Loop Index. This will place an incomplete expression in the Expression Editor. Replace the >Enter name of the loop< with **"Money"** (including quotes) and then at the end of the expression type in **+1**.

6. Click on the OK button.

We need to add one further condition to the event which will check when an object from the Group.Player qualifiers is overlapping the Group.Bonus qualifier. This will only be true when one of the player units is overlapping one of our income generating tiles.

1. Right click on the last condition in event line 30 and select Insert.

2. From the New condition dialog box choose the Group.Player object then Collisions|Overlapping another object, this will bring up the Test a collision dialog, select the Group.Bonus object and click on the OK button.

Now it is time to add the action to this event, and we want to add the value retrieved from the loop and add it to the Counter_Income counter.

1. Move across from the event on line 32 until you are directly under the Counter_Income object, right click the action box and select Add to Counter, in the Expression Evaluator select the 0 value and then click on the Retrieve data from an object button.

2. Locate the Group.Bonus object and then right click and select Values|Values A to M|Retrieve Alterable Value K and then click on the OK button to save this information to the event editor.

   We need a final event in the Income group to handle the disabling of the group.

   1. Click on the New condition text on event line 31. Select the Special object and then Always.

   2. Move across to the Special conditions object, right click the action box and choose Group of Events|Deactivate, in the deactivate dialog box, select (13)-Income and then click on the OK button.

You can see the Income groups events and actions in Figure 14.5.

A group called Income is disabled at the start of the program. You now need to set up some code that will enable it. You want the money to be paid in January of each year, but if you program this to be enabled when the month becomes January, then the money would keep counting upwards when the user does not click on the End Turn button and the month is January. The best option is to

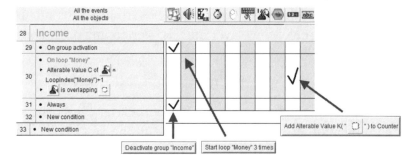

Figure 14.5
The conditions and actions for the Income group.

allow payment only from the next available January. To ensure that it isn't paid on the first January, we can use a flag and set on and off states.

1. Before we continue you can collapse the Income group.

2. To remind you of what the code you are about to add will do, you will first add a comment.

   1. Right click on the event line number 24, which is the comment line Computer Player Moves.

   2. Select Insert|A comment. When the edit text box appears, type in **Not first January – Income**, and click on OK.

We will now create the event which will check to see if it is January and will check to see if a flag is on. At this point, you haven't turned on the flag, so this event will not run when you start the program and the month is automatically January.

1. Right click on the event number 25 and select Insert|A new event.

2. From the New condition dialog box, select the Special object and Compare two general values. When the Compare two general values Expression Evaluator appears, click in the first edit box and then click on the Retrieve data from an object button. Find the String3 string object and select Current number of paragraph displayed.

3. Now select the bottom expression box and type in the value of **1**. Click on the OK button to save the condition.

You need to add a second condition that will check to see if the flag has been set to on. When the flag is on, it means that it is no longer the first January, and the program can run the calculation on the income.

1. Right click on the condition you just added on event line 25 and select Insert.

2. Select the Group.Bonus object, and then select Alterable Values|Flags|Is a Flag on?

3. We will use 0 as the flag, and this is what appears in the Expression Evaluator, so click on the OK button.

Now we need to add the actions; the first is to enable the Income group, and the second is to switch the Group.Bonus flag to off.

1. Move across to the right of event line 25 and right click on the action box under the Special conditions object. Select Group of events|Activate, select the (13)-Income option in the dialog box, and click on OK.

2. Still on the same event line, move directly under the Group.Bonus object, right click the action box, and choose Flags|Set off. The Expression Evaluator appears asking for the flag number; you previously selected 0, so click on the OK button.

You have now added the code to ensure that the Income group only runs when the flag is turned on. This means the very first January will not run the code. You can see the event and its actions in Figure 14.6.

We do not want to turn the flag to on when it is January because this will turn it on for the first January when the program launches. Because we are waiting until the following January, we can switch the Flag on in December, and this will not affect the very first January.

We already have an event for checking when the month is December; we created it to change the year. Find event line 23, which is Paragraph = 12. Move across to the right of this event until you are under the Group.Bonus object. Select Flags|Set on. Leave the number of the flag on 0 and click on the OK button.

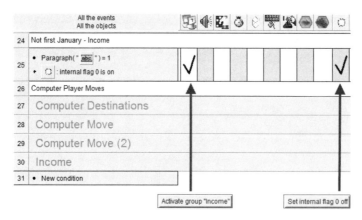

Figure 14.6
The comment and event line for running the Group.Bonus group.

If you now run the code, you will notice no money is added in January, the players units can be moved, and the computer units move in March and August. Once you have waited for the computer units to move and get back to January, as long as you have units on one of the three income-generating tiles, you will get some income. This will continue to be true on every turn.

You can view the completed code by loading and running the money1_-complete.mfa file from the Examples folder.

Paying Income per Area

A similar concept to the example we just created would be to pay the player for any tiles on the map as long as they do not contain computer controlled units on those tiles. This is useful if you want the income to be based on keeping important terrain areas rather than getting the player to go out of his way to capture specific tiles.

In the following example we will show how to create an area-based income system.

First we will set the values of the three tiles. We will use the same tiles we used in the previous example. In your own games, you would apply them to any tiles that you feel are worth something in the game.

1. Load up the file called Money2.mfa from the examples folder.

2. Ensure that you can see the map and units on the Frame Editor.

3. Click on the tile at X2, Y5; this will be the City tile.

4. Click on the Values tab in the object properties.

5. You should see the list of alterable values the entry Income at the bottom. Click on the 0 and enter the value of **50** and press return to save the information to the value slot.

   We will now do this for the other two tiles.

6. Click on the tile at X3, Y1; this is the forest tile.

7. The values tab is already selected.

8. Enter the value of **25** into the Income alterable value slot.

9. Click on the tile at X5 and Y3; this will be the top right corner water tile.

10. Enter the value of **15** into the Income alterable value slot.

Coding Income per Area

You now need to create the code that will handle making money as long as no computer units are situated on top of any income generating tiles. This money will be paid in January of every year, but not in the first year.

1. Click on the Event Editor button.

2. Ensure that all code groups are collapsed.

3. We will now add a new group to contain the income code.

4. Right click on the last event line number, then select Insert|A group of events. In the dialog box, type the title to be **Income 2** and ensure that Active when frame starts is unselected. Click on the OK button.

The group now exists and we need to populate it with code to handle getting the information about which tiles have a unit on it. Then you need to calculate the total income from that and add that to the current income that the player has.

Note

If it is possible to have multiple income systems in a game, that will make it a more complex war game and more of a challenge for the player. If you intend to have multiple income systems within a game, ensure that you use different group names to identify them as well as different flag slots.

Note

It takes time for the computer units to move on the screen, and you may decide it takes too much time when you have 20 or 30 computer units moving at one time. You can change the speed of a moving unit by amending the movement code for that unit and reducing the Restrict actions and the Every 1.00 timing options. Make sure you amend both the every one second condition and all of the movement directions; otherwise, you may find your computer units not moving correctly.

Coding the Income 2 Group

The main issue with the code that you need to create for this income generator system is that you need to loop through three tiles. In previous examples, you looped through all 48 tiles and used the computer controlled unit ID to loop through which tiles are placed on a particular tile qualifier group. Because the three tiles will not have any units placed on top of them to earn money, we cannot use the computer's or the player's unit ID to generate the loop selection.

There is a simple and very effective way around this, and that is to use the unit's alterable values and a process called Spreading Values. The spread value is an action that can populate a value slot such as an alterable value or global value with an incremental value. If you had 100 objects that you wanted to give a unique number to, using spread value would get the first object and apply a value of 1 to it, and so on.

You can see the extra alterable value slot we added to each tile in Figure 14.7.

When the group is enabled, the very first task is to create the spread values into the Group.Bonus items; these are the tiles that contain income values. We only need this event to run once because the alterable value slots will continue to hold these values.

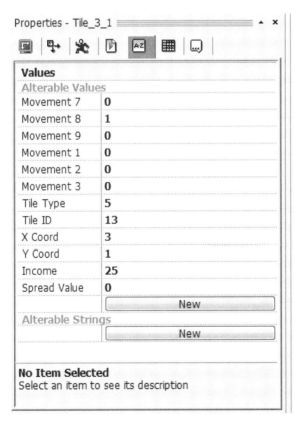

Figure 14.7
The new alterable slot L called Spread Value.

1. Click on the New condition text on event line 29, in the Income 2 group.

2. Select the Special object, then Limit conditions|Run this event once.

3. Move to the right of this new event until you are directly under the Group.Bonus object. Right click the blank action box and select Alterable Values|Spread Values.

4. The Expression Evaluator appears. You need to specify the alterable value slot that you are going to place a value into. Click on the drop down box and select Alterable Value L.

5. In the Enter expression text area, select the 0 value, and click on Retrieve data from an object.

6. Right click on the Special conditions object and select Fast Loops|Get loop index. It will now place an expression into the edit box; you need to delete the >Enter name of the Loop< text and replace it with **"Money"** (including quotes). Because the loop index starts from 0, you must also add a **+1** to the end of the expression. You can see the expression in Figure 14.8.

Now you need to add an event that will check for the group being activated and will specify the loop name and how many times it will run.

1. Click on the New condition text on event line 30.

2. Select the Special object, and choose Group of events|On group activation.

3. Move to the right of this event until you are under the Special conditions object, right click the action box, and select Fast Loops|Start Loop.

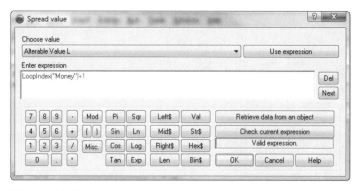

Figure 14.8
The action to spread a value to all items in the loop, using the loop index.

4. When the Expression Evaluator appears, type in the name of the loop between the quote marks, which in this case will be **Money**, and click on the OK button.

5. You will be asked how many times the loop will need to run; in this case, you have three income generating tiles, so type in the value **3**, and click on OK.

Now that you have your spread values and loop activation set, it is time to generate the condition that will tell MMF2 that the event line is the Money loop and to loop through the objects in the Group.Bonus group, while only running the event if there are no computer units overlapping the Group.Bonus object (the tile in that loop).

1. Click on the New condition text on event line 31.

2. Select the Special object and then On loop. In the Expression evaluator type in the name of the loop between the quotes which in this case is **Money**. Click on the OK button.

3. Add a new condition to the same event line.

4. Right click on the condition you just added to event line 31 and select Insert.

5. Find the Group.Bonus object and select Alterable Values|Compare to one of the alterable values.

6. When the Expression Evaluator appears, change the value drop down box to Alterable Value L. Leave Equal to its current value, click on the Enter expression box, and click on Retrieve data from an object. Select the Special object and pick Fast Loops|Get loop index. When the expression appears in the Expression Evaluator, delete the >Enter name of the loop< and type in **"Money"** (including the quote marks). At the end of the expression type in **+1**.

7. Add the final condition to the same event.

8. On event line 31, right click on the condition you just added and select Insert.

9. Select the Group.Enemies group and then Collisions|Overlapping another object. This will then bring up the Test a collision dialog box, select the Group.Bonus object and click on OK.

   We need to change the last condition in that event because at the moment it will run any actions on that event line if an enemy is overlapping any of the income tiles. We only want the player to earn money if there are no computer units currently overlapping the object.

10. Right click on the last condition on event line 31, and select Negate from the pop-up menu.

11. Now that you have the event, you need to add the action to add the money to the Counter_Income counter. This will hold all of the money earned in the game, so you need to add to the value of the counter, which will take into account any money already in the bank.

12. Move across to the right of the event on line 31 until you are directly under the Counter_Income counter. Right click on the action box, and select Add to counter.

13. When the Expression Evaluator appears, select the 0 value, and click on Retrieve data from an object. Find the object Group.Bonus and select Values|Values A to M|Retrieve Alterable Value K.

14. You will be back at the Expression Evaluator, so click on the OK button to save the information to the Event Editor.

One of the issues with groups and certain events is knowing whether they are running correctly. In this example, we are going to add a small sound file that will play when it is January and the loop event has run. This means you can easily see that the code is working because if the sound doesn't play, you know the event is not being activated. You can easily remove the sound from your own war games or replace it with another sound if you require.

1. On event line 31, move across until you are directly under the Sound object, right click on the action box, and select Samples|Play Sample.

2. A play sample dialog box appears. Click on the From a file button. Navigate to the Sound folder, select the pop04 wav sound file, and click on the Open button.

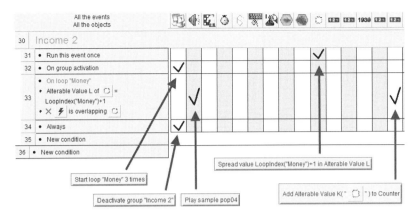

Figure 14.9
The conditions and actions for the Income 2 group.

Finally, you need some code to close the group.

3. Click on the New condition text on event line 32, and select the Special object and then Always.

4. Move across from this event until you are under the Special conditions object, then right click the action box, and select Group of Events|Deactivate. Choose the (13)-Income 2 group and click on OK.

You can see the conditions and actions in Figure 14.9.

As in the previous example, you need to set up an event and a small number of actions to handle the first January.

1. Collapse the Income 2 group.

2. First we will add a comment for our event that will be placed before the groups.

3. Right click on event line number 24, which is the comment line Computer Player Moves. Then select Insert|A comment; when the edit text box appears, type in **Not first January – Income**, and click on OK.

Time to add the event and a flag check.

4. Right click on event number 25 and select Insert|A new event.

5. From the New condition dialog box, select the Special object, and then Compare two general values. The Compare two general values Expression

Evaluator appears, click in the first edit box and then click on the Retrieve data from an object button. Find the String3string object, and select Current number of paragraph displayed.

6. Now select the bottom expression box and type in the value of **1**. Click on the OK button to save the condition.

   You need to add a second condition that will check to see if the flag has been set to on.

7. Right click on the condition you just added on event line 25 and select Insert.

8. Select the Group.Bonus object and then select Alterable Values|Flags|Is a Flag on?

9. We will use 0 as the flag, and this is what appears in the Expression Evaluator, so click on the OK button.

   Now we need to add the actions.

10. Move across to the right of event line 25 and right click on the action box under the Special conditions object. Select Group of events|Activate, select the (13)-Income option in the dialog box and click on OK.

11. Still on the same event line, move directly under the Group.Bonus object, right click the action box, and choose Flags|Set off. The Expression Evaluator appears, it will be asking for the flag number; you previously selected 0, so click on the OK button.

You have now added the code to ensure that the Income 2 group only runs when the flag has been turned on; this means the very first January will not run the code.

We need to activate the Flag to on in December and this will not affect the very first January.

We already have an event for checking when the month is December; we created this to change the year. Find event line 23, which is Paragraph = 12. Move across to the right of this event until you are under the Group.Bonus object. Select Flags|Set on. Leave the number of the flag on 0 and click on the OK button.

Congratulations. You have learned how to add finance to your games. Using finance in your games will give the player a more rewarding game experience.

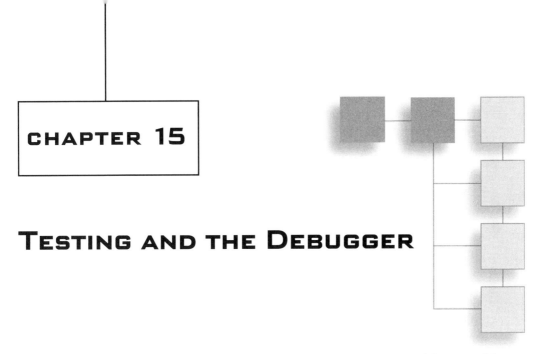

CHAPTER 15

TESTING AND THE DEBUGGER

In this chapter, you will learn how to find and fix program problems and bugs. No matter how hard you try, bugs will appear in any war game you write, but it is very important to ensure that you minimize them before you distribute your war game. We will also offer some advice on how to find problems with your war game by using counters, mouse clicks, and the debugger options.

What Are Bugs?

Computers, and the software used to run them, are made by humans. Unfortunately, no matter how hard we try, we cannot seem to prevent problems with incorrect code or design issues. These issues can cause random crashes and data corruption at any time and can be very infuriating for the user of the PC that's having the problem. Programmers and hardware designers are human, and this means that problems will occur. This is also true when you are programming and making games in MMF2. MMF2 uses a special programming language, and bugs will be introduced due to wrong coding in the Event Editor. You will probably, without knowing it, introduce bugs into your software. The key is making sure you look for them and try to eliminate them where possible.

Why Find Them?

You may have spent a lot of time developing your war game, so you want it to be as good as it can be. You will have a product that is nearly complete, and you will be really excited to try and get it online (or to your friends) as quickly as possible. But when possible, you should try to ensure that you have checked for bugs before releasing your game. This will make a difference in how much your friends and family enjoy playing the game, because if there are problems with it, their enjoyment can be spoiled. You don't want the game playing experience interrupted by errors or problems with the game.

Debugging & Product Releases

There are a number of areas where you might consider fixing bugs or need to ensure that all bugs have been removed. The following distinguishable phases are checked for professional product releases, but even if you are making your game for friends, you can follow this process:

- **General Debugging:** When you create your game, you will test to see if it works. This is just to confirm that you have completed that section of code and then can move on to the next part of the program. There may also be issues with the look and feel and general stability. All of this will be done while you are programming the main part of the game, but you will not be going out of your way to find problems.

- **Alpha Version:** When the product is in a suitable condition and a lot of the functionality has been implemented, you can say your product is at version Alpha. This means that it is still unstable, but it is in a state where a lot of the options work (though not all), and it has the general look and feel of the final product. The product may still have some major bugs and issues, but this is the first version that is considered suitable enough to show people the work in progress (even if you are a hobbyist creator). The Alpha is used to get feedback on how the product sticks together and whether the interface works well enough. This is the final stage of development before the product will be locked down with regards to features and its look and feel. The main issue is that you could continue to keep adding new features and never actually have a final product to release. The end of the Alpha stage is the beginning of the final program and its functionality.

- **Beta:** At the end of the Alpha process, you may have received comments about how the product looks, and if the interface works well. Once you are happy that you have taken the comments into consideration and have made final decisions about the interface (and made those changes to the product), then you enter the Beta stage. The Beta stage is where the product is fully locked down with regards to functionality, look, and feel. During the Beta stage, all that needs to be done is the removal of any bugs within the program. You can start to give this version to your testers, who will then try to locate any problems in the game. Beta testers could be a group of friends, or anyone who has downloaded the game from your website and who replies to you with comments.

- **Post Release:** Once the product has been released, people will use the game on configurations that you may not have expected or in ways that even the Beta testers didn't pick up. There are generally bugs to be fixed once the product is available to a larger number of people.

Note

Beta testers are an essential resource for finding bugs in your war games. Any war game developer who has been working on a product for a while will find it hard to find bugs because they are so used to the product. A new user of a product tries things that the developer just wouldn't think about and so can be a great asset for finding those bugs you never anticipated.

The Debugger

When you run your game in MMF2, you may notice a small bar open on the top left corner of your monitor. This is the Debugger window and its initial job is to tell you how many objects your game has and how much memory it is using. Every program you make contains data: the information stored in an array or the alterable values of each of the terrain tiles. All of this information is essential if you wish to check to see if the values are correct and then any fix issues with your war game if they are not. Using the debugger can help you track down difficult to find bugs in your code, which you may have inadvertently programmed incorrectly.

Starting and Using the Debugger

To make the debugger start, you need to have a program running in MMF2. Locate the file called combat3-complete.mfa in the Examples folder, and load it in to MMF2. Ensure that you are in the Frame Editor for the first frame. If you run the frame or the whole game, the debugger will appear in the top left corner, as shown in Figure 15.1.

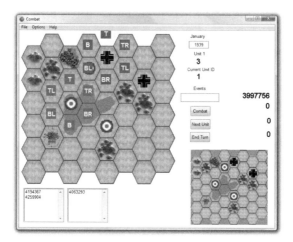

Figure 15.1
The debugger open and ready to use.

Figure 15.2
A closeup of the debugger bar.

Figure 15.2 provides a closer look at what the debugger bar contains.

There are a number of buttons and functionality that you can access:

- If you click on the + icon on the right side of the debugger bar, it will expand the amount of information available that you will be able to see. All options and program data can now be viewed. Within the whole program (each frame, object, etc.) is specific information, be it location on the screen, screen size, current counter values, or string details. The expanded debugger can be seen in Figure 15.3. To collapse it, click on the minus sign that replaced the plus sign when you clicked on expand.

- The first button on the debugger bar (the line with the left pointing arrow) signifies that the program will start from the beginning of the frame once it is clicked. This is very useful if you are trying to track a bug and want to watch what is being changed. You can keep repeating the process until you have found the problem.

Figure 15.3
The expanded debugger, revealing more information.

- The square icon on the debugger bar is the stop button. This stops the frame and program from running, and it closes the running game and the debugger.

- The third icon is the pause button, which will pause your program (nothing will happen on the game's playfield) until you press play to start it back up. This allows you to get to a specific point in the program and then check the result of the current data being stored by MMF2.

- The fourth icon from the left looks like a grayed out right pointing arrow. In fact this is the next step button, which allows you to step through you game code one line at a time. To use this function, you need to pause the program first using the pause button mentioned earlier. This is a very useful option if you want to slowly see what changes are made to your program. (Things can happen very quickly, and you might miss something otherwise).

- The fifth icon is the play button. If you pause the program, you would use this to start it again (playing at normal speed.)

- The display in the middle of the debugger bar shows two bits of useful information: the number of objects being used in the current frame and the number of bytes for the total memory used by the application.

The default information that is shown within the expanded debugger is for the basic application level. What this means is that if you created a blank game, this information is always present (top-level details is separate from anything you might add such as game objects you might have placed in your game). To see what information is contained within the expanded debugger box see Figure 15.4.

Expanding the System folder gives you all standard game information. Frame number is the current frame that is running in the game. The time is the actual time for which that frame has been running (very important in our war game engine because this is reset to different values in combat). You also have another expandable folder, which allows you to see all of the global values being used in the program. At the bottom of the expanded debugger, you will also see three additional buttons that you can use to add and remove items. The first icon is to add items, the second is to delete items and finally, you will see an Edit button, which is used when you want to edit specific data entries.

1. Run the application by pressing F8, then click on the debugger and press the + button. Then click the Add button and you will be able to search through the various types of objects that you can add to your debugger.

Figure 15.4
Basic information that is stored in the debugger.

Figure 15.5
Adding an object from one of four groups.

The file that is loaded will determine the number of group folders you will see; Figure 15.5 contains four.

2. For this example, expand the Active Objects group, and you will see all of the active objects in use on the first frame of your war game (there are quite a few). Scroll down until you find the object called Unit1, select it, and click on the OK button. This object will be added to the debugger, and you can view the object's values as shown in Figure 15.6.

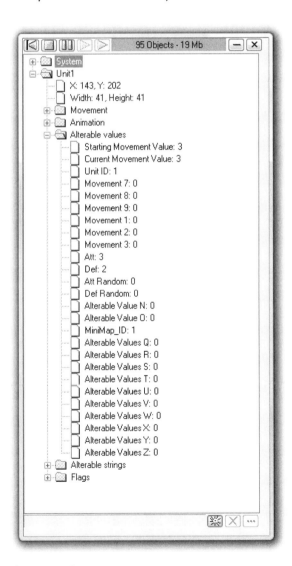

Figure 15.6
The Unit1 object added to the debugger.

Now that you have a list of values for the Unit1 object, you can view them in real-time. This is useful if you want to see if a value is set correctly or not set at all. You can also double click on a value and edit it. This allows you to try different values in a slot to see if your program updates. For example, in the code, perhaps you set the object's position using an alterable value; if you then edit the alterable value, you should see the object move, as long as the code is set to automatically update its position based on this value.

Using Counters or Other Objects

In addition to using the debugger, you can also place objects on your frame and set a value to them in real-time to see that your program is working correctly (or not).

A perfect example of when you might use this is for items such as fixed values or spread values. This is where values are assigned to objects when you have many objects. For example, if you want to know the value of a particular fixed value or other value of any of the 50 objects, you may not want 50 counters on screen to show you if they are set correctly or not.

A useful way is to set a single counter to a value when you click on an object. This is very useful in our war game examples for checking to see if a fixed value is returned correctly. In the following example, we will show you how to return a value to a counter using a mouse click.

1. Open the file called debug-counter.mfa in the Examples folder.

2. Ensure that you are on the Frame Editor for frame 1.

3. Insert a counter object onto the frame and place it somewhere visible when you run the game.

4. Go in to the event editor. Go to the very last event line and click on the New condition text.

5. Select the Mouse pointer and keyboard object and then The mouse|User clicks on an object; select the default options in the User clicks dialog box, and click on OK, then select Group.Good.

6. Move across to the right of this event until you are directly under the counter object you added to the frame. Right click on the action box and

select Set counter. When the expression evaluator appears, click on the 0 value and then click on Retrieve data from an object, find the Group.Good object and pick Retrieve fixed value.

7. The expression will be entered. Click on OK to save this information to the Event Editor.

When you run the program, if you click on any objects that are members of the Group.Good qualifier group, you will see that the counter updates with the fixed value. This can prove very useful when comparing the information for the fixed values in the list objects with the current object you click. For example, when a placeholder object is overlapping a unit, it will enter the information into the list object. Using the mouse click, you can confirm that it is in fact returning the correct value. If the value is different, you know that your code for returning the correct fixed value to the list object was not working correctly.

You can use a similar process for returning other values at any time. Rather than using a key press, you could just display a set of counters that display a particular number at a particular time. One such time might be for the enabling and disabling of groups. Group activation and deactivation can cause your programs many problems if they are not enabled and disabled at the correct times. You can have a set of counters, one for each group, and you could set a value every time that group is enabled and a different value for when it is disabled. This is a simple way of seeing if your groups are being left activated.

Finally, you can use the same process for text boxes as well; you could set a message, very much like the Events text message. You could set a message at particular times of your game so that you, as the developer, know what is happening. You can then easily hide this information when you compile the game to an Exe so that the player does not see this information.

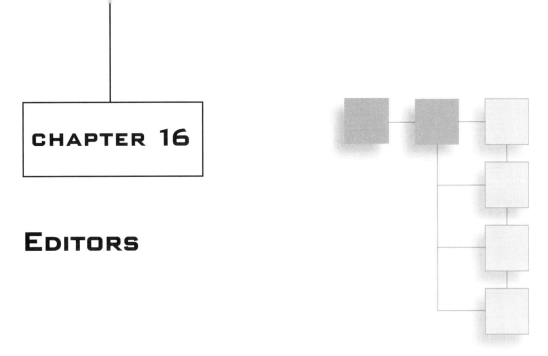

CHAPTER 16

Editors

In a number of the examples created in this book, you manually created data that the program will use. For instance, in some of the movement examples, you created a set of array values that you loaded into MMF at the start of the frame. These values were used as the basis of setting a specific set of movement points for different units on particular tiles. Rather than doing this process manually for each game, you could write an editor and make the process easier. In this chapter, you will look at creating a simple editor to create a set of information for your game.

What Is an Editor?

Editors are used extensively in computer game creation, both in commercial games and in hobbyist creations. An editor is a program that can edit the data for your game directly in a simple interface and allow you to quickly build the data information for your game. This data could be a map in a first-person shooting game or weapon types, weight and cost of an item in a role-playing game, or the actual layout of the game levels.

Even though making an editor requires time, a long-term benefit is usually found in larger games where the levels and data can be built very quickly. For your war game, an editor will not make your war game any quicker, but it will make your game easier to manage. This is especially true when managing the data. Perhaps you have written a war game about the Roman Empire, but you decide you want to transfer the engine to another time period or different units. You could load up a copy of the game and then spend a lot of time manually editing the data, or, alternatively, you could load up your editor, change the data quickly, and then be ready to test your updated game.

Creating an Editor

In this chapter, you will make an editor that creates the terrain movement table information for the player units. The computer uses this information to remove additional movement points over certain tiles. It also uses this information to restrict movement on specific tiles. In Figures 16.1 and 16.2, you can see the information that is within your example file. You can load this file by going to the Examples folder on the CD-ROM and running the editor-normalcode.mfa file. This file is an example of the war game you have already created.

Unit	Water	Grass	Small Mountain	Large Mountain	Forest
Unit1	0	NA	NA	NA	NA
Unit2	NA	0	1	NA	1
Unit3	NA	0	1	NA	1

Figure 16.1
The terrain movement table for the player.

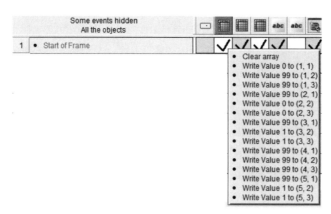

Figure 16.2
The array stored in the event editor.

The aim of the editor is to do the following:

- Create a simple application with an interface that is easy to read and understand

- Load an array file

- Save an array file

- Scroll through the data

- Update the data

- Update the original game to access this array file and use it within the game

We have already created the base editor for you, which has all of the objects on screen, so you can go straight into the programming. You can see a screenshot of the application working in Figure 16.3. You can open this file by going to the Examples folder on the CD-ROM and selecting the file Applicationeditor.mfa.

The editor has the following items on the frame:

- **Unit**: This specifies the actual unit you want to amend.

- **Terrain List box:** This list box displays all of the different terrain types.

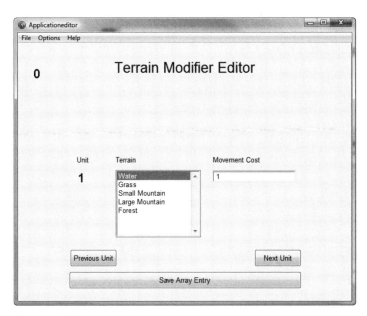

Figure 16.3
The Terrain Modifier Editor window.

- **Movement Cost Edit box**: Here you put in the movement cost for a particular unit on a particular terrain.

- **Previous Unit button**: Move to the previous unit.

- **Next Unit button**: Move to the next unit.

- **Save Array button**: Save the array entry.

In the example, you are going to replicate the array that you used in the war game example, as shown in the array image in Figure 16.2. You've also added an array object to the application and set up its dimensions to be 5,3,1 and as a number array. In your own games, where you may decide to have a larger set of terrain tiles or units, you can increase this figure as required.

If you compare this editor with the table in Figure 16.1 you will notice that you have three units, but many terrains per unit. So, once you select a unit, you need to change the Terrain List box for each type of terrain and enter the movement cost. Once you place all of the values required, you press the Save array button to save the array to a file. This file will be called examplearray.arr, where the .arr extension tells the programmer that this is an array file.

Creating an Array File

The first thing you need to do before you program the editor is to create an array file that you can use. You have to create the array file before you can create the editor. So, you create the look and feel of the editor, write a single event in the event editor to save an array file, and then you can delete this event and write the code to load this newly created file into the editor program.

1. Open the Examples folder on the CD-ROM and copy the file called Applicationeditor.mfa to somewhere onto your PC hard drive.

2. Go to the event editor.

3. Click on the New condition text.

4. Select the Storyboard controls object and then select Start of Frame.

5. Move across to the array object, right-click on the action box, and select Files|Save array to file. A browse dialog box appears. You do not want to browse for the file. Doing so would mean that the file location is stored in a

particular folder on your computer, which means that, if you give someone else these files, then the program will look for the array file using the path on your computer. You can use an expression to fix this though, so click on the Expression button.

6. You are now asked to enter a filename. Click on Retrieve data from an object and then select the Special object. Then choose Filenames| Application pathname, which places the word Apppath$ into the expression evaluator. You are not finished yet, because MMF has obtained the folder path, and you still need to tell the program the name of the file. So, enter +**"examplearray.arr"** onto the end of the path variable. This tells MMF2 to get the path and then add examplearray.arr as the filename. The expression should look like Figure 16.4.

Note

Files that use the apppath variable should be installed on your local hard drive. If the file is on a CD-ROM, then the file will not be able to be created as this CD is read only.

Now that the file can be created, run the program by pressing F8 and check the folder into which you copied the file, and you will see that an array file is created. This means you can now change the program to write, read, and save to this file.

Creating the Editor

Now that you have the array file ready for use, you can continue and create the editor. You should either delete the first event line in the Applicationeditor.mfa file or copy the blank file editorload.mfa to your hard disk. There should be no events at this moment.

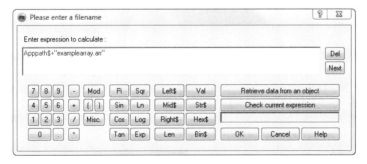

Figure 16.4
The expression to create an array file called examplearray.arr in the same location as the application.

The first thing you need to do is load the array file. You can do this using the Start of Frame condition.

1. Click on the New condition text, select the Storyboard Controls object, and then select Start of Frame.

2. Move across to the array object, then right-click on the action box and choose Files|Load array from file. The selection box appears. Click on the Expression button and then click on the Retrieve data from an object button. Select the Special object and then Filenames|application pathname. MMF enters an expression. Type the rest of the expression, which will be **+examplearray.arr**. Click on OK to save this information to the event editor.

   You now set the first item in the Terrain List Object to be selected.

3. Move across until you are under the List object, right-click, and choose Set current line. In the expression evaluator, type the value **1** and click on OK.

   On the same event line, you need to read in the information for the first entry, which will have the X value of 1 and the Y value of 1, but you do this using the method that you use to read in other entry lines when changing either the list or counter.

4. Move across to the right until you are directly under the Edit object. Right-click and select Editing|Set Text.

5. The expression evaluator appears.

   You are storing numbers in the array, and the edit box stores text, so you need to read in a value and convert it to text.

6. Click on the Str$ button.

   You are now asked to enter a number. You will use the array data as the information that you will load. Because you will drag data in from an array, you need to enter both an X coordinate and a Y coordinate, The action will be made up of the list entry, with a value of 1, and the counter, which is also 1.

7. Be sure that >Enter number here< is selected and then click on Retrieve data from an object.

8. Find the array object and select Read value from XY position. MMF now asks for two bits of information.

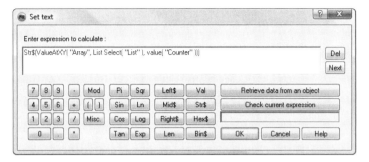

Figure 16.5
The expression for getting the first entry for the unit counter and the first terrain tile in the list.

9. Select the >Enter X offset< option and click on Retrieve data from an object. Find the List object and select Get current line number.

10. Select the >Enter Y offset< option, click on Retrieve data from an object and select the Counter object and then Current Value. The expression is now complete and can be seen in Figure 16.5.

Now, you can program what happens when the user presses the Previous or Next buttons. You will do the following:

- You store the current value in the counter and edit box to the array. This stores the result in temporary memory and means that the user has to press the Save button to save the counter and edit box data permanently to the array.

- Increase or decrease the value of the counter depending on which button is pressed.

- You then set the list item back to 1.

- You load in stored values for the unit and line.

First, you create an event to enable the user to press the Previous button, which is represented by the Button 2 object.

Click on the New condition text.

1. Select the Button 2 object and then select Button clicked.

   Now you are ready to write the value to the array.

2. Move across until you are under the array object, right-click, and select Write|Write value to XY. The expression evaluator appears.

You place the value to write in the Edit box. This value, of course, is a piece of text, so first you have to convert it to a number.

3. Click on the Val button and make sure >Enter string here< is highlighted; then Click on the Retrieve data from an object button. Find the Edit object and select Get Text.

   When you click on the OK button, you are asked for the X coordinate from the array. The X coordinate will be from the current list item selected.

4. Click on the Retrieve data from an object button. Select the list object and then select Get current line number. Click on OK.

   Now, you need to get the current value of the counter for the Y value.

5. Click on Retrieve data from an object; select the Counter object and then select Current Value. Click on the OK button to save the information to the event editor.

   Now that you have written the value to the array, you can decrease the counter. If the counter is already at 1, it won't decrease any further because you set the minimum value.

6. Move across from event line 2 to the Counter object, select Subtract from counter, type the value **1** in the expression evaluator, and click on OK.

   Now that you have set the counter, you want to set the list to line 1.

7. Move across until you are directly under the list object and then select Set current line. In the expression evaluator, type the value **1** and click on OK.

   You now need to read the array to set the edit object with the correct data.

8. Move across to the right until you are directly under the Edit object. Right-click and select Editing|Set Text.

9. In the expression evaluator, click on the Str$ button.

10. Make sure that >Enter number here< is selected and then click on Retrieve data from an object.

11. Find the array object and select Read value from XY position. You are now asked for two bits of information.

12. Select the >Enter X offset< option and click on Retrieve data from an object. Find the List object and select Get current line number.

13. Select the >Enter Y offset< option, click on Retrieve data from an object; select the Counter object and then Current Value.

For the Next button, you want exactly the same events, except rather than subtract from the counter, you add to the counter.

1. Click on the New condition text.

2. Select the Button 3 object and select Button clicked.

   Now you are ready to write the value to the array.

3. Move across until you are under the array object, right-click, and select Write|Write value to XY. The expression evaluator appears.

4. Click on the Val button and make sure the >Enter string here< is highlighted; then Click on the Retrieve data from an object button. Find the Edit object and select Get Text.

5. Click on the Retrieve data from an object button. Select the list object and then Get current line number. Click on OK.

6. Click on Retrieve data from an object, select the Counter object, and then select Current Value. Click on the OK button to save the information to the event editor.

7. Move across from event line 3 to the Counter object, select Add to counter, type the value 1 in the expression evaluator, and click on OK.

8. Move across until you are directly under the list object and then select Set current line. In the expression evaluator, type the value 1 and click on OK.

9. Move across to the right until you are directly under the Edit object. Right-click and select Editing|Set Text.

10. In the expression evaluator, click on the Str$ button.

11. Make sure that >Enter number here< is selected and click on Retrieve data from an object.

12. Find the array object and select Read value from XY position. You are now asked for two bits of information.

13. Select the >Enter X offset< option and click on Retrieve data from an object. Find the List object and select Get current line number.

14. Select the >Enter Y offset< option and click on Retrieve data from an object; select the Counter object and then Current Value.

For the next event, when the user presses the Save button, any information that has been written to the array will be saved to the file.

1. Click on the New condition text on event line 4.

2. Select the Button object and then Button Clicked.

3. Move across until you are under the array object, right-click, and select Write|Write value to XY. The expression evaluator appears.

4. Click on the Val button and make sure >Enter string here< is highlighted; then click on the Retrieve data from an object button. Find the Edit object and select Get Text.

5. Click on the Retrieve data from an object button. Select the list object and then Get current line number. Click on OK.

6. Click on Retrieve data from an object; select the Counter object and then Current Value. Click on the OK button to save the information to the event editor.

Now that you have saved the current entry to the array, you are ready to save the array file.

1. Still on event line four, move across until you are directly under the array object, right-click, and select Files|Save array to file.

2. The file selection box appears. Click on the Expression button to bring up the expression evaluator box.

3. Click on the Retrieve data from an object button.

4. Select the Special object and then Filenames|Application pathname. The expression evaluator will have an expression within it; on the end of the expression, type +"**examplearray.arr**" and then click on OK.

Finally, you now create an event that will check to see when the Terrain list box selection has changed and that will load in the selected list item data and place it in the edit box.

1. Click on the New condition text.

2. Select the list object and then Selection changed?

3. Move across to the right until you are directly under the Edit object. Right-click and select Editing|Set Text.

4. In the expression evaluator, click on the Str$ button.

5. Make sure that >Enter number here< is selected and click on Retrieve data from an object.

6. Find the array object and select Read value from XY position. You are now asked for two bits of information.

7. Select the >Enter X offset< option and click on Retrieve data from an object. Find the List object and select Get current line number.

8. Select the >Enter Y offset< option and click on Retrieve data from an object. Select the Counter object and then Current Value.

You can see the events and actions in Figure 16.6.

You can find the completed editor in the file editorload-complete.mfa in the Examples folder on the CD-ROM.

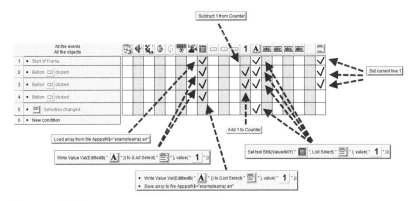

Figure 16.6
Events and actions of the editor program.

If you run the program now, you will be able to enter information and press the Save button to save the terrain data to the array.

Note

When creating editors that other people will use, you may need to change the way the editor program works. In the editor, you will notice that if you have entered information and then click on the next button, any data will be lost. Try adding an event that will save any stored information from the editor into the array.

Changing the War Game File

Now that you have a working editor with an array file filled with data, all you need to do is load this file into the war game file.

1. Load up the file editor-normalcode.mfa located in the Examples folder on the CD-ROM.

2. Be sure you are on frame 1 and then go into the event editor.

3. Find event line 1 and move across until you are under the Player Movement Array array object.

4. Delete all of the actions in this action box. These actions are the manual settings for the array.

Note

Your units may move different distances or move across different terrain tiles if you configure the array values differently in the editor. Once these values are loaded into the current example file, your units may behave differently. These movements are not a concern for the current example and only an issue to be aware of when making your own games using an editor.

5. An empty action box is now under the array. Right-click on the action box and select Files|Load array from file.

6. Click on the Expression button.

7. Click on Retrieve data from an object. Select the Special object and then Filenames|Application pathname.

8. The expression appears in the expression evaluator. Now add +"examplearray.arr". Click on OK to save the information to the event editor.

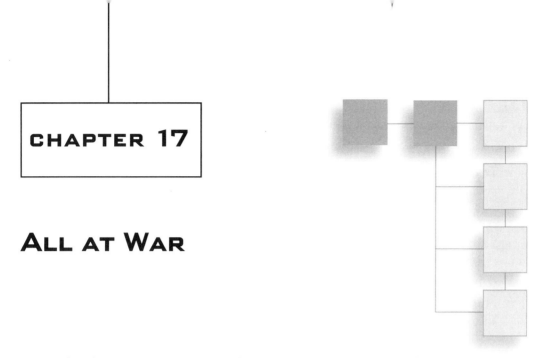

CHAPTER 17

ALL AT WAR

In this book we have concentrated mainly on land based warfare. The majority of the code will directly apply to any war game that you are working on. In this chapter we will look at the other types of war games that you might want to make and any additional considerations that you might need to take into account.

All at Sea

Over the course of history, many sea battles have taken place around the world. Seas were not just used to defend or attack another country but were also used to transfer men, equipment, and resources. In the 1940s the United Kingdom Merchant Navy lost many ships and supplies to the German U-boat submarines.

Nations found that controlling the seas could mean controlling the import and export of goods, and with that they could control money, taxes, and resources in a particular region.

With the different types of technology available through history there are many things that you could do in your own games to have a different slant on your war games.

Types of Sea Equipment

As well as the traditional ships such as battleships and destroyers, some other ship types you might want to use in your game include:

- **Transport Ships:** These can be ships that transport equipment for your armed forces, or merchant ships that are going about their daily work of transporting food and items to markets.

- **Submarines:** These underwater machines accounted for many ships lost at sea throughout the Second World War, and though rarely used in combat, they are still in significant use around the world. Countries such as USA, France, UK, and Russia have nuclear powered and nuclear armed submarines.

- **Aircraft Carriers:** These ships are effectively floating runways. They can carry aircraft, and usually have small numbers of troops, such as marines, ready for precision attacks.

- **Mine Layers:** These are ships that can place explosive mines in the water. These were used extensively in the Second World War. Mines pose a problem for any ship because they are hidden underwater.

- **Mine Sweepers:** These ships can seek out and destroy mines that are hidden underwater.

- **Oil Tankers:** These gigantic ships of the sea can carry large amounts of fuel, which is needed to fuel the modern tanks and other vehicles.

- **Speedboats:** Even today, there are places in the world where fast, small, and maneuverable ships are used to capture merchant ships. These lightly armed ships are popular with modern day pirates.

For ships in the 16th, 17th, and 18th century, you would have different types of ship sizes, number of guns and speed, such as Frigate, Galleon, sloop, ship of the line, and man o' war. There are details about these ships in books and on the internet, but one additional ship type that might be interesting in your games is:

- **Fireship:** It is sometimes difficult to believe that setting a ship on fire and launching it towards enemy ships was a tactic that was commonly used. A cheaply made ship could easily take out a heavily armoured ship that might be difficult to sink in other circumstances. This type of ship/tactic could prove very interesting in a war game, especially with a fire animation and a countdown till it explodes.

Throughout the ages, there have been a multitude of other ship types that could be used in your games, depending on the time period you decide to select. We have not detailed them all as there are too many to mention.

Game Ideas

You do not have to go with the same size tiles in your game, and you do not have to have tiles that just simulate units as ships. There are already a multitude of normal wars and battles for you to consider, so here are a few different ones:

- **Pirates**: You could create your own modern day pirates game. The player could play either the pirates or the opposing side. The aim of the pirates would be to capture a ship, and the player's mission would be to destroy the pirates or prevent them from capturing any ships within a set time frame.

- **Crew Fighting**: Rather than using tiles to signify water and the units to be groups of soldiers, why not have the terrain tiles be two ships locked together? In many early sea battles, one ship would come alongside another ship and the crew would board it to claim the ship as their prize. This meant soldiers jumping from ship to ship while having sword and gun fights. The actual terrain tiles would be the ship itself.

- **Transporter**: The aim of the game could be to get your transport that is laden with goods to arrive at a specific location without being sunk. You do not have to just make all out wars using the war game system that has been detailed in this book. You can take many different styles of games and fit the engine to work around it.

- **Submarine Hunt**: Consider how the paper-based game Battleship works. There is no reason why you cannot create a specialized version of your own. The player can shoot at specific tiles, and the computer controlled units can move invisibly towards the players' ships. Perhaps the submarines don't move but have a countdown number of moves before they shoot. In fact, you could drop the movement engine totally and recreate a more traditional version of Battleship. Some additional coding would be needed to move the computer units around at the start of a new game to ensure that the player does not know where the submarines are.

Look to the Sky

Unlike sea warfare, airplanes and flying machines have only been around for a short amount of time. In the 100 or so years since they were first flown, they have made great advances in technology in speed, aerobatics, armament, and stealth.

Types of Flying Machines

Listed are some of the types of flying vehicles you could have in your games:

- **Helicopters:** The main benefit of helicopters is that they can take off and land without the need for a runway. They can also carry people and cargo to difficult to reach locations. There are many different types of helicopters, such as personnel carriers, rescue helicopters, sea rescue, air ambulances, and attack helicopters. Helicopters can carry rockets, missiles, and standard heavy machine gun weapons.

- **Triplane:** These three-winged planes were the earliest available for combat. They were slow and not very maneuverable in comparison to biplanes. They saw service but were pretty much replaced by the end of the First World War. One of the most iconic Triplane is the Red Baron's red Fokker Dr1.

- **Biplane:** This is a two-wing airplane and was a popular plane in World War I. Popular biplanes included the Bulldog, Sopwith Camel, and Tiger Moth.

- **Monoplane:** This standard in plane design has been in use since the 1930s. There are different types, sizes, and roles for airplanes. World War II saw some truly great planes such as the Spitfire, Messerschmitt, Hurricane, Zero, Junker, Lightning, Lancaster Bomber, He-111, B-17 Flying Fortress, and B52. Since World War II, planes have made great strides in speed and bomb capacity.

- **Hover cars:** Currently, there are no hover cars, but this does not mean you cannot make a game which involves flying vehicles.

- **Barrage**: To prevent enemy aircraft from attacking a particular location, barrage balloons could be used. These were only useful for low flying craft because each balloon was connected to the ground by cables. These cables could get tangled or hit an oncoming aircraft and destroy it.

- **Stealth:** Since radar was introduced in World War II, plane technology has been trying to find ways to prevent airplanes from being spotted by the enemy. The advances in computer technology meant that planes have changed shape.

- **Drones**: With technology becoming more advanced, it is sometimes preferable to put planes in the air with no pilot. These pilotless planes are called drones and have sophisticated camera and telecommunications equipment, which can send pictures and video back to headquarters. It is even possible for the ground crew to send messages to the drone to fire an attached missile at a target. Drones are playing an increasing part in modern day warfare, and have been used in conflicts such as Iraq and Afghanistan.

Game Ideas and Concepts

- **In the Air:** Rather than having your planes flying around the ground, why not have your terrain tiles become the sky. This could be from a top down view as in most war games, but you could also introduce a straight on view, where the higher up the tile, the greater the height the plane has reached.

- **Flak**: Planes can be damaged and destroyed by guns on the ground, so you could add flak explosions as a unit that appears on screen in certain locations.

- **Stealth**: With the current advances in technology and stealth planes, you might find it interesting to create a game based on stealth. Your bomber units could try to destroy another target on screen without being found or destroyed.

- **Hide and Seek**: Using a set of flying drones, your aim is to find a particular computer unit. Once you have found the units in question, you can use the missiles to destroy the target. If you are making a game in which the player's units are limited in attack capability, you could implement different mission criteria and success factors. It doesn't have to just be that the target has been destroyed; perhaps you can have varying missions, where the player needs to ensure that no drones are destroyed or captured if shot down.

- **Rescue:** It is possible to make a game that uses the war game engine as its basis but does not include fighting. An exciting game could be a sea rescue game, where you have to rescue people located on a ship at sea. You could have this as a view of the helicopter and ship units on sea tiles, or a ship as the terrain tiles and rescue crew as the units.

- **Barrage Balloon War:** Your bomber crews have to avoid hitting the balloons and try to hit a set of targets. Perhaps you can also try to take out the balloons. You could also create a game where the player is in control of balloons and items such as ground to air defenses and has to prevent the enemy from causing too many casualties.

Space Wars

Space war games are those games that are played in space. This doesn't mean you cannot have a science fiction based war game on earth or any other planet. For this grouping, we are primarily looking at ideas for a war game played in the depths of space because the general war game engine and concepts apply in space too.

Some technology and other ideas follow:

- **Ship Types:** Space games can contain all manner of ships, straight from your own imagination. Ships could range from large space battleships to small transport shuttles. The larger the ship, the more weapons and shields it has available.

- **Black Holes:** Black holes could provide an area of the map that cannot be moved upon, very much like a mountain or water terrain tile.

- **Worm Holes:** Unlike a traditional war game where a unit has to travel across the length and breadth of the map, worm holes bend the fabric of time and space and allow units to suddenly appear in a different location. Placing one worm hole will provide the entry point, and another will provide an exit point. Worm holes could provide an interesting challenge for the player because they would add strategic importance and advantage in the game.

- **Solar Systems**: You could have many smaller war game maps that reflect certain areas of the solar system. These maps could be part of a bigger game, or they could be level-based.

Game Ideas

- **Ships and Crew**: You can have space games where the ships are the units or where you have the crew fighting on ships. There is no reason why you cannot mix the two styles and have ship unit battles in which, rather than destroying a unit, you could transport the crew to the ship and have a sub level game where you have a crew battle, where they have to take over a specific part of the ship to capture it.

- **Space Race**: You can use many aspects of the Wargame Map object to help you make a slightly different type of game. You could make a hexagon-based map where you have to get all of your rocket parts or space station modules to a particular part of the map. You may have to fight spaceships, armed soldiers, or automated space missile systems.

Reference

There are a large number of references available to you on TV, in movies, fiction and nonfiction books, and the internet. Here is a small selection of TV shows and movies that the author recommends as a good starting point for reference about particular timeframes and subject matter.

Drama Series

- Rome

- The Tudors

- Sharpe

- Band of Brothers

- V The Final Battle

Documentaries

- Battlefield Britain

- 20th Century Battlefields

- Space Race

- World War 1 in Colour

- World War 2 in Colour

- Time Team (Archaeology program)

- Ancient Rome: The Rise and Fall of an Empire

Movies

- Saving Private Ryan

- The Longest Day

- Battle of Britain

- A Bridge Too Far

- Waterloo

- Gettysburg

- James Bond—Moonraker

- Starship Troopers

- Master and Commander: The Far Side of the World

Books

- Time Machine

- War of the Worlds

- Neuromancer

Board & Table Games

- Risk

- Warhammer

- Warhammer 40K

- Stratego

Computer Games

- Total War: Rome

- Empire: Total War

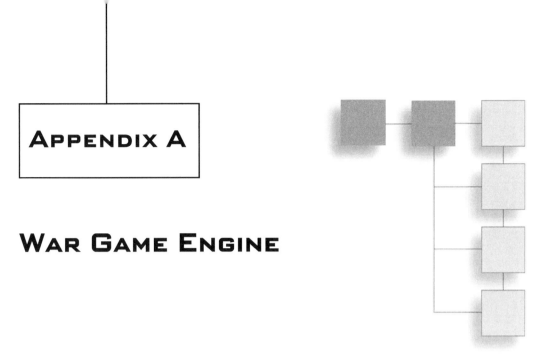

APPENDIX A

WAR GAME ENGINE

This appendix is a quick start guide to the war game engine and its configuration. This will allow you to improve, change, or use this engine quicker once you have read the book, rather than trying to remember what each aspect of the engine has been created for.

Player Units

These are the units that the player will control around the screen. You can see the alterable values for a unit in Figure A.1.

The slots are as follows:

Starting Movement Value: This is the unit's starting movement value. This value is used to reset the current movement value each turn.

Current Movement Value: This is the number of movement value points that the unit has left. This value is reset after each turn by the starting movement value.

Unit ID: A number used to identify the units. This is mainly for the benefit of the player units.

Movement 7: This contains a value of either 0 or 1. If the value is a 0, then the unit can move in this keyboard direction; if it contains a 1, this means the unit cannot move in this direction. The 7 direction means the unit will move in a northwest direction.

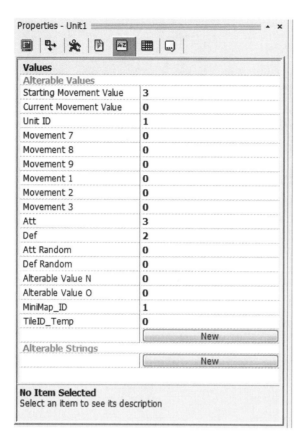

Figure A.1
The alterable value slots for the unit.

Movement 8: This contains a value of either 0 or 1. If the value is a 0, the unit can move in this keyboard direction; if it contains a 1, this means the unit cannot move in this direction. The 8 direction means the unit will move in a northerly direction.

Movement 9: This contains a value of either 0 or 1. If the value is a 0, the unit can move in this keyboard direction; if it contains a 1, this means the unit cannot move in this direction. The 9 direction means the unit will move in a northeast direction.

Movement 1: This contains a value of either 0 or 1. If the value is a 0, the unit can move in this keyboard direction; if it contains a 1, this means the unit cannot move in this direction. The 1 direction means the unit will move in a southwest direction.

Movement 2: This contains a value of either 0 or 1. If the value is a 0, the unit can move in this keyboard direction; if it contains a 1, this means the unit cannot move in this direction. The 2 direction means the unit will move in a southerly direction.

Movement 3: This contains a value of either 0 or 1. If the value is a 0, the unit can move in this keyboard direction; if it contains a 1, this means the unit cannot move in this direction. The 3 direction means the unit will move in a southeast direction.

Att: This is the unit's attack value.

Def: This is the unit's defense value.

Att Random: This is the unit's attack value after a random number between 0 and 10 has been added.

Def Random: This is the unit's defense value after a random number between 0 and 10 has been added.

Alterable Value N: Not currently used.

Alterable Value O: Not currently used.

MiniMap_ID: Unique sequential number for each unit to indentify it on the mini map. We do not use the Unit ID for this because the player units in this example are from 1 to 3, and the enemy units are 1 to 2. This ID is used to ensure that all units have a unique ID number.

TileID_Temp: This will store the tile ID that the unit is currently overlapping.

Computer Units

These are the units that the computer will control around the screen. You can see the alterable values for a unit in Figure A.2.

The slots are as follows:

Starting Movement Value: This is the unit's starting movement value. This value will be used to reset the current movement value each turn.

Current Movement Value: This is the number of movement value points that the unit has left. This value is reset after each turn by the starting movement value.

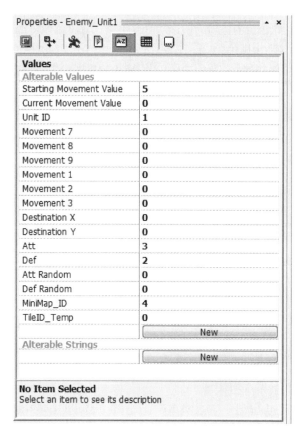

Figure A.2
The alterable value slots for the unit.

Unit ID: A numeric number used to identify the units. This is mainly for the benefit of the player units.

Movement 7: Not used.

Movement 8: Not used.

Movement 9: Not used.

Movement 1: Not used.

Movement 2: Not used.

Movement 3: Not used.

Destination X: The X coordinate of the unit's destination, based on the map tiles.

Destination Y: The Y coordinate of the unit's destination, based on the map tiles.

Att: This is the unit's attack value.

Def: This is the unit's defense value.

Att Random: This is the unit's attack value after a random number between 0 and 10 has been added.

Def Random: This is the unit's defense value after a random number between 0 and 10 has been added.

MiniMap_ID: Unique sequential number for each unit to indentify it on the mini map. We do not use the Unit ID for this because the player units in this example are from 1 to 3, and the enemy units are 1 to 2. This ID is used to ensure that all units have a unique ID number.

TileID_Temp: This stores the tile ID that the unit is currently overlapping.

Terrain Tiles

These are the tiles that make up the main map; you can see the alterable values for a terrain tile in Figure A.3.

The slots are as follows:

Movement 7: This contains a value of either 0 or 1. If the value is a 0, a unit can move in this keyboard direction; if it contains a 1, this means the tile is an edge unit and there are no tiles in that direction.

Movement 8: This contains a value of either 0 or 1. If the value is a 0, a unit can move in this keyboard direction; if it contains a 1, this means the tile is an edge unit and there are no tiles in that direction.

Movement 9: This contains a value of either 0 or 1. If the value is a 0, a unit can move in this keyboard direction; if it contains a 1, this means the tile is an edge unit and there are no tiles in that direction.

Movement 1: This contains a value of either 0 or 1. If the value is a 0, a unit can move in this keyboard direction; if it contains a 1, this means the tile is an edge unit and there are no tiles in that direction.

Movement 2: This contains a value of either 0 or 1. If the value is a 0, a unit can move in this keyboard direction; if it contains a 1, this means the tile is an edge unit and there are no tiles in that direction.

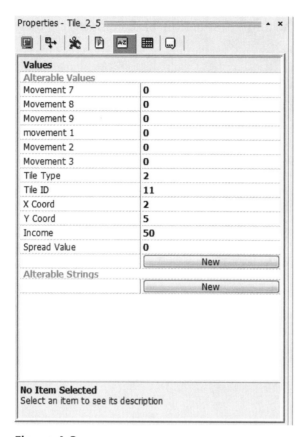

Figure A.3
The alterable value slots for the terrain tiles.

Movement 3: This contains a value of either 0 or 1. If the value is a 0, a unit can move in this keyboard direction; if it contains a 1, this means the tile is an edge unit and there are no tiles in that direction.

Tile Type: This details the tile type. For example, all grass terrain tiles might be configured with a tile type number of 2.

Tile ID: A sequential unique number to indentify the tile.

X Coord: The X coordinate for this particular tile.

Y Coord: The Y coordinate for this particular tile.

Income: The amount of income that can be generated from this tile.

Spread Value: Not Used.

Global Values

Global values are values that are available to the whole game. We have only used a small number of global values so far in the war game, but it is likely that you may want to use more. You can see the values we have used so far in Figure A.4.

The slots are as follows:

Global Value A: Used to set the destination tile number to the global value. This value is used for Enemy_Unit1.

Global Value B: Used to set the destination tile number to the global value. This value is used for Enemy_Unit2.

Global Value C to I: Not currently used.

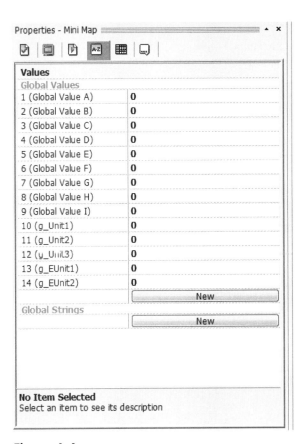

Figure A.4
The global values.

Global Value – g_Unit1: The global value will either be a 0 or a 1. If it is 0, the unit still exists: if it is 1, the unit has been destroyed. This will be used for the mini map to decide if it should delete the corresponding unit.

Global Value – g_Unit2: The global value will either be a 0 or a 1. If it is 0, the unit still exists: if it is 1, the unit has been destroyed. This will be used for the mini map to decide if it should delete the corresponding unit.

Global Value – g_Unit3: The global value will either be a 0 or a 1. If it is 0, the unit still exists: if it is 1, the unit has been destroyed. This will be used for the mini map to decide if it should delete the corresponding unit.

Global Value – g_EUnit1: The global value will either be a 0 or a 1. If it is 0, the unit still exists: if it is 1, the unit has been destroyed. This will be used for the mini map to decide if it should delete the corresponding unit.

Global Value – g_EUnit2: The global value will either be a 0 or a 1. If it is 0, the unit still exists: if it is 1, the unit has been destroyed. This will be used for the mini map to decide if it should delete the corresponding unit.

Note

If you make your game a lot larger, you may need to move some of these global values so that you can keep them all together. This is not such a bad thing, but it will help if you plan your game before you begin making it so you can make the various changes to the engine before you begin.

Phase Order

In the Event Editor we have a number of groups and events. The order in which these groups are activated and deactivated depends on what is happening in the engine at the time.

The general order of the engine is as follows:

Always Running

Update: Always places the tile type that the placeholder unit is overlapping into the alterable value of G for that placeholder unit.

Destroyed: Checks to see if a unit has been destroyed and updates the relevant global values.

Running in Order

The phases don't necessarily work in a precise order because the user may initiate player combat or may click on end turn. So it may work in two different ways depending on the user interaction with the game engine. The following is the general order of play.

Move Player Units: This involves the groups Unit1, Unit2, and Unit3.

Player Combat: Initiates the combat between the player unit and the computer units. This will only work for a unit that is on an adjacent hexagon. This will run the Hit or Miss groups, depending on the success or failure of the attack.

Computer Move: This starts with the running of the Computer Destinations group, which sets up the destinations of any of the computer units. You can consider this the computer order phase. Once the computer destinations group has run then it will run the corresponding unit movement group, in this case Computer Move or Computer Move(2).

Enemy Combat: Once the units have moved they will initiate combat, only if they are adjacent to a player unit.

End of Turn: The end of turn group will run to reset all of the movement values, e.g. the current movement value, back to their starting values.

INDEX

License Agreement/Notice of Limited Warranty

By opening the sealed disc container in this book, you agree to the following terms and conditions. If, upon reading the following license agreement and notice of limited warranty, you cannot agree to the terms and conditions set forth, return the unused book with unopened disc to the place where you purchased it for a refund.

License

The enclosed software is copyrighted by the copyright holder(s) indicated on the software disc. You are licensed to copy the software onto a single computer for use by a single user and to a backup disc. You may not reproduce, make copies, or distribute copies or rent or lease the software in whole or in part, except with written permission of the copyright holder(s). You may transfer the enclosed disc only together with this license, and only if you destroy all other copies of the software and the transferee agrees to the terms of the license. You may not decompile, reverse assemble, or reverse engineer the software.

Notice of Limited Warranty

The enclosed disc is warranted by Course Technology to be free of physical defects in materials and workmanship for a period of sixty (60) days from end user's purchase of the book/disc combination. During the sixty-day term of the limited warranty, Course Technology will provide a replacement disc upon the return of a defective disc.

Limited Liability

THE SOLE REMEDY FOR BREACH OF THIS LIMITED WARRANTY SHALL CONSIST ENTIRELY OF REPLACEMENT OF THE DEFECTIVE DISC. IN NO EVENT SHALL COURSE TECHNOLOGY OR THE AUTHOR BE LIABLE FOR ANY OTHER DAMAGES, INCLUDING LOSS OR CORRUPTION OF DATA, CHANGES IN THE FUNCTIONAL CHARACTERISTICS OF THE HARDWARE OR OPERATING SYSTEM, DELETERIOUS INTERACTION WITH OTHER SOFTWARE, OR ANY OTHER SPECIAL, INCIDENTAL, OR CONSEQUENTIAL DAMAGES THAT MAY ARISE, EVEN IF COURSE TECHNOLOGY AND/OR THE AUTHOR HAS PREVIOUSLY BEEN NOTIFIED THAT THE POSSIBILITY OF SUCH DAMAGES EXISTS.

Disclaimer of Warranties

COURSE TECHNOLOGY AND THE AUTHOR SPECIFICALLY DISCLAIM ANY AND ALL OTHER WARRANTIES, EITHER EXPRESS OR IMPLIED, INCLUDING WARRANTIES OF MERCHANTABILITY, SUITABILITY TO A PARTICULAR TASK OR PURPOSE, OR FREEDOM FROM ERRORS. SOME STATES DO NOT ALLOW FOR EXCLUSION OF IMPLIED WARRANTIES OR LIMITATION OF INCIDENTAL OR CONSEQUENTIAL DAMAGES, SO THESE LIMITATIONS MIGHT NOT APPLY TO YOU.

Other

This Agreement is governed by the laws of the State of Massachusetts without regard to choice of law principles. The United Convention of Contracts for the International Sale of Goods is specifically disclaimed. This Agreement constitutes the entire agreement between you and Course Technology regarding use of the software.